Re-Orienting the Fairy Tale

Series in Fairy-Tale Studies

General Editor

Donald Haase, Wayne State University

Advisory Editors

Cristina Bacchilega, University of Hawaiʻi, Mānoa
Stephen Benson, University of East Anglia
Nancy L. Canepa, Dartmouth College
Anne E. Duggan, Wayne State University
Pauline Greenhill, University of Winnipeg
Christine A. Jones, University of Utah
Janet Langlois, Wayne State University
Ulrich Marzolph, University of Göttingen
Carolina Fernández Rodríguez, University of Oviedo
Maria Tatar, Harvard University
Jack Zipes, University of Minnesota

A complete listing of the books in this series can be found online at wsupress.wayne.edu

Re-Orienting the Fairy Tale

Contemporary Adaptations across Cultures

Edited by
Mayako Murai and Luciana Cardi

Wayne State University Press
Detroit

© 2020 by Wayne State University Press, Detroit, Michigan 48201. All rights reserved. No part of this book may be reproduced without formal permission. Manufactured in the United States of America.

ISBN 978-0-8143-4536-8 (paperback)
ISBN 978-0-8143-4535-1 (hardcover)
ISBN 978-0-8143-4537-5 (e-book)

Library of Congress Control Number: 2020931375

Published with the assistance of a fund established by Thelma Gray James of Wayne State University for the publication of folklore and English studies.

Wayne State University Press
Leonard N. Simons Building
4809 Woodward Avenue
Detroit, Michigan 48201-1309

Visit us online at wsupress.wayne.edu

Contents

Acknowledgments • vii

Introduction • 1
Mayako Murai and Luciana Cardi

Part I. Disorienting Cultural Assumptions

1. Fairy Tales in Site: Wonders of Disorientation, Challenges of Re-Orientation • 15
   Cristina Bacchilega

2. *Moʻolelo Kamahaʻo* 2.0: The Art and Politics of the Modern Hawaiian Wonder Tale • 39
   kuʻualoha hoʻomanawanui

3. Re-Orienting China and America: *Yeh-Shen: A Cinderella Story from China* and Its TV Adaptation • 81
   Roxane Hughes

4. Monstrous Marionette: The Tale of a Japanese Doll by Angela Carter • 111
   Natsumi Ikoma

Part II. Exploring New Uses

5. Japanese Heroine Tales and the Significance of Storytelling in Contemporary Society • 139
   Hatsue Nakawaki

6. Who's Afraid of Derrida & Co.? Modern Theory Meets Three Little Pigs in the Classroom • 169

   Shuli Barzilai

7. Adults Reclaiming Fairy Tales through Cinema: Popular Fairy-Tale Movie Adaptations from the Past Decade • 207

   Aleksandra Szugajew

8. Trespassing the Boundaries of Fairy Tales: Pablo Berger's Silent Film *Snow White* • 235

   Nieves Moreno Redondo

Part III. Promoting Alternative Ethics and Aesthetics

9. Re-Orienting the Fairy Tale, Revising Age? • 265

   Vanessa Joosen

10. Re-Orienting Fairy-Tale Childhood: Child Protagonists as Critical Signifiers of Fairy-Tale Tropes in Transnational Contemporary Cinema • 285

    Michael Brodski

11. Alice on the Edge: Girls' Culture and "Western" Fairy Tales in Japan • 309

    Lucy Fraser

12. Magical Bird Maidens: Reconsidering Romantic Fairy Tales in Japanese Popular Culture • 335

    Masafumi Monden

13. When Princess(es) Will Sing: Girls Rock and Alternative Queer Interpretation • 361

    Katsuhiko Suganuma

14. The Plantation, the Garden, and the Forest: Biocultural Borderlands in Angela Carter's "Penetrating to the Heart of the Forest" • 383

    Daniela Kato

Contributors • 411

Index • 415

Acknowledgments

We are grateful to Donald Haase, Marie Sweetman, and the editorial team at Wayne State University Press for their support and guidance throughout the production process, to the volume's contributors for their incisive work, and to the anonymous reviewers of the manuscript for their helpful suggestions for revisions. We would like to thank Cristina Bacchilega for her thoughtful comments on the draft of the introduction. The material in this volume was first presented at the conference "Re-Orienting the Fairy Tale: Contemporary Fairy-Tale Adaptations across Cultures" organized by the editors and held at Kanagawa University, Japan, in March 2017. This unique encounter of scholars across cultures and disciplines was supported by JSPS KAKENHI Grant Number JP15K02196, the Japan Foundation, and the Institute for Humanities Research at Kanagawa University. Our thanks are also due to Nanae Ōtsuka and Junko Hattori for their dedicated support in helping with the organization and running of the conference, to Davide Burattin at Cactuseed.com for his inspirational design for the conference poster and website, and to Paul Rossiter for his kind support at every stage of the journey.

Introduction

Mayako Murai and Luciana Cardi

Disorienting the Fairy Tale

IN A PROCESS OF multiple retellings spanning centuries—from Giovanni Francesco Straparola's and Giambattista Basile's narratives, moving through the collections of Charles Perrault, the Brothers Grimm, and Hans Christian Andersen, to Walt Disney's animations and countless other cross-cultural adaptations—the fairy tale has powerfully emerged as a polyvalent genre crossing the boundaries between different media, study areas, and sociocultural frameworks. No longer regarded as a predominantly literary genre, the contemporary fairy tale circulates through an extensive network of digital, print, and filmic adaptations that are pervasive in multiple areas of our globalized cultures. As fairy tales have increasingly used the new media platforms to spin their way into the imaginary of mass audiences, the field of fairy-tale studies has constantly expanded by intersecting with different theoretical approaches, including Marxism, gender studies, postmodernism, postcolonialism, translation studies, and ecocriticism. The versatile, encompassing nature of this genre has offered scholars appealing strategies to discuss a wide range of political, ethnic, and identity issues, thus resulting in a large literature aimed at familiarizing readers with the multiple approaches of the new fairy-tale criticism. In the last decade, volumes such as *Grimms' Tales around the Globe* (2014), *The Cambridge Companion to Fairy Tales* (2014), *New Approaches to Teaching Folk and Fairy Tales* (2016), *The Routledge Companion to Media and Fairy-Tale Cultures* (2018), *Teaching Fairy Tales* (2019), and *The Fairy Tale World* (2019) exemplify this trend. Some of them, including *New Approaches to Teaching Folk and Fairy Tales* and *Teaching*

Fairy Tales, explore innovative pedagogical resources and approaches for teaching fairy tales in different educational environments. Others, like *The Cambridge Companion to Fairy Tales*, move from an analysis of the historical significance of the fairy tale as a genre to engage with multiple interpretations of fairy-tale narratives in different study areas. *Grimms' Tales around the Globe*, instead, focuses on the Grimm Brothers' narrative production to investigate its global reception across a wide range of cultures and media, in multilayered processes of adaptation affected by cultural resistance and assimilation. Finally, *The Fairy Tale World* and *The Routledge Companion to Media and Fairy-Tale Cultures* address the reception of the fairy tale around the world in relation to feminism, sexuality, ethnicity, colonialism, and ecocriticism and, at the same time, broaden the scope of fairy-tale studies by engaging with diverse themes throughout the intersection of different fields and media. In consideration of the extensive debate carried out to rethink the scope and the critical approaches of fairy-tale studies in the last decade, there are still some crucial issues that need to be thoroughly addressed in order to "disorient" the cultural and methodological assumptions at the basis of this discipline and "re-orient" fairy-tale studies on a global scale, across multiple cultures, media, and study areas. This twofold operation of disorienting and re-orienting the fairy tale echoes the role of wonder and magic in classic tales and, at the same time, mirrors the strategies employed by postmodern adaptations of traditional narratives. From this perspective, the first step in disorienting fairy-tale studies consists of dispelling the illusions of universality and ahistorical transparency. The very notion of the fairy tale, grounded in the narrative world of the German *märchen* and shaped by European ideological structures, mirrors a hierarchical mapping of the wonder genres. As Cristina Bacchilega (2013) argues, the boundaries of the fairy tale as a genre reflect a Euro-American-centric approach, as if Western scholars could catalog the wonder tales of other cultures from the vantage point of those who have progressed from oral storytelling to the established literary canon of the fairy tale.

> The genre of the "fairy tale" is still generally understood as European and North-American; the Middle East constructed

as the Orient has produced *The Thousand and One Nights*, wonder tales that have become identified with exotic magic and fantasy; most of the rest of the world has or had "folktales" that can become "fairy tales," but are not yet. (Bacchilega, *Fairy Tales* 21)

Disorienting fairy-tale studies thus implies decentering the Euro-American literary fairy-tale tradition and questioning the hierarchical divide between Western tales and other wonder tales. In order to discard familiar scholarly tropes, several scholars—Teverson (2010; 2019), Lau (2016), Bacchilega and Naithani (2018), and Seifert (2018), among the others—have pointed out the colonial and imperialist legacies underlying traditional European tales and their modern adaptations, thus contributing to a pivotal shift of perspectives in the field of fairy-tale studies. However, when it comes to mapping the fairy-tale genre on a global scale, scholars are still confronted with a long-consolidated critical tradition that tends to subordinate Asian, African, and other "peripheral" narratives to a Western viewpoint. In analyses lacking both specificity and depth, Euro-American ideological, methodological, and cultural frames have long been imposed upon fairy tales and fairy-tale adaptations from other cultures, thus overlooking the importance of the environment in which these narratives are produced. For this reason, Donald Haase (2010) and Sadhana Naithani (2006; 2010) urge us to decolonize fairy-tale studies by acknowledging the connections between the institution of folklore as a field of study, the publication of Grimm brothers' collections, the formation of European national identities, and colonial domination.

Disorienting the fairy tale thus consists of resisting the colonialist and Orientalist attitudes toward non-Western tales, avoiding the temptation to analyze them only in relation to a Euro-American canonic discourse. It implies acknowledging the processes of cultural manipulation that have negatively affected the transmission of nonhegemonic narrative capital and have jeopardized scholarly research on non-Western tales. Disorienting the cultural hegemonies at the basis of fairy-tale studies also involves unveiling the sociopolitical conflicts behind the contemporary circulation of fairy tales and exposing the dominant power structures that still tend to perpetuate colonial tropes and neutralize cultural differences. Instead, contemporary fairy-tale scholars need to investigate the complex dynamics shaping both textual and cultural translations, the power relations that regulate the movement of cultural capital across the globe, and the specific characteristics of the sociocultural contexts affecting the production, transmission, and transformation of fairy tales. In order to accomplish this task, fairy-tale studies should benefit from the enormous disorienting potential of "decentering approaches," whether they be indigenous and culturally marginalized perspectives, ecocritical approaches transcending Euro-American anthropocentrism, or analyses of fairy tales in relation to visual and performing arts beyond the centrality of the written text as part of the language imposed by Western colonizers. Among the possible strategies to carry out such study, cross-area and transmedia comparative analysis constitutes an effective means to expose the complexity and the plurality of the fairy tale, thus disorienting the oversimplifying cultural assumptions of Euro-American-centric scholarship.

Such considerations sparked the scholarly debate that was a prelude to this volume, which contains a selection of papers from the international conference "Re-Orienting the Fairy Tale: Contemporary Fairy-Tale Adaptations across Cultures," held at Kanagawa University (Yokohama, Japan) on March 29–30, 2017. This conference, the first of its kind in East Asia, sought to re-orient fairy-tale studies on a global scale by facilitating conversations among fairy-tale researchers with Western and non-Western cultural backgrounds across different media and disciplines. The guiding questions were: What kind of criticisms would be needed to analyze the adaptations of folktales and fairy tales produced in a globalizing world where Western and non-Western cultures interact? What insights would such a comparative analysis bring to the explicit and implicit Eurocentric tendencies in current fairy-tale adaptations and scholarship? In the attempt to address these issues from multiple points of view, we, as the conference organizers, benefited from the critical insights of three keynote speakers from different professional and cultural backgrounds. Cristina Bacchilega has researched and published extensively on fairy tales and their adaptations and has significantly contributed to the scholarly debate on the adaptation of traditional narratives in colonial and decolonial projects. Vanessa Joosen's works on the intertexual dialogue between fairy-tale criticism and retellings in English, German, and Dutch, as well as on the global reception of the Grimms' tales, have been influential in developing intertextual and international approaches to modern fairy-tale adaptations. Japanese novelist and storyteller Hatsue Nakawaki has played an important role in revising the fairy-tale canon in Japan by publishing a series of picture-book retellings of fairy tales from around the world and editing a collection of traditional Japanese fairy tales revolving around brave heroines. In addition to the keynote speakers, each of the participants in the conference made significant contributions to the discussion on re-orienting the fairy tale in panels that explored a wide range of topics, from fairy-tale films across cultures to East-West hybridization, and from non-anthropocentric tales to the intermedial possibilities of fairy tales in classrooms and in picture books. Moving from the fruitful critical debate sparked at the conference, the contributions to this volume seek the re-orientation of fairy-tale studies from different viewpoints, in relation to several media and study areas that have become increasingly relevant to the fairy tale, such as children's studies, age studies, ecofeminism, film studies, performance studies, and anime and manga studies, among others.

The chapters included in the first part, "Disorienting Cultural Assumptions," address the notion of disorienting the fairy tale from multiple perspectives. In "Fairy Tales in Site: Wonders of Disorientation, Challenges of Re-Orientation," Cristina Bacchilega invites us to explore the possibilities related to the uncanny processes of both disorientation and re-orientation taking place in the "journeys" of wonder tales across multiple media and cultures in a globalizing world where Western and non-Western cultures interact. Her analysis encompasses different literary and visual texts, including Sofia Samatar's "Mahliya and Mauhub and the White-Footed Gazelle" (2016), Neil Gaiman's *The Sleeper and the Spindle* (2014), Toni Morrison's *God Help the Child* (2015), and Su Blackwell's "The Woodcutter Hut" (2008).

In "*Moʻolelo Kamahaʻo* 2.0: The Art and Politics of the Modern Hawaiian Wonder Tale," kuʻualoha hoʻomanawanui focuses on the manipulation of the Hawaiian narratives of Maui within the framework of settler colonialism and explains how, in the last few decades, native Hawaiians have reclaimed these cultural figures in alternative adaptations and dance performances. After discussing the factors that have contributed to recent disorienting misrepresentations of Maui, this chapter seeks to re-orient the scholarly debate by contextualizing indigenous storytelling with reference to the ongoing Hawaiian sovereignty movement and the associated cultural revival, thus providing a more culturally appropriate framework for understanding these contemporary adaptations.

In "Re-Orienting China and America: *Yeh-Shen: A Cinderella Story from China* and Its TV Adaptation," Roxane Hughes examines Ai-Ling Louie's and Ed Young's children's book *Yeh-Shen: A Cinderella Story from China* (1982), a retelling of the ninth-century "Yexian Tale," and its TV adaptation (1985). She situates her analysis within the sociocultural framework of ethnic revival leading to the development of Asian American literatures and discusses the ambivalent role of the fairy tale in constructing ethnic identity, a role that mirrors Chinese Americans' equally ambivalent position in the Cold War context of the 1980s.

In "Monstrous Marionette: The Tale of a Japanese Doll by Angela Carter," Natsumi Ikoma analyzes the influences of Japanese literary and performative traditions on Angela Carter's "The Loves of Lady Purple" (1974). This chapter decenters the interpretations of Carter's story as a retelling of Charles Perrault's "Sleeping Beauty" related mainly to the Euro-American genre of Gothic horror; instead, it adds yet another layer of complexity to the analysis of this literary work by discussing the influences of *jōruri*, *bunraku* puppet theater, and Murasaki Shikibu's eleventh-century novel *The Tale of Genji*.

Re-Orienting the Fairy Tale

The following two parts of the book seek to re-orient the fairy tale by examining geopolitical and intercultural dimensions beyond a Euro-American focus and by mapping intertextual connections among multimedia fairy-tale adaptations produced in today's globalizing cultures. On the one hand, from a geopolitical perspective, the choice to hyphenate the term "re-orient" foregrounds the power relations between the "West" and the "East"—two cultural constructions mirroring the Saidian notion of Euro-American society and its Orientalized peripheries—that still operate in the global circulation of fairy tales and their adaptations today. On the other hand, the hyphen is also used to deorientalize the term "orient" itself by underlining the importance of locating our critical standpoint in navigating through newly emerging networks of fairy-tale intertexts across cultures, media, and disciplines. Furthermore, this study seeks to re-orient the term "fairy tale" itself, which has increasingly been considered problematic because of its European origins and the way its use has led to the reinforcement of the cultural authority of Western narrative traditions. In this respect, the editors' choice to retain the term "fairy tale" echoes Andrew Teverson's twofold intention in *The Fairy Tale World* to both "[critique] applications of the term 'fairy tale' that entail homogenising the world's wonder tales according to a Euro-American model or that imply a failure to appreciate or comprehend the cultural specificity of local narrative traditions" *and* to "[hold] out the possibility that this term, now so widely used in English-speaking contexts, can be reclaimed for more dispersed, more decentred, applications" (12).

To re-orient the fairy tale, Haase argues, "we have to practice critical hospitality, to welcome and connect with the stories of others on common ground, both on their own terms and in our own ways, wherever we might encounter them" ("Global or Local" 30). Recent international and interdisciplinary collaborations, such as *The Routledge Companion to Media and Fairy-Tale Cultures* and *The Fairy Tale World*, have significantly contributed to this re-orienting project. To participate in these critical exchanges from another corner of the world, the second and the third part of this volume attempt to re-orient the fairy tale in two ways. First, they explore new areas in education, entertainment, and academic disciplines where fairy tales can be used to promote understanding across diverse cultures. Second, they put an emphasis on the cross- and transcultural analyses of fairy-tale adaptations produced in contemporary Japan as an example of a site where fairy tales from the East and the West are intermingled to create a new fairy-tale culture that would disorient and re-orient the still-dominant Euro-American-centered perspectives. Although Japan-focused fairy-tale criticisms have recently become more visible in English-language fairy-tale scholarship,[1] there still exists a tendency to categorize such works into area studies, especially when they are centered on non-Western materials, a tendency that may result in hindering mutually beneficial interactions across geographical, cultural, and disciplinary borders. Instead, this volume seeks to integrate Japan-oriented views into a wider critical context in order to re-orient geopolitical assumptions in both localized and global fairy-tale research. The aim of this volume is not to claim that its coverage, with an emphasis on Japanese, Euro-American, and indigenous Hawaiian examples, is comprehensive enough but to offer a viable model for transcultural fairy-tale research that would achieve a wider coverage.

"Exploring New Uses," the second part of the volume, critically examines innovative uses of fairy tales in contemporary cultures for education and entertainment for both adults and children. This part opens with Hatsue Nakawaki's "Japanese Heroine Tales and the Significance of Storytelling in Contemporary Society," a chapter based on her keynote lecture at the conference in which she interweaved her fairy-tale analysis with her storytelling. It is important that her storytelling, performed first in Japanese and then followed by English translation, offered an opportunity for the audience, from different cultural backgrounds, to experience an actual storytelling setting in contemporary Japan, giving them what Haase, in his analysis of the paratextual strategies used by recent English translations of Arab tales, calls a "glimpse" of local cultural contexts in which tales are told and received ("Global or Local" 23). Nakawaki's chapter reevaluates the significance of traditional fairy tales and storytelling for children's education, especially regarding gender roles, and stresses the need to provide children with new anthologies that will promote less biased views of gender and cultural differences. Her use of the local term *mukashibanashi* to refer to the genre, like hoʻomanawanui's use of the term *moʻolelo* in this volume, exemplifies a resistance of non-Western narrative traditions to being subsumed under a more culturally dominant rubric. Shuli Barzilai's "Who's Afraid of Derrida & Co.? Modern Theory Meets Three Little Pigs in the Classroom," in contrast, explores the potential of the fairy tale as a pedagogical aid to teach literary theory to university students. Multiple adaptations of a familiar fairy tale, Barzilai argues, function as a mirror reflecting sociocultural trends, inviting students to read literary texts critically. Aleksandra Szugajew's "Adults Reclaiming Fairy Tales through Cinema: Popular Fairy-Tale Movie Adaptations from the Past Decade" outlines the strategies adopted by recent Hollywood live-action fairy-tale films to attract adult audiences. She demonstrates how this new genre offers not only a form of global entertainment but also a forum that invites reflection on various social and cultural issues in today's globalizing world. While also discussing live-action fairy-tale films for adult audiences, Nieves Moreno Redondo's "Trespassing the Boundaries of Fairy Tales: Pablo Berger's Silent Film *Snow White*" focuses on how the Spanish director uses the combined magic of the fairy tale and cinema to reveal the sociocultural stereotypes embedded in the global as well as the national imaginary.

"Promoting Alternative Ethics and Aesthetics," the third and final part of this volume, proposes alternative approaches to fairy tales by integrating important insights from other newly emerging disciplines. These interdisciplinary approaches reveal the intercultural nature of fairy-tale adaptations produced and circulated in a globalizing world. Vanessa Joosen's "Re-Orienting the Fairy Tale, Revising Age?" re-orients fairy-tale studies to incorporate the insights of age studies, an intersection that has not yet been sufficiently explored. By analyzing the construction of age in fairy-tale narratives, Joosen demonstrates that age studies can provide a rich insight into traditional and contemporary fairy tales, and vice versa. Michael Brodski's "Re-Orienting Fairy-Tale Childhood: Child Protagonists as Critical Signifiers of Fairy-Tale Tropes in Transnational Contemporary Cinema" analyzes Western and non-Western live-action films based on traditional fairy tales by combining the analytical frameworks of fairy-tale studies with those of childhood studies and film studies. His exploration of the intersection among the three disciplinary approaches reveals how these contemporary fairy-tale adaptations critique and re-orient the conventional notion of childhood innocence prevalent in Euro-American culture. Lucy Fraser's "Alice on the Edge: Girls' Culture and 'Western' Fairy Tales in Japan" investigates the ways in which Lewis Carroll's *Alice* books have been appropriated by girls' culture in Japan and have produced literary and artistic adaptations that cast an unexpected light on "Western" fairy-tale texts. Fraser's approach illustrates the importance of understanding cultural contexts in analyzing contemporary fairy-tale adaptations circulating across cultures so as not to reproduce or reinforce cultural imbalances. This cross-cultural approach is shared by Masafumi Monden's "Magical Bird Maidens: Reconsidering Romantic Fairy Tales in Japanese Popular Culture." Monden's analysis of the Japanese anime series *Princess Tutu* in the context of "magical girl" *anime* culture in Japan reveals how this work both utilizes the conventional image of fairy-tale princesses and the heteronormative romantic plot they follow and offers an alternative to these conventions, reimagining fairy tales as girl-centered stories embedded in reality. Katsuhiko Suganuma's "When Princess(es) Will Sing: Girls Rock and Alternative Queer Interpretation" also analyzes Japanese pop culture in both national and global contexts. Drawing on queer theory and popular musicology, Suganuma's analysis of the fairy-tale intertexts in the works of the Japanese female band Princess Princess demonstrates that popular music can be a medium through which the queer potential of ostensibly heteronormative traditional fairy tales may emerge. Finally, Daniela Kato's "The Plantation, the Garden, and the Forest: Biocultural Borderlands in Angela Carter's 'Penetrating to the Heart of the Forest'" explores the ecological dimensions of Carter's literary fairy tale and offers an ecofeminist interpretation of a fairy-tale forest as a borderland that lies beyond the nature-culture dichotomy. Kato's analysis redirects the anthropocentric tendency in fairy-tale studies toward a more inclusive, multispecies approach.

On a final note, it seems important that this study is the fruit of the presentations and the conversations that took place at a conference in Yokohama, one of the first Japanese harbor cities where communities of foreigners from Europe and America settled in the nineteenth century, moving into a world that often disoriented their Western perspectives. Likewise, many of the participants to this conference traveled a long way, crossing several national borders and time zones, in an attempt to move beyond Euro-American-centered understandings of fairy-tale studies. It is the editors' hope that this collection conveys the feelings of excitement, energy, and wonder produced in the course of this disorienting experience, all of which helped open up new ways of re-orienting ourselves in the ever-expanding fairy-tale web.

Note

1. See, for example, the special issue of *Marvels & Tales: Journal of Fairy-Tale Studies* on "The Fairy Tale in Japan," guest-edited by Marc Sebastian-Jones (2013), and the works by Fumihiko Kobayashi (2015), Mayako Murai (2015), and Lucy Fraser (2017).

Works Cited

Bacchilega, Cristina, and Sadhana Naithani. "Colonialism, Postcolonialism and Decolonization." *The Routledge Companion to Media and Fairy-Tale Cultures*, edited by Pauline Greenhill, Jill Terry Rudy, Naomi Hamer, and Lauren Bosc, Routledge, 2018, pp. 83–90.

Bacchilega, Cristina. *Fairy Tales Transformed? Twenty-First-Century Adaptations and the Politics of Wonder*. Wayne State University Press, 2013.

Canepa, Nancy, editor. *Teaching Fairy Tales*. Wayne State University Press, 2019.

Fraser, Lucy. *The Pleasures of Metamorphosis: Japanese and English Fairy Tale Transformations of "The Little Mermaid."* Wayne State University Press, 2017.

Greenhill, Pauline, Jill Terry Rudy, Naomi Hamer, and Lauren Bosc, editors. *The Routledge Companion to Media and Fairy-Tale Cultures*. Routledge, 2018.

Haase, Donald. "Decolonizing Fairy-Tale Studies." *Marvels & Tales*, vol. 24, 2010, pp. 17–38.

———. "Global or Local? Where Do Fairy Tales Belong?" *The Fairy Tale World*, edited by Andrew Teverson, Routledge, 2019, pp. 17–32.

Jones, Christa C., and Claudia Schwabe, editors. *New Approaches to Teaching Folk and Fairy Tales*. Utah State University Press, 2016.

Joosen, Vanessa, and Gillian Lathey, editors. *Grimms' Tales around the Globe: The Dynamics of Their International Reception*. Wayne State University Press, 2014.

Kobayashi, Fumihiko. *Japanese Animal-Wife Tales: Narrating Gender Reality in Japanese Folktale Tradition*. Peter Lang, 2015.

Lau, Kimberly J. "Imperial Marvels: Race and the Colonial Imagination in the Fairy Tales of Madame d'Aulnoy." *Narrative Culture*, vol. 3, no. 2, Fall 2016, pp. 141–79.

Murai, Mayako. *From Dog Bridegroom to Wolf Girl: Contemporary Japanese Fairy-Tale Adaptations in Conversation with the West*. Wayne State University Press, 2015.

Naithani, Sadhana. *In Quest of Indian Folktales: Pandit Ram Gharib Chaube and William Crooke*. Indiana University Press, 2006.

———. *The Story-Time of the British Empire: Colonial and Postcolonial Folkloristics*. University Press of Mississippi, 2010.

Sebastian-Jones, Marc, editor. *Marvels & Tales: Journal of Fairy-Tale Studies*, Special Issue: The Fairy Tale in Japan, vol. 27, no. 2, 2013.

Seifert, Lewis C. "Contes et mécomptes: Tahar Ben Jelloun réécrit Charles Perrault." *L'épanchement du conte dans la littérature*, edited by Christiane Connan-Pintado, Presses universitaires de Bordeaux, 2018, pp. 143–53.

Tatar, Maria, editor. *The Cambridge Companion to Fairy Tales*. Cambridge University Press, 2014.

Teverson, Andrew. "'Giants Have Trampled the Earth': Colonialism and the English Tale in Samuel Selvon's *Turn Again Tiger*," *Marvels & Tales*, vol. 24, no. 2, 2010, pp. 198–218.

———, editor. *The Fairy Tale World*. Routledge, 2019.

I

Disorienting Cultural Assumptions

1

Fairy Tales in Site

Wonders of Disorientation, Challenges of Re-Orientation

Cristina Bacchilega

As you enter this reading experience, be mindful: not an argumentative essay, this is a meditation on fairy tales or wonder tales.[1] More specifically, it is a meditation on fairy tales *in site*, that is, as events positioned, produced, and received in specific locations and times.[2] It is a meditation in four movements, or takes, on fairy tales in plain *sight* as well as in a web of unseen relations; fairy tales we *cite* and adapt; fairy-tale *insight* that disorienting adaptations provide; and fairy-tale re-orientation as *incite*ment. Each movement cites and is incited by fairy-tale or wonder-tale texts that were on my mind and in my classroom experience in 2016, when I first drafted this piece. Together these movements assemble my ongoing reflections on Mayako Murai's and Luciana Cardi's question of how to approach "adaptations of folktales and fairy tales produced in a globalizing world where Western and non-Western cultures interact and compete with each other."[3] Movement is a necessary part of this meditation: experiencing located wonder tales is hardly about stories, their producers, or receivers staying in place, but about their taking uncanny journeys and their taking us with them.

Take #1: In and Out of Sight

I contemplate a widely circulating fairy-tale meme, "Life is not a fairy tale. If you lose your shoe at midnight, you're drunk." It is in plain sight, in this case scripted not on a coffee mug but on a shop window, through which I see a fashion display, two female-shaped and white mannequins, one in workday attire, the other in evening dress. Cinderella before and after her makeover? I notice how this shop window functions also as a mirror, reflecting my image as a viewer and possible consumer back to me. Which attire appeals to my desire for recognition or transformation? There is more than glass filtering the experience. This encounter between what is offered for sale and myself (and/or you) is mediated by how I/we respond to the fairy-tale meme and how I/we approach fairy tale as fiction in relation to "real life"—with all this entails, including whether we are already fashioned by fairy-tale symbols, drink alcohol, or notice the irony of the elegantly dressed but shoeless mannequins in the window. While the meme critiques the power of fairy-tale emplotment only to exploit it, the words on the glass surface are variedly refracted in each viewer's eye to facilitate, or not, our becoming consumers. This shop window, then, is more than a two-way mirroring of women and our simulacra. Rather, triangulation is at work, indexed by how the power of the fairy-tale suggestion mediates between me/us and the mannequins, life and fiction, narrative emplotment and high-fashion or consumerist hyperreal.[4] Which tropes of fairy tale and fairy-tale princess do these words and images conjure for me and/or you? The fairy-tale tropes activated in this triangulated mirroring depend in part on how the "fairy-tale princess" image affects our lives—that is, is it desirable or compelling—and on whether the mannequin's simulation is so appealing that it feels more real than we do. The meme on the mirror's surface, then, participates in a much larger, but invisible, fairy-tale web of connections, and only some of these links are activated in the embodied experience and conscious or unconscious mind of any individual viewer.

I have started on a journey of reflection that is not mimesis, wondering how the power structures of triangulation and the potentiality of fairy-tale links may work in both disorienting and re-orienting ways.

Take #2: Why Are You On-Site? Why Are We a Sight?

I am absorbed in an adapted wonder tale that has not yet received much scholarly attention, "The Tale of Mahliya and Mauhub and the White-Footed Gazelle" by Sofia Samatar. Samatar is an award-winning Somali American novelist, short-story writer, poet, and critic who also coedited the electronic *Interfictions: A Journal of Interstitial Arts* (2013–16) and is the author of an essay on film adaptations of the *Arabian Nights* (2016) and the short-story collection *Tender* (2017). "The Tale of Mahliya and Mauhub and the White-Footed Gazelle," first published in *The Starlit Wood* (2016) and then reprinted in *Tender* (2017),[5] is worth reading, discussing, and teaching on numerous accounts. Here, it matters that Samatar describes it as her *adaptation* of a *medieval Arabic tale*, an adaptation that explicitly interacts with the tale's recent and first *translation into English* as "The Story of Mahliya and Mauhub and the White-Footed Gazelle. It Contains Strange and Marvellous Things" (Lyons 2015). This triangulation of tale, translation, and adaptation is significant because the translation, which appeared in Lyons's collection *Tales of the Marvellous and News of the Strange*, "comes into a world that has been primed to receive it by more than three centuries of love for *A Thousand and One Nights*" (Samatar, "Author's Note" 333). Thus, Samatar's 2016 adaptation is produced and received in a wondrous web spun out of a long history of trafficking stories and goods as well as people traveling; and, at the same time, this adaptation is also very much responding to the recent release of the tale's translation as an event, a worldly event in Edward Said's terms, which invites Samatar's also situated response.[6]

Over a thousand years old, the Arabic tale itself is complex, its plot featuring three interlaced and meandering love stories: that of the powerful Egyptian princess Mahliya and prince Mauhub, who was suckled by a lioness and is later turned into a crocodile with pearl earrings; that of the lioness who cared for baby Mauhub and her long-lost lion partner who then becomes Mauhub's messenger to Mahliya; and that of two gazelles that are captured by Mahliya and Mauhub, one a "white-footed gazelle" who is also a prince of jinn, the other a transformed Persian princess. There are also the king of snakes, the queen of jinn crows "who part lovers and companions" (Lyons 412), automata, and many more marvels and tricks. I read it in its English-language translation in Malcolm Lyons's publication, which has been much celebrated for making these inventive and surprising tales finally accessible in English.[7] Aware of how *Tales of the Marvellous and the Strange* could impact scholarly and popular understanding of *The Arabian Nights* and the wonder-tale genre more generally, I had bought the volume but had not read it until prompted by my reading of Samatar.

Samatar's adapted tale, "The Tale of Mahliya and Mauhub and the White-Footed Gazelle," begins with a statement that articulates its multiply mediated provenance as well as its situated occasion:

> This story is at least a thousand years old. Its complete title is "The Tale of Mahliya and Mauhub and the White-Footed Gazelle: It Contains Strange and Marvelous Things." A single copy, probably produced in Egypt or Syria, survives in Istanbul; the first English translation appeared in 2015.
>
> This is not the right way to start a fairy tale, but it's better than sitting here in silence waiting for Mahliya. . . . (321)

Shaped by Samatar, the tale does not begin with a traditional formula—be it "It is said," or "Once upon a time." Rather, we are presented with an authoritative introductory statement that seems to come from an external narrator, possibly a scholar or commentator. But this preamble is actually already part of the tale told in the first person by a modern-day, aged, and bald character who introduces himself as Mahliya's retainer or head servant; he is volunteering to start spinning the "marvelous tale" of the white-footed gazelle to entertain the foreign researcher who is waiting to meet the fabled Mahliya and take her picture, possibly for an English-language publication about the tale in Arabic tradition and present-day storytelling. Before telling a version of the tale, the bald narrator offers various metanarrative takes on it, condensing it, analyzing its structure and tropes, and discussing its genre and its complexities. This teller speaks to the foreign researcher with an authority that is grounded both in research—especially the methods of foreign (that is, western) researchers—and in lived familiarity with this tale and other wonder tales from *The Thousand and One Nights*.

Now, in the Arabic as well as the translated and the adapted tale, when Mahliya first meets Mauhub, she is disguised as a young man who introduces himself as Mahliya's vizier. Mirroring the revelation that Mahliya was masquerading as a man when she first appeared in the medieval tale, Samatar's narrator turns out not to be Mahliya's male head servant but Mahliya herself. This ruse becomes evident when Samatar's I-narrator takes a break from recounting Mahliya's adventures in the third person ("When Mahliya first met Mauhub, she was disguised as a man" [326]) and addresses her narratee directly in a metanarrative sequence entitled "The Wonder Curse":

> My question is this: Why are you people so hungry for marvels? I mean here you are, braving a twelve-hour journey from JFK, one of the world's worst airports, plus a taxi ride through the afternoon traffic, only to sit in an elderly woman's apartment and listen to a story. Really, I felt I had to trick you to make it worth your while! (Hand me my wig, will you? It's under your chair. You'll want another photograph now, I suppose!) Of course, there is a venerable tradition of marvel tales here, a tradition that harbors my own story. But lately it seems to me that there is such a thing as a *wonder curse*, like the literary version of a resource curse. As if, having once tasted the magic of the East, visitors become determined to extract it at any cost.
>
> The link between marvels and money is quite clear. Fabulous tales, astronomical wealth; both are forms of fortune. Perhaps the story is a kind of treasure map. But there is more than one map in the world, my friend. Consider what this tale contains and what it does not. (328)

Situating its telling on the page as an occasion for multiple performances, Samatar maps her tale differently from the traditional tale, as well as from its translation.

In 2015 *Tales of the Marvellous and News of the Strange* had offered English-language readers unprecedented access to medieval Arabic tales that—I quote from the back cover's blurbs—contain "terrifying monsters, lost princes, jewels beyond price, sword-wielding statues, magical transformations and shocking reversals of fortune" and provide "a unique insight into a now-lost elegant, courtly and tolerant Arab world." In contrast, Mahliya, the aged trickster and narrator of her own tale in Samatar's short story, probes into "the western passion for a marvelous, medieval east" (333) and refuses to detach her tale from her experience with Orientalism.

Samatar's Mahliya knows the foreign researcher is chasing after more treasures to which her tale may give him access. In the section of Samatar's metanarrative "What This Tale Contains," Mahliya's list includes "yellow silk, red leather, white marble, red onyx, . . . musk, ebony, . . . carnelian, Bactrian camels, . . . silver, sandalwood, slaves" (328–29)—thus clearly evoking a fetishization that feeds on the once-upon-a-time fantasy of an exotic land whose symbolic and material resources (i.e., marvels) continue to be extracted because they sell. The question, "why are you people so hungry for marvels?" extends beyond the story world to Samatar's readers, as well as to anyone—including myself and, would it be presumptuous of me to say, including many of us—anyone, that is, who enjoys a wondrous tale that calls into being an other world and transports us to it. Does Mahliya's and Samatar's indictment of a persistent Orientalism demand that we reject such enjoyment, that we turn away from wondrous tales that are not homegrown, wherever we recognize our home culture to be? If this is a yes/no absolute question, I would venture to answer in the negative: Samatar's own complex identity stands against an imagined cultural purity; by adapting and commenting on the 2015 English-language translation of a medieval Arabic tale, she adds another layer to its global circulation, and we cannot avoid the entanglements of cultural relations. And yet, in a specific sense, the answer is yes: the power of Samatar's contemporary tale and of Mahliya's first-person telling is to *disorient* those who, in seeking tales of the Other, turn them—consciously or not—into exotic treasures that reaffirm western histories and realities; to disorient all of us away from such a naturalized habit.[8]

Samatar's tale's power lies also in its potential to *re-orient* its English-language readers, whether western or not, to everyday, present-day horrors and wonders in the Arab world to which we may not have been paying as much attention. This potential re-orientation takes the shape of the teller's unexpected invitation to accompany her on an excursion that could lead to re-cognition. What leads up to this invitation? Samatar's shape-shifting teller, Mahliya, lives in twenty-first-century Egypt, and she is well aware of how the foreign researcher's desire to become an authority on the tale participates in reinforcing her people's construction in an ethnographic present (Fabian) that denies them a history and self-determination. In the tale's sequence "What This Tale Does Not Contain," Mahliya's list includes "airports, cigarettes, Internet cafes"; "soap operas based on the works of Naguib Mahfouz, [and] traffic jams"; "street musicians, street protests, cell phones, pictures of bruises taken with cell phones"; "peaceful activists shot down on the street, a poet shot down on the street, the poet who wrote of the streets" (329). The medieval marvels that the foreign researcher came for are juxtaposed with what Samatar identifies in her "Author's Note" as "scenes of contemporary Egypt" and "stories we are less interested in reading" (333).

Samatar's short story ends with Mahliya's invitation to the foreign researcher who had come to add her story and photograph to his treasure trove: "Why don't you let me fly you over the square tonight?" By this point, we readers, like her narratee, have been told that—in the Arabic as well as in the translated and adapted tale—Mahliya was/is also the Queen of Crows, the one "who divides lovers" but reunites them as well (325). In her winged Crow Queen persona, Mahliya flies over Cairo every night, she claims, "watching the city flicker like a broken bulb" and the square turn into "a magic mirror reflecting even the ones who are missing" (332), presumably not only her lost Mauhub but the poet and others shot in the streets. We are not told whether the foreign researcher accepts or not, but the storied invitation has been issued to us as well—the invitation to recognize the complexity and multifariousness of Mahliya, her story, and her world. Accepting it would mean turning away from Orientalist habits whereby "rather than the real person in an unexpected shape, you prefer the magic mirror, which gives you the image you wish to see, although it leaves you grasping nothing but air" (328). It is an invitation that recognizes how imaginative flights of story, nonrealist tales, do not ever merely "report on real life," but, as Marina Warner writes, can "clear the way to changing the experience of living [life]" (27).

As nonrealist narratives or imaginative flights, wonder tales do not simply represent marvelous objects. Often, they thematize wonder as feeling and experience that shake up what we think we know, encourage experiencing the world anew, and inspire imagining what's possible in the world, which is foundational to social change. Adaptations such as Samatar's recognize that wonder tales' immersion in the fantastic triangulates the two-way mirror of history and future in uncanny ways that can work to rearrange dominant economies of fear and desire. While historical and Orientalist entanglements of the west with the east—as Arabic, Middle Eastern, and Asian cultures—structure the wonder-tale imaginary in visible and not-so-visible ways as well as locally and globally, enthusiasm for other cultures, stories, and peoples does not have to result in consuming their resources in ways that impoverish them. It can instead generate new stories and decolonial alliances (Bacchilega 2019).

Take #3: (Un)Homely Insight?

If Samatar's wondrous tale seeks to deobjectify the wonders of the east in order to disturb the hierarchical organization of storytelling traditions, and thus unsettle a hegemonic "politics of knowing" (Ngũgĩ wa Thiong'o 7), it does so from a specific site—the post–Arab Spring and pre-Trump American empire; position—Somali-American woman scholar and fiction writer; and experience—the recent English-language translation event that instigated Samatar's playing Mahliya's tale in a different chord, bringing it back "home" to Egypt.

But does a tale have a home? What does it mean for me or you to feel at home in a tale? What if a tale is represented as part of a structure that is and is not home? I look at Su Blackwell's artwork illustrating the jacket of Marina Warner's *Once upon a Time: A Short History of Fairy Tale*. "The Woodcutter's

Hut" (2008) was part of the 2013 exhibit "Su Blackwell: Stories from the Enchanted Forest" at the Long & Ryle Gallery in London, United Kingdom, featuring "miniature dioramas out of pages, complete with LED lighting [that] recreate enchanting storybook scenes" (Khan). Built out of the pages of a book is a small hut, lit from within and sheltered by a canopy of very tall paper trees; hut and trees are surrounded by a clearing, an apparently deforested area made uneven by "spikey cuts" (Blackwell, personal communication) on the book's flat pages. Words are visible on the walls of the hut and the trees' branches and trunks. The light in the window of the hut makes it look welcoming and warm, like the home one yearns for; the hut's simplicity and isolation make it look poor and primitive, not like the home one yearns for. And the trees surrounding the hut will make it more homey or spooky depending on one's familiarity with them. Against the background screen of tightly packed paper branches is Warner's backlit book title, *Once Upon a Time*, almost as if the light in the hut's window were a modern-day projector as well as the "traditional" source of the formula's magic appeal.

Reproduced on her book jacket, "The Woodcutter's Hut" can only be two-dimensional, but it symbolically functions as a focal point in Marina Warner's multimedial and cross-cultural exploration of the genre as she invites us to "imagine the history of the fairy tale as a map." I quote: "unfurl this imaginary terrain in your mind's eye" (xiii) and take notice not only of its most dazzling landmarks but of the web of story routes that spreads across "centers of talkative storytelling populations" (xiv), plains and cities, ocean and forest, media and audiences. The fairy-tale map she sketches is expansive, and guiding us, Warner writes, are the lights "in the windows of that house in the deep forest ahead of us" (xxiv).

One house, one forest; but not the same house or forest lies ahead for each of us. The house that Warner evokes is and isn't Blackwell's "hut" as they both potentially triangulate with my story house, or yours, and with innumerable other story houses. Guided by the lights of their story house, fairy-tale characters, artists, audiences, and scholars journey, moving across variedly situated spaces of danger and possibility. Even within the Euro-American tradition, it will not be the same house or forest.

Like their adaptations, fairy tales have historically made their way from site to site, carrying a plurality within them. I ask myself, how can any of these story houses in the forest ahead of us be anything but a singularly located yet conglomerate construction of traditions and cross-cultural encounters? And are the windows of these story houses alight with hope for a politics of relation that is rooted not in extraction but in interconnectedness?

Historically, capitalism, sexism, gender binarism, racism, colonialism, and all the -isms have structured fairy-tale mapping and fairy-tale journeying, and scholarship in the last fifty years has remarked on this critically, though unevenly, meaning that sexism has received much more critical attention than Orientalism, racism, and colonialism (Bacchilega and Naithani; Haase; Joosen; Schmiesing; Teverson; Zipes). In her essay "The Frog Sister," Sofia Samatar recounts that

> In 1967, Nongenile Masithathu Zenani, an artist of iintsomi, the Xhosa genre of oral fantasy stories, told a story about a girl and a frog. The girl and the frog were twins, but the mother, horrified at having given birth to a frog, sent it away to be buried in ashes. As for the girl, she couldn't work. *She was just that round thing.* She lay on the floor, inert, until one day, when her mother was away in the fields, a frog knocked at the door. When the frog was with her, the girl could get up and work. *Oh, Child of my mother, you've helped me!* But the frog, frightened of their mother, ran away before she came home, leaving the girl as helpless as before. (203)

Samatar comments: "The girl reveals that her secret power is in fact her rejected sibling. This is the one that was taken and put in the ashes. The small, the inadequately human, the scorned, the repulsive, the trash: this is the source of productivity" (203). For Samatar, the frog sister is like "Dinarzad, or Dunyazad," the minor but enabling "voice to Shahrazad's major one" (204) in *A Thousand and One Nights*.

Extending Samatar's analogy, I see the separation of the sisters as a contrapuntal[9] metanarrative on the Eurocentric emergence of the fairy-tale

Figure 1.1. A collage comprising "The Ice Maiden, 14," "Once Upon a Time, 16," "Sleeping Beauty Castle, 16," "Red Riding Hood, 10," and "The Woodcutters Hut, 08." Artwork by Su Blackwell © 2008–2018.

genre, re-orienting us to its dependence on disavowed family ties with other wonder genres. Traveling to and from different story houses helps me/us to recognize how they are not standing independently of one another and how their *conglomerate* structures are far from independent of social hierarchies and inequities. It helps us to recognize how the homey comfort of one story house may depend on pilfering and trashing another.

Take #4: Re-Orientation as Incitement

Just as interconnectedness does not depend on harmony, re-orientation—even when it follows disorientation—should not lead to a comforting, or reaffirming, return home to the Euro-American tradition as status quo. Take Neil Gaiman's 2014 *The Sleeper and the Spindle*, which meshes a sequel to "Snow White" with an adaptation of "Sleeping Beauty" and is richly illustrated by Chris Riddell and quite popular both in Europe and North America. Featuring a brave unnamed and unmarried queen accompanied by three wise dwarves, this tale ends with the hero choosing not to return to her kingdom in the west, where marriage awaits her. Instead, "They walked to the east, all four of them, away from the sunset and the lands they knew, and into the night" (66). This ending suggests a purposeful disorientation of our expectations for a fairy-tale as well as a Hollywood "into-the-sunset" closing. Its open ending also refigures "the Orient": moving east here means choosing not to conform, crossing a social boundary rather than pushing against the frontier, confronting the unknown as one's ignorance and potential for change.[10]

In my meditation so far on Murai and Cardi's question about "re-orienting the fairy tale," I have reflected on adaptations that play on the Orient and Orientalism and on non-Euro-American tales that provide a contrapuntal reading of the genre. But refiguring western fairy-tale scholarship's relation as anti-Orientalist also requires journeying within the Euro-American fairy-tale territory to re-cognize it, survey it, and know it anew. That is, to challenge Eurocentrism in the study of fairy tales has to involve disorientation and re-orientation as *situated within* the contemporary American fairy-tale map, a tradition that needs to be more forcefully recognized as multiple and as impacting groups of Americans in unequal relation to each other. I move here to consider *God Help the Child* (2015) and how this novel can be read as Toni Morrison's *inciting* take on fairy tale in today's United States.

As fairy-tale scholars we have focused, especially thanks to Jack Zipes's critical work, on Americanization as the commodification and Disneyfication of the European tradition as well as the multimedia production of a fairy-tale formula celebrating heteronormative consumer capitalism. Disneyland's Sleeping Beauty castle, then, has been made to stand for the American story house of fairy tales, its lights and fireworks beckoning not in a forest but in a small-townscape. If there is anything conglomerate about this castle, it consists of its being always already an adaptation, as it relocates a European medieval-like structure to a different continent and also to a theme park, and it projects from its twentieth- and twenty-first-century location a medieval fantasy into our future (Pugh and Aronstein). But what other story houses are assembled not in Disneyland but in the American fairy-tale territory? And what does sighting their lights, a multiplicity of adaptation traditions, within this territory change?

Recently some English-language publications have brought new visibility to the African American tradition. *The Annotated African American Folktales* (Gates and Tatar) asserts the significance of tales that have been "rarely seen as culturally central to the American imagination" (lv), while Emily Zobel Marshall's scholarship (2018) elucidates the politically variable role of these tales' tricksters, in particular Anansi and Brer Rabbit. Focused on stories of racial discrimination and passing, the novel *Boy, Snow, Bird* (2014) by Helen Oyeyemi utilizes African folk narrative forms and African American trickster tropes to expose, as Kimberley Lau writes, "the racial assumptions underpinning the 'Snow White' tradition while also contesting the cultural hegemony of the European fairy tale more generally" (371). These texts and others reassert a storied African American tradition of resistance to slavery, oppression, and discrimination at the same time that they intervene in African Americans' fraught relation to the Euro-American folk and fairy tale. It matters that they do so at a time of heightened racialization and racism in the United States.

Fictional stories emplot real lives, which means that we imagine ourselves in these stories and potentially living them, usually as their heroes (Frank). And the role of "fairy-tale princess" is the most desirable in the hegemonic genre's script. But this two-way mirror, as seen in Carrie May Weems's "Ain't Joking" photographs from the 1980s, does *not* project affirming messages for all. The caption of Weems's "Mirror" reads:

> LOOKING INTO THE MIRROR, THE BLACK WOMAN ASKED, "MIRROR, MIRROR ON THE WALL, WHO'S THE FINEST OF THEM ALL?" THE MIRROR SAYS, "SNOW WHITE, YOU BLACK BITCH, AND DON'T YOU FORGET IT!!!"

This sarcastic citation of the queen's dialog with the magic mirror in "Snow White" replaces "fairest" with "finest"; this puts in evidence the implicit conflation in the fairy-tale "fairest" of beauty and complexion, a conflation the black woman in Weems's artwork rejects but the mirror's words brutally reaffirm.[11]

Toni Morrison's *God Help the Child* does not focus on the exclusion and rejection that black girls and women have felt when attempting to see themselves as fairy-tale princesses. Rather, the novel takes on the social and psychological legacies of this disidentification at a particular time when African Americans face statist violent discrimination within an American society that paradoxically would like to define itself as "post-racial." Morrison introduces us to a "midnight black" (1) American woman. Ostracized by all as a child in the 1990s and abused by her own light-skinned mother, this woman transforms in the early 2000s into a glamorous and publicly celebrated beauty, all thanks to a stylist's advice: always dressed in white, no makeup, with pearl dot earrings, she "makes people think of whipped cream and chocolate soufflé every time they see [her]" (38). Marking her rebranding as rebirth, Lula Ann Bridewell renames herself Bride; and her romance with a beautiful black man named Booker seems to seal her socioeconomic success with happiness. Bride believes she has it made thanks to capitalizing on her color, which seems in the process to have been conveniently emptied out of sociohistorical, cultural, and affective meanings. This Barthesian mythification of Blackness in the supposedly post-racial world of early-twenty-first-century America allows her to become a fairy-tale princess.

Indeed, several reviewers noted that *God Help the Child* presents itself as a "fable" or a "fairy tale."[12] For them, the generic label distances Morrison's story world from contemporary politics and makes wish fulfillment into the novel's core. But I'm thinking of *God Help the Child* as a fairy tale *in site*, not only in triangulation with the Euro-American and African American storytelling traditions but participating in American literary and cultural production in a post-Obama's-second-presidential-election era and alongside of the Black Lives Matter movement; a Black American novel that engages with the fairy-tale genre to unsettle its Euro-American assumed monovocality. So while my brief reflections cannot do justice to the complexity of *God Help the Child*—which is told by various narrators and embraces several points of view—I offer them to foreground the role that fairy tale plays in Morrison's storied meditation on racism today in the United States. I've been teaching Toni Morrison's *God Help the Child* because it calls into question a naturalized "habit of whiteness" (Young)[13] within this tradition; because it *incites* us to break away from the *genre's* hegemonic positioning as a Euro-American practice that is imagined not only as superior to other cultures' wonder genres but also as detached from struggles for social justice.

A disorienting reflection on racism and colorism, *God Help the Child* is no adaptation of a single fairy tale, but there is a fairy-tale aura to it and its female protagonist that quickly loses its shine. Bride, first-person narrator for part of the book, tells how she lost all of it: her looks, confidence, and lover. As Booker puts it later when narrating the same events, "the fairy-tale castle collapsed into the mud and sand on which its vanity was built" (159). When Booker leaves Bride, saying "You not the woman I want," he perhaps intuits that she has not only turned her blackness into a super commodity but also still hates it and herself as Black. Running counter to the "rags to riches" Americanized "Cinderella" tale (Yolen), Bride quickly goes from fairy-tale princess to "scared little black girl" (166), and experiences this painful emotional and social crisis in fairy-tale style, that is, as externalized in bodily changes. Her pubic hair disappeared, her earlobes no longer pierced, her perfect breasts flattened, she finds herself powerless, broken—literally, because of a car accident—displaced from her home, even shot at. Bride's experience as fallen princess calls out the hegemonic fairy tale as tool of assimilation into the white American fantasy of exceptionalism. It is a warning not to go for this exceptionalist story. This novel's disorienting effect, then, is to caution that in a so-called post-racial society the lights in the windows of the Americanized fairy-tale castle are *mis*guiding, that the habit of whiteness continues today to inhabit its halls.

In contrast, the fantastic liminality into which Bride is violently thrust proves to be more conducive to a change that is more genuine than a makeover. Bride's transformation in the final part of the novel does not restore her to the high and isolating social status she had momentarily held as objectified black beauty, but culminates in her being able to live her Blackness as more than color and in a self-affirming community. Eventually, as part of this transformation, Bride realizes and feels that her blackness is "just a color. A genetic trait—not a flaw, not a curse, not a blessing nor a sin" (167), but also grounds her renewed relationship with Booker in their different but specifically Black American experiences of family, loss, mourning, and discrimination. Booker articulates the anti-post-racial intervention of the novel by stating that, especially since scientifically there is no race, "racism without race is a choice" (168).[14] Booker also describes the new Bride as having "changed from one dimension into three—demanding, perceptive, daring" (204). By the end of the novel, Bride is pregnant with Booker's baby and, because their holding hands is about "trust and caring" (206), they feel ready to face their future together. Booker and Bride both have confronted their childhood traumas and taken responsibility for how these traumas "hurtled [them] away from the rip and wave of life" (205). They have not healed, but they have learned from taking care of each other and others, such as Booker's witch-like aunt Queen.

Reviewers have been quick to read this as a fairy-tale ending, and thus a flaw. But they do not notice that the future Bride and Booker imagine for themselves is not the white-fantasy success story the hegemonic fairy tale could offer them only at a high price. Rather, Bride and Booker allow themselves to imagine: "New life. Immune to evil or illness, protected from kidnap, beatings, rape, racism, insult, hurt, self-loathing, abandonment" (207). At least in some regards sharing goals with the real-world Black Lives Matter movement and "working for a world where Black lives are no longer systematically targeted for demise," these fictional characters know that creating this future must depend on "resilience in the face of deadly oppression," a restorative justice that nurtures marginalized difference, and an everyday practice of caring for each other in an intergenerational network (Black Lives Matter).[15] Together, the trope of Bride's fantastic embodied transformations within an otherwise realistic story world, as well as Bride's and Booker's unapologetically Black-centered transformative vision for the future function as Morrison's re-orientation of the fairy tale, which is both critiqued and redeployed to incite social change.

The disorienting and re-orienting strategies of *God Help the Child* intersect. There is a rejection of the "post-racial" and progress-affirming lie that American Disneyfied fairy-tale emplotment sustains. If at first Bride lives out this lie, she quickly realizes its dehumanizing cost. The embodied liminality she then experiences is not a regression; rather, it draws on the trope of eternalized self-reflection that fairy tales are filled with to symbolize violent conflicts and identity breaks that can lead to the transformation of oneself and one's world. And at the center of Morrison's use of this fairy-tale trope lies the exposure to violence Black children have had to endure.[16] While the hegemonic fairy tale is too often instrumentalized as a success story that perpetuates systemic injustices, the hope and the personal as well as social transformation fostered by fairy tales can also be put to use in support of building a just and sustainable future. In Morrison's ending, this vision of the future is focused on the elimination of African American experiences of violence and injustice.

The final line in Morrison's novel comes from Bride's mother, the light-skinned woman who was embarrassed by her "midnight black" child and claimed "Lula Ann needed to learn how to behave, how to keep her head down and not to make trouble" (8). "Sweetness," as she asked her child to call her "instead of 'Mother' or 'Mama'" (7), is now living in a "small, homey, cheaper" nursing home—which she claims to prefer over "those big, expensive nursing homes outside the city" (209); she has some regrets but still holds Bride's color, and not systemic racism, responsible for the discrimination they both suffered. Sweetness—who does not acknowledge how her daughter's letters address her as "S."—is skeptical of any possibility for real change, especially for Black women like Bride; declining responsibility, in the end she calls on God to help Bride's and Booker's Black baby. As she still believes they should accept their place and keep their heads down, Sweetness's story house remains unchanged. The effect of Sweetness's closing words, her hands-off skepticism and dependence on some outside power for hope, is double: it marks the future imagined by Bride and Booker as no "happily ever after," but it also foregrounds what in fairy-tale studies we call the "heroic optimism" (Carter xx) of small or otherwise socially marginalized characters.[17] Structural injustice takes on new forms across time and space, and activist fairy-tale adaptations take us on imaginative flights as an incitement to reject this naturalized cycle.

While presenting this composition as meditation may exonerate me from generating conclusions, I hope it communicates my scholar-teacher commitment. Fairy tales and wonder tales are too often dismissed as simple stories for children, supernatural remainders of the past, or innocuous entertainment. But historically and in their contemporary adaptations, these tales disorient and re-orient us, guiding us in the forests and urbanscapes of our dreams and nightmares, beckoning us to journey across inner and social barriers, projecting alternative futures, and affecting our sense of what is possible. All good stories do this to some extent, but the fantastic in its varied forms is enabled by a double vision that transforms "things as they are." I agree with Marek Oziewicz in *Justice in Young Adult Speculative Fiction* that nonrealist fiction in general is an excellent "tool to conduct thought experiments" to expand our thinking and imagining "beyond the limits of the given" (12); and according to Oziewicz, it is not accidental that we are globally experiencing an "explosion of the fantastic" in a "tightly interconnected world where we either achieve justice or we will be doomed to a vicious circle of escalating conflicts" (14). Scholarly commitment to reading fairy-tale adaptations *in site* is one way to foreground their participation in struggles for social justice as well as the hope some of them offer for an interconnectedness not based on perpetuating exploitation.

Notes

1. I will be using these terms interchangeably. This is not to say that there are not other wonder genres that are quite distinct from fairy tales.

2. From the Latin, *in situ*.

3. I want to thank Mayako Murai and Luciana Cardi for envisioning and organizing "Re-Orienting the Fairy Tale: Contemporary Fairy-Tale Adaptations across Cultures," which in my experience offered an unprecedented opportunity for international encounters and exchanges.

4. For triangulation and mirrors, I'm referring back to my discussion in *Postmodern Fairy Tales* of reflection, framing, and refraction. I'm also thinking of feminist readings of the magic mirror in "Snow White," where the relationship between the queen and her stepdaughter is mediated by the mirror's voice, which puts the two women in competition with one another by asserting which one is more desirable from the perspective of patriarchal power. Based on whose authority and desire, then, will the viewer recognize herself or not in the phantasmatic fairy tale? My references here are Arthur Frank for "emplotment" and Jean Baudrillard for "hyperreal."

5. It also appeared in the electronic *Lightspeed: Science Fiction and Fantasy* (issue 89, October 2017). I wish to thank Veronica Schanoes for recommending the story to me.

6. Said insisted on how "all texts" are "worldly and circumstantial" (*Orientalism* 23), that is, bound to the world because they are events that have "sensuous particularity as well as historical contingency" (*The World, the Text, and the Critic* 39). Colonialism, imperialism, and globalization are some of the power structures impacting which tales of wonder have traveled and with what authority since the 1500s at least.

7. Malcolm Lyons's volume first appeared in hardcover in November 2014, but its 2015 edition was more broadly reviewed, and thus I refer to it as an event. For different takes in the United Kingdom and the United States on Lyons's translation and its eventfulness, see Robert Irwin ("The earliest known Arabic

short stories have just been translated into English for the first time" in the *Independent*, www.independent.co.uk/arts-entertainment/books/features/the-earliest-known-arabic-short-stories-in-the-world-have-just-been-translated-into-english-for-the-9859833.html), Anthony Sattin ("A treasure-trove of grisly Arab tales may appeal more to an Isis fighter than your average British reader" in the *Spectator*, www.spectator.co.uk/2014/12/a-treasure-trove-of-grisly-arab-tales-may-appeal-more-to-an-isis-fighter-than-your-average-british-reader/), Amanda Craig ("Tales of the Marvellous and News of the Strange review – powerful stories from ancient Arabia" in the *Guardian*, www.theguardian.com/books/2014/dec/14/tales-of-the-marvellous-news-of-the-strange-review-malcolm-c-lyons), Michael Dirda ("In these medieval Arab tales, a heavy dollop of spice" in the *Washington Post* www.washingtonpost.com/entertainment/books/medieval-arab-fantasy-tales-arabian-nights-styled-stories-spiced-with-sex/2015/04/01/83f5798c-d3f8-11e4-a62f-ee745911a4ff_story.html?utm_term=.215b148389bf), and Genevieve Valentine ("'Tales of the Marvellous' Is Indeed Very Strange" in *NPR Reviews*, www.npr.org/2015/02/18/385193561/tales-of-the-marvellous-is-indeed-very-strange).

8. About unwittingly reproducing the tropes of "Arabian fantasy," Samatar's understated comment in an interview is: "If you do all of that without thinking about what is happening in those places now, and the relationship between the place you are in and what is happening in those places now, if you're not doing that thinking and it's nowhere visible in the work that you're doing, I do think it's kind of weak" (Duffy).

    Please note that Samatar's adaptation does not offer an explicit characterization of the foreign researcher's gender; in my meditation I take the liberty of asserting my hunch that this researcher is male.

9. In *Culture and Imperialism*, Edward Said reads Jane Austen's *Mansfield Park* as being about not only the estate owned by the Bertram family in England but also about this estate's dependency on colonial structures as the family's wealth derives from sugar plantations in Antigua. The text represents an imperial perspective as sovereign, but a contrapuntal reading takes a perspective external to it and foregrounds what the text has ignored or minimized.

10. In the conference talk on which this essay draws, I discussed Neil Gaiman's *The Sleeper and the Spindle* at much more length. Gaiman is a British author who lives in the United States some of the time. As with most English-language popular-culture adaptations, one can hardly say that its author's

nationality defines *The Sleeper and the Spindle*. Its story world is mapped as a fantasy world where, however, east and west matter.

11. Kimberly Lau discusses the various meanings of "fairest" in her excellent essay on Helen Oyeyemi's *Boy, Snow, Bird,* another recent novel that thematizes race and gender in the twentieth-century United States by drawing on fairy tale. Racial discrimination is a persistent problem in the world as well as in mainstream globalized fairy-tale culture à la Disney, where children of color have a hard time recognizing themselves.

12. A "modern-day fable" (*NPR Books*, April 22, 2015), for some reviewers *God Help the Child* "echoes the fairy tale" (*The Oregonian*, April 28, 2015), while for others it is "a modern fairy tale" (*Entertainment News*, April 21, 2015). A book club question online reads, "*Kirkus Reviews* said of the book, 'As in the darkest fairy tales, there will be fire and death.' In what other ways is *God Help the Child* like a fairy tale?" ("*God Help the Child*").

13. In her 2015 book, Helen Young shows how "habits of whiteness" informed the very emergence of modern fantasy in the nineteenth century as a Eurocentric genre with roots in European medieval times. Nnedi Okorafor's "The Magical Negro" is a wonderfully parodic short story exposing this habit. I do not have the space here to elaborate on this thought, but in contrast to fantasy, fairy tales—as wonder tales and folktales—have inhabited and moved across multiple cultures. That we can map the genre, historically and geopolitically, as a conglomerate of traditions and cross-cultural encounters means that the "habit of whiteness" is by comparison more easily breakable. Lau shows this happening in Oyeyemi's novel's use of African American traditions. I am suggesting Morrison's strategy is to root the fairy-tale plot in African American needs and desires.

14. See Gras for a strong reading of the novel as refuting the existence of a postracial and postfeminist American reality.

15. I don't mean to push this parallel any further. Unlike Black Lives Matter, which articulates its support for extended-family and queer-affirmative networks, Morrison's characters remain tied to a heteronormative future and family structure. Their action is also limited to personal relationships and not necessarily extending to the public or political sphere.

16. By the end of the novel Bride has also built relationships across racial barriers, and these relationships are based not on the shared pain she and other mistreated youth have suffered but on how they each choose to resist being

objectified and isolated because of their color. Specifically, Morrison's focus extends to the abuse of white children in the figure of Rain, a character whose "milk-white skin, ebony hair" (100) associate her with Snow White. The important bond that Bride and Rain form cannot be part of my focused meditation, but merits attention within the framework of relationality.

17. Angela Carter does not define "heroic optimism" more than "as if to say, one day, we might be happy, even if it won't last" (xx). Carter's resonant phrase, characteristic of the hopeful and resilient "what if?" space of fairy tales, appeared originally in her *Virago Book of Fairy Tales* (1990), which was recently reprinted as *Angela Carter's Book of Fairy Tales*.

Works Cited

Bacchilega, Cristina. "'Decolonizing' the Canon: Critical Challenges to Eurocentrism." *The Fairy Tale World*, edited by Andrew Teverson, Routledge, 2019, pp. 33–44.

Bacchilega, C., and Naithani, S. "Colonialism/Postcolonialism/Decolonization." *The Routledge Companion to Media and Fairy-Tale Cultures*, edited by Pauline Greenhill, Jill Terry Rudy, Naomi Hamer, and Lauren Bosc, Routledge, 2018, pp. 83–90.

Baudrillard, Jean. *Simulacra and Simulation*. Translated by Sheila Glazer, University of Michigan Press, 1995.

Black Lives Matter: About. blacklivesmatter.com/about/. Accessed 28 January 2018.

Blackwell, Su. Personal email communication. 11 December 2017.

Carter, Angela, editor. *Angela Carter's Book of Fairy Tales*. Virago, 2005.

Duffy, Peter A. "Sofia Samatar's Arabian Fantasies Get Dosed in Reality." *Wired*, 3 June, 2017, www.wired.com/2017/06/geeks-guide-sofia-samatar/. Accessed 26 January 2018.

Fabian, Johannes. *Time and the Other: How Anthropology Makes Its Object*. Columbia University Press, 1983.

Frank, Arthur W. *Letting Stories Breathe: A Socio-Narratology*. University of Chicago Press, 2010.

Gaiman, Neil. *The Sleeper and the Spindle*. Illustrated by Chris Riddell, Bloomsbury, 2014.

Gates, Henry Louis Jr., and Maria Tatar, editors. *The Annotated African American Folktales*. W. W. Norton, 2017.

"*God Help the Child* by Toni Morrison." *Vintage Books & Anchor Books Reading Group Center*, knopfdoubleday.com/guide/9780307594174/god-help-the-child/. Accessed 12 December 2017.

Gras, Delphine. "Post What? Disarticulating Post Discourses in Toni Morrison's *God Help the Child*." *Humanities,* vol. 5, no. 80, 2016, mdpi.com/2076-0787/5/4/80. Accessed 13 December 2017.

Haase, Donald. "Decolonizing Fairy-Tale Studies." *Marvels & Tales*, vol. 24, no. 1, 2010, pp. 17–38.

Joosen, Vanessa. *Critical and Creative Perspectives on Fairy Tales: An Intertextual Dialogue between Fairy-Tale Scholarship and Postmodern Retellings*. Wayne State University Press, 2011.

Khan, Tabish. "Art Review: Stories from the Enchanted Forest at Long & Ryle." *Londonist*, londonist.com/2012/11/art-review-stories-from-the-enchanted-forest-long-ryle. Accessed 10 December 2017.

Lau, Kimberly. "Snow White and the Trickster: Race and Genre in Helen Oyeyemi's *Boy, Snow, Bird*." *Western Folklore*, vol. 75, no. 3–4, 2016, pp. 371–96.

Lyons, Malcolm C., translator. "The Story of Mahliya and Mauhub and the White-Footed Gazelle. It Contains Strange and Marvellous Things." *Tales of the Marvellous and News of the Strange: A Medieval Arab Fantasy Collection*, Penguin, 2015, pp. 395–440.

Morrison, Toni. *God Help the Child*. Random House, 2015.

Ngũgĩ wa Thiong'o. *Globalectics: Theory and the Politics of Knowing*. Columbia University Press, 2012.

Okorafor, Nnedi. "The Magical Negro." *Dark Matter: Reading the Bones*, edited by Sheree R. Thompson, Aspect, 2004, pp. 91–94.

Oyeyemi, Helen. *Boy, Snow, Bird*. Riverhead Books Penguin, 2014.

Oziewicz, Marek. *Justice in Young Adult Speculative Fiction: A Cognitive Reading*. Routledge, 2015.

Pugh, Tyson, and Susan Aronstein, editors. *The Disney Middle Ages: A Fairy-Tale and Fantasy Past*. Palgrave Macmillan, 2012.

Said, Edward W. *Orientalism*. Pantheon, 1978.

———. *The World, the Text, and the Critic*. Harvard University Press, 1983.

———. *Culture and Imperialism*. Chatto & Windus, 1993.

Samatar, Sofia. "The Frog Sister." *Fantasy Magazine, Women Destroy Fantasy! Special Issue*, no. 58, October 2014, pp. 203–5. Also online in www.fantasy-magazine.com/products-page/issue-58-women-destroy-fantasy-special-issue/.

———. "The Tale of Mahliya and Mauhub and the White-Footed Gazelle," *The Starlit Wood*, edited by Dominik Parisien and Navah Wolfe, Saga Press, 2016, pp. 321–32.

———. "Author's Note." *The Starlit Wood*, edited by Dominik Parisien and Navah Wolfe, Saga Press, 2016, pp. 333.

———. "Spectacle of the Other: Recreating *A Thousand and One Nights* in Film." *Fairy-Tale Films Beyond Disney: International Perspectives*, edited by Jack Zipes, Pauline Greenhill, and Kendra Magnus-Johnston, Routledge, 2016, pp. 34–47.

———. *Tender: Stories*. Small Beer Press, 2017.

Schmiesing, Ann. "Blackness in the Grimms' Fairy Tales." *Marvels & Tales*, vol. 15, no. 2, 2016, pp. 210–233.

Su Blackwell Studio. www.sublackwell.co.uk/

Teverson, Andrew, editor. *The Fairy Tale World*. Routledge, 2019.

Warner, Marina. *Once Upon a Time: A Short History of Fairy Tale*. Oxford University Press, 2014.

Weems, Carrie Mae. "Mirror." *Ain't Joking (1987-88)*, carriemaeweems.net/galleries/aint-jokin.html

Yolen, Jane. "America's Cinderella." 1977. *Cinderella: A Casebook*, edited by Alan Dundes, University of Wisconsin Press, 1982, pp. 294–304.

Young, Helen. *Race and Popular Fantasy Literature: The Habit of Whiteness*. Routledge, 2015.

Zipes, Jack. *The Irresistible Fairy Tale: The Cultural and Social History of a Genre*. Princeton University Press, 2012.

Zobel Marshall, Emily. "'Nothing but Pleasant Memories of the Discipline of Slavery': The Trickster and the Dynamics of Racial Representation." *Marvels & Tales: Journal of Fairy-Tale Studies*, vol. 32, no. 1, 2018, pp. 59–75.

2

Moʻolelo Kamahaʻo 2.0

The Art and Politics of the Modern Hawaiian Wonder Tale

kuʻualoha hoʻomanawanui

Moʻolelo is an Indigenous Hawaiian[1] word that describes a broad category of stories, histories, and narratives that span oral, written, and now digital formats, multiple languages (such as Hawaiian and English), and time periods (ancient to contemporary). *Moʻolelo kamahaʻo*, which literally translates to "wonder tale," is one way to describe Hawaiian oral traditions that contain elements of wonder, stories with their own culturally rooted orientation distinct from European *märchen*, or "fairy tales."[2] *Moʻolelo* have always been an important cultural form of crafting and passing on knowledge, orienting Native Hawaiians to understand, practice, and continue sharing across generations. *Moʻolelo kamahaʻo* is a category of Hawaiian *moʻolelo* worthy of closer study, particularly within the context of re-orienting non-European wonder tales, so that the intent of such *moʻolelo* can be *reimagined*. Such re-orientation provides new insights and meanings into *moʻolelo kamahaʻo* that simultaneously expand and complicate the western concept of a wonder tale.

Like other traditional stories of *Moana Nui* (the broader Pacific[3]), Hawaiian *moʻolelo* have been passed down across generations through performative modes (storytelling, including dance, chant, and song), visual ones (textiles, visual arts), and, once western literacy (reading and writing) was introduced, literature (printed text). Some, like those for the shape-shifting *kupua* (demigod, culture hero) Māui, who is often paired with Hina (a moon goddess who is alternately his mother, sister, or wife), have deep roots extending into Oceania and possibly into Asia, that complement more localized versions, variants, and retellings composed in and connected to specific places and cultures like Hawaiʻi. With western colonial expansion into Moana Nui in the eighteenth to nineteenth centuries, *haole* (Euro-American) explorers and settlers began collecting *moʻolelo* and publishing them in collections of tales in their colonial languages (primarily English, French, and German) to be exported to their home countries for consumption. These versions were often highly summarized, with subjective editorial remarks that often denigrated the Indigenous peoples and their stories as "primitive." In this way, Indigenous *moʻolelo* were re-oriented to support *haole* hierarchical ideals of human intelligence and advancement based on false ideas of "race" and culture to justify colonialism.

This chapter explores the development of *moʻolelo kamahaʻo* adaptations by Indigenous artists that shift the settler colonial *moʻolelo kamahaʻo* by returning to Indigenous representations, focusing on the wondrous Moana Nui ancestors Māui and Hina. While discussing variants of Māui *moʻolelo* from Oceania outside of Hawaiʻi, this essay is written from a specifically Hawaiian perspective, in part because of different indigenous language terms for story, history, and narratives, such as *tala* (Tongan, Samoan), *kōrero* or *pūrākau* (Māori), and *ʻaʻamu* or *ʻaʻai* (Tahitian), none of which are equivalent to *moʻolelo* or to each other. Re-orienting *moʻolelo* from settler colonial to Indigenous perspectives, Noenoe Silva argues, "free[s] our ancestral stories from the captured state, such that they become healthy frameworks for our own communal self-understanding, antidotes to the poisonous stereotypes of the colonizer" (160).

Prior to the nineteenth century, *moʻolelo* were performed and visually represented; these form the basis for later print adaptations. When western literacy was formally introduced in Hawaiʻi in the 1820s, Hawaiians began recording *moʻolelo* in the Hawaiian language for a primarily Hawaiian audience. Over time, such *moʻolelo* were collected, translated into English, and published by *haole* settlers who recast legendary heroes and ancestors such as Māui as a sometimes feckless, other times brutal figure, without acknowledging the original Hawaiian sources. In this way, *moʻolelo kamahaʻo* became a tool of the settler colonization project that disoriented the scope and purpose of the original *moʻolelo*. Like other Indigenous Pacific peoples, Hawaiians have continually resisted such efforts by continuing to affirm our own intellectual and creative traditions through new modes of storytelling that reflect the original *moʻolelo* of our illustrious *kūpuna* (ancestors). Cristina Bacchilega addresses this point in her work on twenty-first-century adaptations of wonder tales when she writes that in some contemporary literary traditions, such as those of Oceania, "a direct engagement with the fairy tale may be less common," in part because there is more interest by Pacific peoples "in revitalizing and popularizing homegrown wonder genres and indigenous epistemologies in order to decolonize the telling of stories and history both" (Bacchilega Kindle loc. 3678). Thus,

> while the translation of European fairy tales and of the *Arabian Nights* into Hawaiian had its influence on nineteenth-century Hawaiian literature (Bacchilega 2007), generally speaking, the fairy tale is not a genre of choice in Hawaiian adaptation projects today, possibly because the reframing of Hawaiian *moʻolelo* as fairy tale continues to have currency in popular imagination to disparaging effects. (Bacchilega Kindle loc. 3685)

Bacchilega references Disney's *Lilo and Stitch* (2002), but its most recent Oceanic animated feature film, *Moana* (2016) is also highly relevant. Such efforts at re-orienting the *moʻolelo* once disoriented by settler colonialism are part of the continuing effort at reaffirming cultural identity and pride as a *lāhui* (people, nation), promoting indigenous and culturally based education that refutes the damage done to previous generations through an imposed colonial education system, and remembering and reclaiming the intellectual and creative genealogy of our *kūpuna* as part of asserting claims for rebuilding and restoring political sovereignty.

The metaphor of orientation is quite appropriate in discussing *moʻolelo kamahaʻo*, those of Māui (and Hina) in particular, as it is a key concept of long-distance navigation Polynesian cultures are renowned for. Oceania was settled by the brave, intelligent, ancient voyagers, who traversed thousands of miles of open ocean, navigating through keen observation of constellations and other natural phenomenon to guide them to their destinations, often tiny dots of low-lying islands flung across the vastness of Moana Nui, the largest geographical feature on earth. Yet orienting themselves through reading constellations and other signs of nature created what Tongan anthropologist ʻEpeli Hauʻofa has described as "a sea of islands" connected by the ocean, rather than separated by it, as was the predominant view of western scholars (152). Much of western scholarship in myriad disciplines, and as part of an ongoing project of settler colonialism, and what Patrick Wolfe calls "the elimination of the native" (387) has worked across time to disorient and disconnect Indigenous peoples from our traditional knowledge, environment, and culture, which includes our *moʻolelo*, since they contain core elements of traditional knowledge and culture.

From nineteenth-century collected tales to twenty-first-century computer-generated imagery (CGI) animated movies, *moʻolelo kamahaʻo* continue to be manipulated to tell disoriented narratives that often misrepresent the peoples and cultures from which they come. For example, the announcement of Disney's animated feature film *Moana* early in 2014 prompted revisiting the issue of poor representation of indigenous people, culture, and stories in settler colonial storytelling, versus no representation at all. Settler colonial storytelling juggernauts like Disney (Pixar, Dream Works, etc.) are powerful economic and cultural forces that have shaped imaginations for generations now, including those of Indigenous children. As Thomas King argues, "The truth about stories is that's all that we are" (3). In this regard, the misrepresentation of Indigenous peoples, cultures, and stories, including wonder tales, skews everyone's perceptions of such, often with damaging results. In part, such misrepresentations perpetuate colonial tropes and stereotypes that influence how Indigenous peoples, such as Hawaiians, are (mis)perceived by others. It also continues the cultural hegemony of settler colonialism that has the power to produce, disseminate, and reinforce such narratives, resulting in Indigenous peoples being misunderstood by others and our own selves, unable to escape from these narratives and powerless to assert our own culturally rooted narratives at the same level. The mainstream media (news and entertainment) is a powerful and pervasive tool that works with other industries of western capitalism, such as tourism, product merchandising (including toys), and real estate. On the one hand, the narrative exotifies and stereotypes Hawaiʻi as a place (tropical paradise), its people (Noble Savage, golden people), and its culture ("the Aloha state," "Aloha Spirit") to lure in tourist dollars and foreign investment.

On the other hand, the settler colonial project exploits the land, people, and culture through its prostitution, as Hawaiian nationalist, scholar, and poet Haunani Kay Trask (1993) argues, dismissing Hawaiians as archaic, and our assertion of *aloha ʻāina* (patriotism, caring for and protecting the land, especially from development), kinship to the *ʻāina* (land), and political independence and self-determination from the United States as ridiculous. Thus, while settler colonialism profits from such exploitation, Hawaiians remain landless, homeless, criminalized, undereducated, unhealthy, demoralized, displaced, and destitute in our own homeland (McDougall and Nordstrom).

In this context, highlighting Indigenous presentations and re-presentations of traditional stories, such as *moʻolelo kamahaʻo*, is critical, as Indigenous truth-telling through *moʻolelo*, as Lakota scholar Waziyatawin (2010) argues, provides engaging counter-narratives—or re-orientations—that challenge the misportrayal of damaging settler colonial narratives, offering more powerful, inspiring narratives with more positive results, particularly for Indigenous peoples. Daniel Heath Justice (2018) points out that in the context of settler colonialism and the severe damage done to Indigenous peoples and our stories, there are stories that wound and stories that heal. Stories that wound are settler colonial narratives that negatively stereotype and disparage Indigenous peoples and cultures. Stories that heal are a reassertion of Indigenous knowledge and perspectives encoded in our *moʻolelo*. In short, the reason Indigenous stories matter is because Indigenous people matter, people who were not meant to survive what David Stannard (1989) has referred to as the American Holocaust of colonial expansion. Through asserting our stories of healing, we re-orient ourselves back to our ancestral knowledge as survivors, not victims. As Steven Winduo argues, "Indigenous communities in Oceania have always used [traditional stories] to explain our political and cultural environment[s] . . . [a] tradition [that] continues today in the cultural production of many Pacific writers, artists, and filmmakers, [whose] 'texts' are often saturated with social and political discourse that challenge the hegemony of western ideology, tradition, and power" (1).

Māui, an admired, popular, and important shape-shifting demigod and trickster hero, traces his origins to other parts of Oceania. He is associated with a number of wondrous feats and phenomena, sometimes with the assistance of Hina, and is an important figure of old cultural and oral traditions, including navigation and wayfinding, a powerful Oceanic deity and ancestor.

Over time, *moʻolelo kamahaʻo* have undergone multiple kinds of adaptations. In recent decades, an increase in political and cultural activism has led to cultural empowerment, including the steady blossoming of culturally based and indigenous-language revitalization efforts in education systems such as Kohanga Reo (*lit.* language nest) in Aotearoa (New Zealand) and the Kula Kaiāpuni Hawaiian language immersion public schools in Hawaiʻi, which have been long, hard-fought political battles for more native linguistic, cultural, and educational autonomy. Within this larger political context, Indigenous Pacific peoples have worked to reclaim the mana of our traditional *moʻolelo* in their myriad forms, while also working to encourage new ones. Thus, Māui, Hina, and other important cultural figures in myriad alternative adaptations, such as children's literature, cartoon animation, graphic novels, and stage drama have blossomed. These Indigenous re-presentations of Oceanic *moʻolelo kamahaʻo* have intentionally countered settler colonial adaptations by asserting a culturally based resistance to U.S. assimilation that factors into the ongoing Hawaiian sovereignty movement, *aloha ʻāina* nationalism, and continued cultural revival, including *ʻāina*-based and experiential education. Thus, understanding the culturally based, political underpinning of *moʻolelo kamahaʻo* such as that for Māui and Hina provides a more culturally centered and appropriate interpretation of modern Indigenous adaptations and their purpose. New media adaptations of Indigenous-focused *moʻolelo kamahaʻo* help to re-orient them in two ways: first, to re-present them to Indigenous audiences by reclaiming them from damaging, settler versions, and second, to re-present them to non-Indigenous settler and global audiences in a way that dispels negative settler colonial stereotypes.

Nā Moʻolelo Kamahaʻo o Māui, ke Kupuʻeu Leleʻoi o Hawaiʻi (The Traditional Wonder Tales of Māui, the "Hawaiian Superman")

Auē! He toa nui Māuipeutini rā i!

Ho! A mighty warrior-hero is Māui of a thousand glorious deeds!
(Stimson 12)

Māui and Hina *moʻolelo* are "one of the strongest links" of indigenous wonder tales found across Moana Nui (William D. Westervelt in Luomala 10); as demonstrated in the above epigraph, he is a celebrated *toa nui*, great warrior-hero remembered for his multitudinous (*tini*) accomplishments. Celebrating Māui through epithets such as *"peu tini"* (a thousand deeds), a Tuamotuan variation of Māuitinihanga (Māori) demonstrates ancient kinship and cultural connections across the vast Pacific region, while hinting as well to his superb wayfinding skills. Māui and Hina *moʻolelo* are found throughout Polynesia, in Melanesia (Fiji, Vanuatu), and in Micronesia (Kiribati), and purportedly trace beyond Oceania into the Philippines, India, Malaysia, and China. There are numerous wondrous feats associated with Māui and Hina across Oceania that vary in scope and detail. Highlights include:

- A miraculous birth (Māui from his mother Hina)
- Fishing up islands
- Lifting the sky
- Snaring the sun, creating seasons (assisting his mother Hina; aided by sister Hina)

- Discovering fire for human use (assisting his mother Hina)
- Originating kite flying
- Wondrous battles, such as with Peʻapeʻa the eight-eyed bat (saving a kidnapped Hina), and Pīmoe, the supernatural *ulua* (crevalle) fish
- Seeking immortality (why humans are mortal)
- Being aided by Manaiakalani, a "magical" fishhook
- *Kupua* (demigod) status
- Shape-shifting ability

Rather than explicate these wondrous deeds of Māui in detail, which have been well documented elsewhere[4], I will highlight selected examples of Māui and Hina *moʻolelo* retold or represented in contemporary Indigenous storytelling contexts.

New media representations of *moʻolelo kamahaʻo* for Māui and Hina include performance modes, including songs, dance, stage productions, and animated and live-action film; visual images; and print genres, such as children's picture books, comics, and graphic novels. Many of the printed texts are published in indigenous languages such as Māori language in Aotearoa (New Zealand) and Hawaiian language in Hawaiʻi, in the colonial language (English or French), or bilingually with the indigenous and colonial languages. Similarly, performance and film productions are also rendered in the native language, the colonial language, or both.

Re-Orienting *Moʻolelo Kamahaʻo*: The Cultural and Political Renaissance of the 1990s

In Hawaiʻi as elsewhere in Oceania, the 1990s marked the beginning of a cultural, political, and educational renaissance, the result of decades of cultural and political advocacy to reestablish the Hawaiian language as a foundation of educational and cultural practices. The year 1993 commemorated the centennial of the illegal overthrow of the Hawaiian kingdom, when Queen

Liliʻuokalani (1838–1917) was unceremoniously deposed by a faction of *haole* men in their own bid for land and power.

New performance modes retelling—and reaffirming—important, traditional *moʻolelo*, including *moʻolelo kamahaʻo*, appeared in myriad forms, including performance such as *mele* (song) and hula drama, visual arts, and literature. The political and cultural activism of the 1990s was, collectively, a deepening of Hawaiians looking to the past to navigate toward the future, re-oriented in part through our traditional *moʻolelo*.

Māui, the Hawaiian Superman

In 1993, Hawaiian musician Del Beazley composed what quickly became a hugely popular song, "Hawaiian Supʻpah [super] Man," a *mele hoʻohanohano* (honorific song) celebrating the wondrous accomplishments of the legendary Māui using contemporary Hawaiian music and channels of dissemination (live performances, radio airplay, recordings, such as CDs, and MP3s). Recorded and performed by Israel Kamakawiwoʻole, "Maui Hawaiian Supʻpah Man" demonstrates the importance of adapting Hawaiian language stories to English (the dominant language forcibly imposed through over a century of oppressive settler colonial policies, resulting in many Hawaiians losing fluency in our native language) while maintaining a cultural viewpoint that preserves the integrity of the traditional cultural superhero. The first part of the *mele* references two of Māui's important and wondrous accomplishments listed above—fishing up the Hawaiian Islands with his "magic" fishhook, Manaiakalani, and creating seasons through slowing the sun part of year, so his mother Hina's *kapa* (cloth made from the soft inner bark of specific plants) could dry properly. He is then historicized as an ancient figure "before Clark Kent," Superman's human alter ego, a more contemporary and fictional western superhero. The second part of the *mele* celebrates another important feat of Māui—discovering the secret of fire, which, until that time, had been kept secret by the crafty ʻ*alae* (Hawaiian mudhen).

Pīnaʻi (repetition) in the chorus is a *meiwi* (poetic device, strategy) that emphasizes Māui's heroic status, the ultimate "mystical, marvelous, magical . . . hero" who is so amazing, there is no one else who can compare; *pīnaʻi* is also evident through consonance, with repeated "m" sounds:

> Mischievous, marvelous, magical Māui, hero of this land
> The one, the only, the ultimate Hawaiian Sup'pah Man
> Māui, oh Māui, oh Māui, Hawaiian Sup'pah Man. (lyrics transcribed by author)

By contextualizing Māui's amazing accomplishments through a contemporary American hero figure, Superman, familiar to Hawaiian and other youth because of Americanization and the pervasive saturation of western culture, Beazley finds a connecting point for Hawaiian youth living within the constraints of settler colonialism to their traditional culture and hero figures, providing a comfortable and inviting way—via catchy, contemporary Hawaiian pop music—to explore decolonization via the story of an ancestor superhero. Through his wondrous deeds, Māui exhibits behaviors considered virtuous and admirable in Hawaiian culture: he seeks to act on behalf of his *kūpuna* (elders), represented by his mother Hina and grandmother, in slowing the sun (creating seasons), fishing up islands to live on, and discovering the secret of fire so people can cook food. These wondrous deeds reflect key Hawaiian cultural values, including *aloha* (compassion) and *mālama* (caring). He exhibits the admired and desirable values of *ʻeleu* (quick) and *ʻaʻapo* (smart) in figuring out how to do these tasks, using braids of Hina's hair to weave a special rope to snare the sun; this wondrous rope has the power to not be incinerated by the sun when it gets too close to it, imbuing Māui's heroic masculine feat with feminine *mana* (power, often sacred and spiritual).

The *mele* was an important part of the blossoming cultural identity and political agency of the 1990s. It provided an important reminder in 1993 of the brilliance and depth of Hawaiian history and genealogy of not just the overthrow of Queen Liliʻuokalani a century before, but of her illustrious ancestors, including Māui, who is named in her royal, sacred genealogy known as Kumulipo, an integral *koʻihonua* (cosmogonic genealogy) documenting a

Hawaiian account of evolution and the origin of the universe.[5] It was one of several important performance-based adaptations of *Māui moʻolelo* that contributed to a re-orientation of Native Hawaiian identity, culture, and politics, as much as it re-oriented the telling and understanding of the *moʻolelo* itself.

Stage Performances: Hula Dramas

Kamehameha Schools, a private Hawaiian educational institution founded in 1887 for Native Hawaiian students, began a song contest for students in 1920, which, since the mid-1960s, has included a *hōʻike* (performance) between the competition and the awards ceremony. Each year, the *hōʻike* is organized around a theme, which has included *moʻolelo kamahaʻo*; in 1997, the *hōʻike* theme focused on Māui and Hina *moʻolelo*. The *hōʻike* features student performers, with *hula kahiko* (traditional-style hula dance) and *hula ʻauana* (modern-style hula) performed to live music, including songs and chants to which the hula dances are choreographed. The song contest is broadcast live each year on television, and in recent years, livestreamed on the World Wide Web. A video recording of the 1997 performance is preserved on YouTube.[6]

The 1997 Kamehameha Schools Hōʻike featured five scenes associated with Māui: his unusual birth, his reunification with his brothers, fishing up islands, discovering the secret of fire, and snaring the sun. The production is narrated from Hina's perspective, an important element of Māui's story in the production, as Hina's voice is often absent in the telling of this *moʻolelo*. Each scene contains at least one *mele* or a hula related to the segment of the *moʻolelo*, and features different members of the ensemble. For example, in recounting the experience of Māui's unusual birth, Hina describes what she thinks is his stillborn body and how she comes up with his name, Māui-a-ka-malo (Māui of the loincloth), alternately known as Māui-a-Kalana (or Māui-Akalana, Māui of [the father] Akalana).

> There was little Māui, Māuiakamalo, a shapeless mass, barely breathing, barely human. At that moment, I was the only one in

the world who could find beauty in this forsaken child. . . . The direction of the wind changed, and somehow I knew I couldn't keep Māui, not here in the land of men. My sisters helped me as I made my way down to the sea. I pressed my face up against him one last time. (audio transcribed by author; 00:16–1:38)

Hina then calls upon Kanaloa, god of the ocean, "Oh Kanaloa, guardian of the sea, receive my son into your bosom" (1:39). The performance segues into a hula, where the dancers personify the ocean, *pololia* (jellyfish), *mālolo* (flying fish), and sea birds, who take the infant Māui from his mother's arms and carry him to Kuaihelani, the ancient, mythical homeland of the gods, where he is raised. Hina wraps him in one of his father (A)kalana's red *malo*, hence his names Māuiakamalo and Māuiakalana. The scene reaffirms Māui's *kupua*, or wondrous status, cared for by the natural elements, and the interrelation between land, people, and deities.

Such presentations of *moʻolelo kamahaʻo* are important reorientations, particularly for Indigenous peoples consumed by settler colonialism, in keeping our history and culture visible, vibrant, and alive for current and future generations, spurring their own creativity as well as knowledge. Katrina-Ann Oliveira (2014) discusses the importance of *performance cartographies* in the construction of Hawaiian knowledge that functions, in part, as a way to orient knowledge. Performance through hula (dance), for example, is a way to record, remember, and pass down various kinds of cultural knowledge, including *inoa ʻāina* (place names, or names of geological features on the land and in the sea), *moʻolelo* (historical accounts), *moʻokūʻauhau* (genealogies), and *hoʻokele* (navigation), which are all relevant to the Māui (and Hina) *moʻolelo*. The section of the *moʻolelo* described above recounts Māui's exceptional beginnings, a *hōʻailona* (symbol) of his hero status to come. Moreover, indigenous performative modes based on performance and language (the *mele* or chants to which the hula are danced) are mnemonic devices, particularly in modern times, for people living generations after a heroic figure like Māui to remember and celebrate his achievements on behalf of humans. "Conversely," Oliveira writes, "the names of *aliʻi* not carried on through

Figure 2.1. The infant Māui, wrapped in his father Akalana's red *malo*, is taken by his ocean guardians (dancers clothed in blue and white, representing the sea) to be raised in the mythical home of the gods, Kuaihelani. Kamehameha Schools Song Contest Hōʻike 1997. Video still.

such performative cartographies are forgotten in due time, and their place in history is replaced by the memory of a more famous *aliʻi*" (Kindle loc. 1846). This is applicable to Māui, as *moʻolelo* record his deeds and connections to lands throughout Moana Nui and across the Hawaiian archipelago. Moreover, as Oliveira explains,

> Kupa o ka ʻāina [natives of specific locations] were caretakers of the moʻolelo attached to their kulāiwi [native lands]. Moʻolelo were memorized and passed down generation after generation, reinforcing an akua connection and embedding an air of importance to the places enumerated in the moʻolelo. The island of Maui is named after the demigod Māui; thus, the name bestows much mana [spiritual power] upon it.... With pride, Kānaka ulitized performance cartographies to map their places and to record their legacies. (Kindle loc. 2070; 2383).

The following year, playwright Tammy Hailiʻōpua Baker and her husband, Chris Kaliko Baker, and their nonprofit theater company, Hālau Hanakeaka, produced the play *Māuiakamalo, ka Hoʻokala Kupua o ka Moku*

(Māui of the loincloth, the Hawaiian hero of the islands). The Bakers are at the forefront of reviving *hana keaka* (Hawaiian stage plays), writing, directing, and producing them primarily in the Hawaiian language and focusing on traditional themes and *moʻolelo*. *Māuiakamalo* is one of the first of such plays. The Bakers' work combines the acting and format of western theater with important Hawaiian cultural performance genres, such as *mele* and hula, that function, in part, as performance cartographies. The play toured the Hawaiian Islands throughout 1998, reaching audiences across the archipelago. In 2000 it was performed at the Pacific Arts Festival in Noumea, New Caledonia, introducing a modern, Hawaiian performance of Māui and Hina *moʻolelo* to a much larger Pacific audience.

A published section of the script begins with the end of act 1, scene 8, where Māui's brothers are preparing to depart on a fishing trip. Act 1, scene 9 opens with a *mele* chanted by the four *ʻalae* mudhens who hold the secret of fire, named Kaʻalaehuapī, Kaʻalaehuaiki, Kaʻalaehuaʻole, and Kaʻalaehuanui in the play. The female *ʻalae* birds are roasting bananas. Māui approaches the *ʻalae* and tries to coax the secret of fire from them, but they are unwilling to share it, teasing him first with incorrect information. Angered, he grabs Kaʻalaehuapī and begins to strangle her, until she finally reveals the secret. This scene is an enactment of the episode in the *moʻolelo* told in the second verse of Beazley's *mele* "Hawaiian Sup'pah Man."

Collectively, it is important to compare the three works and their use of language, and the dynamic use of English, Hawaiian Creole English

Figure 2.2. Māui attempts to learn the secret of fire making from the *ʻalae* mudhens. Hālau Hanakeaka's *Māuiakamalo* stage play. Video still.

(HCE) or "pidgin" as it is commonly called in Hawai'i, and Hawaiian, as each are used politically. Beazley's composition and Kamakawiwo'ole's performance of "Hawaiian Sup'pah Man" make Māui's story accessible in English and HCE for those not fluent in Hawaiian. The *mele* also identifies the target audience, which is made up of what in Hawai'i are called "Locals," often considered Native Hawaiians, part-Hawaiians, and plantation-rooted immigrants, primarily Chinese, Japanese, Filipino, Korean, and Puerto Rican descendants of immigrants imported as labor for the sugar and later pineapple plantations. The general gloss of "Local" excludes *haole*, although many locals have intermixed with each other, *haole*, and other ethnicities over time. It is through this ethnic and cultural intermixing that HCE was born. These languages reflect the reality of multiple generations of Hawaiians educated in the settler colonial–imposed English language, beginning in 1896 after the overthrow of the independent kingdom, when Hawaiian was outlawed as a medium of instruction in public schools by the *haole*-run Republic of Hawai'i. HCE stabilized in the early 1900s, an outgrowth of the influx of diverse ethnic immigrant groups brought to work sugar plantations who sought to communicate with each other while simultaneously rejecting the American-imposed "standard" English. HCE became a language of solidarity and "local" identity whose adherents were comprised of Native Hawaiians and plantation immigrants who resisted American political and socioeconomic power through their refusal to adopt English. Georganne Nordstrom describes the political intent of HCE as "rhetorical sovereignty," an integral practice employed to resist English (318). The rendering of "super" (for "Superman") as "sup'pah" is a clear marker of HCE influence, as is the pronunciation of other words in the song by Kamakawiwo'ole. Both English and HCE are often used in contemporary Hawaiian reggae compositions, as reggae is viewed as a genre of music that resonates with the oppression of brown people across tropical island environments, creating a transcultural alliance through its adoption across Oceania (ho'omanawanui). Thus, the melody is reggae-influenced modern pop, and it is not considered a song suitable for hula and has not been choreographed as such. In this way, it reflects not only a contemporary "Local" identity rooted in Native Hawaiian legend, language, and place but also a more modern, mixed–ethnic identity culture that claims a genre of music (reggae) by other working-class brown people, thus reflecting resistance against colonial oppression. By interweaving an old Native Hawaiian *moʻolelo* celebrating a pre-Christian wonder hero with a melody and rhythm associated with anticolonial resistance told in HCE, Beazely re-orients the tale away from settler colonial retellings that use English writing as a medium. As a *mele*, it is meant to be performed, taking it back to the oral tradition but, as it is retold in HCE rather than the Hawaiian language, it is a linguistic re-orientation inclusive of modern Hawaiian and "Local" identities.

The Kamehameha Schools Hōʻike is presented bilingually, with English language narration and *mele* composed and performed in Hawaiian, a long-standing central feature of *hula kahiko*. The bilingual aspect of the Kamehameha performance allows for the enjoyment of the production by a wider audience; the narration in English provides the context for the performance of *mele* and hula in Hawaiian for those who are not fluent but who would expect to see hula presented in the Hawaiian language. The Bakers' work, however, reasserts the Hawaiian language as an important vehicle for Hawaiian storytelling, presenting traditional *moʻolelo* as modern storytelling in performance. Their linguistic re-orientation of the performance back to the Hawaiian language reflects the contemporary Hawaiian cultural and political renaissance, which began in the 1960s and was reaffirmed in the 1990s, of which the revitalization of the Hawaiian language is a key component. In doing so, the play re-orients the audience (and performers) to a mode of storytelling more aligned to traditional cultural practice, not only because it is presented in the Hawaiian language but also because of how the *moʻolelo* is presented. For example, there is no specific number of *ʻalae* birds in the original *moʻolelo*, nor are the *ʻalae* always named. In *Mauiākamalo*, there are four named *ʻalae*. Four is an important number in Hawaiian culture, representing *pono* (balance, harmony) in a multitude of ways. The four names for the *ʻalae* represent important cultural (and traditional storytelling) concepts, such as *ʻēkoʻa* (dyads)—Kaʻalaehuaiki means "the small fruit mudhen," which is balanced by Kaʻalaehuanui, "the large fruit mudhen." The "large fruit" (*hua nui*) metaphorically means someone or something productive. This concept is contrasted with Kaʻalaehuaʻole, "the unproductive mudhen," whose name also means "worthless." On the one hand, Kaʻalaehuapī's name references the red-beaked and red-breasted mudhen as ʻalae huapī as a synonym for the ʻalae ʻula (red mudhen), which is distinct from the ʻalae kea (white mudhen). Yet pī also means stingy, and the kaona (metaphoric, veiled, poetic) meaning refers to the mudhen's stinginess with fire, and not wanting to share that knowledge with Māui. The red (ʻula) and white (kea) colors of the ʻalae hens are also dyads that oppose and complement each other—in Hawaiian culture, both are sacred colors associated with different akua (deities). For example, red is a color of the highest ranking aliʻi, and the war god Kūkāʻilimoku (island-snatching Kū); an alternate form of Kū is Kūʻula (red Kū), a fishing deity and stone-attracting fish. Lono, a god of fertility and agriculture and an antithesis of Kū, was associated with white, particularly in the annual fall harvest festival, called Makahiki.

The number four reflects the four directions (north, south, east, and west) and the four main male gods, who are also found throughout Polynesia, Kāne (or Tāne), Kū (or Tū), Lono (or Rono, Rongo, Roʻo), and Kanaloa (or Tangaroa, Taʻaroa). Collectively, they regulated Hawaiian society in traditional times (prior to the overthrow of the ʻAikapu after the death of Kamehameha I in 1819). They also embody and regulate key natural elements, such as sunlight and fresh water (Kāne), staple vegetable crops such as kalo (taro) (Kāne), ʻuala (sweet potatoes), puaʻa (pork) (Lono), the ocean and everything associated with it, including seafood (Kanaloa), and healing, agricultural practices, and warfare (Kū). Counting or grouping by four is kāuna, a traditional formulistic number. Thus, the use of kāuna applied to the ʻalae mudhens is one way the moʻolelo is re-oriented back to its cultural roots.

Like Beazley's mele, pīnaʻi or repetition is also present throughout. When the scene opens, the ʻalae chant a mele that evokes the fire, and they tease humans for not possessing the knowledge of fire making. The mele is performed in act 1 scene 9, and is repeated in act 1, scene 10, as the ʻalae boast about tricking Māui—

'Ena'ena lapalapa ka hau malo'o i 'ena'ena lā
'Ena'ena 'ole ho'i ke ao kanaka lā
'O ke ao kanaka lā, ka po'e nele ho'i hā
Kāhāhā, kāhāhā, kāhāhā nele lākou lā. (Baker 111, 117)

Red hot, blazing, the dry *hau* (hibiscus) tinder is ablaze
The realm of humans, however, is not [it is cold and dark]
In the human world, the people are truly lacking [the knowledge of fire making]
Surprising, puzzled, astonished they are truly lacking. (my translation)

The composition is a modern one that reflects traditional *mele*. For example, *pīna'i* is visible in the repetition of sounds and words, which emphasize the meaning; the "ah" sound in particular, through words such as *'ena'ena* (blazing, glowing, red hot), *kanaka* (people), and *kāhāhā* (surprising, puzzling, astonishing; a teasing interjection) demonstrates the focus of the *mele*, which is that the *'alae* are boasting about their knowledge of fire and scoffing at the ignorance of humans who lack it. The Hawaiian word *'ā* (pronounced "ah") means "fiery, burning," and connotes jealousy or anger. As such, the words and sounds are *kaona* (metaphoric, having veiled meaning) that foreshadow the rising tension between Māui and the *'alae*, as his anger and frustration with the crafty mudhens comes to a head, a fact that is choreographed through a hula.

As fluency in Hawaiian continues to increase, a wider audience able to appreciate stage plays in the Hawaiian language continues to grow. For example, in 2016, Hālau Hanakeaka staged the *mo'olelo* of Lā'ieikawai, the first ever Hawaiian-language production featured on the main stage of the University of Hawai'i at Mānoa's Kennedy Theater; all performances were quickly sold out. Beyond a burgeoning of Hawaiian arts, the politics of Hawaiian language as a cornerstone of cultural identity is still under threat within the settler state of Hawai'i. Continued visibility of the Hawaiian language in all venues, including retellings of *mo'olelo kamaha'o* helps re-orient the ways Hawaiian culture is carried from the past into the future, a continuing insistence on keeping *moʻolelo*, language, and other elements of traditional culture visible and vital.

Visual Storytelling

It has long been acknowledged that contemporary Hawaiian and Pacific literatures trace their literary lineages to oral roots. But as Pacific studies scholar Teresia Teaiwa points out, there is a visual aspect to traditional stories. Teaiwa argues that there is an "abundance of visual" cultural production in traditional Moana Nui cultures to argue for Pacific literature to acknowledge a "theory of polygenesis" of elements beyond the oral (such as the visual) (731). Teaiwa's essay focuses on traditional visual culture, including textile designs and the practice of *tātau* (tattooing), among others. Yet her argument is applicable to modern visual arts as viable modes of storytelling. A number of Indigenous Pacific artists use a variety of media to retell—and re-orient—*moʻolelo kamahaʻo*. Two examples of Māui snaring the sun are represented in visual works by Tahiti-based Bobby Holcomb and Hawaiʻi-based Herb Kawainui Kāne.

Bobby Holcomb (1947–1991) was born in Honolulu to a part Hawaiian mother and African American father. He made his way to Maeva on the island of Huahine in French Polynesia in 1976 where he lived and worked as a visual artist, teacher, and musician. Internationally known, Holcomb is considered a key figure in contemporary Tahitian art with a politicized foundation of Māʻohi (Indigenous) identity, "reflect[ing] the rise and the affirmation of a contemporary art form known as *l'Art du Fenua* (art of the land/nation)" that became revitalized with protests against the French government's nuclear testing program in French Polynesia, beginning in the 1960s (Deso 162). Holcomb painted many *atua* (deities) and legendary figures, including at least two of Māui, one with his sister Hina, titled "O Maui Tiitii o te Ra e o Hinahina Toto Io (Māui—with-the-topknot-[son of]-the-sun and [his sister] Hina-hina-toto-io)."[7] This painting depicts a Tahitian version of Māui snaring the sun and creating seasons, as the sun "caused the days and nights to be irregular," so Māui "regulated the sun by seizing it by its rays"

(Henry 348). "Sun caught in snare" is identified as A728 in the ATU Motif-Index of Folk-Literature. Māuiti'iti'i is the sixth son (all named Māui) of Tangaroaitepō and Uahea; Hinahinatotoio is his youngest sibling and the only girl, a favorite in the family. In other Tahitian versions, Māui is also the son of *te rā* (the sun). Māui uses ropes fashioned from Hinahinatotoio's braided hair to slow the sun, allowing his mother to cook food and for people to have longer, more productive days. In his quest, Māui helps his priestly, oldest brother, Māuimua, establish temples of worship across the islands. In this way, Māui's wondrous deeds have an integral religious component, one that recognizes traditional Tahitian cosmogony, where Māui's ancestor Ta'aroa was "the greatest of gods, [who had] the power which created the world . . . and people" (Luomala 146). The painting shows Māui holding a long, braided rope made from Hina's hair, which is wrapped around the sun on one end, snaring it. Māui grips the rope with both hands, as this is an arduous feat. His left hand is extended toward his sister, kneeling before him, his right grips the rope to his *piko* (navel). The other end of the rope is still attached to Hina's *po'o* (head).

In Holcomb's version of the *mo'olelo*, Māui is unable to accomplish this wondrous task without the aid of powerful, female mana represented by Hina. As Māui's sister, Hinahinatotoio has similar godly power, and together their mana creates a balanced dyad of complementary opposites that is an integral concept in traditional eastern Polynesian religions (Tahiti, Hawai'i). Gaëtan Deso notes that the relationship between the two as siblings is visually represented by the rope extending from Hina's head to the sun through Māui's *pito* (navel), expressed in the term "*pito hōʻē*," or "one navel (one origin)," which is also linked to the sun "that allows life to emerge" (170). Moreover, the navel (*pito, piko*) and head (*upoʻo, poʻo*) are two important centers of mana; the *poʻo* is itself a *piko* (center) of the body, as the source of memory, intellectual thought, logic, creativity, and knowledge, and thus considered sacred—no one should touch the head of another unless intimately related (parent to child, for example), and the head should never be touched in any act of aggression or negativity, even in intimate relationships (slapping the head of a child, for example, was considered a horrific offense, even by a parent). The navel is a second important *piko* of the body, connecting a

Figure 2.3. Māui snares the sun using a rope made from his sister Hinahina's hair. Bobby Holcomb, *Maui and His Sister Hinahinatotoio*, photo of original painting. Image courtesy of Dorothy Lubin-Levy.

member of one generation to the mother, and symbolically to the ancestors. The navel is also considered "a vital energy centre" of the body, and of Māui (Leimbach 11). Visually represented this way, Hina's *poʻo* and her *lauoho* (hair) represent *mana wahine* (female power, female empowerment), and Māui's holding the rope of her hair to his *piko* represents not just *mana kāne* (male power), but also *mana kūpuna* (power and empowerment through the ancestors).

In a heavily Christianized (Catholic) contemporary culture, the image reorients modern Tahitian audiences to traditional, pre-Christian *moʻolelo*, reminding us all about the wondrous power and deeds of our ancestors, who descended from deities and who created our own concepts of cosmogony. It is *kūʻē*, or resistant to settler colonial hegemony embodied in institutional practices such as the Christian church, as well as educational institutions, created and run by settlers, that utilized western stories for the betterment of Indigenous peoples.[8] Deso writes that "Holcomb was aware that pre-colonial Polynesian culture functioned on the basis of oral tradition, and he was able to define and reinterpret certain facts through his songs and his pictorial works" (167).[9]

Consistent with Holcomb's style, the image is painted in warm hues of oranges, yellows, browns, and creams, with line details in black. The colors are indicative of traditional dye colors pulled from natural plant elements in traditional textile production in Oceania, taking these colors into a new medium. Bruno Saura writes, "[w]arm tones dominate" Holcomb's work, as he "wanted to use the natural colours of Hawaiian or Tahitian costumes" (111). Māui wears traditional male clothing—a *malo* and *kīhei* (garment worn over one shoulder). He sports long hair worn in a *pū* (topknot), a traditional hairstyle for men. He is presented as a strong, brave, and intelligent young man, a positive role model for contemporary youth. Hina wears traditional women's clothing—a *kīkepa* (a type of sarong) and a *kīhei*. Deso interprets the "white garb" added "to the more or less dark ochres" for the purpose of "attract[ing] the viewer's gaze" (170). While the visual contrast is eye-catching, white is also a traditional color worn, one often associated with chiefs and deities because of the rarity of materials used in manufacturing white tapa.

Hinahinatotoio's long, wavy hair is worn loosely; it is likened to the shimmering rays of the sun. She sits cradling some leaves that resemble *ʻawa* (kava, a plant native to the Pacific that has narcotic qualities used in medicine and for relaxation).[10] The leaves represent plants, associated with the earth mother, and traditional medicine (manufactured from plants), as Hina is a deity associated with healing and cultural ceremony in relation to offerings to Māui as a *kupua*.

Long hair was often worn by men as well as women, because hair is considered a source of personal mana. While the long hair of Polynesian women was fetishized by early *haole* explorers and settlers in their writing and artwork, a now normalized representation of Polynesian female identity, the long hair of men was harshly criticized as a mark of savagery by Christian missionaries. To cut one's hair was to cut off a source of mana. This is why, in part, cutting of hair under Christian influence and insistence occurred, as long hair, especially for men, was viewed as a pagan and anti-Christian practice, where the Christian God held all mana, not humans, and not non-Christian deities.

Māui stands in profile looking up toward the sun, while Hina sits on her knees looking down toward the earth. Their positions depict another layer of *ʻēkoʻa*, that of standing (*kū*) related to the male strand of *pono* (dualism). This parallels the male strand represented by the sun in the *lani* (heavens, atmosphere), which is Wākea, the Hawaiian sky father, known in other parts of Polynesia as Ātea, Vātea, or Rangi. Māui standing is balanced by Hina sitting; Hina's name also means "prostrate" or "fallen from an upright position" in Hawaiian, reflecting the female strand of *pono* that balances the male strand. Moreover, the earth, known as Papahānaumoku (the foundation that births islands) in Hawaiian and Papatūanuku in Aotearoa (New Zealand), balances Wākea, the sky father. The Hawaiian concept of *pono* as balance is clearly depicted in the image in multiple ways; the inclusion of Hina in this integral Māui *moʻolelo* demonstrates the Indigenous storytelling perspective as inclusive, rather than Māui being represented alone. These concepts align with and complement each other in dyads, as represented below:

female	male
left	right
Hina	Māui
long hair down, straight	long hair up, coiled in a topknot
kneeling/sitting	standing
facing forward	profile (facing sideways to the left)
prostrate, horizontal	upright, vertical

moon	sun
earth	heavens, atmosphere
looking down to the earth	looking up to the sky
earth mother	sky father
Papahānaumoku (Papatūanuku)	Wākea (Ātea, Vātea, Rangi)

Lastly, Holcomb's images are often framed by geometric patterns common in Polynesian tattoo, tapa, and other designs, imbuing his contemporary art with traditional motifs that were and remain culturally coded symbols that can be read and interpreted in a variety of ways. Saura argues that Holcomb "acquired and elaborated on the technique of taking a motif from the ancient *tapa* designs he used with a painting and making it serve as a frame. Often it was a detail from plant life, or perhaps a geometric figure, like triangles repeated and reversed" (111). Deso explains that this is because these designs "permit the composition to be 'dressed' in exactly the same way that those designs used to 'dress' *Māʻohi* bodies" (169–70). Deso summarizes Holcomb's important contribution to re-orienting Polynesian *moʻolelo kamahaʻo*:

> Holcomb took delight in producing graphic works that depicted Polynesian life such as it was narrated in oral histories. This is important, because Holcomb gave concrete expression to traditional stories and he is one of the few sources of artistic illustrations for French Polynesian legends. . . . Holcomb produced autonomous works, comprehensible to all who were aware of these stories. As he stated, ". . . I want to show another way to paint Polynesia. A Polynesian way" (*La Depeche de Tahiti*, 1978, quoted in Saura and Levy 2013: 135; author's translation from the original French). (168–69)

Like Holcomb, Herb Kawainui Kāne (1928–2011) is a well-known, celebrated Hawaiian artist; Kāne is most noted for his visual depictions of Hawaiian history. Kāne's "Māui Snaring the Sun" is a visual representation of this important Māui *moʻolelo* that Holcomb represents, but from a different Polynesian perspective. In the painting, Māui is depicted as an *aliʻi nui*, a high-ranking chief, symbolically represented by the adornments he is wearing, a *mahiʻole* (helmet worn by warrior chiefs) and *ʻahu ʻula* (feather cloak worn by *aliʻi nui*), reflecting his illustrious chiefly and godly ancestry. He is standing on a mountain summit above the clouds, suggesting Haleakalā, the dormant volcano and highest point on the Hawaiian island of Maui, named for the culture hero-ancestor, and the location where Māui accomplishes this wondrous feat in Hawaiʻi. A woven *ʻupena* (net) with the sun snared is gripped firmly in his strong hands. Māui's long hair flows freely under the *mahiʻole* helmet, although his body position leaning back, called *kīkiʻi*, alludes to the topknot hairstyle Māui is associated with, the *kiʻikiʻi* (*kīkiʻi* is the contraction of *kiʻikiʻi*). In the background, the constellation Ka Makau Nui o Māui (the great fishhook of Māui) is clearly visible in the heavens.

Māui is depicted as a young, strong, vibrant, and confident figure. Traditional Hawaiian geometric designs are incorporated into the *ʻahu ʻula* Māui wears, as well as into the way the rays of the sun are rendered in triangular shapes. The holes in the net are rendered as diamonds, the combination of two triangles. Even the triangular shapes of the jagged rocky mountaintop of Haleakalā Māui stands on suggest these motifs. Circular and spiral designs, also common in Polynesian geometric designs, are used to suggest the swirling motion of the clouds surrounding the peak of Haleakalā at Māui's feet, as well as the heat waves of the sun. Moreover, the circling spiral patterns radiating out from the sun suggest the watermark pattern, often more textual than visible, in Hawaiian *kapa*. Kāne's colors are also natural, the vibrant yellow of the sun and Māui's royal regalia catching the eye. These are complemented with shades of orange, pink, and deepening blue radiating out from the sun, representing the depth of space, with the left upper corner of the image rendered in a deep blackish-blue, Māui's fishhook constellation clearly visible, evoking another wondrous *moʻolelo* associated with him.

In some *moʻolelo*, Māui uses his "magical" fishhook, named Manaiakalani, to hook a supernatural *ulua* (crevalle) named Pīmoe, whom he defeats and uses to pull up islands out of the vast, deep sea, a feat no one else in Polynesia, not even the great ocean god Kanaloa (alternately Tangaroa or

Figure 2.4. *Māui Snaring the Sun*. Herbert Kawainui Kāne. Photo of original painting. Courtesy of Nancy Baker. Copyright Herbert K. Kane, LLC.

Taʻaroa), accomplishes. Māui then casts his magical hook into the heavens, where it forms the constellation Ka Makau Nui o Māui, known in the west as Scorpio. The celestial fishhook is part of the star line Manaiakalani (alternately "the chief's fishing line" or "coming from the heavens").[11] It is an important tool of orientation in Pacific navigation and wayfinding, not only in ancient culture but even today. The traditional, double-hulled long-distance voyaging canoe Hōkūleʻa, which completed a multiyear voyage around the world (2014–18) and is called "Mālama Honua" (caring for the earth), carried a message of traditional knowledge, sustainability, and the dangers of climate change. The participants of the Mālama Honua voyage also tested and proved the science behind traditional practices, such as voyaging and associated *moʻolelo*, including those for Māui as an ancient master navigator renowned across Moana Nui.

Saura notes that Holcomb's paintings "are a call to honour the past" (115). Most notable was his attraction to myths and traditions, Tahitian wonder tales, and "their capacity to inspire images"; moreover, Saura concludes, "[i]n another time and place, he might have applied the same talent and enthusiasm to illustrating Grimm's fairy tales or Aesop's fables" (115). Kāne's artwork also honors the past with an intent to keep *moʻolelo kamahaʻo* alive in new storytelling media that recall the wonderful and wondrous deeds of the ancestors with a view to inspiring current and future generations.

In 2011, Pacific Resources for Education and Learning (PREL) launched its E Hoʻomau (to carry on) series, which includes both animated video and graphic novel versions of *moʻolelo kamahaʻo*, including *Why Māui Snared the Sun*. The art in the graphic novel is taken from stills of the animated production. The *moʻolelo* is told as a frame story, with "Aunty" at the beach with several nieces and nephews. Aunty's nephew Ikaika arrives late because he had to help his mother with chores, including laundry, and he grumbles about how long it takes. This provides an opportunity for Aunty to (re)tell this important deed of Māui. The *moʻolelo* is told primarily in English with some Hawaiian words (the sun, for example, is named Kalā, "the sun"). The frame story highlights oral storytelling tradition, particularly from the older generation, represented by Aunty, to subsequent generations. Because Ikaika is irritated with doing chores, Aunty tells the story of Māui snaring the sun because he wanted to help his mother in her daily activities, particularly making *kapa* cloth, equated with the modern task of doing laundry. Set in a modern time period, the *moʻolelo* provides ancestral perspectives on the importance of working together for the benefit of others, beginning with family, and extending out to the wider community. Part of why Māui is remembered and celebrated is because he models *pono* behavior. Māui's selfless actions are more important in the era of the continued assault against Indigenous peoples and cultures via settler colonialism, which prioritizes individual rights over familiar, community responsibilities. At the end of the story, Ikaika thus understands his familial responsibilities and addresses the sun directly, telling him not to forget to show up, because Ikaika (meaning "strong") knows where Kalā lives.

Like the artistic images in both Holcomb's and Kāne's work, the artwork of *Why Māui Snared the Sun* uses warm, natural hues. The land is a neutral earth brown with white misty clouds, and the sky at sunrise is depicted in shades of orange and yellow. When Māui ascends the summit, Haleakalā is more specifically represented than in Kāne's painting, the landscape populated with *hinahina*, the native silversword plant that thrives in the alpine environment of the mountain's high, cool slopes and nowhere else in the world.

Māui is clothed in a traditional *malo* and has loose, shorter hair than in Holcomb's or Kāne's images. He also holds a *koʻi*, a traditional adze in one hand, which he later uses to fasten the ropes to snare Kalā. Kalā is personified with a face; his mouth is open in a grimace, his face marked by geometric motifs that suggest a *moko* (Māori facial tattoo often worn by men). Two related sounds are represented by alphabetic text bilingually—the sleeping sun emits a series of "z's," indicating him "snoozing," and what looks like a series of "'o's," *ʻoʻoʻoʻō*, the Hawaiian word for a rooster's crow, an onomatopoeia; both the "z's" and the rooster crow represent early morning, as does the orange sunrise-coloring of the sky.

There are related teaching tools, such as a glossary, questions, and scientific information in the graphic novel version for cross-cultural comparison. The inclusion of educational materials is a key part of the *moʻolelo* featured in the E Hoʻomau series, which is meant to appeal to and engage Hawaiian and other youth. The production of the *moʻolelo* in two media demonstrates the adaptability of the *moʻolelo*, as well as reflects a desire to reach a wider audience. Animated adaptations are a return to oral traditions as well as adapting performative modes of storytelling in a new way. Increasingly, Indigenous peoples are learning digital storytelling techniques that will expand the telling and retelling of our *moʻolelo* in new and diverse ways.

Figure 2.5. PREL, *Why Maui Snared the Sun*. Video still.

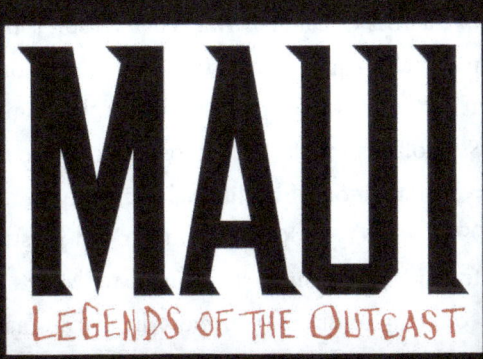

Figure 2.6. Chris Slane and Robert Sullivan, *Māui: Legends of the Outcast*, a graphic novel.

Graphic novels are increasing in popularity overall, and in the retelling of *moʻolelo kamahaʻo* across Oceania. Perhaps one reason is the centering of the storytelling on visual images, which stimulate the imagination, as well as the reduction of text, which reflects the orality of the original tales. *Why Māui Snared the Sun* follows the darker, almost apocalyptic retelling in the Māori graphic novel adaptation of traditional Māui stories, *Māui: Legends of the Outcast* (1997), written by Robert Sullivan and illustrated by Chris Slade. It is presented in English and includes many of Māui's feats, from his miraculous birth to trying to discover immortality for humans by tricking Hinenuiitepō, the goddess of death.

Three culturally symbolic colors in Māori culture are black, white, and red. In a discussion of the national Māori flag, which features these colors, black symbolizes *te korekore*, a period of nothingness in Māori cosmogony that is the time before night, "the realm of Potential Being [that] represents the long darkness from whence the world emerged. It represents the heavens. The male element is formless, floating and passive" (Te Kawariki). White symbolizes *te ao marama*, "the realm of Being and Light. It is the Physical Word. White also symbolizes purity, harmony, enlightenment, and balance" (Te Kawariki). Red symbolizes *te whei ao*, "the realm of Coming into Being. It symbolizes the female element. It also represents active, flashing, southern, falling, emergence, forest, land, and gestation. Red is Papatuanuku, the Earth Mother, the sustainer of all living things. Red is the colour of earth from which the first human was made" (Te Kawariki). This color scheme frames the collection of stories, enhancing the cultural symbolism visually depicted in the *moʻolelo*. The gritty font and edgy drawings emphasize the hostility in Māui's encounters that reflects the level of struggle and violence in the Māori stories that begin with his perceived death and the disposal of his infant "corpse" into the sea, where it is rescued and nurtured by elements of nature. The red coloring is a metaphoric connection to Papakūanuku and his gestation, as is the shape of his infant body curled into a fetal position. This curved shape of his body alludes to the koru, the curled, yet unfurled fern tip that "represents the unfolding of new life"; it represents as well "rebirth and continuity, and offers the promise of renewal and hope for the future" (Te Kawariki). Collectively, the colors black, white, and red, and the stylized, geometric shape of the koru on the national Māori flag connect cultural, artistic elements with elements of the *whenua* (land; similar to *fenua* in Tahiti, and *'āina* in Hawai'i). In contemporary contexts, such symbols meld Indigenous identity, politics, and art with and through the re-presentation of ancient *mo'olelo kamaha'o* in the assertion of cultural strength, presence, and pride as distinct First Peoples of colonized nations.

In a discussion on Indigenous comics, Bryan Kamaoli Kuwada quotes Rocco Veraci, who notes that "comics are not expected to deliver significant social or political criticism and therefore possess what I call a 'powerful marginality' insofar as they are freer to express subversive or unpopular political ideas" (112). Kuwada argues that it is "[t]his 'powerful marginality' [that] has drawn many native people to the comic form . . . moving them to produce graphic novels and comics [including *Maui: Legends of the Outcast*] . . . that tell their own stories and present their own heroes" (112). Kuwada also cites Tony Chavarria, who calls this appeal of the comic (visual) form of storytelling in Indigenous cultures "only natural that this marginal art appeals to oft-marginalized indigenous people, for both have been regarded as a primitive and malignant presence on the American landscape" (112). Kuwada explains that comics help to free the reader, in part, in thinking and reimagining differently (113). What this medium does, I assert, is return the reader to a more visual and thus performative mode of storytelling, and an embodying of the *mo'olelo*.

In 2005, Robert Wiri (Māori) and Zak Waipara (Māori) published *Ka Kimi a Māui i ōna Mātua (Māui Searches for His Parents)*. Wiri and Waipara's printed text is accompanied by a CD that contains a short, animated version of the *mo'olelo*. Their text is presented bilingually, in Māori and English. Also in 2005, Jason Te Puia (Māori) published *He Kōrero mo Māui, pukapuka 1 (The Legend of Māui, book 1)*. It was published as two separate texts, one in Māori, one in English, featuring the same stories and artwork in each. Te Puia's work features Māui fishing up islands, snaring the sun, and battling a giant *tuna* (fresh water eel).

Throughout each, the visual depictions of Māui help the viewer and reader reimagine Māui as a heroic figure. Each rendition depicts Māui as a smart, fit, capable, tough, hero figure who uses intelligence, strength, courage, and compassion for his mother and his people to make life better for them. The incorporation of culturally specific design motifs that visually represent Indigenous Pacific ideas of symmetry and beauty also marks socio-spatial aspects of time and space. Tongan anthropologist Tēvita Kaʻili draws on ʻōkusitino Mahina's *tā-vā* (time-space) theory of reality in reference to Tongan (and in extension, Oceanic) art, arguing, "tauhi vā [the indigenous Tongan art of mediating socio-spatial conflicts] is an indigenous artistic device that uses symmetry to reconcile sociospatial conflicts and create harmonious and beautiful sociospatial relations. . . . In Tongan and all Moanan cultures, indigenous artists rhythmically or symmetrically mark tā in vā to produce harmony, and above all, beauty," which are expressed in everything from tātau (tattooing) to music, dance, and literature (Kaʻili *Marking Indigeneity*, Kindle loc. 390).

Collectively, these works by Indigenous Moana Nui artists provide a stark contrast to Disney's Māui, highlighting his struggle against the dark forces trying to destroy him and his perseverance in overcoming his circumstances. Thus, these Indigenous works help to re-orient and steer us on a more *pono* (just) pathway from the disoriented (and disorienting) Disney caricature. These portrayals highlight the magic and wonder that is Māui, which is a far cry from Disney's overweight, unfit, thieving, misogynistic clown, who is anything but a hero, let alone a superman. Disney's Māui and everything he stands for in traditional Moana Nui cultures follows the colonial trope of the emasculated buffoon. Cultural anthropologist Brian Dawson critiques Disney's racist history in a comparison of *Song of the South*'s Uncle Remus and *Moana*'s Māui: both function as storytellers, but while Uncle Remus is a fictitious character, Māui is a historical figure, "a tangible, traceable, genealogical ancestor to many in Oceania, which is the indigenous counter narrative to Disney's U.S. *Moana*" ("Zip-a-dee-do-dah"). Dawson quotes Tevita Kaʻili, who explains Māui's traditional role representing the ordinary person's fight "against all forms of injustices, from ageism to xenophobia. Through his wisdom as a grand-master trickster of Oceania, he transformed society from [unequal] to [equal]" (Kaʻili "The Demigod Maui").

Dawson goes on to argue that Disney "decided to de-deify him," transforming him into a fictitious character akin to Uncle Remus, "bringing back if not perpetuating, that 'ridiculous idealization' of a 'noble savage,'" resulting in "a bad exploitation of Oceania" ("Zip-a-dee-do-dah"). Dawson concludes that in their misrepresentation of Māui, "Disney even has the impudence to now call him the 'once-mighty demigod'" ("Zip-a-dee-do-dah").

As Kaʻili explains, there is much more to be concerned about with Disney's misportrayal of Māui than physical characteristics. What is at stake is his role in Indigenous Moana Nui societies in the past, and his meaning in the present. Thus, critiques of the physical stereotypes and representation of Māui are important. However, it is important not to "overlook one of the grand messages of Maui's stories, which is to **advocate for justice by transforming society**" ("The Demigod Maui").

Kaʻili describes Māui's accomplishments as *"heliaki,* beautiful poetic expressions of resisting oppression and fighting for injustice for the benefit of humanity (Māhina 1992; 2003)" ("The Demigod Maui"). *Heliaki* is a traditional Tongan poetic device that resonates with previous discussions of traditional Hawaiian *meiwi*. Tongan poet Konai Helu Thaman describes *heliaki* as "the use of natural features as symbolic referents of persons and/or personal traits and various other cultural/social phenomena," which requires the viewer, listener, or reader to have an intimate understanding of "the social and cultural contexts" of art under discussion (46). Elsewhere Kaʻili discusses Māui's important role in mediating time, with a goal of "[creating] harmony within social spaces," which "has deep historical roots in Moana cultures" (Kaʻili "The Demigod Maui," Kindle loc. 582). In the Tongan tradition of *heliaki*, the *moʻolelo* of Māui slowing the sun suggests the possibility "that the paramount chief did not give his people enough time to do their work. [Therefore] Maui mediated (or symmetrized) the conflicting times by demanding that the paramount chief extend the working time . . . [which] resulted in harmonious social spaces (*vālelei*) between the people and their chief." (Kaʻili "The Demigod Maui," Kindle loc. 603)

In addition, Māui represents a universal hero within the specific cultural context of Oceania and provides a way for contemporary Pacific peoples to remember our ancestors and history and re-orient ourselves to the culture values of the past, through our own wondrous figures. Kaʻili argues that while Māui tales are specific to individual places and culture groups within

Oceania, what is critical is that his function as a *kupuna* (ancestor), *kupua* (wondrous figure), and *kupuʻeu* (hero) are more universal. For example, Māui's ethos is found in a range of other historical figures around the world, from Martin Luther King Jr., Mother Teresa, Mahatma Gandhi, and Nelson Mandela to Cesar Chavez, Harvey Milk, and Rosa Parks, amongst others, who, like Māui, "accomplish the daunting task of transforming society." In addition, contrary to Disney's and other nonindigenous representations, Māui "depend[s] upon the goddess Hina for power, guidance, and support," and, as Oceanic descendants of Māui and Hina, "[w]e, like Maui, must look to our ancestors for guidance and our allies for support and solidarity." Kaʻili concludes that, "The systems of domination, such as racism, exploitation of the poor, hate crimes, brutalizing of women and men of color, and retaliatory violence, all of which are oppressive forces in our society, call for the rise of a new Maui" ("The Demigod Maui"). New Māuis materialize every day, inspired by our *kupuna*, the *kupua* and *kupuʻeu* Māui. In 2014, a collective of Indigenous Moana Nui scholars, activists, and cultural practitioners called "Mana Moana: We are Moana, We are Māui" formed to provide informed, culturally rooted critiques of Disney's *Moana* from numerous perspectives.[12] Alongside Indigenous Oceania artists, we collectively seek to remember, reaffirm, reimagine, rearticulate, and reorient our lives to find meaning and value in our cultural traditions, including *moʻolelo kamahaʻo* as a way to *hoʻi i ka piko* (return to the navel or source) of our cultural mana. In doing so, Indigenous-produced reimaginings of traditional *moʻolelo* such as Māui and Hina counter disorienting settler colonial representations, and provide a renewed, reinvigorated Indigenous wonder tale.

In a 2010 symposium, "Folktales and Fairy Tales: Translation, Colonialism, and Cinema," Jack Zipes called for us to "De-Disneyfy Disney" by looking beyond Disney at the development of the fairy-tale film. We can extend Zipes's call to look beyond Disney in other ways. Almost every map of the world focuses on its continental features centering Europe, Asia, and Africa or the Americas. Such colonial, land-based perspectives often chop the Pacific Ocean in half, diminishing its mana and that of the over thirty thousand islands, ten million people, and one thousand languages and cultures and the stories held within them. This "sea of islands," as Hauʻofa describes it, is a purposeful and thus political label that intentionally counters the western colonial perspective of the ocean as a barrier to connection and exploration. From an indigenous Oceanic perspective, Hauʻofa's term recognizes the ocean as a pathway that facilitates connection, validating thousands of years of oceanic wayfinding and voyaging (another reason Disney's *Moana* is disorienting). Māui is a powerful ancestor-deity who is not so powerful that he can escape traveling with a canoe, even though he can also create islands. As Disney announced its animated feature film *Moana* in 2014, a version now familiar to audiences worldwide, Rotuman film maker, storyteller, playwright and scholar Vilsoni Hereniko was staging his own oceanic wonder tale, *Moana, the Rising of the Sea*.[13] Hereniko's *Moana* focuses on the devastating effects of climate change already decimating Pacific islands and peoples. A film adaptation of the original stage play has allowed the message to travel further than the immediate audiences who witnessed the play, a powerful testimony of Indigenous Pacific peoples' experiences. As Marshallese poet Kathy Jetnil-Kijiner says in her poignant poem "Tell Them," "we don't want to leave / we've never wanted to leave / and that we / are nothing / without our islands" (66–67). As an ancient, esteemed navigator-ancestor, Indigenous Moana Nui representations of Māui today demonstrate the continuity of Indigenous knowledge, imagination, and futures.

Haʻina ʻia mai ana ka Puana (Conclusion)

Moʻolelo kamahaʻo are, like other genres of *moʻolelo*, part of the "social cultural texts" that constitute social and political imaginings (Winduo 1). Thus, understanding the political underpinning of *moʻolelo kamahaʻo* such as Māui and Hina, and closely examining artistic, visual, and performative representations of such provide a more culturally appropriate interpretation of modern adaptations and their purpose, which is, like all stories, to remember, retell, and sometimes reshape our understanding and celebration of our past, for Indigenous peoples as we navigate toward (re)imagining a decolonial and decolonized future. Contemporary Indigenous adaptations and retellings of *moʻolelo kamahaʻo*, such as those for Māui, are responses to earlier settler colonial adaptations that disoriented the original *moʻolelo*. As such, they are a re-orienting of our *moʻolelo*, informed by long-standing cultural traditions, meant to reinvigorate the *moʻolelo* with the culturally centered knowledge eroded or replaced by settler colonial reimaginings. Thus, there is power to disorient, as well as re-orient, stories—crucial for Indigenous peoples, as our *moʻolelo* as story and history live through us, and are a vital part of our identity.[14] Gerald Vizenor has discussed the idea of "survivance," in part, as "an active sense of presence, the continuance of native stories, [and] not a mere reaction" to settler colonialism (vii). Hawaiian author Lehua Parker has authored new versions of European wonder tales. Recently, she discovered, in trying to create a Hawaiian adaptation of Hans Christian Andersen's *The Little Mermaid*, that *moʻolelo* and fairy tales are not the same. She writes, "the story has fought me at every turn, refusing to fit into the mold of a western fairy tale. I've struggled, writing and rewriting, and eventually throwing out 90% of what was in my original manuscript." Parker's experience demonstrates, in part, the vastly different orientation of European and Oceanic wonder tales, each pointing in different directions, embodying different orientations. To orient one's self is to find one's position or place *in relation to new and unfamiliar surroundings;* to find direction, to adjust to a specific need or circumstance. The continuity of indigenous wonder tales is part of the larger resurgence of such endeavors by Indigenous Pacific peoples as we continue to traverse the vast Pacific first traveled by our *kūpuna* millennia before us.

Notes

1. Throughout this chapter, *Hawaiian* refers to *Kanaka Maoli,* or Native Hawaiian people and culture. Kanaka Maoli are the Indigenous First Peoples of the Hawaiian archipelago who migrated from other parts of the Pacific, specifically Polynesia, centuries ago and settled the islands, creating a distinct language and cultural practices.

2. Hawaiian literature scholar Marie Alohalani Brown defines a Hawaiian wonder tale as *kaʻao*, which is also applicable here. Hawaiian terms are as difficult to define as western ones (*märchen*, fairy tale, wonder tale), in part because of the connotation of *kaʻao* as completely fabricated, a purely "fanciful tale," and *moʻolelo* carrying the meaning of history. Much work in this area of Hawaiian literary scholarship remains. For further discussion, see Brown.

3. Moana Nui is an Indigenous Polynesian term that is synonymous to the Pacific and Oceania, and the three are used interchangeably in this chapter. Some cultures, such as the Māori of Aotearoa (New Zealand) have more specific terms, such as Moana Nui a Kiwa (the great ocean of Kiwa); Kiwa is an esteemed Māori ancestor who was a great navigator and adventurer.

4. Anthropologist Katharine Luomala's *Maui of a Thousand Tricks: His Oceanic and European Biographers* and William D. Westervelt's *Legends of Maui, A Demi-God of Polynesia and His Mother Hina* (Hawaiian Gazette Co., 1910) are examples of some of the first collections of Māui *moʻolelo* across Oceania. Other collections are more specific to island groups, such as Lilikalā Kameʻeleihiwa and Dietrich Varez, *Māui the Mischief Maker,* Bishop Museum Press, 1991 (Hawaiʻi); Ron Bacon, *Māori Legends, The Māui Stories,* Shortland, 1984 (Aotearoa New Zealand); E. E. Colcott, "Legends from Tonga: The Maui," *Folklore,* vol. 32, no. 1, 31 March 1921, pp. 45–58 (Tonga); and Teuira Henry, *Ancient Tahiti*, Bishop Museum Press, 1928 (Tahiti).

5. Queen Liliʻuokalani is the first to translate and publish in English (1898) her Kumulipo, which kept her sacred genealogy and thus her right to rule Hawaiʻi.

6. See 1997 Kamehameha Schools Song Contest Hōʻike, YouTube, www.youtube.com/watch?v=vooqywOqA5U.

7. Another name for Hinahinatotoio is Māuipōtiʻi, or [the] girl Māui; pōtiʻi (pōtiki) means girl in the Society [Islands] dialect, and means the youngest, and often favorite sibling in Māori (*pōtiki*) and Hawaiian (*pōkiʻi*) (Luomala 144).

8. This occurred in Hawaiʻi in the nineteenth century when *haole* newspaper publisher Henry Whitney published Hawaiian-language translations of European fairy tales such as Snow White (*Kahaunani*), Cinderella (*Lehuahi*), and the Frog Prince (*Ka Moo Alii*), amongst others, as an expressed settler strategy seeking "the betterment" of Native Hawaiians. This was, in part, a reaction against rival Kanaka Maoli publishers who featured traditional Hawaiian *moʻolelo* in their newspapers (Brown 212).

9. More widely known for his music than his art, Holcomb also composed a song in the Tahitian language for Māui's snaring of the sun, "O Māui tiʻi o te Rā" (Māuitiʻi[tiʻi] of the Sun). The audio and performative adaptation of his visual imaging of the moʻolelo is oriented toward Polynesian orality; it features a Tahitian "double strum" ʻukulele rhythm that adds a rhythmic, sonic layer of Māʻohi cultural motifs. It was recorded on his CD *Bobby* (Océane Production, 1991). Lyrics and translations are found on the website *Paroles de Chansons Tahititennes,* paroles.webfenua.com/chanson.php?id=126. An audio recording is accessible online via YouTube, www.youtube.com/watch?v=w7nHn-9TEbg.

10. The Tahitian blog *Tehivarereata* features Tahitian *ava* (kava) plants. tehivarereata.over-blog.com/article-34993904.html.

11. archive.hokulea.com/ike/hookele/hawaiian_star_lines.html#manaiakalani

12. An archive of published work by Mana Moana scholars can be found at the Mana Moana website, manamoana.wordpress.com/.

13. Ironically, Hereniko was involved in Disney's production of *Moana* as well. Personal communication.

14. See Brandy Nālani McDougall, "Ola (i) Nā Moʻolelo: Living Moʻolelo." *Tedx-Manoa,* 2012. www.youtube.com/watch?v=K69_kuqBiX8.

Works Cited

Bacchilega, Cristina. *Fairy Tales Transformed? Twenty-First-Century Adaptations and the Politics of Wonder.* Wayne State University Press, 2013.

Baker, Hailiʻōpua, and Kaliko Baker. "From Māuiakamalo." *Hawaiʻi Review,* vol. 56, 2001, 109–24.

———. "Māuiakamalo." Vimeo, uploaded by ʻĀina Paikai, 25 June 2013, vimeo.com/69139487. Accessed 30 July 2018.

Beazley, Del. "Hawaiian Supʻpah Man." *Huapala,* www.huapala.org/Mau/Maui_Superman.html. Accessed 30 July 2018.

Brown, Marie Alohalani. "The Politics and Poetics of Märchen in Hawaiian-Language Newspapers." *The Fairy Tale World,* edited by Andrew Teverson, Routledge, 2019.

Dawson, Brian. "Zip-a-Dee-Doo-Dah: From Uncle Remus to Maui." *Huffington Post,* 29 November 2016, www.huffingtonpost.com/entry/zip-a-dee-doo

-dah-from-uncle-remus-to-maui_us_57ff37f5e4b06f314afeadda. Accessed 30 July 2018.

Deso, Gaëtan. "Neo-Polynesian Artist Bobby Holcomb, Herald of Cultural Renewal in French Polynesia." *Journal of New Zealand & Pacific Studies*, vol. 5 no. 2, 2017, pp. 161–73.

Hauʻofa, ʻEpeli. "Our Sea of Islands." *Contemporary Pacific*, vol. 6, no. 1, Spring 1994, pp. 147–61.

Helu Thaman, Konai. "Of Daffodils and Heilala: Understanding (Cultural) Context in Pacific Literature." *Navigating Islands and Continents, Contestations and Conversations in and around the Pacific*, edited by Cynthia Franklin, Ruth Hsu, and Suzanne Kosanke, University of Hawaiʻi Press, 2000, pp. 40–50.

Henry, Teuira. *Ancient Tahiti*. 1928. Krauss Reprints, 1971.

hoʻomanawanui, kuʻualoha. "From Ocean to O-shen: Reggae, Rap and Hip Hop in Hawaiʻi." *Crossing Waters, Crossing Worlds, the African Diaspora in Indian Country*, edited by Tiya Miles and Sharon Holland, Duke University Press, 2006.

Jetnil-Kijiner, Kathy. "Tell Them." *Iep Jāltok: Poems from a Marshallese Daughter*, University of Arizona Press, 2017.

Justice, Daniel Heath. *Why Indigenous Literature Matters*. Wilfrid Laurier Press, 2018.

Kaʻili, Tēvita. *Marking Indigeneity: The Tongan Art of Sociospatial Relations*. University of Arizona Press, 2017.

———. "The Demigod Maui: Modern Day Lessons from Ancient Tales of Oceania." *Huffington Post*, 15 July 2016. www.huffingtonpost.com/entry/the-demigod-maui-modern-day-lessons-from-ancient-tales_us_5788c6e7e4b0cbf01e9f8508. Accessed 30 July 2018.

Kamehameha Schools Song Contest Hōʻike. 1997. "Māui." YouTube, uploaded by chadepp, 23 March 2013, www.youtube.com/watch?v=vooqywOqA5U. Accessed 30 July 2018.

Kane, Herb Kawainui. "Maui Snares the Sun." *Herb Kawainui Kane*, herbkanehawaii.com. Accessed 30 July 2018.

King, Thomas. *The Truth About Stories*. University of Minnesota Press, 2008.

Kuwada, Bryan Kamaoli. "Find Mana in the Mundane: Telling Hawaiian Moʻolelo in Comics." *Anglistica*, vol. 14, no. 2, 2010, pp. 107–17.

Leimbach, Claire. *Bobby, Visions Polynésiennes*. Pacific Bridge Publishing, 1992.

Luomala, Katharine. *Maui of a Thousand Tricks*. Bishop Museum Press, 1949.

McDougall, Brandy Nālani. "Ola (i) Nā Moʻolelo: Living Moʻolelo." *TedxManoa*, 2012. YouTube, www.youtube.com/watch?v=K69_kuqBiX8. Accessed 30 July 2018.

McDougall, Brandy Nālani, and Georganne Nordstrom. "Stealing the Piko, (Re) placing Kānaka Maoli at Disney's Aulani Resort." *Huihui, Navigating Art and Literature in the Pacific*, University of Hawaiʻi Press, 2014.

Nordstrom, Georganne. "Pidgin as Rhetorical Sovereignty: Articulating Indigenous and Minority Rhetorical Practices with the Language Politics of Place." *College English*, vol. 77, no. 4, March 2015, pp. 317–37.

Oliveira, Katrina-Ann R. Kapāʻanaokalāokeola Nākoa. *Ancestral Places, Understanding Kanaka Geographies*. Oregon State University Press, 2014.

Pacific Resources for Education and Learning (PREL). *Why Māui Snared the Sun*. Oiwi TV, 7 February 2012, oiwi.tv/keiki/why-maui-snared-the-sun/. Accessed 30 July 2018.

Parker, Lehua. "Moʻolelo Aren't Your Granny's Fairy Tales." *Lehua Parker*, 23 July 2018, www.lehuaparker.com/2018/07/23/moolelo-arent-your-grannys-fairy-tales/. Accessed 30 July 2018.

Polynesian Voyaging Society. "The Mālama Honua Worldwide Voyage Continues into 2018." *Polynesian Voyaging Society*, www.hokulea.com/worldwide-voyage/. Accessed 30 July 2018.

Saura, Bruno. "Maker of Dreams." *Mānoa*, vol. 17, no. 2, 2005, pp. 107–15.

Silva, Noenoe. "Pele, Hiʻiaka, and Haumea: Women and Power in Two Hawaiian Moʻolelo." *Pacific Studies*, vol. 30, no. 1–2, 2007, pp. 159–80.

Stannard, David. *American Holocaust: The Conquest of the New World*. Oxford University Press, 1989.

Stimson, J. F., translator. *The Legends of Maui and Tahiki*. Bernice Pauahi Bishop Museum Bulletin 127, 1934.

Sullivan, Robert, and Chris Slade. *Māui: Legends of the Outcast*. Godwit, 1997.

Teaiwa, Teresia. "What Remains to Be Seen: Reclaiming the Visual Roots of Pacific Literature." *PMLA*, vol. 125, no. 3, May 2010, pp. 730–36.

Te Kawariki. *Twenty Years of Protest Action, 1979–1999*. Te Kawariki, 1999.

Te Puia, Jason. *He Kōrero mo Māui, pukapuka 1 (The Legend of Maui, book 1)*. Reed, 2005.

Trask, Haunani Kay. "Lovely Hula Hands, Corporate Tourism and the Prostitutionization of Hawaiian Culture." *From a Native Daughter, Colonialism and Sovereignty in Hawaiʻi*. Common Courage Press, 1993.

Vizenor, Gerald. *Manifest Manners: Narratives on Postindian Survivance*. Bison Books, 1994.

Waziyatawin. *Maka Cokaya Kin (The Center of the Earth): From the Clay We Rise.* Edited by Cristina Bacchilega, Vilsoni Hereniko, Noenoe Silva, and kuʻualoha hoʻomanawanui. ScholarSpace, University of Hawaiʻi at Mānoa, 2010.

Winduo, Steven. "Reconstituting Indigenous Oceanic Folktales." *Folktales and Fairy Tales: Translation, Colonialism, and Cinema*, edited by Cristina Bacchilega, Vilsoni Hereniko, Noenoe Silva, and kuʻualoha hoʻomanawanui. ScholarSpace, University of Hawaiʻi at Mānoa, 2010.

Wiri, Robert, and Zak Waipara. *Ka Kimi a Māui i ōna Mātua.* Emissary Media and Film, 2005.

Wolfe, Patrick. "Settler Colonialism and the Elimination of the Native." *Journal of Genocide Research, vol.* 8, no. 4, December 2006, pp. 387–409.

Zipes, Jack. "De-Disneyfying Disney: Notes of the Development of the Fairy-Tale Film." *Folktales and Fairy Tales: Translation, Colonialism, and Cinema*, edited by Cristina Bacchilega, Vilsoni Hereniko, Noenoe Silva, and kuʻualoha hoʻomanawanui. ScholarSpace, University of Hawaiʻi at Mānoa, 2010.

3

Re-Orienting China and America

Yeh-Shen: A Cinderella Story from China and Its TV Adaptation

Roxane Hughes

RELEASED IN 1982, AI-LING Louie's *Yeh-Shen: A Cinderella Story from China*, illustrated by Ed Young, introduces Duan Chengshi's ninth-century Yexian tale[1] to an audience of American children at a time of countercultural movements and political changes in the United States. The Civil Rights movement of the 1950s and 1960s, the Immigration Act of 1965 that changed the demographics of the United States, and the ethnic revival that ensued in the 1970s led to the development of ethnic American literatures. Eager to recover their erased history and cultural heritage, as well as write their familial and personal stories at cultural crossroads, ethnic American writers developed a multiplicity of texts that slowly revised and decentered the Eurocentric American canon.

By recovering and sharing the Yexian tale that was transmitted to her by her grandmother, Louie presents her family's cultural legacy to a wider audience of American children, while drawing cross-cultural connections between East and West through its Cinderella story line. Yet, by presenting it as a "Chinese Cinderella Story" from the outset, Louie Westernizes Duan's tale to foster her Western audience's interest and curiosity. Although following the general plot of the Yexian tale and foregrounding its Chinese setting, Louie's rewriting adapts the story to its Eurocentric American context by alluding to Charles Perrault's "Cendrillon ou la petite pantoufle de verre" and the Grimm brothers' 1847 "Aschenputtel." In so doing, Louie endows the Yexian tale with a Western fairy-tale happily-ever-after twist to appeal to young American readers. Contrastingly, the illustrations made by Ed Young oppose the Westernization of Louie's retelling and re-orient the reader toward the Chinese background of the Yexian tale.

The visual and verbal interaction presented in *Yeh-Shen* proposes therefore two complementing and counterpointing narratives, as defined by Maria Nikolajeva and Carole Scott in *How Picturebooks Work*. On the one hand, the two narrative lines are *complementary*, as words and images fill in the gaps left by one another (12). On the other, they are *counterpointing, asymmetrical*, if not *conflicting*, allowing for multiple contrasting and ambivalent readings (12, 17). As a result, the word-image interaction in *Yeh-Shen* not only combines Eastern and Western Cinderella story lines and motifs but also offers an ambivalent Cinderella tale that refuses fixity and opens up various interpretations. The visual and verbal narratives of this picture book thus work together to transform the predominantly Western Cinderella story diffused in the United States into a text of *multiple* cultures,[2] and invite its American readers to explore the importance of cross-cultural exchanges and understandings at a time of national and cultural conflicts.

Yet, this cross-cultural retelling also foregrounds the political and cultural constraints of its time. Despite Louie and Young's endeavor to build cross-cultural connections, the cultural re-orientation presented in *Yeh-Shen* also reinstates Orientalist assumptions widely diffused in the United States in the 1980s. The cross-cultural underpinning of Young's illustrations certainly nods to Duan's text, which already locates the origins of the Yexian story *elsewhere*. But Young's creative touch also presents an amalgamation of Asian cultural symbols often collapsing into one single and undistinguishable entity throughout the picture book. This continues the single story[3] of a unique and homogeneous Asian culture passed as *Chinese* and emphasizes the restrictions of the publishing industry for Asian American writers and artists in the 1980s.

The constraining background of Louie and Young's book production is enhanced when analyzed in conversation with its TV adaptation released in 1985 by PBS as part of *CBS Storybreak*, a Saturday-morning children's program broadcasting animations of contemporaneous picture books. PBS's animated adaptation transforms the Yexian tale into an offensive play of Orientalist stereotypes. This American show inscribes narratives of China in the familiar Western colonialist tradition of Orientalism, vilifying Chinese cultural difference and belittling China in the Cold War context of the 1980s.

Put together, Louie and Young's *Yeh-Shen* and its TV adaptation provide a contextual reading of the political and cultural conflicts pervading the United States in the 1980s, as it struggled to maintain its Eurocentric hegemonic structure in the wake of emerging internal ethnic countercultural movements and external Communist threats. The conflicting narratives of these two retellings ultimately underline the ambivalent role of the fairy tale in constructing and deconstructing stereotypes and cultural identities. A cross-cultural perspective that takes into consideration the sociohistorical, cultural, and political contexts of fairy tale production and diffusion and capitalizes on the ambivalent function of cross-cultural retellings is crucial to understanding, exposing, deconstructing, and altering persisting oppressive practices as well as limiting geographical and cultural boundaries.

Revisiting the Cross-Cultural Origins of the Yexian Tale

The earliest version of the Yexian tale is found in Chinese scholar Duan Chengshi's *Youyang Zazu*, a ninth-century collection of miscellanies. Literally meaning "miscellaneous morsels" from Youyang (Reed, *Tang* 1), a mountain in modern-day Hunan, Duan's title underlines the *palatability* or entertaining function of the stories told (2),[4] while already locating the Yexian tale, and the other recorded entries in this volume, in distant times and places.[5] As Victor Mair explains in the introductory notes to his English translation,

> according to legend, certain scholars who were fleeing from "the burning of books" carried out by the First Emperor of the Qin dynasty (221–207 B.C.E.) sought refuge in [Youyang]. Upon arrival, they deposited the texts they brought with them in a cave on the mountain. These writings (which presumably survived nowhere else) were later discovered by people who had wandered into the cave. Because of this legend, the name Youyang came to signify rare and old books from far away. (363–64)

The symbolic connotation of Duan's title is complemented by the eclectic books (*juan*) of the collection that reveal Duan's interest in the foreign and exotic.[6] Divided into multiple encyclopedic entries, these books present miscellaneous Chinese and distant legends, anecdotes, and tales dating from the Tang (618–907) and pre-Tang dynasties (Reed, *Tang* 1). This wide range of stories from mundane topics to supernatural accounts is complemented by practical notes on matters such as "medicinal herbs, perfume, tattoo and language" (1). Gathered from oral and written sources, as well as first-hand experiences (2–3), this encyclopedic compilation of anecdotes, tales, and notes points to the circulation of stories and cultural traditions brought about by the development of extensive trade routes connecting Asia to other parts of the world during the Tang dynasty (Mair 364; Reed, *Tang* 3).

The Yexian tale reflects the oral circulation and transmission of folktales in this time of economic trade and cultural exchange. Following two tales respectively located in modern-day Korea and Henan Province, Duan's Yexian tale,[7] set in the so-called South in pre-Qin time (221–207 BCE) (see Jameson 75; Mair 364; Waley 227), appears as an old and foreign folktale passed down from one generation to the next among the people of the South. Although Duan leaves this South unmapped, Mair and his predecessor Arthur Waley have hypothetically located it in contemporary Guangxi (Mair 367n25; Waley 229), which was inhabited by indigenous tribes before the region was incorporated into the expanding Chinese empire during the Qin dynasty (Ebrey 82–83). The concluding lines of Duan's tale also foreground how this story was passed down to him by Li Shiyuan, a former servant at his court and "member of a tribal community in Yongzhou" (modern-day Nanning), who could remember "many strange tales from the south" (Mair 366). Mair connects Li's origins to the Zhuang, a large minority group speaking a language akin to Thai, who used to live in modern-day Nanning when Duan wrote the *Youyang Zazu* (367n25).[8]

The Yexian tale narrates the story of Yexian, a young girl left in her wicked stepmother's hands at her parents' death. Yexian finds temporary comfort in the company of a fish living in the pond behind their abode. Annoyed by Yexian's distraction, the stepmother kills the fish and buries its fish bones in the house's cesspit. When mourning for the loss of her friend, Yexian receives a visit from a magical being who reveals the stepmother's treacherous act and informs her of the fish bones' magical ability to grant her wishes. In order to attend the cave festival in which marriage matches are made, Yexian asks the fish bones for resplendent clothing and slippers. As she is forced to run away from the festival when her stepsister seems to recognize her, Yexian loses a slipper, which is then found and sold to the king of the neighboring kingdom called Tuohan. After unsuccessfully trying the shoe on all the women of Tuohan, the king extends his search to the neighboring cave region in which Yexian lives, ultimately finding her. While Yexian marries the king, the stepmother and stepsister are retributively killed by flying stones and buried in a tomb ironically used as a matchmaking shrine. Despite Yexian's marriage to the king, the tale concludes on a dark note. Thirsty for riches and power, the king abuses the fish bones' magical ability for his own end. When the fish bones lose their power to grant wishes after a year, the sea buries them and the waves wash them away. Similarly to the fish bones, Yexian vanishes at the end, the story open-endingly concluding with the king's kingdom being looted by his troops.

References to the so-called Tuohan kingdom have also spurred Western translators to claim a "non-Sinitic" origin for the Yexian tale (Mair 366n1). Mair reads Tuohan as a "transcription of Dvāravatī/Dvārapati or Tavoy, Southeast Asian kingdoms that flourished during the Tang period and whose names were transcribed by Chinese in a nearly identical fashion, one which is very close to the transcription given here in our text" (366n10). The connection to the kingdom of Dvaravati was already made by Waley in

1947, as he argued that the Yexian tale did not originate in southern China among the native peoples of the Guangxi area,[9] who "had no 'kingdom of [Tuohan] lying off their shores,'" but instead "with the people of Dvaravati, who had as their close neighbor an island kingdom called Tuohan" (232). Waley's and Mair's respective references to Dvaravati not only presuppose an older Southeast Asian origin for the Yexian tale, but also foreground the important role of trade in its oral diffusion, the kingdom of Dvaravati being, in Mair's words, an "important transshipment poin[t] for long-distance trade between East and West" from the sixth to the thirteenth centuries (366n10). This alludes to potential Eastern and Western cross-cultural influences for the Yexian tale. In response to this modern attempt to situate the Yexian tale geographically, Dorothy Ko warns us, however, of the difficulty of "map[ping] the geography in the story onto the real world" (*Every Step* 28), despite the topographical elements figuring in Duan's tale. She reminds us of the role played by the South in many fantastic tales, as well as in Daoist and other folk religions; and this was a South that had already been the birthplace of many immortals, kings, and other heroes in Chinese poetry and literature by the Tang dynasty (28).

Although the temporal and geographical context of the Yexian tale remains uncertain, its moralistic tone, when read in contrast to the other marvel tales recorded in *Youyang Zazu*, points to other cultural and literary influences. As Reed explains in her *Chinese Chronicles of the Strange*, the Yexian tale (third entry, book 1, volume 2) appears more complicated in form and content than the more traditional Tang *chuanqi* tales found in their *juan* (book) and throughout the *Youyang Zazu* (11–12).[10] *Chuanqi* tales[11] were orally transmitted folkloric marvel tales dealing with human interactions with the supernatural set in particular times and places. They were told from a somewhat realistic perspective despite their fictional content, and often framed by formulaic expressions attesting to their verisimilitude, authenticity, and authority (see Nienhauser xiii–xxiii; Ming 76–82; Idema and Haft 134–39). Duan's tale follows *chuanqi* patterns in its formulaic beginning and ending crediting its oral transmission and source. Moreover, its narration of the human and supernatural encounter between Yexian and the fish serves to approach difficult human relationships—familial, marital, and gender-based.

Yet, contrary to traditional *chuanqi* stories, the Yexian tale is endowed with a moralistic tone in its critique addressed to society. On the one hand, the tale follows Yexian's rags-to-riches progression as the fish spirit frees her from her stepmother and enables her to marry the king, while the stepmother and her daughter are killed in retribution. Yexian's interaction with the fish highlights the abuse of Yexian at the hands of her stepmother, as well as the "good overcome evil" motif (Reed, *Tang* 12) dominating the story—a recurring motif found in many Cinderella variants across the world. On the other hand, the presence of the fish bones also serves to expose the constraining gender roles and expectations governing Yexian's society. Yexian's marriage does not appear liberating, despite Yexian's wish to find a suitable husband. Not only does Yexian disappear from the narration after marrying the king of Tuohan, as the tale shifts to focus on the king's unquenchable greed and abuse of the fish bones' magical power, but the kingdom itself collapses in looters' hands, leaving Yexian's fate uncertain. This dark ending complicates the rags-to-riches progression of the tale and offers a social critique regarding uneven relationships of power. The moralistic message of the Yexian tale thus sets it apart from the other *chuanqi* tales of the *Youyang Zazu*. More hybrid in form and content than the other tales of the collection, the Yexian tale can be placed in a larger folkloric and cross-cultural context.

Situating the origins of the Yexian tale in a cross-cultural background is crucial for critically engaging with its adaptations in the United States as a Cinderella story in the 1980s. Complicating the Chinese origins of this tale not only contributes to expanding our understanding of the role of fairy tales in constructing and deconstructing culture(s), but also sheds light on processes of self-ethnicization or Orientalization in settings of diaspora, and the inherent tensions between diasporic populations and Western societies at times of conflicting relationships. Decentering the Yexian tale also offers a better look at the persisting constructions of Eastern and Western cultures in dualistic terms despite the fluidity of geographic and cultural borders.

Constructing and Deconstructing China: *Yeh-Shen* and the Cross-Cultural Transformation of the Yexian Tale

The Yexian tale reached the English-speaking world through R. D. Jameson's translation and commentary published under the title "Cinderella in China" (*Three Lectures on Chinese Folklore* 1932), and Waley's annotated translation provided in his article "The Chinese Cinderella Story" (1947). The Yexian tale was more broadly diffused outside of the academic realm in the early 1980s in the United States with the publication of Ai-Ling Louie and Ed Young's picture book *Yeh-Shen: A Cinderella Story from China*.[12] In addition to reflecting the growing interest in the Cinderella story and its cultural variants in the West, as well as the increasing diffusion of postmodern retellings of the Cinderella story,[13] Louie and Young's retelling of the Yexian tale echoes the countercultural movements of the 1970s and 1980s. Following the civil rights movement, the establishment of more favorable immigration laws, and the counterculture of the Vietnam War era, but also the restructuring of university curricula and the birth of ethnic American studies, ethnic American writers strove to tell their stories in their own terms to oppose their discrimination and erasure from the American national, cultural, political, social, and artistic scenes. As explained in the preface to *Yeh-Shen*, the Yexian tale has held cultural, communal, and personal significance for Louie from a young age, this story being transmitted in her family for over three generations ("About the Author"). The discovery of a manuscript of the Yexian tale dating from the Qing dynasty (1644–1911)[14] spurred her, years later, to translate and pass it down to the children of her community.[15]

Published by Puffin Books, "one of the most prestigious children's paperback publishers in the United States" ("Puffin"), *Yeh-Shen* has reached a broad readership beyond the Chinese American community, inviting children from multicultural backgrounds to approach their world differently and cross-culturally. The spectrum of this broader readership might have encouraged Louie to adapt the Yexian tale to her Western audience, interweaving in her retelling elements from Charles Perrault's "Cendrillon ou la petite pantoufle de verre," and the Grimm brothers' 1847 "Aschenputtel."

Echoing Perrault, Louie emphasizes Yexian's unusual beauty in the opening of her tale:[16] "[Yeh-Shen] was a bright child and lovely too, with skin as smooth as ivory and dark pools for eyes. Her stepmother was jealous of all this beauty and goodness, for her own daughter was not pretty at all" (Louie). While Duan emphasizes Yexian's skill at "fishing for gold," (Ko, *Every Step* 26), he does not refer to her beauty. In contrast, Louie makes Yexian's beauty an integral part of the plot, as the stepmother sees Yexian's good looks as a hindrance to her own daughter's chance to find a suitable husband.[17] Moreover, comparing Yexian's skin to ivory and exaggerating the darkness and depth of her eyes, metaphorically described as "dark pools," Louie, *à la Disney*, exoticizes Yexian's appearance.

Allusions to Perrault return in Louie's adaptation when Yexian loses the shoe while running away from the festival to escape her sister's suspicious and inquisitive look. In Duan's Yexian tale no mention is made of Yexian's transformation from her resplendent attire into her rags when she loses the shoe. Yexian is simply said to return to her cave. In her retelling, Louie, echoing Perrault, foregrounds Yexian's magical transfiguration: "No sooner had the shoe fallen from her foot than all her fine clothes turned back to rags. Only one thing remained—a tiny golden shoe" (Louie).[18] With this allusion to Perrault, Louie strengthens the supernatural nature of the Yexian tale, while dramatizing the shoe loss episode. Louie anticipates the dramatic disappearance of the fish spirit when Yexian reaches home, as she is unable to return the borrowed slippers. In so doing, Louie endows this dramatic turn with an added moral and didacticism for her young audience: Yexian's negligence leads to the disappearance of her "only friend," the text says (Louie). Saddened by the loss of her spiritual companion, Yexian is determined to find the lost slipper at all cost and return the pair to the fish bones. Her determination to do the right thing recalls Perrault's *moralité* that stresses the importance of kindness and goodness over beauty.[19]

Similarly to Perrault's and the Grimms' Cinderella stories, Louie's plot evolves toward a happy ending. Louie changes the dark ending of the Yexian tale into a positive happily-ever-after conclusion by transforming Duan's violent, abusive, and greedy king into a more positive character. No longer deploying violence to find the owner of the slipper he was given as a gift by a merchant,[20] Louie's king uses strategy to bring Yexian forward on her own, as his early search efforts remained inconclusive.[21] Similarly, Louie's king appears sensitive and more humane, as he is said to find "true love" (Louie) in Yexian as soon as she fits the shoes and transforms into a beautiful sight.

Moreover, Louie's *Yeh-Shen* erases any reference to the king's greed and abuse of the fish bones' magical ability to grant riches, and to the looting of the Tuohan kingdom that leaves Yexian's fate uncertain in Duan's version. Louie concludes on Yexian's marriage to the king and the retributive justice met by the stepmother and her daughter, crushed in their caves by stones: "fate was not so gentle with her stepmother and stepsister," Louie's retelling reads. "Since they had been unkind to his beloved, the king would not permit Yeh-Shen to bring them to his palace. They remained in their cave home, where one day, it is said, they were crushed to death in a shower of flying stones" (Louie). Louie nods to Perrault's ending in which Cendrillon invites her stepsisters to come and live in the prince's palace with her. Yet, Louie's version makes Yexian passive, as it is the king who speaks up and forbids the sister to come along. Louie's revised ending also recalls the conclusion of the Grimms' 1847 "Aschenputtel," the German tale ending with the stepsisters' eyes being pierced by pigeons on Aschenputtel's wedding day. This allusion contributes to affirming Yexian's passivity. Like Aschenputtel, despite the happy ending inferred by her marriage, Yexian remains in the background of the story, a passive object of both the king's desire and nature's magical forces. Louie's Westernized story line remains therefore conservative for its time compared to the feminist retellings of the Cinderella story increasingly diffused in the West by the early 1980s.[22]

While Louie combines East and West by interweaving elements from Perrault's "Cendrillon" and the Grimms' "Aschenputtel" within the Yexian story, Young's illustrations return to the Asian cross-cultural underpinning of Duan's Yexian tale. Young relegates typical Cinderella motifs to the background and presents the tale from the dominating perspective of the fish—an important cultural symbol in many Asian cultures. Although complementing and enhancing the text, Young's illustrations serve as cultural counterpoints to the narration (see Nikolajeva and Scott 12), enabling a multiplicity of different readings and interpretations. Read together, the plot and its illustrations present alternative and ambivalent ways of telling and seeing (see Trumpener 57), which invites readers to explore and experience the Cinderella tale differently.

The friction between the verbal and the visual can be seen in *Yeh-Shen* as the juxtaposed text and images tell a different story. For instance, the stepmother and daughter—essential parts of the plot in Duan's tale and Louie's retelling—are left unrepresented beyond their vague appearance when Yexian loses her slipper, and beyond the related illustration of the tomb in which they are buried at the end. Similarly, whereas the lost shoe is given emphasis, Yexian is never shown fitting it in front of the king. The episode is implied and replaced by an arm and hand symbolically pounding at Yexian's door, followed by an image of the king's face expressing mesmerization at the sight of Yexian dressed in her beautiful attire. Although this illustration erases Yexian's physicality to foreground the king's fascination, Yexian triumphantly appears at the center of the next page majestically dressed in a blue-green cloak and adorned with shining jewelry. Contrasting with the previous fragmented depiction of the king's hand and head, Young's emphatic representation of Yexian's body revises the subordinate position she is conferred in Louie's text.

This visual emphasis on Yexian is furthered by the asymmetrical distribution between the text and image on the adjoining pages. Young's focal representation of Yexian is complemented by one sentence appearing on the top corner of the left page: "Her loveliness made her seem a heavenly being, and the king suddenly knew in his heart that he had found his true love" (Louie). Although Louie underlines Yexian's heavenly beauty in the first part of the sentence, the king is positioned at the center of the action. Louie quickly turns to the king and *his* happiness, linguistically and narratively, while consigning Yexian to the side. Contrastingly, Young's illustration, filling up the right page, puts Yexian at the center of the reader's attention, magnifying her beauty and reintegrating her presence in the marriage plot of the Cinderella story. Young's drawing does not extend, however, to portray Yexian's feet shod in the tiny golden slippers, which moves the focus away from her feet to reinforce her striking presence. Young's omission of some of the key features of the Cinderella story speaks of his transformative and deterritorializing agenda,[23] the ideological focus of his adaptation reorienting the Yexian tale toward different cultural (con)texts.

Far from Westernizing the Yexian tale, however, Young's illustrations present a case of sinicization, if not Asianization, as he grounds his visual retelling in a Chinese culture that exceeds the cultural setting of Duan's tale. Young made two trips to China to research the traditional costumes and customs of the people living in the area and time in which Duan's Yexian tale is set ("About the Author"). Yet, the question remains regarding which people, costumes, and customs he took as models for his drawings, the temporal and geographical setting of the tale being quite ambiguous, if not mythical, in *Youyang Zazu*. As a result, the Chinese historical context of Young's illustrations remains debatable. Likewise, the use of compartmentalized panels combining words and images vaguely evokes painted screens and scrolls—a "Chinese painting philosophy," as Young calls it ("About Ed"), that, however, refuses cultural and historical identification. The artistic design of his work, more than Chinese, is elusively *Asian*.

The Asianization of Young's illustration culminates in the haunting presence of the fish. Young's fish departs from the carp with golden eyes and red fins described in Duan's tale (Reed, *Chronicles* 111). Having the silhouette of a carp, yet endowed with a multiplicity of colors evolving throughout the narration, Young's fish recalls the Japanese *Nishikigoi*, more commonly known as koi fish, a subspecies of the Eastern carp *Cyprinus carpio* that made its way to Eurasia through trade long before the publication of *Youyang Zazu* (Tamadechi 8, 14).[24] According to Michugo Tamadechi, the Eastern carp gained a variety of colors over time through natural breeding and mutation, though the literature and records documenting this transformation are scarce in China and Japan (16–20). It is only in the 1800s that extensive breeding started, especially in Japan, leading to the multiplicity of colors and mutation varieties that we have today (20–21). Indeed, the carp of Chinese and Japanese stories and myths before the nineteenth century mostly referred to wild uncolored carps, which were praised for their ability to swim upstream and their resulting symbolism of perseverance (16).

The multiplicity of colors permeating Young's illustrations brings the fish of the Yexian tale to new cultural grounds. By endowing the fish with a variety of cultural symbols that refuse clear geographical and temporal boundaries, Young evokes the cross-cultural Asian origins of the Yexian tale implicit in Duan's version. Yet, in addition to drawing connections between Asian cultures and simultaneously decentering the Western plot of the Cinderella story, this cross-cultural fish also contributes, more negatively, to presenting a reductive single story of Asia that omits cultural, historical, and geographical distinctions.

However, despite the Orientalist connotation of this cultural mixing, Young's illustrations offer an alternative mode of storytelling, as the images seem to tell the tale from the fish's perspective. Key elements of the plot and characters, with the exception of Yexian, are represented as part of, if not engulfed by, the fish. This engulfing points to the fish's supernatural ability to control the action and ultimately alter the story line. Literally filtered through the fish, Young's pictorial interpretation presents a fairy tale grounded in nature, as well as a nature rife with (cross-)cultural and folkloric significance.

Contrastingly, Yexian appears by the fish's side in the early representations. This separation does not alter the fish's dominance and roles as mediator and storyteller but accentuates its intervening power. The opening illustration highlights the fish's developing friendship with Yexian and its increasing control over the action through a collage of two images—Yexian embracing her dying mother in the forefront and an imposing representation of the fish in the back. With its purple color, the fish comes to symbolize both heaven and grief (see Eberhard 299). The fish's purple shade resonates with Yexian's sorrow at her mother's deathbed, while reinforcing the spiritual fusion between the mother and the fish hinted at in this drawing, as the fish thereafter takes on the role of Yexian's new spiritual and material guardian. This association is furthered as the mother appears in the fish's eye in the background illustration. Shaped as a window, the fish's eye captures the departing mother, curved up and holding a wooden banister, her upper body and head surrounded by a halo. This visual juxtaposition spurs the reader to view the fish as a substitute for the dying mother, literally keeping an eye on Yexian and accompanying her in her life of toil.[25]

This substitute motherly protection is amplified as the next illustration represents a juxtaposition of Yexian and the fish, whose bodies are respectively curved, if not entwined, Yexian bending down to perform some washing tasks, the fish appearing in a crescent shape, his head and tail rising out of the water to hold, if not protect, Yexian. Forming together a type of circle, Yexian and the fish are represented in an embrace that mirrors the hug between mother and daughter seen in the previous image. Its vivid shade of green, symbolic of springtime, nature, and life (Eberhard 159; Welch 506), also strengthens the fish's nurturing presence.[26] Young presents a nurturing nature tending to the ones in need, while simultaneously guiding and influencing, if not determining, human behavior, as the fish comes to supernaturally oversee Yexian's actions and future.

The fish's nurturing presence is evoked once again in Young's representation of the fish's magical ability. Transforming into a half-fish, half-human creature once Yexian collects its bones from the cesspit, Young's nurturing fish blurs the lines between humans and animals, nature and culture, reality and magic. Whereas the creature's body remains a fish, the head is conferred human features, as it appears bald, with a long whitening beard and white hairy eyebrows that recall artistic representations of Confucian sages or literati in Chinese art. The fish's anthropomorphization also complicates the connection made between the fish and Yexian's deceased mother in the early drawings, as it destabilizes gender boundaries. This confused state of metamorphosis is further exemplified by the fish's changing color from green to yellow. Its greenish body and yellowish head are surrounded by a yellow halo that evokes both earth and heaven,[27] a blurring that amplifies the fish's natural and nurturing presence as well as its supernatural ability and authority.

Binaries separating the human and the animal, the natural and the supernatural, as well as gender boundaries are also revised and complicated at the end of *Yeh-Shen* when Yexian becomes one with the fish, her silhouette and clothing physically merging with the fish after fitting the shoe. In addition to symbolizing the fish's accomplishment of its ultimate task and

Yexian's self-realization, this merging similarly evokes cross-cultural connections once again exceeding the context of the Yexian tale. The fish in Chinese culture commonly stands for wealth and abundance, the characters for fish and wealth being similarly pronounced in Mandarin (Perkins 57). This symbolic pairing between fish and wealth is also present in other Asian cultural representations (see Chwalowski 455–61; Ball 189–204), especially in the fish's emblematic association with fertility—due to its ability to reproduce rapidly (Perkins 57)—and marital bliss, fishes usually swimming in pairs (57). By becoming one with the fish at the end, Yexian, in her rich outfit, transforms into the symbolic embodiment of wealth. This representational embodiment of abundance is complemented by the textual reference to her marriage to the king that follows and the symbol of marital prosperity, if not fertility, suggested by this union. Yet, Young simultaneously complicates this association, as Yexian and the king are not represented side by side, as two fish metaphorically swimming together, but on two different and separated pages.[28] This separation stresses Yexian's self-realization and accomplishment over her connubial happiness.

By representing the fish as a carp—thus remaining consistent with Duan's text—Young also endows it with the carp's symbolism of perseverance and achievement as depicted in the Chinese legend of the Dragon Gate—symbols also expanding cross-culturally beyond this Chinese account. Legend has it that a carp reached the top of a waterfall after swimming upstream, where it found a closed gate. Persevering in its effort, the carp jumped up the gate and transformed into a dragon.[29] The transformation from fish to dragon exemplifies the fish's determination, strength, and achievement regardless of the struggles previously endured. The carp's cultural representation of perseverance and achievement plays a crucial role in Young's drawings, as the fish comes to accompany, if not epitomize, Yexian's persistence and tenacity in the face of hardship.

Yexian's personal achievement is furthered in Young's illustration, as she not only becomes one with the fish but simultaneously transforms into a type of bird when she puts on the "feathered cloak" and "azure gown" she received from the fish bones (Louie). While Duan's version points to kingfisher feathers, which denote feminine beauty (Welch 137), Young's illustration depicts a cloak seemingly made of peacock feathers, the peacock symbolizing elegance, as well as rank, wealth, and power (Welch 143–44). Yexian's more ambiguous blue-green cloak in *Yeh-Shen* accentuates her beauty, as well as her achievement and newly gained status. Becoming both fish and bird, Yexian figuratively rises above her life of toil, free from the physical bondage that kept her tied to her stepmother.[30]

Accordingly, the interaction of text and images in *Yeh-Shen* decenters Western Cinderella motifs. This picture book offers a cross-cultural Cinderella story that narratively interweaves the Yexian tale with Perrault's "Cendrillon" and the Grimms' "Aschenputtel," and visually contextualizes this Chinese American retelling in a larger Asian context that exceeds the setting of Duan's Yexian tale. The multicolored carp permeating the drawings complicates the Chinese roots of the tale by invoking natural and folkloric symbols that surpass the limits of cultural boundaries. In so doing, Young revisits the Yexian tale and the Cinderella story by putting forth a nature rife with cross-cultural symbolic meaning, thus inviting a more complex reading of the Cinderella story as a text of multiple cultures in the West. This artistic disorienting comes, however, with a negative twist. Young's cross-cultural mixing of Asian symbols oversimplifies and presents Asian cultures as somewhat interchangeable or similar. As a result, Young's cross-cultural representations also point to the dangers of reductive cultural amalgamation and stereotyping.

Orientalizing the Yexian Tale on the American Screen

Released three years after Louie and Young's illustrated book, the *CBS Storybreak* animated TV adaptation "Yeh-Shen: A Cinderella Story from China," while diffusing the Yexian tale to a larger American audience and including Asian American actors and staff members in its production,[31] simultaneously uses and perverts the Yexian tale to diffuse Orientalist stereotypes in the never-ending Cold War context of the 1980s. Whereas CBS commentator Bob Keisha introduces Louie and Young's picture book, as well as the Yexian tale more generally, as a Chinese *Cinderella* story, he similarly emphasizes its "surprising" "difference" from the story known in the United States.[32] He also underlines its temporal distance, being a "thousand years older" than its presupposed Western counterpart ("Yeh-Shen"). Keisha's introductory words, more than drawing cross-cultural connections, magnify China's difference by inserting the Yexian tale in a constructed narrative of curiosity and wonder rife with Orientalist overtone.

This enraptured attention to the strange and mysterious Oriental, who fascinates and frightens, is extended in "Yeh-Shen" through the visual displays of Chinese otherness meant to transport the audience to the physically and temporally distant China of the Yexian tale. The southern cave region of Duan's tale is coarsely outlined in a style imitative of classical Chinese landscape paintings featuring high and sharp rocky mountains arising in the foggy distance, sprinkled with curvy trees and isolated pagodas or temples, and interspersed with rivers and parceled fields. Although evoking the "Chinese painting philosophy" of Young's work ("About Ed"), the setting of this TV adaptation contrasts with the abstract and subtle brushstroke-style of Young's illustrations that elude geographical representations. Conforming to standardized, if not fixed, artistic representations of China, the Chinese landscape of "Yeh-Shen" thus verges on the stereotypical; stereotypes additionally stressed by the Oriental instrumental music playing in the background.

Similarly, moving away from the historical underpinning of Young's illustrations outlining tribal—but somewhat atemporal—clothing and headdresses, the protagonists' hairstyles and costumes in the CBS adaptation Orientalize their bodies and culture through a display of contrasts and stereotypes that evoke and exceed the *evil and ugly* vs. *kind and beautiful* motif of the Cinderella story. Characters, even the flat ones filling the background, are depicted in an exaggerated Orientalist fashion. The numerous farmers and lower-class men shown throughout the episode are portrayed with stereotypical conical hats, and long shirts on ample trousers, as well as amplified phenotypes: exaggerated round or elongated faces with angular jaws, yellow skin, big ears, flat noses, thin and arched eyebrows, as well as exaggerated Fu Manchu–style mustaches—here represented as rather short and thin strands of hair growing far apart on each side corner of the mouth.

Although exoticized, the king with his colorful clothing and accessories is set apart from this monotonous and stereotypical crowd of Chinese men filling the space. His long white robe with Oriental patterns in blue and red hues worn on blue trousers, his high boots, prominent shoulder pads, and white-and-blue head scarf mark his respectability and good looks. Likewise, the king's phenotypes appear toned down, if not Westernized, and his face more harmonious and charming than the other male protagonists'. In distinguishing lower- and upper-class men, "Yeh-Shen" not only paints a grotesque portrait of Orientalist masculinity predominantly depicted as rural but also underlines the success story of Yexian, who gets to marry the king, the only representative of respectability and good looks.

Likewise, Yexian, the stepmother, and the stepsister are portrayed through a play of stereotypes of the opposing caricatures of the China Doll (Yexian) and the Dragon Lady (stepmother and daughter), two major stereotypes of Chinese femininity diffused in the United States since the mid-nineteenth century. As for the king and his male subjects, these Orientalist stereotypes magnify the associative pairing of evil with ugly and kind with beautiful well-known in the United States through Disney's adaptation of Perrault's "Cendrillon." Yexian's costumes and more favorable phenotypes highlight her exotic beauty, which complements her submissive and subservient character in depicting her as an Oriental doll. Conversely to her whiter skin and more neutral phenotypes that emphasize her Europeanization, her dark, thick, long, and manicured hair, tied in a voluminous ponytail and decorated with pink flowers, simultaneously accentuates her exoticism. Even her so-called rags, equally curated, reinforce her visual harmony.[33]

Her exotic beauty culminates, however, when she dons the clothing she receives from the fish bones to attend the festival. As soon as the stepmother and sister leave, the fish bones dissipate in a cloud of golden smoke to transform into golden shoes, whose pattern recalls the scales of a fish. Whereas these shoes hint at the golden slippers of Duan's text, they remain historically and culturally inaccurate. In addition to resembling the platform shoes Manchu women wore during the Qing dynasty (1644–1911) (see Ko, "Bondage"), about two thousand years after the time of the Yexian tale, they equally resemble open brass oil lamps with elongated nozzles and elevated bases. This visual parallel amplifies the magic of the scene as well as the fish bones' ability to grant Yexian's wishes, thus aligning the fish with the Oriental figure of the genie.

Yexian's exoticism is furthered by her dress that contrasts with the blue feathery coat of Duan's tale and Louie and Young's retelling. She wears instead a more *sexy* tight-fitting yellow dress ornamented with a dark yellow fabric overlay in the abstract shape of fish bones. Her dress is complemented by accessories: prominent dark-blue shoulder pads in the angular shape of a fishtail, an equally triangular golden headdress garnished with pink roses, and floor-length blue scarves attached to her forearms, vaguely resembling fish fins, with tassels at each extremity. Although wearing the fish as in Young's illustration, Yexian predominantly appears as an extravagant, exotic princess, whose Disneyfied attire evades historical and cultural references but stirs the young audience's curiosity and imagination, while allowing them to identify with her.

The *chinoiserie* of the stepmother's and daughter's outfits contrasts with Yexian's fantasy dress that evades cultural association. While the stepmother wears a green knee-length skirt and blouse buttoned on the right side and adorned with a high collar, the stepdaughter wears a discordant and tasteless purple and green cheongsam—a traditional long, tight-fitting dress with high splits on each side—on top of blue trousers. Both women similarly wear grotesque imitations of the Chinese cheongsam, headdresses, and platform shoes to the festival. The Orientalism of the stepmother's and sister's clothing, when read in contrast to Yexian's more Western attire, adds a level to the associative pairing of evil and ugly. Evilness and ugliness are also visually linked to the two women's so-called *Chineseness*.

Likewise, the stepmother's and sister's exaggerated racial phenotypes accentuate their Oriental difference, threatening look, and evilness. Their wrinkly dark-yellow faces are oval and elongated with excessively pointy chins. Their lips and ears are disproportionately big, their noses flattened and wide, their cheekbones particularly protruding, and their slanted eyes drippy. Their strikingly high-arched eyebrows complement their distasteful and offensive representations by magnifying their aggressiveness and evilness.[34] Their respective hairstyles—the daughter wearing her thin and depleted hair in a high and disheveled ponytail, the mother tying her grey-streaked black hair in two loops at the back of the skull—reinforce their grotesque appearances. Mother and daughter appear indeed as parodic versions of the stereotypical Chinese female villain known as Dragon Lady in the West—an alluring yet deceitful and evil femme fatale—here deprived of any beauty and charm. The exaggerated Oriental evilness and ridicule of mother and daughter, while underlining Yexian's exotic yet Westernized beauty, kindness and rags-to-riches progression, simultaneously magnify the vilification of China conveyed in this TV adaptation.[35]

Read in this context, Yexian's rags-to-riches development is also conferred ideological significance. Yexian's marriage to the king, yet continued passivity as she declares subservience to her husband-to-be,[36] complemented with the defeat of her evil *dragon* stepmother, speaks of the reinstitution of the Oriental Doll as desirable model of Chinese femininity and behavior, despite Yexian's partial Europeanization. More than adapting Louie and Young's picture book to the screen and diffusing the Yexian tale to a varied audience of American children, PBS's animated adaptation essentializes and fixes China in a perpetual state of passivity and inferiority in the Cold War context of the 1980s.

Putting Louie and Young's children's book in conversation with its animated adaptation enables us to fathom what Martine Hennard Dutheil de la Rochère, Gillian Lathey, and Monika Woźniak have called the "transformative dimension" (14) of the Cinderella story constantly re-adapted to different social, cultural, historical, and cultural contexts (15), as well as explore the political, social, and cultural conflicts that the fairy tale genre covers and uncovers. Louie and Young's cross-cultural and multivocal retelling, in addition to decentering the Eurocentric Cinderella story diffused in the United States, points to the Asian American diasporic community's endeavor to open up dialogue and intercultural exchanges at this time of (trans-)national conflicts. In so doing, *Yeh-Shen* opposes power differentials to move the American nation toward a more integrated and socially cohesive society.

Yet, Louie and Young nevertheless fall short in countering colonialist forces, as *Yeh-Shen* also presents an amalgamation of Asian cultures passed as *Chinese*, as suggested by the title of the picture book. This *melting-pot* technique continues to propagate in the West the presumption of a monolithic Asian culture, while reductively associating Asia with its largest and most populated country, China. This raises the question of the constraints of the publishing industry for Asian American writers and artists in the 1980s, as Louie and Young's simultaneous Westernized and Orientalized adaptation of the Yexian tale seems to cater to the taste of an American audience deeply influenced by Disney and quite prejudiced against Asian populations.

The stereotypes left in the background of Louie and Young's *Yeh-Shen* are more fully developed in the PBS adaptation. Although evoking Disney's battle between the ugly female villain and the beautiful, kind, and hardworking heroine, this screen adaptation reestablishes and conveys Orientalist stereotypes to a wide American audience, ultimately countering Louie and Young's attempt at drawing more positive cross-cultural connections between East and West through the Cinderella story in times of political conflicts.

Although *Yeh-Shen* and its TV adaptation are products of their times, their respective design and story line, as well as their connection and interaction, highlight the power and limits of the fairy tale in a cross-cultural context. Constantly building on, rewriting, and transforming previous texts produced in specific settings and contexts, and continuously endowed with new symbolic, if not ideological, significance to match with arising concerns, the fairy tale appears as an inevitably ambivalent genre that constructs and deconstructs, rewrites and creates anew, negotiates and articulates culture(s). In its ambivalent, plural, polyvalent, and multivocal forms, the fairy tale thus has the power to reproduce or strengthen inequalities, but also to question and subvert them, or, in other words, to disorient cultural hegemonies and re-orient the reader toward new possibilities of social justice, as Cristina Bacchilega has argued (*Fairy Tales* 27).[37] In contexts of cross-cultural encounters, it is crucial to keep this ambivalence in mind and pay attention to the often conflicting and constraining sociohistorical and political contexts of their productions and diffusions. Theorizing ambivalence in the context of fairy-tale studies would be a good step in this direction.

Notes

1. I generally use the contemporary pinyin spelling "Yexian" except when quoting the original titles of Louie and Young's book and its TV adaptation.

2. I allude here to Martine Hennard Dutheil de la Rochère, Gillian Lathey, and Monika Woźniak's term "text of culture(s)" used in their introduction to *Cinderella Across Cultures* (2).

3. The term "single story" was used by Chimamanda Ngozi Adichie in her TED talk "The Danger of a Single Story" (2009) to describe the Western reductive construction of Africa as monolithically poor, economically and politically unstable, as well as primitive and barbaric.

4. As Carrie E. Reed claims: "*Za* means miscellaneous. *Zu* means a platter for sacrificial meat, and, by extension, the offerings of tasty meat morsels themselves. Duan implies in his brief authorial preface that the entries in his work, metaphorically revealed out of the depths of the secret cave, are intended as delicious morsels that may help to make scholar's reading more palatable" (*Tang* 2).

5. The temporal and physical distance implied by Duan's geographic and symbolic reference to Youyang is captured in Western translators' transcriptions Miscellany of Forgotten Lore (Waley 226), and Miscellaneous Morsels of Lost Lore (Mair 364).

6. *Youyang Zazu* is divided into two volumes of twenty and ten books, respectively, each also divided into multiple entries. See Reed's *Tang Miscellany*, pp. 25–42.

7. The Yexian tale is found in the second, or sequel, volume of the *Youyang Zazu*, in the third entry of its first *juan* (book) entitled "Zhi Nuogao" (sequel to the Records of Nuogao). For a translation and more information on the "Records of Nuogao," see Reed's *Chinese Chronicles*.

8. For more on the tale's connection to the Zhuang, see Beauchamp's "Asian Origins." Waley also argues that the story "belonged to certain aborigines in the extreme south of China" (226).

9. In contrast to Mair and Waley, Jameson situates Tuohan "in the middle of the great sea southwest of Linyi" (77), which he identifies as Annam, present-day Vietnam (95n10). He estimates this island as being "over three-months travel from the [Jiaozhiao] country (French-Indo China)" (77).

10. The preceding Korean tale (first entry, book 1, volume 2) is as complicated in form and content as the Yexian tale. These two tales do not match with the other *chuanqi* tales present in their *juan* and throughout the *Youyang Zazu*. This tale narrates the story of two brothers. Pang Yi asks his young and wealthy brother for silkworm eggs and grains. His brother honors his request, but preliminarily boils the eggs and grains. Only one silkworm egg hatches and one stalk grows, but both grow to gigantic size. The stalk is soon broken and taken by a bird. Pang Yi follows the bird to a little cave in the mountain where he finds and steals a magic golden awl that grants all his wishes. Pang Yi's brother, jealous of his success, boils silkworm eggs and grains for his own end. Only one egg hatches and one stalk grows. The stalk is similarly taken by a bird, whom he follows. Arriving at the same cave where Pang Yi found the awl, the brother is greeted by angry goblins who accuse him of stealing their awl. As a punishment, they ask him to build a twenty-foot-long pile of chaff. As the brother is unable to do so, the goblins pull his nose till it reaches the size of an elephant's trunk. Soon after the brother dies of shame. The story concludes on a note regarding Pang Yi's descendants, who continue to ask the awl for riches until one day the awl disappears during a thunderstorm. See Reed, *Chinese Chronicles*, pp. 109–10. The highly moralistic message of the Korean tale and the Yexian tale, set almost back-to-back in the *Youyang Zazu*, further highlights their foreign origins.

11. *Chuanqi* meaning "transmissions of the strange" (Nienhauser xiii).

12. The Yexian tale was also subsequently used by Chinese American writer Adeline Yen Mah in her autobiographical novel *Chinese Cinderella: The True Story of an Unwanted Daughter* (1999) and her juvenile book series *Chinese Cinderella*.

13. See, for instance, Jane Yolen's "America's Cinderella" (1977), and Alan Dundes's edited collection *Cinderella: A Casebook* (1982). For more on postmodern and feminist fairy tales, see Cristina Bacchilega's *Postmodern Fairy Tales* (1997), and Donald Haase's edited volume *Fairy Tales and Feminism* (2004).

14. The manuscript is reproduced at the beginning of *Yeh-Shen*.

15. Louie also developed in 2007 a children's book series entitled *Amazing Asian Americans*, few biographies of Asian American artists being written for a younger readership. The series has been published since 2012 under her own Dragoneagle Press (www.dragoneagle.com).

16. Perrault highlights how Cendrillon, despite her rags, looked more beautiful than her sisters who were dressed in resplendent clothing. The French text reads: "cependant Cendrillon avec ses méchants habits ne laissait pas d'être cent fois plus belle que ses sœurs, quoique vêtues très magnifiquement" (66).

17. The stepmother "hoped to find a husband for her own daughter and did not want any man to see the beauteous Yeh-Shen first" (Louie).

18. "Cendrillon arriva chez elle bien essoufflée, sans carrosse, sans laquais, et avec ses méchants habits, rien ne lui étant resté de toute sa magnificence qu'une de ses petites pantoufles, la pareille de celle qu'elle avait laisse tomber" (Perrault 76).

19. "La beauté, pour le sexe, est un rare trésor. / De l'admirer jamais on ne se lasse; / Mais ce qu'on nomme bonne grâce / Est sans prix, et vaut mieux encore" (Perrault 80).

20. Duan's version reads: "The king of Tohan suspected that the cave dweller had gotten the shoe in some improper way, so he imprisoned and tortured him, but he never did end up finding out where it had come from. After that, the king threw the shoe down by the wayside, and went through houses everywhere to arrest people. If there was a woman who could wear it, the king's men were to take her into custody and inform the king" (Reed, *Chronicles* 112).

21. From here onward, Louie's plot regarding the shoe search differs from Duan's Yexian tale. In Duan's account, the king, who receives the lost slipper, orders his men to find the owner of the shoe at all costs. After searching for the owner in the king's kingdom in vain, the king's men extend their search to the neighboring kingdom. Going from door to door to ask every woman in each household to try on the tiny shoe, they eventually find Yexian. In Louie's version, Yexian's lost shoe is found and sold to the king of the Tuohan kingdom, as it is in Duan's tale. The shoe search process differs, however, as the king, unable to find the owner of the shoe, decides to leave the shoe in a pavilion by the side of the road where it was found to let the owner come forward on her own. Hidden nearby, the king observes the site in the hope of finding his match. Contrary to other women who come to try on the shoe during the day, Yexian timidly comes to pick up the shoe at night. Struck by the beauty of her face, as well as by her tiny feet, the king follows Yexian home. The king pounds at the door and kindly asks Yexian to put on the golden slippers. It is then that Yexian transforms once again into her resplendent outfit. The Yexian tale that

Louie heard as a child might have differed slightly from Duan's ninth-century version, as the Yexian tale was told and retold in China over time.

22. As Hennard, Lathey, and Woźniak observe, "since the 1970s, second-wave feminists have debated the representation of gender roles, behaviors, and social expectations encoded in fairy tales, raised the issue of female agency and desire, and questioned the heteronormative model of romance, marriage, and family exemplified by Sleeping Beauty, Snow White and Cinderella" (11). See as well Haase's *Fairy Tales and Feminism*.

23. I allude here to Hennard, Lathey, and Woźniak, who emphasize the "manifold de-territorializations" of the Cinderella tale as it has been adapted to different sociocultural, political, and historical contexts (15).

24. This Eastern carp made its way to Eurasia about 2000 years ago (Tamadechi 14).

25. A cross-cultural connection can be made between Young's illustration of the fish as motherly substitute and the Grimms' tale in which the hazel tree serves as a substitute for Aschenputtel's deceased mother.

26. This embrace between Yexian and the fish carries a double meaning. Louie's juxtaposed text also introduces the treachery of the stepmother, who donned Yexian's clothes to trick the fish and kill it. From this perspective, what appears as an embrace between Yexian and the fish/deceased mother can also be seen as a wrestling match between the stepmother and the fish; or, in other words, between Yexian's mother and stepmother. This double reading foregrounds the richness of Young's illustrations, which offer multiple, nuanced readings enabling cross-cultural connections between Cinderella stories and beyond.

27. Yellow symbolizes the earth (Eberhard 402), but also Chinese emperors called "Sons of Heaven" in the Mandate of Heaven, the spiritual and political principle defining the emperor's role and place as ruler of the universe (Ebrey 179).

28. Contrastingly, Yexian symbolically swims by the fish's side in the early drawings, a fact that stresses their special friendship and connection.

29. See, for instance, Mah, *China*, p. 2.

30. Yexian's transformation is given added cultural and religious significance, fish and bird being connected in the Buddhist tradition for their ability to adapt to water and air, and their resulting association with freedom (Ripley 192).

For instance, as Katherine M. Ball explains in her analysis of animal representations in Asian arts, the fish, able to swim in all directions, symbolizes the spiritual freedom of those emancipated from desires and attachments (204).

31. Although directed by Ray Patterson, "Yeh-Shen" was managed by Taiwanese American director James Wang (Wang Film Productions). Similarly, Iwao Takamoto, a Japanese American animator who began his career with Walt Disney in 1945, where he notably participated in designing *Cinderella*, worked on the creative design of "Yeh-Shen." Also, a majority of Asian American voice actors contributed to "Yeh-Shen" (e.g., Michael Chan, Ernest Harrada, Emily Kuroda, Janice Motoike, George Takei, and Brian Tochi) (see "CBS Storybook, Yeh-Shen"). This testifies to the progress already made in the 1980s regarding the integration of Asian American artists, professionals, and actors in American cinematic and TV productions, Asian Americans being barred from the American screen before the 1960s.

32. By mentioning the existence of one Cinderella story Americans know—that he does not identify—Keisha presents the Cinderella tale as monolithic and homogeneous, thus obscuring the multiplicity of Cinderella stories diffused in the West.

33. Yexian wears dark-blue pants, an orange-red long-sleeved shirt, long white socks, black slippers, and a beige apron. The complementarity of her blue pants and orange shirt foregrounds her visual harmony.

34. Their evil appearances are complemented by their threatening words, laughs, and gestures, as well as by their ominous positions toward Yexian. The stepmother is predominantly represented from the bottom up to make her bigger and more intimidating in moments of tension.

35. This demeaning association of the characters' Chineseness and evilness can also be seen through the Chinese-accented English spoken by the stepmother, who stands out visually and vocally compared to the other characters, even her own daughter.

36. Yexian submissively answers to the king's proposal: "If I am destined to be your queen then I am happy beyond belief. I will do everything to fulfill your trust and love" ("Yeh-Shen").

37. For a discussion of fairy tales' multivocality, and transformational power, see Bacchilega's *Fairy Tales Transformed?* (1–30), where she lays out the

foundation for rethinking fairy tales and immersing "the practice of reading intertextuality in social changes" (27).

Works Cited

"About Ed." *Ed Young*, 2006, edyoungart.com/about.html.

Adichie, Chimamanda Ngozi, "The Danger of a Single Story." *TEDGlobal*, 2009, www.ted.com/talks/chimamanda_adichie_the_danger_of_a_single_story.

"Ai-Ling Louie: About the Author." *Penguin Random House*, 2017, www.penguinrandomhouse.com/authors/247964/ai-ling-louie.

Bacchilega, Cristina. *Fairy Tales Transformed? Twenty-First-Century Adaptations and the Politics of Wonder*. Wayne State University Press, 2013.

———. *Postmodern Fairy Tales: Gender and Narrative Strategies*. University of Pennsylvania Press, 1997.

Ball, Katherine M. "The Fish." 1927. *Animal Motifs in Asian Art: An Illustrated Guide to their Meanings and Aesthetics*, Dover Publications, 2004, pp. 189–204. Originally published by John Lane The Bodley Head.

Beauchamp, Fay. "Asian Origins of Cinderella: The Zhuang Storyteller of Guangxi." *Oral Tradition*, vol. 25, no. 2, 2010, pp. 447–96.

"CBS Storybreak, Yeh-Shen: A Cinderella Story from China." *IMDb*, 1990–2017, www.imdb.com/title/tt1369041/fullcredits?ref_=tt_ov_st_sm.

Chwalowski, Farrin. "Fish: the Buddha Symbol." *Symbols in Arts, Religion and Culture: The Soul of Nature*. Cambridge Scholar Publishing, 2016, pp. 455–61.

Duan, Chengshi (段成式). *Youyang Zazu* 酉阳杂俎. Shangaiguji Chubanshe, 2012.

Dundes, Alan, editor. *Cinderella: A Casebook*. Garland, 1982.

Eberhard, Wolfram. *Dictionary of Chinese Symbols: Hidden Symbols in Chinese Life and Thought*. 1986. Translated from German by G. L. Campbell, Taylor and Francis, 2006. Originally published by Routledge and Kegan Paul.

Ebrey, Patricia Buckley. *The Cambridge Illustrated History of China*. 1996, 2nd ed., Cambridge University Press, 2010.

Grimm, Jacob, and Wilhelm Grimm. "Aschenputtel." *Kinder- und Hausmärchen*, edited by Hans-Jörg Uther, Eugen Diederichs Verlag, 1996, pp. 120–28.

Haase, Donald, editor. *Fairy Tales and Feminism: New Approaches*. Wayne State University Press, 2004.

Hennard, Martine Dutheil de la Rochère, Gillian Lathey, and Monika Woźniak. "Introduction: Cinderella Across Cultures." *Cinderella Across Cultures: New Directions and Interdisciplinary Perspectives*, edited by Martine Dutheil de la Rochère Hennard, Gillian Lathey, and Monika Woźniak, Wayne State University Press, 2016, pp. 1–24.

Idema, Wilt, and Lloyd Haft. "The Form and Content of Chuanqi." *A Guide to Chinese Literature*, University of Michigan Press, 1997, pp. 134–39.

Jameson, R. D. "Cinderella in China." *Cinderella: A Folklore Casebook*, edited by Alan Dundes, Garland Publishing, 1982, pp. 14–29. Originally published in *Three Lectures on Chinese Folklore*, North China Union Language School, 1932, pp. 47–85.

Ko, Dorothy. "Bondage in Time: Footbinding and Fashion Theory." *Modern Chinese Literary and Cultural Studies in the Age of Theory: Reimagining a Field*, edited by Rew Chow, Duke University Press, 2000, pp. 199–226.

———. *Every Step a Lotus: Shoes for Bound Feet*. Bata Show Foundation, University of California Press, 2001.

Louie, Ai-Ling. *Yeh-Shen: A Cinderella Story from China*. Illustrated by Ed Young, Puffin Books, 1982.

Mah, Adeline Yen. *China: Land of Dragons and Emperors*. Allen & Unwin, 2008.

———. *Chinese Cinderella: The True Story of an Unwanted Daughter*. Dell Publishing, 1999.

Mair, Victor. "The First Recorded Cinderella Story." *Hawai'i Reader in Traditional Chinese Culture*, edited by Mair et al., University of Hawai'i Press, 2005, pp. 363–67.

Ming, Dong Gu. *Chinese Theories of Fiction: A Non-Western Narrative System*. State University of New York Press, 2006.

Nienhauser, William H. Jr. *Tang Dynasty Tales: A Guided Reader*. World Scientific, 2010.

Nikolajeva, Maria, and Carole Scott. *How Picturebooks Work*. Garland Publishing, 2001.

Perkins, Dorothy. *Encyclopedia of China: History and Culture*. Routledge, 2013.

Perrault, Charles. "Cendrillon ou la petite pantoufle de verre." *Histoires ou contes du temps passé avec des moralités*, Amsterdam, 1721, pp. 64–82.

"Puffin." *Penguin Books USA*, Penguin Random House, 2017, www.penguin.com/publishers/puffin/.

Reed, Carrie E. *Chinese Chronicles of the Strange: The "Nuogao ji."* Peter Lang, 2001. Asian Thought and Culture, vol. 44.

———. *A Tang Miscellany: An Introduction to* Youyang Zazu. Asian Thought and Culture, vol. 57, Peter Lang, 2003.

Ripley, Doré. "The Maiden with a Thousand Slippers: Animal Helpers and the Hero(ine)'s Journey." *Goddesses in World Culture, Volume 1: Asia and Africa*, edited by Patricia Monaghan, Praeger, 2011, pp. 185–200.

Tamadechi, Michugo. *The Cult of the Koi*. 1990. 2nd expanded edition, TFH Publications, 1994.

Trumpener, Katie. "Picture Worlds and Ways of Seeing." *Cambridge Companion to Children's Literature*, edited by M. O. Grenby and Andrea Immei, Cambridge University Press, 2009, pp. 55–75.

Waley, Arthur. "The Chinese Cinderella Story." *Folklore*, vol. 58, no. 1, March 1947, pp. 226–38.

Welch, Patricia Bjaaland. *Chinese Art: A Guide to Motifs and Visual Imagery*. Tuttle Publishing, 2013.

"Yeh-Shen: A Cinderella Story from China." Directed by Ray Patterson, written by Ai-Ling Louie and Macolm Marmorstein, *CBS Storybreak*, 6 April 1985.

Yolen, Jane. "America's Cinderella." *Children's Literature in Education*, vol. 8, no. 1, March 1977, pp. 21–29.

4

Monstrous Marionette

The Tale of a Japanese Doll by Angela Carter

Natsumi Ikoma

Introduction

THE LITERARY GENRE OF fairy tales is what British author Angela Carter (1940–92) often utilizes to address archaic human desires from deconstructive and feminist perspectives. Many of her later retellings collected in *The Bloody Chamber* (1979), for instance, have positively empowering story lines that defy oppressive morals entailed in many traditional fairy tales and free heroines from domesticity and sexual oppression. However, "The Loves of Lady Purple," a short story of a marionette coming to life, collected in *Fireworks* (1974), is darker and more ambivalent. As one of her first experiments in utilizing a fairy-tale framework, it shares a subversive plot with many of her later works where the objectified heroine's revenge is achieved, although the marionette's complete liberation is not realized in this story, and there has been debate among Carter scholars as to whether this story is a success from a feminist perspective.

This chapter seeks to introduce alternative readings of this story that has, by many (Gamble 105; Gruss 207; Wisker 185), been considered a pessimistic Gothic fairy tale, by locating it within the genealogy of doll narratives both in the West and in Japan. I would also argue that this story was particularly inspired by Japanese literature and culture—especially influential were *bunraku* puppet theatre and *The Tale of Genji*—which allowed Carter to delve more deeply into the already rich realm of the doll metaphor and its strong relation to desire, sexuality, violence, and prostitution. This story showcases how modern fairy tales have been enriched by diverse cultural interactions, creating more complex, diachronic, international, and intertextual texts that invite the reader to engage in a deeper exploration of other cultures.

Doll Narratives

The Western literary obsession with the metamorphosis of dolls into animate beings dates back to as early as ancient Rome, when Ovid described the story of Pygmalion, a sculptor who falls in love with his own sculpture, in the Tenth Book of *Metamorphoses*. Since then, inanimate objects coming to life have been narrated by many writers, including E. T. A. Hoffmann. The fairy-tale genre is especially rich with tales of metamorphoses, among which the motif of a doll transforming into a human being is especially fertile, as "Pinocchio" attests to. If we include doll-like women in our consideration, fairy tales are populated with many inanimate or asleep women coming to life or an awakened state by the magical hand of the hero, as seen in "Sleeping Beauty" and "Snow White," to mention but a couple. There are opposite cases, too: naughty women turning into dolls can be seen at the end of the Madame de Beaumont version of "The Beauty and the Beast," when the evil sisters are turned into statues as punishment for their wickedness.

When the transformation of a female character into an object (or vice versa) takes place, the story almost always revolves around the theme of sexuality and marriage. In Greek mythology, Daphne turns herself into a laurel tree in refusal of Apollo's sexual pursuit. But whether or not Daphne successfully stops herself from becoming an object of desire is highly dubious, as she has become a highly popular topic in art ever since, and her transformation has been depicted, painted, and sculpted, over and over. We may perhaps even say that she became an object of desire precisely because she transformed herself into a tree, attesting to the strange attraction to inanimate women.

In a similar twist, Nathaniel, the protagonist in E. T. A. Hoffmann's short story "The Sandman," falls for Olympia, an automaton, when his fiancée, Clara, opposes his delusional story about Coppelius being "the sandman." Clara says to Nathaniel:

> "Yes, Nathaniel, you are right; Coppelius is an evil, inimical force, he can do terrible things, he is like demonic power that has stepped visibly into life—but only so long as you fail to banish him from your mind. As long as you believe in him he continues to exist and act—his power is only your belief in him." (103)

Nathaniel, to this reasonable and sane advice, becomes furious, and calls Clara a "lifeless, accursed automaton" (106). When he meets Olympia, he desires her so intensely, he forgets about his betrothal completely and falls head over heels in love. Hoffmann describes how Nathaniel held her / its hand and "spoke passionately of his love in words incomprehensible to either of them. Yet she, perhaps, understood, for she gazed fixedly into his eyes and sighed time after time: 'Ah, ah, ah!'" (114). What we witness here is an interchange of the inanimate and the animate in Nathaniel's mind; an inanimate automaton, who lacks agency, becomes desirable, because it will not, and cannot, defy him, whereas an animate woman who can, and does, defy him is treated as a "cold" "automaton" (106). In Nathaniel's case, his feelings are reflected in the way he describes their eyes—the tell-tale signs: Olympia's mechanical eyes are "full of love and desire" (114), whereas Clara's eyes are "death" (105), although to a sane person they must be the opposite. Hoffmann's story is a clear demonstration of how the formation of narcissistic desire works: Nathaniel desires whoever listens to his story and accepts his gaze. He wants to be "understood." Neither questions nor criticism are allowed here. In such a framework, necrophilia is peremptory, and it is the inevitable consequence that an automaton, with eyes that automatically reflect Nathaniel's self-love back to him, is preferred to a real, living woman whose eyes express their own inner feelings. What he pursues is, just like Narcissus whom Jacques Lacan analyzes does, what reflects the ideal image of himself, the one that gives him a sense of mastery and totality as in "the primary identification by which the ego is formed in the mirror stage" (Evans 120). In fairy tales, therefore, Sleeping Beauty and Snow White could not be more ideal as they lie asleep, shutting their potentially defiant eyes that might threaten the hero's ego. These sleeping heroines do not defy the hero. They just obediently accept his kiss, and happily marry him.

Counter-Narratives with Defiant Heroines

Feminist artists, writers, and theorists have problematized this image of ideal womanhood in literature and art, casting into light the narrative as well as symbolic attempts at reversing the animate / inanimate binary as a way of patriarchal control of wayward and defiant women.[1] Henrik Ibsen's *A Doll's House* is a prototype of such a counter-narrative, and George Bernard Shaw, influenced by Ibsen, created *Pygmalion*, which is also a fine example of a counter-narrative. When Eliza turns from a vulgar flower girl into a sophisticated lady through the speech training administered by Professor Higgins, she follows the typical development / magical transformation of a traditional fairy-tale heroine. From Professor Higgins's perspective, Eliza transforms from a less-than-human creature to an animate, desirable woman. However, from Eliza's point of view, what happens is quite the opposite. She becomes a programmed automaton who speaks only what Professor Higgins wants her to speak. Shaw's ending is liberating, therefore, when Eliza walks out on Professor Higgins, refusing to be slighted as his doll, and demonstrates her independence from him.

Angela Carter is also famous for her deconstructive and feminist counter-narratives utilizing the fairy-tale genre. In a way similar to Bernard Shaw's *Pygmalion*, many of her retellings of fairy tales collected in *The Bloody Chamber* have positively empowering plots, and their heroines are portrayed not as mere victims but active participants and agents with their own will. Especially emphasized is the heroine's sexual liberation. The heroine of "The Bloody Chamber," unlike the heroine of the original story, "Bluebeard," by Charles Perrault, is not punished for her sexual curiosity, nor is she rescued by male characters. And in "The Tiger's Bride," a retelling of "The Beauty and the Beast," the heroine chooses to transform into a beast herself to stay with the Beast. Carter also problematizes necrophilia or semi-necrophilia in her stories, such as *The Infernal Desire Machines of Doctor Hoffman* (1972), "The Snow Child" (1979), and *Nights at the Circus* (1984), in which she critically draws sexual intercourse with a passive (asleep or dead) woman as patriarchal control over women.

"The Loves of Lady Purple"

"The Loves of Lady Purple," a short story of Carter's collected in *Fireworks*, published shortly after her return from a two-year stay in Japan, is, however, more controversial, because in this story it seems the heroine's complete liberation is not achieved.

To briefly summarize the story, Lady Purple is the principal marionette among the entourage of the Asiatic Professor, a puppet master in a traveling fairground, where "the grotesque is the order of the day" (25). Sumptuously clad and delicately made, Lady Purple turns very lifelike at the masterful hands of the Professor, and "appear[s] wholly real and yet entirely other" (26). Nightly, she acts out an erotic story of love and lust, titled, "*The Notorious Amours of Lady Purple, the Shameless Oriental Venus*" (27), which tells a nightmarish story of an orphan girl growing into a sadistic prostitute and then into a murderer, to "the image of irresistible evil" (32), who brings destruction to men. But years of outrageous devouring consume her as well, and in the final scene on stage, aged Lady Purple turns into nothing but a monstrous hag, devoid of all humanity, engaging in necrophilic sex with bloated corpses on a seashore. When the show is over, the Professor takes her home and kisses her goodnight before falling asleep next to her. But one night, she comes to life during the kiss, sucks the life out of him, drains his blood, frees herself from the strings, and sets fire to the house before heading for the brothel in town.

This ending has sparked controversy, as Lady Purple becoming a prostitute in the end is not considered liberating by many.[2] Indeed, it is deemed as becoming a slave-like woman, who is exploited and manipulated. In reading Carter's story, however, we need to trace back through the genealogy of doll narratives, not confining ourselves to a modern socioeconomic analysis, or to the Western literary tradition, because, when analyzed in conjunction with Ovid's story of Pygmalion, its remake by George Bernard Shaw, Hoffmann's "The Sandman," and Japanese doll narratives, the critical significance of the topic of prostitution surfaces.

Prostitution

In Ovid's *Metamorphoses*, the original Pygmalion is described as someone who becomes disinterested in women when he witnesses the Propoetides, the daughters of Propoetus, prostitute themselves in public.[3] Disgusted and disenchanted by these women, Pygmalion falls in love with the sculpture he himself creates, and he marries her when she turns into a real woman by the magic of Venus. In this framework, the ideal image is entirely generated within Pygmalion's narcissistic desire to sexually monopolize a "pure" woman, who is the counterimage of what he negates: the prostitutes. The contrast cannot be clearer: the former is pure and clean, the latter degenerate and corrupt. Pygmalion's love for his statue is born out of his misogyny and self-love, which conditions that he can only love a nonhuman, a statue of his own creation.

Bernard Shaw's *Pygmalion* is a conscious counter-narrative of Ovid's tale, in which the theme of prostitution is repeatedly insinuated around Eliza, the flower girl. As Lisa Shahriari points out, this story "plays upon ideas of prostitution and reform in its subtext" and "is littered with references to prostitution" (68).[4] In this reading, Professor Higgins's program is not merely speech therapy for Eliza but can be viewed as an attempt to reform Eliza from the prostitution business, thus trying to make a "pure" lady out of a degenerate, filthy, common prostitute. His possessive, manipulative, and self-centered desire is finally denied, however, and his scorn for Eliza is refuted by her, when she accuses him of being disrespectful, treating her as if she were "dirt under [his] feet" (292). She says:

> "Oh! if I only could go back to my flower basket! I should be independent of both you and father and all the world! Why did you take my independence from me? Why did I give it up? I'm a slave now, for all my fine clothes." (290)

In the minds of the original Pygmalion and possibly of Shaw's Professor Higgins, prostitutes are the worst kind of women, and they should be despised and repelled. In opposition to these "evil" images of prostitutes, the ideal woman's image is constructed—the statue and the lady, respectively. They are the antithesis of prostitutes: doll-women are docile, chaste, pure, innocent, do only what the creator makes them do, and reside in the realm of "love"; prostitutes, on the other hand, are vile, degenerate, cunning, cheating, and cannot be monopolized, and their realm is "sex." Men can own doll-women, but cannot own prostitutes—they can only purchase them for a while. Doll-women are stable, while prostitutes are elusive. The former deserves the worthy "love" of the male protagonist, whereas prostitutes do not. What the tale of Pygmalion by Ovid reveals and Shaw's retelling implies is how the binary opposition of doll-women / prostitutes forms two sides of the same coin, and how a male-centered formation of the "ideal woman" presupposes a disgust and fear for prostitutes and what they symbolize—an untamable female sexuality. When Shaw's Eliza utters her regret at abandoning her former profession, she may be clarifying that prostitution can be a better alternative to becoming a lady, because the former at least promises her independence.

In a similar fashion to Shaw, who defends the prostitutes' choice of profession to sustain their livelihood more clearly in the preface of *Mrs. Warren's Profession*, Angela Carter describes a prostitute as "a fair tradesman and her explicit acceptance of contractual obligation implicit in all sexual relationships mocks the fraud of the 'honest' woman who will give nothing at all in return for goods and money . . ." (*The Sadeian Woman* 58). She also argues wives and prostitutes are not fundamentally different, as "all wives of necessity fuck by contract" though "[p]rostitutes are at least decently paid on the nail and boast fewer illusions about a hireling status that has no veneer of social acceptability" (9).

Similarly, in *Nights at the Circus*, Fevvers, the heroine, calls Baudelaire "a poor fellow who loved whores not for the pleasure of it but, as he perceived it, the horror of it, as if we was, not working women doing it for money but damned souls who did it solely to lure men to their dooms, as if we'd got nothing better to do. . . . Yet we were all suffragists in that house" (38). Carter and Shaw share the view that prostitution is just a job for women with fewer opportunities and it has nothing to do with their moral degeneracy or innate vice. From their point of view, any disrespect or moral judgment toward prostitutes should be condemned as signs of prejudice, narcissistic self-love, and misogyny in the accuser.

Taking into account Carter's view on prostitutes, Lady Purple becoming a prostitute at the end of the story may not necessarily be a pessimistic ending but a liberating one. Still, the words Carter chooses to describe this ending are rather ambiguous. Lady Purple does not look fully human with her free will. Rather, she "began her next performance with an apparent improvisation which was, in reality, only a variation upon a theme" (*Fireworks* 36). Her actions were rather unnatural and mechanical when "[h]er every motion was instinct with a wonderful, reptilian liquidity" (37), and "the leprous whiteness of her face gave her the appearance of a corpse animated solely by demonic will" (38).

Apparently, Lady Purple here, though she looks alive and human, is described by Carter as not entirely human but as something that performs femininity with a "wonderful" dexterity. And the description of Lady Purple above as having "reptilian liquidity" and "leprous whiteness" seems to be the description of a *bunraku* puppet, by which Angela Carter was so intrigued when she was in Japan (Araki, Personal interview).[5]

It may be quite off the mark, therefore, to try to read a feminist story of liberation in "The Loves of Lady Purple." Lady Purple may certainly look like a woman who, for years, has been in bondage under the control of a selfish, obsessive man, and finds freedom at last. However, Lady Purple has never been a real woman. She has been an artificial doll from the beginning, and has no authentic human self to return to. Though Carter did not view prostitution as immoral, when Fevvers of *Nights at the Circus* gives "economic necessity" as the only reason for a woman to become a prostitute (39), the profession's liberating nature is surely not stressed. The narrator of "The Loves of Lady Purple," as if to tease the predictable perplexity in the reader, explains:

> But whether she was renewed or newly born, returning to life or becoming alive, awakening from a dream or coalescing into the form of a fantasy generated in her wooden skull by the mere repetition so many times of the same invariable actions, the brain beneath the reviving hair contained only the scantiest notion of the possibilities now open to it. All that had seeped into the wood was the notion that she might perform the forms of life not so much by the skill of another as by her own desire that she did so, and she did not possess enough equipment to comprehend the complex circularity of the logic which inspired her for she had only been a marionette. (*Fireworks* 37)

Lady Purple is as she has been made: a doll, an automaton. She has never been a real woman, and she cannot become one now. Therefore, in the final desolate scene, she heads for the brothel "like a homing pigeon" (38), as though she is following her trained route, the programmed way.

Lady Purple makes sense when she is considered as a symbol of the doll / prostitute dyad in the Pygmalion narrative. The Asiatic Professor creates Lady Purple at once as the most beautiful doll, the epitome of femininity, and as a horrible prostitute riddled with disease who devours men. His jealous ownership of Lady Purple shows clear necrophilic desire when he is to "lay her, naked, in her coffin-shaped case" and "see how defenselessly bald she was beneath [her wig]," then "kiss his doll good night" (35). Lady Purple, by his hand, performs necrophilia on stage upon many corpses, but in actuality, the Professor enjoys her sole ownership. She is, indeed, ideal for him, catering to his necrophilic desire to own a doll-woman. Carter deliberately makes Lady Purple transform into a devouring monster to demonstrate the two sides of "femininity"—a pure doll and a vile prostitute—both of which are constructed in the mind of the Professor out of narcissism and misogyny.

Bunraku Puppet Theatre

As I briefly touched upon above, it is not only by the Western narrative tradition that Angela Carter was inspired. Another significant inspiration comes from *bunraku* puppet theatre.[6] As argued in the previous section, Lady Purple is a demonstration of a doll and a prostitute, two opposite, yet complementary, images of woman, fabricated in the mind of narcissistic and misogynous men. As if to prove that Lady Purple is a male construction, Carter makes Lady Purple voiced and motioned by a man, a puppeteer who calls himself the Asiatic Professor. Although Lady Purple is manipulated by strings, the performance style comes from *bunraku* puppet theater in Japan, in which puppets are controlled by three male masters and voiced by male singers, all of which are within a definitive hierarchy. The headmaster is allowed to reveal his face, but two minor puppeteers conceal their entire bodies and faces in black costumes. The transformation from a beautiful woman to an evil ugly monster is also a popular *bunraku* stage trick. The Japanese element of this story is further visible when the puppeteer is described as having "the wistful charm of a Japanese flower which only blossoms when dropped in water" (*Fireworks* 26), indicating that Carter utilizes here the aesthetics of masochistic repression and serenity appreciated in Japonisme.

The feminine performance of the *bunraku* puppet is spun solely by the hands of men, as no women are allowed on the stage of authentic *bunraku* theater. It is similar to the performance of *kabuki* actors in female roles. *Kabuki* and *bunraku* are twin theatrical traditions, sharing parts of their history and some repertoire, and having influenced each other in their development and performance style. They also share the eventual exclusion of women from the stage and the monopoly of feminine performance by men.[7] Thus, in the theater of the Asiatic Professor, "the Professor allowed no one else to touch her" (*Fireworks* 27). In *kabuki* and *bunraku* today, their famed feminine performances are entirely guarded as men's jurisdiction: created, trained, maintained, worshipped, and handed down by generations of men, as the "ideal femininity" in men's imagination, like the statue created by Pygmalion. This idealized notion of femininity has been denied to women in *bunraku* and *kabuki* theaters, and we may sense behind this notion a disgust for real women, similar to the one Pygmalion has.[8]

Roland Barthes analyzes in his *Empire of Signs* (1970) that "the Oriental transvestite does not copy Woman but signifies her: not bogged down in the model, but detached from its signified" (53). Barthes rightly grasps that the femininity on show in Japanese theater is detached from the actuality of women. It is rather a signifier of femininity, in a poststructuralist sense, where the signified is void. Barthes continues:

> the refinement of the code, its precision, indifferent to any extended copy of an organic type (to provoke the real, physical body of a young woman), have as their effect — or justification — to absorb and eliminate all feminine reality in the subtle diffraction of the signifier: signified but not represented, Woman is an idea, not a nature. (91)

Barthes's analysis of "femininity" in the Japanese theater tradition, of it being an idea, a concept quite detached from the feminine reality of a live woman, is in line with Carter's. Carter repeatedly exaggerates the "miraculous inhumanity" (*Fireworks* 33) of Lady Purple, and how she is unrelated to real women:

> Her actions were not so much an intimation as a distillation and intensification of those of a born woman and so she could become the quintessence of eroticism, for no woman born would have dared to be so blatantly seductive. (26–27)

She also describes her as "the most beautiful of women, the image of that woman whom only a man's memory and imagination can devise" (35). Lady Purple in Carter's story is created, deliberately and evidently, as a male construct.

Each marionette of the Professor that represents a prostitute "was as absolutely circumscribed as a figure in rhetoric, reduced by the rigorous discipline of her vocation to the nameless essence of the idea of woman, a metaphysical abstraction of the female which could, on payment of a specific fee, be instantly translated into an oblivion either sweet or terrible" (30). We can see the connection between doll and prostitute clearly stated here. I analyzed in a previous section that a doll and a prostitute are the antithesis of each other and two sides of the same coin. Carter's description above further advances the theory, suggesting a more complex structure behind their relation: prostitutes are artificial beings to begin with, who perform "femininity" as male customers wish. They are supposed to act out male fantasy, only this fantasy often involves the enactment of what male customers wish to deny as part of their "ordinary" self. Prostitutes are considered "evil" because they perform "evilness" that male customers transfer onto them. Both ideal doll-women and vile prostitutes are male constructions, and Carter's Lady Purple is an embodiment of this structure. Lady Purple in the end merely performs what Juliette performs in Sade's story, "a method of profane mastery of the instruments of power. She is a woman who acts according to the precepts and also the practice of a man's world and so she does not suffer. Instead, she causes suffering. . . . She is a New Woman in the mode of irony" (*The Sadeian Woman* 79).

Bunraku, Kabuki, and Prostitution

"The Loves of Lady Purple" features puppetry and may seem to have been influenced solely by the *bunraku* tradition. However, as I stated earlier, *bunraku* and *kabuki* are twin traditions, as it were, and they greatly influenced each other in their development. The female *bunraku* puppets' movement and female *kabuki* actors' movement both reflect the notion of "ideal femininity" constructed and developed in their shared history. It is noteworthy, then, that the histories of both *bunraku* and *kabuki* are not distant from prostitution. One of the origins of *bunraku* puppet theatre is an old puppetry tradition performed by performance groups called *kugutsu*. Ōe no Masafusa, a historian in the eleventh century, described them as performing tribes who, upon the summons from the upper classes, served various ceremonial roles in which men mainly handled puppets and played instruments, while women sang, danced, and prostituted (Tanigawa and Yamato 242). Many documents in the tenth and eleventh centuries record these performing groups. From the Heian period, it was documented that *kugutsu* women performed music, singing, and dancing during the day, and slept with customers at night. However, Sanae Fukutō points out that it is important to note that prostitutes in this period were not looked down upon (*Kodai* 74–75). Many of them nurtured regular relationships with aristocrats, often accompanying them on their travels and serving them as their maids, and sometimes even married them. They were, in fact, interchangeable with lower-class ladies in court in those days, and their lifestyles were not so different, as these lower-class ladies were engaged in prostitution, too. Prostitution, in those days, was not an exceptional thing to do. Their lives were unstable, and they relied on financial support from male aristocrats with whom they managed to have affairs (Fukutō, "Kugutsu-me" 427). Fukutō maintains it was not until the thirteenth century, when the patriarchal household system among the warrior class seeped through the whole society, that the disdain and contempt for prostitutes became prevalent (*Kodai* 229–43).

Kugutsu groups often had strong ties with shrines and temples, as dolls were supposed to be receptacles of gods and spirits.[9] The most famous example is Nishinomiya Shrine, which protected *kugutsu* people by letting them live on its site. According to Jane Marie Law, *kugutsu* traveled while performing puppetry with wooden puppets in the shape of the folk religion deity Ebisu, spreading their beliefs around Japan, and this puppetry is said to be the origin of *bunraku* puppetry (111). Nishinomiya Shrine in Hyōgo prefecture enshrines Momodayū (or Hyakudayū) as one of its gods, and it has attracted worshippers among puppet masters and prostitutes. The puppetry performance by *kugutsu* became popular in the early seventeenth century, when it was combined with another art form, *jōruri*, which was to be developed into the art of *bunraku* as we know it now.

Jōruri had its own association with prostitution. It was originally an aural narrative performance, a typical story being the tale of Princess Jōruri: a sad, romantic story involving the legendary Princess Jōruri and the famous historic figure Ushiwakamaru, who later came to be known as Yoshitsune Minamoto, a great warlord. It was accompanied by string instruments only at first, then later with puppets, when the performance came to be known as *ningyō-jōruri* (doll *jōruri*). There were many groups performing this art in the Edo period, among which the Bunraku Theatre in Ōsaka survived into the Meiji era, and it became the name of this art form itself (Ningyō Jōruri Bunrakuza). Princess Jōruri's historicity is rather obscure; some say she was a daughter of a wealthy landowner, but many say she was a mythic character created out of a commonplace story of a prostitute in those days who had a brief relationship with an upper-class man. We see here that prostitution surfaces as the origin of *bunraku* theater from both sides: puppetry and *jōruri*.

The origin of *kabuki* is also rich in associations with prostitution. *Kabuki* derived its meaning from the term "*kabuki-mono*," meaning men with a strange, queer, or odd manner. These men appeared at the beginning of the Edo era, around the early seventeenth century, and in defiance of the regime, they wore strange clothes (sometimes cross-dressing) and engaged in violence. They were at once popular and abhorred. Their way of life was taken up by a female performer, Okuni, who set up a theatre of *kabuki* dance in Kyoto in 1603, in which female performers wore male costumes in *kabuki-mono* fashion. After its success, similar theaters were established in many places. According to Kōsaku Yamashita, these female performers were prostitutes by profession, and *kabuki* dance in male costume was their way of advertisement (158). Once they became very popular, the government repeatedly issued official notices to prohibit their act—considered an affront to public decency—until its disappearance. In lieu of female *kabuki*, a new *kabuki* appeared in which young male actors performed in *kabuki-mono* fashion. Yet, again, their performance was highly sexual, and they often prostituted themselves, so the government again issued prohibitions. After the banning of the boys' *kabuki* in 1652, another version of male *kabuki* was created, which, with the approval of the government, was developed into the sophisticated art form we see today, having absorbed many aspects of *bunraku* into its repertoire, and at the same time having shed its association with prostitution completely (Japan Arts Council).

Kabuki and *bunraku* share prostitution as part of their origin, and with it, gender-crossing as another important part of both arts. However, women's cross-dressing was prohibited and taken away by the government, whereas men's cross-dressing was approved and authorized. This may suggest how gender-crossing has been, and still is, regulated in Japan in these arts. It also makes us wonder why puppetry, the performance of gender, and prostitution are so closely tied. Perhaps the use of the body suggests eroticism, or perhaps the Japanese concept of the body as a mere receptacle plays a role.[10] Either way, the Japanese concept of "ideal femininity" is epitomized in the performances of *bunraku* female puppets and *kabuki* female actors, both of which reflect the manner of prostitutes—their shared ancestry. Whether or not Angela Carter was familiar with the history and origins of *bunraku* and *kabuki* is unclear, though she mentions *bunraku* in "People as Pictures" (*Shaking a Leg* 234) and *kabuki* in "Lorenzo the Closet-Queen" (*Shaking a Leg* 499), and Sōzō Araki, who was her boyfriend when she was in Japan, remembers talking about *kabuki* in length with her after she went to see a *kabuki* performance one day with a friend (Araki, *Seduced* 64–65). In writing about Japanese culture, if Carter did research—as she always did—by reading numerous volumes of books and journals, it would not be surprising if she learned about their histories. And she would have used these materials to create her own story, in which the wooden body of Lady Purple, the ultimate prostitute, contains only a demonic will, born out of the misogynistic fear of female sexuality.

Lady Purple and Lady Murasaki

Another Japanese vein in this story comes from *The Tale of Genji*, created in the tenth century. Carter had read *The Tale of Genji*, translated by Arthur

Waley, by the time she wrote this story, and named her puppet after Genji's heroine who shares its name with the author, Lady Murasaki ("*murasaki*" is "purple" in Japanese). Lady Murasaki, the character, in *The Tale of Genji* leads a sorrowful life, as one of the many wives of the hero, Prince Genji. First, she was kidnapped by Prince Genji when she was still a small child. Genji raised her to become a desirable woman, and one night, to her shock and dismay, he made her his wife. In Heian court culture, where men and women were segregated and did not meet face-to-face unless they were intimate, forceful sexual encounters were not uncommon. Courtship was customarily done only by correspondence, without actually seeing each other, and a wooing man might one night venture to sneak into the woman's room to sleep with her. But in Lady Murasaki's case, Genji develops a father-daughter relationship with her at first, and then makes her his wife, which is felt as a betrayal of her trust, though she had no power to say no to him. He had a string of affairs with numerous mistresses, which again was normal in the Heian era, and later married a princess, who overshadowed Lady Murasaki in rank and status.

Initially, Lady Murasaki in *The Tale of Genji* and Lady Purple in Carter's tale may look entirely different, but if one observes carefully, *The Tale of Genji* can be categorized as a doll narrative, since Lady Murasaki is raised to fulfill the image of Genji's ideal woman. In Japanese, a doll is termed *ningyō* (as in *ningyō-jōruri*), literally "a human form" or "a substitute." Lady Murasaki is a human form to substitute for Genji's unattainable love: his mother-in-law, Fujitsubo. And indeed, Lady Murasaki is treated like an object from the beginning. Genji kidnaps her without asking for her consent, because, upon seeing her as a little girl for the first time, Genji "wondered what she would be like when she grew up" and "it suddenly occurred to him that she bore no small resemblance to one whom he had loved with all his being" (84). Again, the theme of ownership comes up here. Lady Murasaki is a doll who is raised to look like Genji's ideal woman, only for Genji himself. After obtaining Lady Murasaki, however, Genji keeps falling for one woman after another, trying to find the elusive image of his loved one, the perfect woman. Although Lady Murasaki may seem to monopolize Genji's affection, he is always looking elsewhere, because his ideal woman is unattainable.

The theme of prostitution can also be found in this tale. Lady Murasaki is one of many women with whom Genji has relationships. She might be one of the more fortunate ones, as she manages to establish a long-term relationship with him. However, she is, in the end, superseded by a lady who is more properly ranked. As I wrote before, the lives of the ladies in court in the Heian period were unstable, as they relied on support from men, whose affection they needed to secure through romantic affairs. The tale describes how Lady Murasaki and other women of Genji's are in similarly pitiful situations, even when Lady Murasaki is in a supposedly steady relationship with Genji. Lady Murasaki is, after all, a bought woman, who has to secure Genji's support in order to survive.

In her review of *The Tale of Genj*, newly translated by Edward G. Seidensticker in 1976, Carter writes, "the Heian court, from the point of view of one of those ladies in elegant competition, is really a meat-market with a particularly pretty décor . . ." (*Shaking a Leg* 264). Despite all of its elegance and sophistication, Carter perceived the horrible inhumanity described in the tale. Ladies of Genji are cuts of meat that are compared, priced, and sold. With this realization, she writes that "[i]t is curious that this wonderful and ancient novel that Seidensticker's translation makes so voluptuously deliciously readable should have so little hope in it" (264). *The Tale of Genji* is a story told from the point of view of a woman who strives to become the perfect doll. It is no wonder that there is so little hope in it, because for a woman to become a doll is an impossibility when a doll is the antithesis of a real woman.

Sleeping Beauty

Another Japanese source may be found in Yasunari Kawabata's disturbing doll narrative, "House of the Sleeping Beauties" (1961). Angela Carter obtained the English translation of this story from Kawabata himself while she was in Japan and kept the copy on her bookshelf.[11] Although this story may not seem like a doll narrative initially, it is clear that the ambiguities among the sleeping beauties, the dolls, and the prostitutes are further complicated within the story.

The protagonist, an aged man named Eguchi, visits an inn, where he sleeps with one virgin girl after another, all of whom have been drugged into a deep sleep and do not wake up until after the guest leaves the bedroom. The inn only accepts men old enough to have lost their sexual potency, and the guests are strictly prohibited to taint the virginity of the girls, but otherwise can do anything with them. They can act out any fantasy with the sleeping girls without embarrassing themselves, as the girls will not wake up to reproach them, complain, or call them disgusting. The girls in the story are indeed ideal dolls, like Pygmalion's statue: pure but available, alive but inanimate. Eguchi says he has not lost his potency, and fantasizes of breaking the rule and deflowering the girls, but in the end, does nothing but meekly sleep beside them, only using their bodies to trigger memories of the women in his past. He sees in them his mother, daughters, and past girlfriends, and projects on their sleeping bodies all sorts of erotic fantasies, including incestuous and violent ones. He calls the girls words like "witch" (39), "slave maiden" (42), or "incarnation of a Buddha" (68), according to the emotion they stir in him. He wants to murder them, to rape them, thinking they deserve to be raped, or to worship them. The sleeping girls are convenient and ideal receptacles for his self-centered emotions; they are virgin prostitutes, the perfect, oxymoronic ideal. Kawabata writes:

> One elbow on the pillow, he gazed at [the hand of the girl]. As if it were alive, he muttered to himself. It was of course alive, and he meant only to say how very pretty it was; but once he had uttered them the words took on an ominous ring. Though this girl lost in sleep had not put an end to the hours of her life, had she not lost them, had them sink into bottomless depths? She was not a living doll, for there could be no living doll; but, so as not to shame an old man no longer a man, she had been made into a living toy. (20)

As Eguchi calls this inn a "bawdy house," the story is clearly about prostitutes and prostitution in an extremely disturbing, and perhaps, from the protagonist's point of view, idealized form. The dilemma within the doll / prostitute dyad—that the dolls are pure and clean but inanimate and dead, whereas the prostitutes are animate and can arouse sexual desire but are filthy and potentially threatening—is resolved perfectly in this story. These girls are "pure" virgins and real, and yet, as with prostitutes, the customers can project any sexual fantasy onto their bodies without fear of retribution.

As the title of the story suggests, Kawabata's tale is inspired by the Western fairy tale, "Sleeping Beauty."[12] Yet, it is worth noting that the story posits these doll-women and death in close vicinity, bringing the theme of necrophilia to the fore. One day, a guest dies while he is in bed with one of the girls. And then Eguchi encounters a girl's death while he is sleeping by her. The narrative addresses the ambiguous distinction between the animate and the inanimate. However alluring they may be, these living dolls are not really living, the narrative seems to suggest. Or it may also suggest that they bring death to men, showing that even these sleeping girls cannot entirely eradicate the fear Eguchi feels for women.

According to Araki, Kawabata was not on the list of Angela Carter's favorite authors in Japan. Certainly, the pedophilic and necrophilic values this story exhibits are what Carter is known to criticize. Whether she liked him or not, it seems certain that she had read this story and received inspiration for her own stories of sleeping beauties, including "The Loves of Lady Purple" and "The Snow Pavillion," in which dolls and prostitutes are analogized. When Lady Purple brings death to the self-centered puppet master and returns all sorts of fear projected onto her back to him, "The Loves of Lady Purple" certainly produces a counter-narrative to "House of the Sleeping Beauties."

Female Impersonator

Yet another Japanese influence upon "The Loves of Lady Purple" comes from a more personal arena. Around the time when Carter created the blueprint of this story, she was living with a Japanese man, Sōzō Araki, whom I briefly mentioned earlier. He was a young man, four years her junior, whom she met in a Shinjuku café and fell in love with. Their relationship was intense, and it greatly affected Carter's literary style.[13]

Carter wrote a story, "A Souvenir of Japan," based on her relationship with Araki, in which the narrator analyzes:

> I had never been so absolutely the mysterious other. I had become a kind of phoenix, a fabulous beast; I was an outlandish jewel. He found me, I think, inexpressibly exotic. But I often felt like a female impersonator. (*Fireworks* 7)

In this excerpt, we can find the imposition of "femininity" as an image of the other in Japanese society, within which the narrator, it seems, was trapped. Even though she was already a woman, the narrator tells us, she felt compelled to "act as a woman," as if her femininity was not authentic, and she had to realize the ideal woman in her lover's imagination. The alienation was double, because she was both a foreign woman and expected to be a fabulously exotic doll. It is no coincidence, therefore, that Lady Purple's play "was entirely exotic" (*Fireworks* 27), as no real woman can be that—only marionettes can. Similarly, the narrator of "Flesh and the Mirror" tells us that she had to perform in accordance with a script that was written by someone else:

> I no longer understood the logic of my own performance. My script had been scrambled behind my back. The cameraman was drunk. The director had a *crise de nerfs* and been taken away to a sanatorium. (*Fireworks* 68)

In the end, Carter came to describe in one of her journals with a term borrowed from Wallace Stevens that she and her Japanese lover ended up becoming "philosophic assassins" (Stevens 256) of each other.[14] Molding herself entirely to her lover's desire, she became a demonic possession, like Lady Purple, reflecting his desire and fear of Woman. In a battle of egos, both trying to control the other, he became her assassin, but she also could not help becoming the woman that devoured him. When Sōzō broke up with her, after a year and a half of turbulence, Angela went berserk and abused him physically and verbally (Araki, *Seduced* 139). Lady Purple, therefore, can be read as a story that reflects the author's personal experience. It portrays a possible ending at which Carter might have arrived. In this story of a monstrous marionette who cannot go beyond devouring people, Carter's own devastating relationship with a Japanese man is reflected. The sobering description of the story's ending is like that of a morning after a hard-drinking party or a drugged orgy, when the previous night's spree seems like a horrible nightmare, when "the place, deserted, with curds of vomit, the refuse of revelry, underfoot, look[s] utterly desolate" (*Fireworks* 38).

Conclusion

"The Loves of Lady Purple" certainly is the product of cultural interactions, and therefore, it benefits from being analyzed from non-Western perspectives. So far, the story has been predominantly analyzed from a Western perspective, which labels this tale as Gothic horror, and Lady Purple as a revengeful, vampiric woman. Such arguments are valid, but the Japanese influence at the basis of this story has continued to be neglected. In today's globalizing world, many adaptations of folktales and fairy tales are influenced by non-Western cultures, among which Carter's tales are exemplary. These works are waiting for a comparative analysis to excavate their full literary potential. While current Eurocentric tendencies may limit us in our understanding of fairy tales and their adaptations, comparative analyses could generate new understandings of these works, of the world, and of the power of literature.

The platform of fairy-tale narratives served Angela Carter in enabling her to mix Western doll narratives, the Pygmalion narrative in particular, with Japanese doll narratives through incorporating her cultural analyses of *bunraku*, *kabuki*, *The Tale of Genji*, and "House of the Sleeping Beauties." What surfaced from these combined analyses is a strong connection between doll narratives and the theme of prostitution. It is remarkable that all the Japanese influences analyzed in this chapter have especially strong ties to prostitution while they describe "ideal femininity."

Skillfully incorporating these multilayered Japanese imageries of the ideal women / prostitutes dyad, Carter created a story that stresses the artificiality of the "femininity" trapped in a doll / prostitute dichotomy. Lady Purple was not made a doll prostitute at random but rather because dolls and prostitutes form a set. She devours her puppeteer not for revenge but because of this dichotomy she is part of, which has fear of female monstrosity at its basis. She goes to a brothel at the end of the story, because it is where she belongs and she has nowhere else to go. The story conveys the confining atmosphere of a world contaminated by the contradictory concept of misogynous "femininity."

As we have seen, this story showcases how modern fairy tales have been enriched by various inspirations as diverse as have been analyzed in this chapter, creating more complex, diachronic, international, and intertextual texts to fit the perusal of contemporary readers in the globalizing world, inviting them into deeper exploration of other cultures. The story never offers a single straightforward interpretation, but ambiguous and contradictory ones that challenge the reader's prejudices and misconceptions about the world. "The Loves of Lady Purple" certainly is a story developed from the author's exposure to other cultures, and through comparative analysis, it shows the full potential of the positively magical and empowering imagination of the Carterian literary universe.

Notes

The research for this article was supported by JSPS KAKENHI 24520307 and 16KK0035.

1. There are numerous such attempts, but Elisabeth Bronfen's *Over Her Dead Body* is one fine example.

2. For instance, Gamble writes, "this story is a perfect demonstration of the point Carter makes in *The Sadeian Women* that a 'free woman in an unfree society will be a monster' (p.27)" (104) and "Lady Purple's rapacious desires lock her

into a savage cycle of endless replication and self-destruction which makes her the very epitome of the Sadeian subject" (105).

3. "The obscene Propoetides had dared / Deny Venus' divinity. For that / The goddess' rage, it's said, made them the first / Strumpets to prostitute their bodies' charms. / As shame retreated and their cheeks grew hard, / They turned with little change to stones of flint. / Pygmalion had seen these women spend / Their days in wickedness, and horrified / At all the countless vices nature gives / To womankind lived celibate and long / Lacked the companionship of married love" (Ovid 232).

4. Interestingly, in one scene of the Theatre Guild production of *Pygmalion* (1926), Eliza appeared on stage in Japanese *kimono*. It is suggestive, considering the association of Japanese *kimono* and prostitutes propagated by Madame Sadayakko (Kawakami Sadayakko), an actress and former *geisha* who toured Europe at the beginning of the twentieth century, and Giacomo Puccini's *Madame Butterfly*. See en.wikipedia.org/wiki/Pygmalion_(play)#/media/File:Pygmalion-Fontanne-Travers-1926.jpg.

5. Carter writes several blueprints of this story in her journal. In one of them she specifies Lady Purple as a *bunraku* puppet (*Angela Carter Papers: Journal*).

6. See note 5.

7. Originally, *kabuki* was an all-female erotic performance, but it was banned by the government around 1629. Today, there are some small groups of female *kabuki* actors, but they remain minor and unofficial. *Bunraku* started as simple puppeteering done by men and women. The history of puppeteering in Japan dates back to the ninth century. As it became more stylized, however, it grew into an all-male tradition. Presently, there are some female *bunraku* groups, but they are by far the minority.

8. Yukio Mishima's short story, "Onnagata," reflects this disgust for real women in the *kabuki* world. For details, please see: Natsumi Ikoma, "Carter and Japanese Signs: *Bunraku*, Mishima, *Irezumi*, and Sozo Araki."

9. There are many folklores in Japan of a doll coming to life, that attest to people's belief that dolls have souls. Lafcadio Hearn records one of the stories in *Glimpses of Unfamiliar Japan*, "Notes of Kitzuki," chapter 11, x–xi, 216–19. Even today, we hear a popular horror story of a "Rika-chan" doll, having been mass-produced in the 1970s and then abandoned, coming to life and cursing

the chance finder. There are many shrines and temples in Japan that perform "*ningyō-kuyō*," the ritual to calm the souls of disused dolls.

10. The term "utsusemi" or "utsushimi," found in many documents in Japan as early as the eighth century, denotes "the current body," and it is based on the belief that our spirits migrate from one life to another and our current body is only a temporary receptacle.

11. The copy she owned has an autograph of the author, Yasunari Kawabata, and a dedication to Angela Carter. The Angela Carter library, archived at the University of East Anglia, holds its photocopy.

12. The original title of "House of the Sleeping Beauties" is "*Nemureru Bijo*" (Sleeping Beauty).

13. See Natsumi Ikoma's "Her Side of the Story (Afterword by the Translator)" in Sozo Araki's *Seduced by Japan: A Memoir of the Days Spent with Angela Carter* for more details.

14. See *Angela Carter Papers: Journal*.

Works Cited

Araki, Sozo. Personal interview. Tokyo. 23 September 2010.
———. *Seduced by Japan: A Memoir of the Days spent with Angela Carter*. Translated by Natsumi Ikoma, Eihosha, 2017.
Barthes, Roland. *Empire of Signs*. 1970. Translated by Edward Howard, Hill and Wang, 1992.
Bronfen, Elisabeth. *Over Her Dead Body: Death, Femininity and the Aesthetic*. Manchester University Press, 1992.
Carter, Angela. *Angela Carter Papers: Journal*. British Library, London, Carter MS 88899/1/93.
———. *The Bloody Chamber*. 1979. Vintage, 1995.
———. *Fireworks*. 1974. Virago, 1988.
———. *The Infernal Desire Machine of Doctor Hoffman*. 1972. Penguin, 1982.
———. *Nights at the Circus*. 1984. Vintage, 1994.
———. *The Sadeian Woman: An Exercise in Cultural History*. 1979. Virago, 1997.
———. *Shaking a Leg: Collected Writings*. 1997. Penguin, 1998.
———. "The Snow Child." 1979. *The Bloody Chamber*, Vintage, 1995, pp. 91–92.

———. "The Snow Pavillion." 1995. *Burning Your Boats: Collected Stories*, Vintage, 1996, pp. 514–31.

Evans, Dylan. *An Introductory Dictionary of Lacanian Psychoanalysis*. Routledge, 1996.

Fukutō, Sanae. *Kodai Chūsei no Geinō to Baibaishun: Ukareme kara Keisei e* [*Performance and Prostitution in Ancient to Early Modern Japan: From Ukareme to Keisei*]. Akashi Shoten, 2012.

———. "Kugutsu-me no Tohjo to Henyo: Nihon ni okeru Baibaishun" ["The Appearance and Transfiguration of Kugutsume: Prostitution in Japan"]. *Saitama Gakuen Daigaku Kiyou Ningengakubu-hen*, vol. 10, 2010, pp. 421–36.

Gamble, Sarah. *Angela Carter: Writing from the Front Line*. Edinburgh University Press, 1997.

Gruss, Susanne. *The Pleasure of the Feminist Text: Reading Michele Roberts and Angela Carter*. Rodopi, 2009.

Hearn, Lafcadio. *Glimpses of Unfamiliar Japan*. 1894. Tuttle Publishing, 2009.

Hoffmann, E. T. A. "The Sandman." *Tales of Hoffmann*. Selected and translated by R. J. Hollingdale, Penguin, 1982.

Ibsen, Henrik. "A Doll's House." 1879. *A Doll's House and Other Plays*, translated by Deborah Dawkin and Erik Skuggevik, Penguin, 2016.

Ikoma, Natsumi. "Carter and Japanese Signs: *Bunraku*, Mishima, Irezumi, and Sozo Araki." *Pyrotechnics: The Incandescent Imagination of Angela Carter*, edited by Mulvey-Roberts and Charlotte Crofts, Palgrave Macmillan, forthcoming.

———. "Her Side of the Story (Afterword by the Translator)." *Seduced by Japan*, by Sozo Araki, pp. 153–75.

Japan Arts Council. "*Kabuki* no Rekishi" ["History of *Kabuki*"]. *Kabuki: Kabuki eno Izanai* [*Kabuki: An Invitation to Kabuki*], 2007, www.ntj.jac.go.jp/unesco/kabuki/jp/2/2_01.html. Accessed 13 October 2017.

Kawabata, Yasunari. "House of the Sleeping Beauties." 1961. *House of the Sleeping Beauties and Other Stories*. Translated by Edward G. Seidensticker, Kodansha International and Quadriga Press, 1969.

Law, Jane Marie. *Puppets of Nostalgia: The Life, Death, and Rebirth of the Japanese Awaji Ningyô Tradition*. Princeton University Press, 1997.

Murasaki Shikibu. *The Tale of Genji*. Translated by Arthur Waley, 5th ed., vol. 1, George Allen & Unwin, 1973.

Ningyō Jōruri Bunrakuza. "*Bunraku* no Miryoku" ["The Charm of *Bunraku*"]. *Ningyō Jōruri Bunrakuza*. bunrakuza.com/whatsbunraku. Accessed 13 October 2017.

Ovid. *Metamorphoses*. Translated by A. D. Melville, Oxford University Press, 1986.

Shahriari, Lisa. *Encyclopedia of Prostitution and Sex Work: A–N*. Edited by Melissa Hope Ditmore, vol. 1, Greenwood Publishing Group, 2006.

Shaw, George Bernard. *Pygmalion*. 1913. Rev. ed., Penguin, 2003.

Stevens, Wallace. *The Collected Poems*. 1954. Vintage, 1990.

Tanigawa, Kenichi, and Iwao Yamato, editors. *Geinō Hyōhakumin* [*Performing Vagabonds*]. Yamato Shobo, 2013.

Yamashita, Kōsaku. "Kabuki Torishimari to Yakusha no Mibun" ["Regulation over Kabuki and the Social Status of Actors in the Edo Era"]. *Kōchi Daigaku Gakujutsu Kenkyū Hōkoku (Jinbun Kagaku)*, vol. 45, 1996, pp. 157–65.

Wisker, Gina. "Behind Locked Doors: Angela Carter, Horror and the Influence of Edgar Allan Poe." *Re-Visiting Angela Carter: Texts, Contexts, Intertexts*, edited by Rebecca Munford, Palgrave Macmillan, 2006, pp. 178–98.

II

Exploring New Uses

5

Japanese Heroine Tales and the Significance of Storytelling in Contemporary Society

Hatsue Nakawaki

Introduction

IN JAPAN TODAY, MUKASHIBANASHI (lit. tales of old times) with male protagonists are better known than those in which female protagonists play active roles. As I will demonstrate below, female protagonists in widely known tales tend to be nonhuman beings. However, in the transcriptions of orally transmitted tales, tales with female protagonists can be found in various parts of Japan. I am a novelist, and I also research mukashibanashi, rewrite them, and tell them to both children and adults. When I do storytelling, I choose to retell tales that have active heroines and that end happily.[1] In contemporary diversified society, it is necessary to reselect and transmit mukashibanashi with female protagonists from the perspective of women living today. This is also related to the significance of telling mukashibanashi not only about women but also about other socially marginalized people in contemporary society, such as children and old people. In this chapter, I will consider Japanese heroine tales by taking two tales as examples in order to explore the significance of telling mukashibanashi in contemporary society.

The Definition and the Transmission of Mukashibanashi in Japan

First, I will provide a survey of the definition and the transmission of mukashibanashi in Japan. Western folk and fairy tales began to be imported to Japan at the end of the nineteenth century.[2] With an influx of Western tales, however, Japanese tales did not wane, and tales originating both in Japan and in the West are equally popular still today.

In defining mukashibanashi in Japan, this chapter follows the definition given in Japanese folklore studies because it was mainly by folklorists that oral tales were recorded in Japan. In Japanese folklore studies, mukashibanashi are defined as "tales that have been transmitted by common people in their everyday lives" and "whose transmissions can be identified as mainly oral, that is, the tales that have been definitively established as narratives by means of oral transmission even when they might have originated or been transmitted via written records"; a further criteria is that they are tales "whose transmitters intend to entertain the audience through storytelling" and "that have narrative structures" (Inada et al. 917). The German term "*Volksmärchen*" is understood as "referring only to those kinds of folk narratives that have certain styles or types, and it is these kinds of narratives that Japanese folklore studies calls mukashibanashi."[3] Because the English term "fairy tale" includes literary tales and refers to a wide range of narrative forms, and "folktale" does not include literary tales but refers only to all kinds of folk narratives, neither of these terms coincides with the mukashibanashi (Ōtsuka Minzoku Gakkai 701), which are gathered in the major collections, *Nihon mukashibanashi taisei*, edited by Keigo Seki, and *Nihon mukashibanashi tsūkan*, edited by Kōji Inada and Toshio Ozawa.[4] It is the mukashibanashi from these two collections that I will discuss in this chapter.

It is important to understand how mukashibanashi have been transmitted in Japan. Today, a large number of picture books and other books based on mukashibanashi, especially for young children, are being published. Since the Meiji era,[5] mukashibanashi have always been included in textbooks teaching Japanese language. Japanese readers have become familiar with Japanese and non-Japanese mukashibanashi equally, and aware that the latter are from foreign countries. For example, a textbook for first-year elementary school pupils may contain both the Japanese tale "The Rolling Rice Ball" and the Russian tale "The Enormous Turnip."[6] Tales such as Charles Perrault's "Cinderella," the Brothers Grimm's "Snow White," and Joseph Jacob's "The Three Little Pigs" have frequently been translated into Japanese since the Meiji era and have been as popular as Japanese mukashibanashi.

What is more, the influx of these European tales has not caused domestic tales to decline; rather, they have been received as completely different but equally good tales. As can be seen in Japanese textbooks, even seven-year-old children are expected to be able to distinguish between Japanese and European tales, and, in my own experience as a storyteller, even many preschool children can distinguish between these two kinds of tales. For example, when I asked children what kind of tales they wanted to hear, they would ask for either "tales of princesses," referring to Western fairy tales, or "tales of old men and women," meaning Japanese mukashibanashi. I believe that the ability to make such a distinction allows these tales from totally different cultures to coexist in Japan. In this sense, it can be said that a great number and a wide variety of tales have been told in Japan.

One reason why such a distinction can be possible is due to the rich and diverse ways in which mukashibanashi have been transmitted in Japan. Japanese mukashibanashi began to spread in the form of picture books in the late-Muromachi period and frequently appeared in the forms of *Nara-ehon* (handwritten illustrated books and scrolls produced between the late-Muromachi and early-Edo periods) and *akahon* (inexpensive storybooks with red covers produced in the Edo era).[7] Canonical tales became established in their currently known forms between the late-Edo era and the Meiji period.[8] From the Meiji period onward, canonical tales were repeatedly published in such publications as the *chirimen-bon* (crepe-paper book) series of Japanese Fairy Tales,[9] which are illustrated picture books of Japanese mukashibanashi in translation produced for readers abroad, the then immensely popular *Nihon mukashibanashi* collection edited and retold by Sazanami Iwaya,[10] and textbooks teaching Japanese in modern school education. Especially after the use of government-approved textbooks was enforced in schools in 1903, mukashibanashi became widespread throughout Japan.[11] The tales included in these books roughly coincide with those generally known today, which I refer to as "canonical" mukashibanashi in this chapter.

These canonical tales have several characteristics that are distinctively different from tales in other parts of the world, especially the West. These characteristics are the predominance of tales that have male or aged protagonists,[12] as well as the predominance of moralistic tales. Moreover, Japanese tales do not always end happily, and even when they do, they tend to end not with marriage but with the acquisition of wealth or security. These tendencies have been pointed out as characteristic of Japanese mukashibanashi. In Europe and other parts of the world, there are relatively more tales that have female protagonists. Max Lüthi, for example, observes that the protagonists in the tales collected and retold by the Grimms are predominantly women (Lüthi, *Mukashibanashi no honshitsu* 190–92). This is not always the case, however: tales that have old men and women as protagonists are found in Russia, Mongolia, and Thailand, although in smaller numbers. Nevertheless, in these regions, the tale type called "The Old Man Next Door," often found in Japan, is rarely found.[13] Tales in other parts of the world tend to be less moralistic than in Japan and often feature princesses, princes, and witches and end with happy marriages. In the case of animal bride and bridegroom tales, the interspecies couple are rarely permanently united in Japan, whereas in other parts of the world the protagonist sets out to search for his or her partner after separation, and they are often reunited. European folktale scholars have also observed that Japanese tales are more similar to legends and are moralistic (Ozawa, *Gaikoku*). Lutz Röhrich states that Japanese tales lack the element of salvation found in German tales and that they are "neither happy tales nor tales of wish fulfillment" (Röhrich 74). It can be said that these differences between Japanese mukashibanashi and tales in other parts of the world, especially Europe, make it easy for the Japanese to distinguish between the two. Furthermore, because they are different, Japanese children have found both kinds of tales necessary and have familiarized themselves with both.

There are also, however, many tales that have never been included in the canon. Spaces for storytelling had long existed in Japanese households and local communities, even if they did not survive the period of rapid economic growth in the 1970s. The existence of these storytelling spaces allowed other kinds of mukashibanashi not included in the canon to be disseminated across many regions in Japan richly and profusely. Moreover, fortunately, folklore studies was established relatively early in Japan, compared to other non-Western countries, and many tales have been recorded in methodologically sound ways since the 1910s. People who recorded tales included those who were not affiliated with academic institutions and lived in remote areas throughout Japan. *Nihon mukashibanashi tsūkan* (Inada and Ozawa), the most comprehensive collection to date, contains about sixty thousand tales and 1,211 tale types.

However, the records of these tales, which mainly have been transmitted orally, began to be neglected after oral storytelling declined at the end of the period of rapid economic growth in the 1970s. As a result, they were not told, published, or included in textbooks and are now barely known. Some claim that folklorists are partly responsible for this decline. Masami Ishii, for example, states that:

> Folklorists did not try to return the tales to local communities. They simply assumed that mukashibanashi would disappear sooner or later. They seem to have believed that, if the tales they collected were returned to the communities, it would disrupt their research. As a result, folklorists monopolized mukashibanashi, which were put to sleep in university offices and libraries. (48)

Among these tales, there are many tales that differ from the mukashibanashi canonized in the course of modernization in Japan, that have active female protagonists, and that are not moralistic. In this chapter, I refer to those tales that have been transmitted orally among the common people as "oral" mukashibanashi, to be distinguished from canonical ones.

Japanese Heroine Tales

In order to better understand the characteristics of Japanese heroine tales, we should first note that most of the canonical mukashibanashi have male protagonists, and those with female protagonists are very rare. Take, for instance, a picture-book series of twenty-four Japanese tales published by Shōgakkan in 2009–10.[14] The tales in this series were selected according to the choices made by readers who had small children and who were asked by the publisher which mukashibanashi they would like to read themselves and to read to their children and which tales they knew; these twenty-four tales can thus be considered to be among the canonical mukashibanashi in contemporary Japan.[15] This picture-book series contains eight tales from the *chirimen-bon* Japanese Fairy Tale First Series, which consists of twenty tales, and eleven tales from Iwaya's collection mentioned above.

Of the twenty-four tales that comprise Shōgakkan's series, the following four are not considered in my analysis below: "The Monkey and the Crab," whose protagonists are animals, "Kachi Kachi Mountain," whose protagonist changes from an old man to a hare, and two tales that have a couple as protagonists. Sixteen tales out of the remaining twenty have men as protagonists, such as the hero of "Momotarō," who is born from a peach and slays ogres, and the hero in "The Old Man Who Made Flowers Bloom," who takes care of a dog and becomes happy with the help of the grateful dog. Although "The Tongue-Cut Sparrow" features an old woman, she is described as evil in contrast to her husband, who looks after the sparrow injured by his wife and is shown as a kind old man.

There are only four tales with female protagonists: "The Farting Bride," "The Tale of Princess Kaguya," "The Crane Wife," and "The Snow Maiden." However, Princess Kaguya can barely be considered human, as she is born from a bamboo tree and goes back to the moon at the end of the tale. The protagonist in "The Crane Wife," who, in return for his kindness, visits a man in the form of a young woman, is actually a crane. The heroine of "The Snow Maiden," another animal bride tale, is a snow maiden and, biologically speaking, is not a terrestrial being. The only human heroine is the bride who becomes happy by extravagantly breaking wind in "The Farting Bride." As these examples make clear, canonical Japanese tales that have female protagonists tend to be either animal bride tales or, if they are human heroines, jocular tales.

As oral storytelling declined in Japan in the 1970s, TV programs also began to play a significant role in transmitting Japanese tales and legends to children. The highly popular TV animation series *Manga Nippon mukashibanashi* started in 1975 and broadcasted more than 1,400 tales and legends until 1995. This series, especially at the beginning, mainly aired standard mukashibanashi and reflected the tendency to feature more tales and legends with male protagonists than those with female protagonists. For example, of the twenty-four tales aired in 1975, apart from four tales in which the gender of the protagonists is not clear, as many as seventeen tales have male protagonists, while only three, namely, "The Snow Maiden," "The Crane Wife," and "The Tale of Princess Kaguya," have female protagonists.

In contrast, heroine tales abound in the West. "Snow White" and "Cinderella," the variants of which can be found in Europe and other parts of the world, have female protagonists who are clearly human. However, the young and beautiful heroines in these tales usually remain passive throughout the story and only become happy when they get married at the end of the story. This has been criticized from contemporary women's perspectives as reflecting a patriarchal view of women, in that the endorsement of passive and patient heroines in "Snow White" and "Cinderella" as models of feminine virtue plays a part in establishing gender roles.[16] Similarly, one of the influences that mukashibanashi exert has to do with establishing gender roles. The predominance of active male characters and the contrast between the good old man and the bad old woman in Japanese tales are clear examples.

However, there are Japanese tales that have active female human protagonists, although the number is smaller than that of those that have male protagonists. These tales are now unknown to most people because they rarely appear in textbooks and picture books, which shows the enormous impact of the publishing industry on mukashibanashi. Among these, there are tales that merely reverse the gender of the protagonists. For example, the version of "The Tongue-Cut Sparrow" I included in the collection I edited in 2012, *Onnanoko no mukashibanashi* [*Girls' Folktales*], reverses the roles of the old woman and the old man. This type of tale has been told mainly in Akita Prefecture and surrounding regions in the northeastern and central districts along the coast of the Japan Sea. The story of "The Straw Millionaire," in which a poor young man becomes rich by exchanging a straw with one thing after another, and the story of "The Search for the Nara Pear," in which a son kills a monster and brings back a pear for his ailing mother, also have variants with female protagonists. In the next section, I will analyze two oral tales in which human heroines play an active part and that do not end with a happy marriage. I will also compare them with Japanese tale collections and picture scrolls based on folklore as well as with heroine tales in the Western tradition in order to clarify the distinctive features of Japanese heroine tales.

Tales about Stepdaughters and Marriage between Different Species

I will first examine tales about stepdaughters and marriage between different species, especially in terms of how marriage is treated in these tales. Female protagonists most often appear in tales about stepchildren. This tendency can be observed all over the world, and this type of tale seems to be one of the most commonly found tales. "Cinderella" is one example. The heroine is bullied by her stepmother and her stepsisters but eventually becomes happy by being chosen by the prince. Such tales about stepchildren can also be found in Japan, but the one I am going to retell below does not follow this pattern, and this variant can only be found in Japan.[17]

"Otsuki, Ohoshi" (or "Little Moon, Little Star")

Once upon a time, there lived two sisters. The elder sister was called Otsuki, or Little Moon, and the younger sister was called Ohoshi, or Little Star. Otsuki was the previous mother's child, and Ohoshi was the present mother's child. The present mother could not hate Otsuki more.

One day, the father set out on a long journey. Believing that this was the best time to kill Otsuki, the mother made a cake containing poison and gave it to Otsuki. She made a cake containing sugar for Ohoshi and said, "Ohoshi, Ohoshi. Otsuki's cake has poison in it, so don't eat her cake."

Ohoshi nodded and, receiving her cake, she went out to play with Otsuki. Then she divided her cake into two to share and made Otsuki throw away her cake in a bamboo bush. A flock of sparrows flew down to eat the cake and immediately died of poison.

When Otsuki came home safely, the mother called Ohoshi again and said, "Ohoshi, Ohoshi, I've decided to kill Otsuki by dropping a stone mortar from the ceiling on her bed, so you must pretend to know nothing about it."

Ohoshi nodded, but when evening came, she secretly called Otsuki and made her sleep with her in her own bed. She put a big gourd filled with red dye in Ohoshi's bed and covered it with the duvet.

At midnight, the mother dropped the stone mortar from the ceiling. The stone mortar fell on Otsuki's bed and crushed the gourd, spattering red dye on the mother's face. Believing that it was Otsuki's blood, the mother rejoiced that now the obstacle was gone and went back to her bed to sleep.

When morning came, Otsuki and Ohoshi got up and appeared in front of the mother together. The mother was very surprised by this and went to the stone carver's house to have him make a large stone box with a lid. She then called Ohoshi and said, "Ohoshi, Ohoshi, I've decided to put Otsuki in a stone box and abandon her on the farthest mountain. When your father comes home, you must pretend to know nothing about it."

Ohoshi nodded, but she secretly went to the stone carver's house and asked him to make a small hole at the bottom of the box.

On a cold snowy day, the stone box was ready, and Otsuki was placed in the box. Ohoshi filled a bag with rape seeds and secretly gave it to Otsuki, saying, "Sister, sister, please drop these rape seeds through the hole in the box as you go. When spring comes, I will surely come and rescue you."

Otsuki was carried in the stone box by evil men over a mountain and a valley, then another mountain, till she reached the farthest mountain, where the stone box was buried in the ground.

When spring came, Ohoshi said to her mother, "Mother, Mother, I am going to go to the mountain to gather some corn parsley, so please make some rice balls for me." Then she went out carrying a lot of rice balls and a little ax for chopping wood.

When she arrived at the edge of the village, she saw some rape flowers. Ohoshi followed those flowers, walking over a mountain and a valley, and another mountain, till she arrived at a spot where rape flowers were blossoming in a circle.

Ohoshi dug into the ground with the ax and saw the lid of the stone box. She opened the box and found Otsuki in it. Otsuki cried so much that she became blind. In tears, Ohoshi helped Otsuki sit up. The moment tears from Ohoshi's left eye dropped into Otsuki's right eye and tears from Ohoshi's right eye dropped into Otsuki's left eye, Otsuki's eyes opened wide and clear.

After Ohoshi made Otsuki eat the rice balls and drink the water she scooped from a mountain stream, Otsuki regained her energy.

At that moment, the prince of a castle passed by on his hunting trip. When they told him what had happened, he took pity on them, so he took them back to his castle and made them live comfortably.

One day, when Otsuki and Ohoshi were looking out of the window of the castle, a blind old man passed by and sang a song while beating a gong:

As precious as heaven and earth
What has become of Otsuki and Ohoshi?
If Otsuki and Ohoshi were with me
Why do I beat this gong?
Clang, clang, clang,

Hearing this, Otsuki and Ohoshi thought that it must be their father and ran out. When he had got home from his journey, Otsuki and Ohoshi were gone, so he cried his eyes blind and had been wandering around looking for them.

As the three were holding each other in tears, Otsuki's tears dropped into his right eye, and Ohoshi's tears dropped into his left eye. Immediately, his eyes opened wide and clear.

Seeing this, the prince was overjoyed and let the father live in his castle too.

The three lived in the castle happily, and when they died, they ascended to heaven. The father was turned into the sun, Otsuki into the moon, and Ohoshi into a star. The mother became so ashamed of what she did that she buried herself in the ground and was turned into a mole.

Dondoharae[18]—or: that is the end of the story.[19]

This tale has been frequently told in the northeastern districts of Japan, such as Iwate Prefecture and Miyagi Prefecture. What is remarkable about this tale is that it is the stepmother's biological daughter who helps Otsuki. Whereas in "Cinderella," another tale about a stepdaughter, the stepmother's biological daughters either bully the heroine in company with their mother or obey their mother as bystanders, the heroine of "Otsuki, Ohoshi" deceives her stepmother and behaves actively. We can even say that Ohoshi, rather than Otsuki, is the protagonist, for Ohoshi plays a very active role, while Otsuki only does what her sister tells her to do. Also, the ways in which the stepmother tries to kill Otsuki are very cruel. She does not use any magic but does the deed with her own hand. It is much worse than the way the stepmother bullies Cinderella by working her hard, slandering her, and leaving her behind when they go to the ball. If Ohoshi had not helped, Otsuki would certainly have been killed, and the story would have ended there.

Moreover, when the prince appears, we may expect there will be a marriage, but, since there is only one prince for two daughters, they do not marry. Instead, the story ends happily when the two sisters are reunited with their father and are transformed into the moon, a star, and the sun. Unlike "Cinderella," which ends with the marriage between the stepdaughter and the prince, this tale ends with the daughters' reunion with their father, which emphasizes the love between the father and the daughters, rather than the love between a couple.

This tale may seem rather new but can be found in the picture scroll called *Hakone gongen emaki*, produced as early as the first half of the fourteenth century (Yokoyama and Matsumoto). The names of the characters are different, but, as in "Otsuki, Ohoshi," the stepmother tries to kill her stepdaughter by taking her to a faraway place and dropping her into a deep hole. Her stepsister comes and rescues her. Two princes pass by and rescue the stepdaughter from the hole with the help of five hundred huntsmen. As there happen to be two princes, the two daughters marry them and become princesses. Just at that point, the girls' father, who does not go blind in this picture scroll version, appears. This ending seems happy enough, but in addition to this, the five characters—two princes, two princesses, and their father—come to be revered as gods of Hakone and Izu, which are districts in Kanagawa Prefecture. From this literary version dated about seven hundred years ago, it can be said that marriage was once part of "Otsuki, Ohoshi." However, marriage rarely appears in the oral versions still told today.

We can find many similar cases where the medieval picture scroll stories differ from the oral tales handed down to us today. One example is "Urashima Tarō." In this tale, the hero rescues a turtle, is taken to an undersea palace, and is welcomed by the princess Otohime. After three days, he goes home to find that three hundred years have passed. When he opens the forbidden casket given to him by the princess, smoke rises from it and turns him into an old man. In the medieval picture scroll, Urashima Tarō marries Otohime. This is why he spends as long as three years at the undersea palace. In the oral tale told today, he only spends three days there because marriage does not take place; wonderful food and dancing fish alone are perhaps not enough to keep him entertained for more than three days (Ōshima 414–24).

The tradition of picture scroll stories since the Kamakura era led to the *Nara-ehon* in the late-Muromachi era,[20] which were also often based on traditional tales. What characterizes these medieval picture scrolls and picture books up until the mid-Edo era is the predominance of heroine tales, which usually end with the happy marriage of maltreated heroines, as in "Hachikazuki" and "Ochikubo." These stories are also similar to Western folktales in this respect. In his analysis of the Brothers Grimm's tales, which are by far the most popular tales in the West, Lüthi points out that the protagonists are predominantly female and that tales with male protagonists are "categorized as jocular tales," and this is "probably because those who told the stories to the Grimms were mostly women" (Lüthi, *Mukashibanashi: Sono bigaku* 190–91). This remark is suggestive in that it is the exact opposite of the canonical mukashibanashi, where male protagonists are predominant and heroine tales belong either to animal bride tales or to jocular tales.

Another important point concerns the gender of those tellers who memorized and transmitted tales. In fact, in Japan, women were the main authors of prose literature written in *hiragana* (as opposed to Chinese characters, which were used mainly by male writers). Recent research on *Nara-ehon* by Tōru Ishikawa (2009) revealed that, although most of the authors of medieval picture scrolls and *Nara-ehon* are anonymous, women were sometimes in charge of pictures and texts, at least up until the mid-Edo era. Women seem to have been absent from publishing after that period, and it can be assumed that women did not take part in publishing mukashibanashi or selecting school textbooks in the Meiji era because women did not have the right to vote and were given little opportunity to receive university education at the time.[21] This may be reflected in the fact that not a single tale from those heroine tales that end with a happy marriage, which were popular from the medieval to the mid-Edo periods, is included in the contemporary canon of mukashibanashi.

Besides marriage, these medieval picture scrolls have one more element that modern oral tales do not have. Orally transmitted animal bridegroom tales lack the element of struggle between sisters, or more precisely, the motif of the false bride. In other parts of the world, as in "Beauty and the Beast," the elder sisters become envious of the youngest sister who marries a nonhuman partner and they plan to separate the couple, or, as in "The Three Oranges," another girl kills the bride and replaces her. In Japanese tales about interspecies marriage still told today, however, there are no female characters who are passionate enough to either make the couple separate or replace the bride.[22]

Again, however, we can find this motif of the envious sister in a medieval picture scroll called *Amewakahiko zōshi* produced in the fifteenth century (Yokoyama and Matsumoto, "Amewakahiko"). When the two elder sisters find out that the giant snake whom the youngest sister, the Third Princess, married is actually a handsome man called Amewakahiko, they trick the heroine into opening a forbidden box in order to separate the couple. This motif does not appear in the oral version of "The Snake Husband" told today.

In Japanese tales of marriage between different species, protagonists do not search for their partners who have left them. The only exception is the protagonist in "The Celestial Maiden," also known as "Tanabata," meaning "star festival." All the other characters simply give up. When the nonhuman partner is female, as in "The Crane Wife" or "The Snow Maiden," the male protagonist gives up. On the other hand, when the nonhuman partner is male in such forms as a snake, a monkey, or a wild boar, the female protagonist kills him in the end. It seems that, when the protagonist is female, it is expected that she may give birth to a child, and this makes the interspecies marriage emphatically unacceptable. This, however, used to be accepted in ancient Japan, as there exists a tale about a child born from an interspecies union (Kurano and Takeda 181–83).

These tales represent the forms of mukashibanashi told in contemporary Japan. Even in animal bride and bridegroom tales, which revolve around the theme of marriage, romantic love and romantic feelings are not described, and rivals in love do not appear. This is one element that clearly distinguishes Japanese tales from those in other countries, not only in Europe but also in other countries in Asia.

Likewise, in tales about stepdaughters, neither romance nor marriage is involved, so sisters do not become rivals; rather than competing with each other, they even help each other, like Otsuki and Ohoshi. Compared to the medieval picture scroll, the modern oral tale of "Otsuki, Ohoshi" emphasizes the sisterly affection of Ohoshi, who goes out to rescue her stepsister by herself. Love in this tale is the love among family members, between sisters, and between parent and child. In "Otsuki, Ohoshi," tears open the eyes of the elder sister and the father, whereas in "Rapunzel" tears open the eyes of the heroine's once-lost husband.

Tales about Women with Great Strength

There are also tales about active human heroines who have special abilities that have traditionally been considered uncharacteristic of women. The following tale belongs to a tale type rarely found in the West.

"The Farting Guardian"

Once upon a time, there lived a girl who farted during her sleep. Her farts were unusual and sounded as if somebody was roaring, "Who's that, who's that!" So, when she was ripe for marriage, nobody wanted to marry her.

Then a rich man visited her and said, "I want to hire you as a guardian against our burglar." So she was hired by the rich man.

The rich man's house was burgled every night, but on that night, the master felt reassured and slept soundly because he had hired the farting guardian. The girl also slept.

Then the burglar came as usual. When the burglar heard a roar, "Who's that, who's that!" he was alarmed and stopped to take in the situation.

But, long as he waited, nobody appeared. He could only see a sleeping girl in the room, so he wondered and entered the room and found out that the roar was in fact the girl's fart. The burglar brought in a stopper made of oak and plugged her bottom with it. Then her roaring fart stopped.

The burglar thought now was the time and filled a big wrapping cloth with a lot of valuable objects. Just as he was about to go out heaving the bundle, the oak stopper popped out, and there came a tremendous roar, "Who's that, who's that!" which was so loud that it did not sound like a fart. The burglar was so startled that he abandoned the bundle and fled without taking anything.

Next morning, the master said to the girl, "Thanks to you, we didn't get anything stolen. I will pay you handsomely, so please be our guardian for ever."

So the girl received a lot of money for doing nothing other than sleeping at night and farting.

Various things happened a long time ago. *Mukasha mukkuri kayatte, hanasha hanekuri kayattato.*[23] (Nakawaki, Onnanoko 17–21)[24]

Wind-breaking tales also appear in medieval picture scrolls and can be traced as far back as the mid-fifteenth century (Yokoyama and Matsumoto, "Fukutomi"). Many tales about breaking wind have been told in East Asia. Interestingly, there are slight differences among them. In Korea and China, sweet-smelling farts tend to be valued. In Japan, what matters is how wonderful or interesting the farts sound. These vulgar tales are said to be rarely found in Europe, though "The Farting Guardian" can be regarded as a variant of ATU 1453, "The Flatulent Girl," which can be found in Finland, Spain, and Hungary (Uther 228–29). Nevertheless, it is in Japan that this tale type has been richly transmitted.

In Japanese tales, there are many tales in which women play a lively role by means of breaking wind extravagantly. "The Farting Bride," one of the canonical mukashibanashi, tells the story of a bride who is driven out of her home for blowing away her husband and her mother-in-law with an enormous fart. On her way back to her parents' house, she obtains dresses and other everyday goods as well as rice and is brought back to her husband's house, where he recognizes her worth, and they live happily ever after. People seem to have enjoyed such tales because they are unexpected. It is usually considered improbable that women should break wind in public. In other words, these tales have been enjoyed precisely because it has been commonly assumed that women should be discreet and are not supposed to do such a thing.

There are also tales in which women behave unexpectedly by displaying great strength or sharp intelligence. In either case, the emphasis is placed on the unexpectedness of the heroines' possession of such abilities in spite of being women. Although tales about women's intelligence are told all around the world, tales about women's physical strength are rarely told in the West. According to Inada, the wind-breaking tale has its origin in the tale about great strength, which was adapted at a certain point in history (Inada, "Chikara" 209). *Nihon ryōiki*, a Buddhist tale collection written by the priest Kyōkai in the early ninth century, contains tales about a woman who has unexpected physical strength (Endō and Kasuga). This tale can also be found in orally transmitted tales in various areas of Japan, although the number is smaller than that of the wind-breaking tale. These two tale types share a similar plot pattern. In either case, the common assumption that women should be discreet makes these tales entertaining. As mentioned above, "The Farting Bride" is still widely known today, which may suggest that the same assumption about women's discreetness is still held firmly in contemporary Japan.

This tendency found in mukashibanashi may be related to the fact that Japan ranks 114 out of 144 countries in the World Economic Forum's 2017

Global Gender Gap Index. In addition, it may help suggest the reason for the existence in Japan of an electronic device that covers the sound of urinating in ladies' toilets, something that can be rarely found in other countries. This device produces a recorded flushing sound to hide the sound of urinating. Japanese women used to flush water continuously in public toilets in order to cover the sound that they feel ashamed of being heard by others. Because this was regarded as a waste of water, this electronic device was invented. The device is called "Otohime," which literally means "Sound Princess" and which, cleverly enough, is also the same sound as the name of the princess in the undersea palace in "Urashima Tarō."

As this little device symbolizes, generally speaking, Japanese women wish to be always discreet and are also expected to be discreet by society to the extent that they must hide the sounds that their bodies make. In this way, women's own wishes and society's expectations together restrict their behavior, resulting in the social condition that ranks exceptionally low in the Global Gender Gap Index.

Moreover, this situation is not new. Murasaki Shikibu, the author of the early-eleventh-century novel *Genji monogatari* (The Tale of Genji), and Sei Shōnagon, the author of *Makura no sōshi* (The Pillow Book, c1001), both lamented that to be a woman was detrimental about a thousand years ago (Sōgo Joseishi Kenkyūkai 42–44). Although the tale about a woman with great strength mentioned above was written almost 1,200 years ago, it describes how obediently the strong heroine served her husband, suggesting that a wife's obedience to her husband was regarded as a virtue at that time.

Another factor in Japanese mukashibanashi that shows this kind of conventionally held assumption about women's discreetness is that the tales that contain the motif of "Love Like Salt," found widely throughout the world, have rarely been told in Japan despite the fact that they have been told in neighboring countries like Korea and China, with whom Japan shares many tales. This motif, famous for its appearance in Shakespeare's *King Lear*, concerns the father, often the king, who asks his daughters how much they love him and, when the youngest daughter answers, "I love you as I love salt," drives her out for comparing him to such a trivial thing. The youngest daughter later invites her father to her wedding and serves him unsalted dishes, making him realize his ignorance and apologize to her. In another variant, the father asks his daughters to whom they owe their present lives, and dismisses the daughter who replies, "my own power," but later realizes his ignorance. In Japan, tales like "The Charcoal Burner *Choja*" and the tale type known as "Remarriage with Good Fortune Evenly Divided between Man and Woman," in which the husband asks his wife (or sometimes, though less often, the father asks his daughter) "to whom she owes her present life" and dismisses her for her answer, have been told mainly in the Ryūkyū Islands. In these tales, the woman who has become happy with her second husband's ability or her own luck does not usually tell the truth to force her former husband (or her father) to realize his ignorance. He may realize by chance that the now happy woman is his former wife (or daughter) or may not even realize at all. This differs significantly from the heroine of "Love Like Salt," who invites her father to her wedding, makes him eat unsalted dishes, tells him the reason for her conduct, and makes him apologize to her. In a variant of "The Charcoal Burner *Choja*" found among a tribe in China, the heroine declares to her father the king, "My good fortune is not given to me by anyone, and I will carve out my own fortune," and is driven out of the palace. She marries a charcoal burner and finally makes her father recognize that she was right. Even though this tale shares almost the same plot as the Japanese variant, there is an overt conflict between the father and the daughter (Li 134–43).

Nevertheless, in the West, where women are not expected to be "discreet" in the same way as women in Japan are, heroines are usually passive and obedient, and their stories end with a happy marriage. On the other hand, the farting woman can always blow away everything and thus attains happiness; the heroine of "The Farting Bride" is driven out of her husband's house because of her enormous farts but overcomes her hardship by blowing away rain clouds, moving a large ship, and driving away an army. And, importantly, the happiness of such women does not have to involve marriage, as in "The Farting Guardian" (Nakawaki, *Onnanoko* 199). Today, we no longer regard marriage between a man and a woman as the only goal to achieve in order to lead a happy life. Love and marriage are not obligatory, and it is up to each individual to choose what form it takes to be happy. Happiness for women—and of course for men—does not necessarily mean marriage. These orally transmitted tales, which do not end with a happy marriage, indicate to us that there are various ways of living happily and encourage those women—and those men who live in this society with women—who try to carve out their own futures in this diversified society.

The Significance of Storytelling in Contemporary Society

Traditional storytelling spaces have been long lost in many parts of the world. This process happened relatively late in Japan, where these spaces persisted as late as the 1970s. Hideo Hanabe, one of the leading folklorists, who has researched mukashibanashi over a long period, claims that the folkloristic methodology has come to an end in the field of mukashibanashi studies (Hanabe, "Mukashibanashi"). It is true that folklorists can no longer "gather" a lot of new tales in traditional storytelling spaces and boast of their achievement. No new mukashibanashi will be created because spaces where anonymous storytellers used to tell tales have disappeared, leaving no possibility for such storytellers—who also created tales—to create mukashibanashi. Therefore, today, we can only record tales told by the remaining few storytellers, who are by no means anonymous. On the other hand, there are numerous tales that have been recorded mainly by folklorists that remain virtually unexamined. As Hanabe states, even though the part of research conducted through repeated visits and fieldwork is over ("Mukashibanashi"), research utilizing the vast amount of recorded material that has been accumulated so far has only just begun in Japan.

For the general public, the demand for mukashibanashi will certainly become stronger. This is because children genuinely love mukashibanashi. I have felt this throughout my storytelling career. Kyōko Matsuoka, who has played a significant role in conveying the pleasure of books and stories to children as the founder of the Tokyo Children's Library, observes that children react to mukashibanashi more strongly than to other literary stories. When I tell mukashibanashi to children, I feel as if they were sucked into the tales. This feeling must be felt by any storyteller, leaving a profound impression on them. Matsuoka also states that mukashibanashi do not choose their audience and attract, "virtually without exception, a wide range of children between five and twelve who have varied experiences, abilities, and interests" (Matsuoka 1–2). This observation is often made by storytellers, including myself.[25] In fact, *Ohanashi no rōsoku* [*The Candle of Stories*], an anthology of stories suitable for storytelling edited by the Tokyo Children's Library (*Tokyo Kodomo Toshokan*), mainly consists of folktales from around the world. Ruriko Masaki, one of the leading storytellers in Japan, states: "Basically, stories suitable for storytelling should have a clearly distinguishable protagonist, have a beginning that creates expectations for things to happen, which is followed by actions in response to these expectations, progress towards the climax, and have a satisfying closure. Most mukashibanashi meet this condition" (Masaki 22). In these new storytelling spaces that are different from the traditional ones, mukashibanashi is still needed.

Why, then, does mukashibanashi attract children's minds so strongly? Lüthi's work on European folktales shows that the folktale has a highly sophisticated literary form and that the style specific to the folktale attracts the audience's minds (Lüthi, *Yōroppa*). In folktales, as he observes, the audience can empathize with the protagonists because time, place, and people are not specified, and these protagonists perform a series of actions following a single plot and develop the story. The folktale has a specific style of narration, which appeals to the audience's feelings.

One of the stylistic elements of the folktale is that the folktale often has a protagonist who is a stepchild or the youngest child. This is because they are in the weakest position in a family. Although Lüthi states that he does not know if his analysis applies to Japanese tales, Ozawa argues that Lüthi's theory is also applicable to Japanese mukashibanashi (Ozawa, "Yakusha" 296), and I agree with this view. Lüthi states that folktales "feature as protagonists those who are at the bottom of society" (Lüthi, *Mukashibanashi no honshitsu* 63) and that "the blind, the youngest son, the orphan, the lost . . . these are the real protagonists of folktales" (Lüthi, *Yōroppa* 149). Seen in this light, the old, childless couple who are the main characters in many Japanese tales are also in the same category: old people with no one to depend on are the socially disadvantaged. Women also can be regarded as the socially disadvantaged as compared to men, so a stepdaughter, who often appears in folktales, is the weakest presence in a family. In hearing such tales, children who are still small and weak can empathize with the disadvantaged protagonist and experience happiness. These protagonists, even if they find the world frightening or hard, are able to succeed or obtain happiness in the end. In other words, folktales give hope to children who will go out into the world; they feel that, however weak they are, they will be accepted as they are. Psychological studies have proved that children can develop trust in others and confidence in themselves by being accepted as they are.[26]

As for the relationship between the audience's minds and the folktale, Lüthi argues that "while the *Märchen* fills children's minds with trust, legends make them anxious. For children to develop their selves, they need trust first of all—trust in themselves and trust in the world into which they will enter as they grow up and which will take them in" (Lüthi, *Mukashibanashi* 332). In the case of Japanese mukashibanashi studies, Inada claims: "That boundless optimism of the mukashibanashi is the very feeling of children who will transform the present into the future. Today's mukashibanashi is a gift for children from our ancestors" (Inada, *Mukashibanashi wa ikiteiru* 232).

Many unfortunate things are happening all over the world. We may feel paralyzed by their absurdity at times. However, folktales, and our ancestors who have handed them down to us, tell stories in which the protagonist becomes happy, and in which things will get better: "Whatever the situation, this world is worth living in, so trust this and *live*." This is where the significance of storytelling lies in contemporary society.

Conclusion

In this chapter, I have made the following three points. First, there has been a rich tradition of heroine tales among the orally transmitted mukashibanashi in Japan, many of which have remained outside the canon. Second, in medieval literary tales, tales including romance, an element rarely found in canonized tales, can be found. Finally, the significance of telling mukashibanashi in contemporary society lies in the mukashibanashi's ability to give us hope for a better future and to encourage us as we are by telling tales about the socially disadvantaged, including women, children, and old people, who all become happy in the end.

If traditional storytelling spaces still existed, tales would have become more refined to align themselves with contemporary audiences' needs, thereby constituting a new set of mukashibanashi. However, this is no longer possible. Nevertheless, tales that would be accepted by today's diversified society can be found among the corpus of tales that have been recorded so far. It is easy for writers who can modernize and recreate traditional tales to create stories that would be accepted by contemporary society. However, there are things that can be conveyed through the style characteristic of traditional mukashibanashi that fill audiences with a sense of trust and encourage them by featuring a disadvantaged protagonist who attains happiness in the end. Therefore, we need to reselect various tales from the perspective of today's values and to transmit them. In Europe, too, even after the Brothers Grimm's tales became predominant, many orally transmitted folktales were recorded by such scholars as Achille Millien and Paul Delarue in France, Gastone Venturelli in Italy, and Svend Gruntvig in Denmark, to name but a few. These oral tales include many tales in which active heroines attain happiness that does not take the form of marriage. Such diverse tales have been also recorded in many parts of the world other than Europe.[27] Hopefully, these tales will be put to good use.

As time passes and storytellers change, mukashibanashi will be reselected and transformed. In today's society, telling tales of various women—and at the same time men, or humans beyond gender distinctions—and of various forms of happiness is needed. Interestingly, Lüthi, in one of his late works observes that "in *Märchen*, tales that do not make a distinction between male and female protagonists are much stronger and more definite than those that do" (Lüthi, *Mukashibanashi* 295). It is true that, as I made clear in my collection (Nakawaki, *Onnanoko*), the gender of protagonists in mukashibanashi can be easily exchangeable. That this is true internationally is evident in the example of "Cinderella," which has been disseminated widely and has variants with male protagonists in many parts of the world, including Japan. What is important in mukashibanashi is not whether the protagonist is a woman or a man. Rather, it is a genre of narrative that treats the subject of a kind of human *existence* much wider than the one determined by gender.

It may be true that traditional storytelling spaces have disappeared and the form of oral transmission of tales has been lost. However, new kinds of storytelling spaces are being born in many places, and other forms of transmission of tales, such as publication and film adaptations, will continue to flourish. Today, we are also participating in the process of transmitting tales. Children are waiting to hear mukashibanashi at this very moment. What we hand down to people in the future in the form of mukashibanashi is given into our hands. I hope that this chapter will assist in making decisions in this area.

(Translated by Mayako Murai)

Notes

1. See Nakawaki, *Onnanoko no mukashibanashi* (2012) and *Chā-chan no mukashibanashi* (2016).

2. For example, Hiroshi Nomura states that the Brothers Grimm's tales were first introduced to Japan in *Seiyō koji shinsen sōwa*, translated by Ryōhō Suga in 1887, which includes ten tales by the Grimms probably translated into Japanese from their English translation (Nomura 208).

3. All quotations from works cited in Japanese in the works cited list are given in the translator's own translation.

4. This chapter also considers those tales that were recorded elsewhere but not included in these collections.

5. The Meiji era is the period between 1868 and 1912.

6. See *Kokugo 1 Jō* (2018).

7. The Muromachi era is the period between 1338 and 1573, and the Edo era is the period between 1603 and 1867.

8. Annotated editions of mukashibanashi published in the late-Edo era, *Enseki Zasshi* (1810) by Bakin Takizawa and *Hina no Ukegi* (c. 1848) by Norikiyo Umetsuji, both contain "The Monkey and the Crab," "Momotarō," "The Tongue-Cut Sparrow," "The Old Man Who Made Flowers Bloom," "Kachi Kachi Mountain," and "Urashima Tarō."

9. The *chirimen-bon* Japanese Fairy Tale Series was conceived by Takejirō Hasegawa, who ran the publishing company Kōbunsha, and began to be published in 1885. This series contains "The Mouse's Wedding," "The Old Man and the Devils," and "The Wonderful Tea-Kettle (The Good Fortune Kettle)," in addition to the six tales in the annotated mukashibanashi books mentioned above. The heroine tales included in this series are "Princess Splendor (The Tale of Princess Kaguya)," "The Wooden Bowl (Hachikazuki)," which is a variant of "Cinderella," and "The Matsuyama Mirror," which tells the tale of a girl who is bullied by her stepmother but is rewarded for her filial devotion in the end.

10. Iwaya's anthology includes the six tales in the annotated mukashibanashi books mentioned above and "The Old Man and the Devils," "The Good Fortune Tea Kettle," "Little One Inch," and "The Mouse's Wedding." "The Matsuyama Mirror" is the only tale with a female protagonist.

11. The government-approved textbooks teaching Japanese included "Urashima Tarō," "The Monkey and the Crab," "Momotaro," "The Old Man and the Devils," "The Old Man Who Made Flowers Bloom," "The Tongue-Cut Sparrow," "Kachi Kachi Mountain," "The Mouse's Wedding," and "Little One Inch," together with many moralistic tales from Aesop's fables such as "The Dog and Its Reflection," "The Tortoise and the Hare," "The Honest Woodcutter," and "The North Wind and the Sun." "The Matsuyama Mirror" and "The Tale of Princess Kaguya" are the only heroine tales (Kaigo *Nihon* vol. 4). Songs for school music education also had a significant influence on the transmission of mukashibanashi. Government-approved textbooks teaching songs included tales adapted for songs such as "Momotarō," "The Old Man Who Made Flowers Bloom," "Urashima Tarō," and "The Tongue-Cut Sparrow," none of which have female protagonists (Kaigo, *Nihon* vol. 25). These songs have been transmitted to children today.

12. This has been pointed out by scholars. Inada traces the history of tales with aged protagonists to ancient times and observes that this form "spreads through all types of mukashibanashi including mukashibanashi in complete form, jocular tales, animal tales, and formula tales" (Inada, "Jiji" 15).

13. Hideo Hanabe states that "tales featuring the old man next door, which are widely spread throughout Japan, can only rarely be found in Korea, China, Ainu communities, and Northeast Asia, and cannot be found in other parts of the world" (Hanabe, "Moji" 20). It is interesting that he points out that "the tale type 'The Old Man Next Door,' still unformed in medieval tales, used to reflect women and people in varied professions and positions as active agents before it came to be consolidated into 'The Old Man.' In the process of oral storytelling, these characters came to be absorbed into 'The Old Man Next Door'" (26). However, it seems inaccurate to attribute the reasons for this to the social change brought about by what Inada describes as "the maturation through designating children as suitable audiences" (Inada et al. 653) and the social background in which "families gradually became established and the atmosphere within families that separated inside and outside for convenience started to exert a considerable influence on oral storytelling with the development of the village system" (Hanabe "Moji" 26). In fact, it was not only in Japan that folktales had children as audiences and the village system had been established. This is an important subject for future investigations in mukashibanashi studies.

14. See Chiba 2009–10.

15. The author also contributed *Yuki onna* (2009), a retelling of the tale told by Toshiko Endō and recorded by Hiroko Fujida in Fukushima Prefecture.

16. For example, see the Japanese translations of Colette Dowling's *The Cinderella Complex: Women's Hidden Fear of Independence* (1981) and Elissa Melamed's *Mirror, Mirror: The Terror of Not Being Young* (1983).

17. Variants of this tale can be found in northern Cameroon, where only two tales of that kind have been recorded (Eguchi). Although it is not as widely told as in Japan, this needs to be investigated further.

18. The last phrase is a set phrase to conclude a tale in Iwate Prefecture and has no particular meaning.

19. This is an abbreviated version of the retelling by Nakawaki (Nakawaki, *Onnanoko* 110–21). Permission to translate and reproduce this tale granted by Nakawaki and Kaiseisha.

20. The Kamakura era is the period between 1192 and 1333.

21. University education began in Japan in 1877, but it was not until 1913 that women were admitted to university. Women gained suffrage as late as in 1946.

22. "Urikohime (Princess Melon)," although it is not an animal bride tale, contains the motif of "The False Bride." Inada ("Urihime") investigates the transmission of the motif of "The False Bride" in Japan and reveals that this motif is divided into two tales, "Urikohime" in the mainland and "The Elder Sister and the Younger Sister" in the Ainu and Ryūkyū regions. Hiroko Kenmochi ("Urikohime") discusses the relationship between "The Three Oranges," which has the motif of "The False Bride" and is found widely in Europe, and "Urikohime." The transmission of this motif is an interesting subject to be pursued further.

23. The last phrase is a set phrase to conclude a tale in Kōchi Prefecture and has no particular meaning.

24. Permission to translate and reproduce this tale granted by Nakawaki and Kaiseisha.

25. In my experience as an occasional storyteller, I once felt this feeling when I told the British folktale "Molly Whuppie" to audiences ranging from two- to seventy-year-olds.

26. See, for example, Erik H. Erikson (*Identity*) and Masami Sasaki (*Kodomo*).

27. Some of these recorded tales have been translated into Japanese in the folk narrative series published by Miyaishoten.

Works Cited

Chiba, Mikio, et al. *Nihon meisaku ohanashi ehon*, 24 vols., Shōgakkan, 2009–10.

Eguchi, Kazuhisa. "Hokubu Kamerūn, Furube-zoku no minkansetsuwa: Ādamāwa chihō to Berue chihō no hanashi." *Kokuritsu Minzokugaku Hakubutsukan chōsahōkokusho*, vol. 45, 2003, pp. 354–58.

Endō, Yoshiki, and Kazuo Kasuga, editors. *Nihon ryōiki: Nihon koten bungaku taikei*. Vol. 70, Iwanamishoten, 1967, pp. 183–85, 257–61.

Erikson, Erik H. *Identity and the Life Cycle*. International Universities Press, 1959.

Hanabe, Hideo. "Moji to katari no media." *Mukashibanashi: Kenkyū to shiryō*, vol. 34, 1997, pp. 20–27.

———. "Mukashibanashi kenkyū niokeru minzokugakuteki hōhō wa owattaka." *Nihon minzokugaku*, vol. 281, 2015, pp. 36–46.

Inada, Kōji. "Chikara onna to hehiri yome." *Mukashibanashi no jidai*. Chikumashobō, 1985, pp. 195–219.

———. "Jiji to baba tono hanashi: Kankei mukashibanashi o kangaeru." *Mukashibanashi kenkyū nyūmon*. Miyaishoten, 1976, pp. 1–21.

———. *Mukashibanashi wa ikiteiru*. Chikuma Gakugei Bunko, 1996.

———. Urihime keifu hō. *Mukashibanashi no genryū*. Miyaishoten, 1997, pp. 232–60.

Inada, Kōji, et al., editors. *Nihon mukashibanashi jiten*. Kōbundō, 1977.

Inada, Kōji, and Toshio Ozawa, editors. *Nihon mukashibanashi tsūkan*. Dōhōshashuppan, 1977–90.

Ishii, Masami. "Mukashibanashi o mirai e tsunagu kichōna syuppan." *Yonde agetai Aomori no mukashibanashi 10: Daija no tanomi*. Retold by Tatsuji Sasaki and Ryōko Muraka. Aomoriken Bungeikyōkai Syuppanbu, 2012, pp. 48–50.

Ishikawa, Tōru. *Nara-ehon to emaki no tenkai*. Miyaishoten, 2009.

Iwaya, Sazanami. *Nihon mukashibanashi*. Annotated by Nobumichi Ueda. Tōyōbunko, 2001.

Kaigo, Tokiomi, editor. *Nihon kyōkasho taikei kindai hen*. Vol. 4, Kōdansha, 1964.

———, editor. *Nihon kyōkasho taikei kindai hen*. Vol. 25, Kōdansha, 1965.

Kenmochi, Hiroko. "'Urikohime': Wakei bunseki oyobi 'Mittsu no orenji' tono hikaku." *Kōshōbungei kenkyū*, vol. 11, 1998, pp. 45–57.

Kurano, Kenji, and Yuukichi Takeda, editors. *Kojiki norito*. Iwanamishoten, 1958.

Li, Xinghua, editor. "Ōjo to sumiyaki." *Chūgoku shōsū minozoku no mukashibanashi: Pē-zoku minkankoji densetsushū*. Translated by Hisako Kimishima, Miyaishoten, 1980, pp. 134–43.

Lüthi, Max. 1962. *Mukashibanashi no honshitsu: Mukashi arutokoro ni*. Translated by Hiroshi Nomura, Chikumashōbō, 1994. [*Once Upon a Time: On the Nature of Fairy Tales*. Translated by Lee Chadeayne and Paul Gottwald, Frederick Ungar, 1970.]

———. 1975. *Mukashibanashi: Sono bigaku to ningenzō*. Translated by Toshio Ozawa, Iwanamishoten, 1985. [*The Fairytale as Art Form and Portrait of Man*. Translated by Jon Erickson, Indiana University Press, 1987.]

———. 1981. *Yōroppa no mukashibanashi: Sono katachi to honshitsu*. Translated by Toshio Ozawa, Iwanamibunko, 2017. [*The European Folktale: Form and Nature*. Translated by John D. Niles, Institute for the Study of Human Issues, 1982.]

Masaki, Ruriko. *Sutōrīteringu: Gendai niokeru ohanashi*. Jidōtoshokan Kenkyūkai, 1987.

Matsuoka, Kyōko. *Mukashibanashi wo kangaeru*. Nihon Editā Sukūru Shuppanbu, 1985.

Mutsurō, Kai, et al. *Kokugo 1 jō: Kazaguruma*. Mitsumuratoshoshuppan, 2018.

Nakawaki, Hatsue. *Chā-chan no mukashibanashi* [*Chā-chan's Folktales: Collection of Japanese Regional Folktales*]. Fukuinkanshoten, 2016.

———. *Onnanoko no mukashibanashi: Nihon ni tsutawaru totteoki no ohanashi* [*Girls' Folktales: The Best Japanese Tales You Never Heard*]. Kaiseisha, 2012.

Nomura, Hiroshi. *Gurimu dōwa: Kodomo ni kikasete yoika?* Chikumashōbō, 1989.

Ōshima, Tatehiko, editor. "Urashima Tarō." *Otogizōshi shū*, Shōgakkan, 1974, pp. 414–24.

Ōtsuka Minzoku Gakkai. *Nihon minzoku jiten*. Kōbundō, 1974.

Ozawa, Toshio. *Gaikoku no mukashibanashi kenkyūsha ga mita Nihon no mukashibanashi*. Mukashibanashi Daigaku Syuppankai, 1995.

———. "Yakusha atogaki." *Yōroppa no mukashibanashi: Sono katachi to honshitsu*. By Max Lüthi, translated by Ozawa Toshio, Iwanamibunko, 2017, pp. 293–97.

Rörich, Lutz. "Doitsujin no me kara mita Nihon no mukashibanashi." Ozawa, *Gaikoku*, pp. 68–77.

Sasaki, Masami. *Kodomo eno manazashi*. Fukuinkanshoten, 1998.

Seki, Keigo. *Nihon mukashibanashi taisei*. Kadokawashoten, 1978–80.

Sōgō Joseishi Kenkyūkai, editor. *Shiryō niyoru Nihon josei no ayumi*. Yoshikawakōbundō, 2000.

Tokyo Kodomo Toshokan, editor. *Ohanashi no rōsoku*. Tokyo Kodomo Toshokan, 1973–.

Uther, Hans-Jörg. *The Types of International Folktales: A Classification and Bibliography, Based on the System of Antti Aarne and Stith Thompson*. Suomalainen Tiedeakatemia, Academia Scientiarum Fennica, 2011.

Yokoyama, Shigeru, and Takashi Matsumoto, editors. "Amewakahiko zōshi." *Muromachijidai monogatari taisei*, vol. 2, Kadokawashoten, 1974, pp. 13–18.

———. "Fukutomi zōshi" and "Fukutomi monogatari." *Muromachijidai monogatari taisei*, vol. 11, Kadokawashoten, 1983, pp. 335–52.

———. "Hakone gongen engi emaki." *Muromachijidai monogatari taisei*, vol. 10, Kadokawashoten, 1982, pp. 277–87.

6

Who's Afraid of Derrida & Co.?

Modern Theory Meets Three Little Pigs in the Classroom

Shuli Barzilai

A Start-Up Story

THE FIRST CLASS OF my compulsory course on "Modern Literary Theory" was a non-encounter. The mainly silent students whose body language expressed boredom, disease, or anxiety sat opposite the screen I diligently filled with abstract concepts. For several days before our next meeting, I worried the problem: how to captivate my captive audience? How to generate interest in a reputedly bone-dry yet demanding subject? So I tried out another stratagem, and it assumed a fairy-tale form in two senses. First, drawing on adaptations of the tale type designated "Blowing the House In" (ATU 124), I used the tale to explicate varied theoretical approaches; second, happily, the conjunction of "highbrow" theory with "lowbrow" texts not only defused initial apprehensions and biases but also facilitated lively classroom discussions. This combination had an unexpected additional advantage. Through encounters with an endearing (and enduring) tale about three anthropomorphic pigs, students increasingly grasped the relevance of its multiple adaptations and re-orientations for understanding contemporary sociocultural trends and issues. The tale's high malleability, its plasticine-like capacity to be reworked and reshaped while retaining an identifiable shape, I proposed, might explain its durability and centrality in Western culture at large. Each variant holds up a kind of mirror not to nature but to nurture; through this medium, we reflect on the ways we were, are, and want (the world) to be. The odd coupling of "Modern Theory" with "The Three Little Pigs" thus evolved into an ongoing lesson in the permutations of cultural criticism.

But why choose variants of "The Three Little Pigs" among all the popular folk- and fairy tales just as readily available? Rather than presenting an academic rationale, this choice, I admit, was intuitive and contingent on circumstance. Many years ago, I found in some bookstore a "Peepshow Book"—a pop-up version whose front and back covers tied together forming a kind of mobile lantern. My children were fascinated and asked to be retold the story with such frequency that it evidently had, beyond its attractive format, a meaningful resonance for them.[1] It proved impossible, however, to find a Hebrew-language version, or a version in any language, in the place I inhabit: the holy city of Jerusalem. Perhaps because the pig is an unclean and proscribed animal for both Jews and Muslims, local bookstores were all three-little-pigless. So in those fabled pre-Internet times, my resource was the children's shelves in bookstores abroad that I explored whenever traveling. Gradually, the collection grew, to the delight and interest of auditors of all ages. When the "Modern Literary Theory" class required swift remedial intervention, I called upon "The Three Little Pigs" for help, which they deftly and immediately provided.

The Well-Wrought Churn

My threefold starting points were: Cleanth Brooks's "Keats' Sylvan Historian: History without Footnotes," in *The Well Wrought Urn: Studies in the Structure of Poetry* (1947), followed by William Wimsatt and Monroe Beardsley's "The Intentional Fallacy" and "The Affective Fallacy," in *The*

Verbal Icon: Studies in the Meaning of Poetry (1954). As the subtitles of these influential volumes indicate, the New Critics favored poetry above other generic milieus. What motivated this partiality for poetry? The genre apparently afforded ample opportunity for the New Criticism to validate itself via detailed, quasi-scientific analyses of formal devices ("studies in the *structure* of poetry") together with thematic content ("studies in the *meaning* of poetry").

But this explanation generates further questions. What impelled this drive toward "objective" methods that excluded not just readers and authors but any factors other than the text itself? Why try to re-form literary criticism so that it resembled a "hard" science? Although varied explanations may be forthcoming, it is useful to recall the *Zeitgeist*, the defining spirit of the mid-twentieth century: the geopolitical background of the New Criticism was the Cold War era.[2] The long-standing rivalry between the United States and the Soviet Union openly began in 1947, the same year that *The Well Wrought Urn* appeared, and the superpowers' struggle for political, economic, and technological ascendancy placed unprecedented emphasis on scientific achievement. After the Soviet Union launched the first artificial satellite, "Sputnik," in 1957, the space race conferred even greater prestige on the sciences. These historic developments, intensified by the media attention surrounding them, arguably inflected (or infected) literary studies during this period.

After discussing the exemplary essays just mentioned, and bearing in mind the New Critical predilection for poetry, we turned to an old English ballad in which a fox and geese enact the plot of "Blowing the House In":

> There was once a Goose at the point of death,
>   So she called her three daughters near,
>   And desired them all, with her latest breath,
>   Her last dying words to hear.
> "There's a Mr. Fox," said she, "that I know,
>   Who lives in a covert hard by,
>   To our race he has proved a deadly foe,
>   So beware of his treachery."

> "Build houses, ere long, of stone or of bricks,
>   And get tiles for your roofs, I pray;
>   For I know, of old, Mr. Reynard's tricks,
>   And I fear he may come any day."

After Mother Goose's demise, her daughters—Gobble, Goosey, and Ganderee—forge an alliance against their foe. But Gobble, the youngest and silliest, soon comes to "a very bad end" because, being lazy and silly, she "would not to her mother attend"; instead of bricks, she makes an open nest with wooden boards. You can imagine what happens next: "She only had time to hiss once or twice / Ere [Fox] snapped off her lily-white head." And so it goes with Goosey, too, until Ganderee alone remains. Unlike her feather-brained sisters, however, this clever goose heeds mother's advice.

A deadly game of cat and mouse, so to speak, accelerates in quatrain after quatrain. But when the fox fails to prevail, he conceives a wily plan that will get him inside Ganderee's house: "Quick, quick, let me in! oh, for once be kind, / For the huntsman's horn I hear; / Oh, hide me in any snug place you can find." Summon up the wolf's "Little pig, little pig, let me come in" for an analgous appeal for entry with malicious intent. The goose agrees to hide the fox inside her butter churn. Here's how she outfoxes him:

> Then into the churn the Fox quickly got;
>   But, ere the Goose put on the top,
>   A kettle she brought of water quite hot,
>   And poured in every drop.
>
> Then the Fox cried out, "O! I burn, I burn,
>   And I feel in a pitiful plight;"
>   But the Goose held fast the lid of the churn,
>   So Reynard he died that night.

Heeding the injunction to look for meaning only within the text, we note its moral coda adds an allegorical dimension that subsequent storytellers recast for other edifying purposes: "Mankind have an enemy whom they well know, / Who tempts them in every way; / But they, too, at length shall o'ercome this foe, / If wisdom's right law they obey." Instead of humankind versus the devil, you may substitute "USA" versus "USSR" (and vice versa) for an interrelated parable.

In this course segment, dubbed "The Well-Wrought Churn," we consider the traditional ballad as a plot-driven poem that recounts tragic or comic events building up to a dramatic conclusion. To generate a sense of fast-paced urgency, ballads are often structured in monosyllabic rhymed quatrains, with each line containing three or four stresses. In reading this ballad as formalist critics, we analyze significant rhymes, such as the framing "know / [thy] foe," identify the generic *abab* pattern, and scrutinize the climactic irony—the New Criticism loves irony and paradox—in which (feminized) prey outwits (male) predator. Eater and eaten change places. In yet other words, she foils her foe and cooks his goose.

Two Roads Diverged

After the New Criticism, it is possible to proceed in divergent directions. On the one hand, the fight to the death between seemingly asymmetrical adversaries leads thematically to Freud's paradigm-shifting interpretation of the murderous rivalry between fathers and sons in *The Interpretation of Dreams* (1900) and his amplifications of the Oedipal complex in such writings as *Totem and Taboo* (1913). The focus of psychoanalytic theory on "*man*kind" raises the issue of women's development and societal role, as epitomized by the (in)famous question attributed to Freud: "Was will das Weib?"—variously translated as "What does [the/a] woman want?"[3] Thus the road via psychoanalytic criticism cogently leads to the impact of the feminist movement and, from there, to queer theory.

On the other hand, the striving after ever-more-exact, definitive modes of analysis that would confer the validity of truth on interpretation leads both methodologically and chronologically to Ferdinand de Saussure's *Course in General Linguistics* (1916) and structuralism. Saussurian theory informs in due course such essays as Claude Lévi-Strauss's "Structural Study of Myth"

(1955), as well as Roman Jakobson and Lévi-Strauss's "Charles Baudelaire's 'Les Chats'" (1962), which became an influential showpiece for the exactitude of structuralist approaches to poetry. From structuralism, the path to poststructuralism and, from there, to postcolonialism is direct enough.

So which way to go? Unlike the regretful (or, perhaps, contented) speaker of Robert Frost's "The Road Not Taken," who chose unalterably between forked roads, I propose that we travel both, though not, of course, simultaneously. "The Three Little Pigs" shows us the way. Following the approximate chronology of the storybooks at hand, and knowing we will return to the road not taken, we proceed from the New Criticism to psychoanalytic criticism and then to critiques of phallogocentric thinking. Subsequently, we backtrack and explore Saussure's linguistic theories and their formative effects.

Father versus Sons

In reconstructing the primordial origins of social organization and religion in *Totem and Taboo*, Freud invokes "a violent and jealous father" who, in order to keep all the women for himself, kills or drives away his sons as soon as they mature. To leave their mark and multiply, it becomes imperative for them to band together and slay the primal father. As Freud recounts this momentous event, "One day the brothers who had been driven out came together, killed and devoured their father and so made an end of the patriarchal horde.... [The] father had doubtless been the feared and envied model of each one of the company of brothers: and in the act of devouring him they accomplished their identification with him, and ... acquired a portion of his strength" (141–42).

Freud's articulation of the sons' slaying of the father (or what Lacan calls "the only myth" of the modern age [*Seminar* 176]) lends itself well to the drama enacted between the wolf and three pigs. Read psychoanalytically, the paradigm of feared father versus fearful sons underpins the fairy-tale plot, and lurking behind its manifest presentation lies a timeless generational conflict. After all, why "*little* pigs" when a hungry wolf would want to devour *any* pigs? The adjective denotes an (up)rising generation. The story's happy outcome, for the sons, perhaps clarifies its unconscious appeal to generations of young and not-so-young audiences.

However, as I point out, in the variant collected in folklorist Joseph Jacobs's *English Fairy Tales* (1898; fig. 6.1), based on the first print version in James Orchard Halliwell's *Nursery Rhymes and Nursery Tales* (1843),[4] the plot unfolds otherwise: it is every man for himself and only the fittest survives. Instead of banding together, each pig stands alone, and so the wolf-father devours two pigs after obliterating their flimsy houses before meeting his match. Versions in which all three pigs survive may represent an alternative folkloric tradition, or bowdlerized adaptations of Jacobs's rendition,

Figure 6.1. Joseph Jacobs's *English Fairy Tales* (1898). Public domain.

designed to conceal or camouflage the realities fulminating behind the overt story.

Be that as it may, the colored ink drawings in Paul Galdone's *The Three Little Pigs* (1970), which adheres to Jacobs's text, vividly serve my expositional purposes. The first-page illustration shows a doleful separation between teary-eyed sow and weepy piglets marking the end of the pre-Oedipal stage: "She had no money to keep them, so she sent them off to seek their fortune" (fig. 6.2). The pigs are literally, visually down in the mouth. (Looking ahead, the feminization of poverty is imaged here as a single mother with piglets to feed and no breadwinner in sight.) But things look up when each homeless pig, in turn, meets a man with a different load—straw, sticks, and brick—and builds a house. Soon enough, however, the enemy comes knocking at the door. A constant feature in Galdone's drawings is the wolf's long red tongue and big bushy tail, as opposed to the pigs' blunt snouts and short, skinny appendages (fig. 6.3). The symbolism, consciously intended or not, is self-evident; as one student quipped, "it's the story of the three little pricks." So the well-endowed wolf easily overpowers the two puerile pigs. The third one represents another story. Using brains instead of brawn, this alpha pig *is* a match for the wolf-father and defeats him three times. The wolf, enraged, declares: "I'm going to climb down your chimney and eat you up!" No sooner does the pig hear him on the roof, then he boils up a cauldron of water: "as the wolf was coming down the chimney, the little pig took the cover off the pot, and in fell the wolf. The little pig quickly put on the cover again, boiled up the wolf, and ate him for supper."

In the accompanying image, when the smiling survivor puts the lid on, the only remnant of his adversary is the bushy tail sticking out of the pot (fig. 6.4). Perhaps it will serve him as a token and memento of the totemic father who once owned it. Among Freud's several self-revised theories, he never altered his account of the slaying of the primal father followed by the totem meal. It is as if the anonymous author-inventor of "Blowing the House In" had somehow read *Totem and Taboo* before telling an analogous story.

Figure 6.2. "She had no money to keep them, so she sent them off to seek their fortune." Illustration from *The Three Little Pigs* by Paul Galdone, Clarion Books, 1970. Copyright © 1970 by Paul Galdone, renewed 1998 by Joanna C. Galdone. Reproduced by permission of Houghton Mifflin Harcourt Publishing Company. All rights reserved.

When the little pig heard the wolf on the roof—

Figure 6.3. Illustration from *The Three Little Pigs* by Paul Galdone, Clarion Books, 1970. Copyright © 1970 by Paul Galdone, renewed 1998 by Joanna C. Galdone. Reproduced by permission of Houghton Mifflin Harcourt Publishing Company. All rights reserved.

We're Comin' Out of the Kitchen!

In traditional tale variants, the sole female character quickly vanishes from view, even though her poverty sets the plot in motion. The story sequence is played out among male antagonists. Our next project, then, re-orients this tale by underscoring its masculinist bias, often ignored or overlooked due to hegemonic narrative conventions, as well as by studying critical essays and retellings that reflect the changes achieved through the

Figure 6.4. "The little pig quickly put on the cover again, boiled up the wolf, and ate him for supper." Illustration from *The Three Little Pigs* by Paul Galdone, Clarion Books, 1970. Copyright © 1970 by Paul Galdone, renewed 1998 by Joanna C. Galdone. Reproduced by permission of Houghton Mifflin Harcourt Publishing Company. All rights reserved.

successive "waves" of the feminist movement. The wide range of notable feminist writings made selection quite difficult; nevertheless, considerations of coherence and continuity led me to Shoshana Felman's "Women and Madness: The Critical Phallacy" (1975) and Luce Irigaray's "Women on the Market (*Le marché des femmes*)" (1978). Both punning titles present opportunities for discussion.

Felman's inventive spelling of "phallacy" constitutes a portmanteau (like the contemporary "podcast" combining iPod and broadcast) that mixes and matches two words, blending their sounds and meanings. However, speaking of "The Critical Phallacy" also invokes two theoretical contexts: the one is the American critics Wimsatt and Beardsley's authoritative essays on the intentional and affective fallacies; the other, the French psychoanalyst Jacques Lacan's identification of the phallus as the "privileged signifier" that enables the subject's entry into the symbolic order of language and culture ("Signification" 287). Lacan distinguishes between the positions said to "govern the relations between the sexes": namely, "a 'to be' and a 'to have'" the phallus. In theory, all subjects are marked by the desire *to be the phallus*—that is, to be the object of the desire of the Other—and *to have the phallus* insofar as those in the masculine position wield this symbolization of power, prowess, and vitality over others. In social practice, however, although these dual trends intermingle in human beings, the one desire is strongly identified with femininity and the other, with masculinity (289–90).

Felman's essay presents critical and metacritical analyses of several texts, which we scrutinize before focusing on an aspect of her critique that is highly significant for our discussions. Briefly delineated, Felman begins by comparing between American feminist Phyllis Chesler's *Women and Madness* (1973) and French feminist Luce Irigaray's *Speculum of the Other Woman* (1974). "In contrast to Phyllis Chesler," Felman observes, "Luce Irigaray interrogates not the empirical voice of women and their subjective testimony, but the key theoretical writings of men—fundamental texts in philosophy and in psychoanalysis—which, in one way or another, involve the concept of femininity" (3). Felman then closely reads Honoré de Balzac's three-part novella *Adieu* (1830) and two scholarly commentaries published in a 1974 edition intended to introduce the book and explain its importance. Most strikingly, Felman writes, both commentaries concentrate only on *Adieu*'s second part, about a war episode: "The main plot, which consists of the story of a woman's madness (episodes I and III), is somehow completely neglected in favor of the subplot (episode II), a historical narrative whose function is to describe the events which preceded and occasioned the madness. The 'explication' thus excludes two things: the madness and the woman.

Viewed through the eyes of the two academic critics, *Adieu* becomes a story about the suffering of men" (5). This "forgetting" or elision is not merely symptomatic of particularized oversights but of a widespread sociocultural phenomenon: a "censorship mechanism" that produces "a symbolic eradication of women from the world of literature" (6).

By way of analogy, we recall the male-centered plot of "The Three Little Pigs" and its omission of the mother's story, except for cursory mention of her failure to provide for her offspring. The word "piggish" assumes extratextual associations in this context. To alleviate the oppressive atmosphere that has settled like a pall in the classroom, I promise our prospects will lighten up when we turn to the story as retold by Steven Kellogg. But, before the pleasures of the text, there remains more preliminary work to be done.

Hence we invoke the phallocentrism of Freudian and Lacanian psychoanalysis already discussed, as well as the categorization of women's social role in Lévi-Strauss's *Elementary Structures of Kinship* (1949), which posits the circulation and exchange of women as "gifts" between men in both primitive and contemporary societies. We then move fast forward to Irigaray's critique of psychoanalysis and the structuralist analysis of women as "infrastructure," as commodities and objects of transaction, in representative passages from "Women on the Market":

> [A]ll the social regimes of 'History' are based on the exploitation of one 'class' of producers, namely, women. Whose reproductive use value (reproductive of children and of the labor force) and whose constitution as exchange value underwrite the symbolic order as such, without any compensation in kind going to them for that 'work.' For such compensation would imply a double system of exchange, that is, a shattering of the monopolization of the proper name (and of what it signifies as appropriative power) by father-men. (173)

Irigaray's tone in this passage, with its characteristic intermingling of outrage and irony, matches a rhetorical strategy that brandishes a rejection of "proper" language—the grammar of the fathers—and a frequent deployment of quotation marks of protest. Added to her critique of the symbolic paternal order, Irigaray urges women to surmount their conditioning as commodity-objects, to take part in the sociopolitical economy, and to reinvent themselves as agent-subjects who carry out transactions and exchanges. But, as she states in her cautiously utopian conclusion, "Not by reproducing, by copying the 'phallocratic' models that have the force of law today, but by socializing in a different way the relation to nature, matter, the body, language, and desire" (191).

"*Le marché des femmes*," aptly translated as "Women on the Market," may thus be read as prestaging the clarion call of Irigaray's closing statement. Typically, the English idiom means available for sale, as in: several attractive commodities/properties/women are coming on the market. However, it is also used to denote agency, as in: she is on the market for a new car, indicating that *she* wants to buy something; and, similarly: "The land acquired by women on the market often escapes the restrictions and limitations placed on customary land by men-dominated family and lineages" (World Bank 138). The preposition "on" becomes a cognate of "in" or "atop," as in the *Guardian's* headline, "Changing Faces: Three Women making their Mark on the Beauty Market," whose URL switches "in" for "on": "changing-faces-women-making-their-mark-in-the-beauty-market" (Fetto). Likewise, Irigaray's polyvalent title in French denotes not only women for sale but also women as sellers and buyers. Moreover, the past participle of the verb "*marcher*" (to walk, advance, go), is "*marché*," suggesting women on the march, no longer merchandise but, rather, moving onward.

In reading Felman and Irigaray against the hegemonic establishment, Kellogg's adaptation of "Blowing the House In" provides an illustration of second-wave feminism—of a woman doing it for herself with financial finesse and mercantile success. No wimpy, weepy old sow, Serafina abounds in entrepreneurial spirit. She starts up a thriving business (saying "I want to bring WAFFLES to the world!"), educates her piglets at Hog Hollow Academy, and, handing over her successful "Wheeled Wafflery" to them, she retires to the Gulf of Pasta ("If you ever need my help, you can call me there"). Clearly, Serafina needs nobody's help. The wafflery prospers, and life hums along: Percy weaves a cozy straw bungalow, Pete assembles a log cabin, and Prudence constructs a brick house.

But utopias are boring, narratively speaking, and so along comes a dystopic wolf named "Tempesto" to upset the happy waffle cart: "I HATE waffles! . . . I want YOU!" Soon the wolf is battering at the pigs' doors and huffing away: "The two brothers were blown clear to the brick cottage, where Prudence whisked them safely inside." Tempesto promises to "blast this pigsty into pebbles," but falling short of his promise, he decides to descend the chimney. Mother to the rescue! Her well-timed return saves the day and the three pigs too. Serafina strategically positions a waffle iron in the fireplace, so that rather than turning piggies into sausages, the wolf becomes a WOLFFLE. But, although temptingly smothered in butter and maple syrup, the three pigs do not eat him up. Instead, after retiring Tempesto to the Gulf of Pasta to mellow on the beach, they happily wed and rapidly (re)produce a commercial dynasty: world-wide-waffles or, for short, www. "My dream has come true," announces Serafina.

We're Comin' Out of the Kitchen?

To pause and take stock: no ambiguity surrounds the "women on the market" in this instance. Sisters *are* standing on their own two feet. This is a story precisely designed "to celebrate," and instantiate, "The conscious liberation of the female state! / Mothers, daughters and their daughters too" ("Sisters"). Nonetheless, some ambivalence may persist among readers, for women are not exactly coming out of the kitchen here. On the contrary, Serafina takes the kitchen with her everywhere she goes: "Each morning at dawn the family pushed Serafina's invention [a waffle iron on wheels] from hamlet to hamlet, delighting passersby." This observation begets arguments that bring us to interrogate the notion of "the female state": what kind of nation or identity is that?

In Kellogg's version, traditional sex-gender roles are not so much undermined or challenged as straightforwardly reversed and thereby indirectly endorsed. Opposites, I underscore, are often close enough. This retelling reinforces binary divisions by opposing energetic, ambitious Serafina and pragmatic, well-defended Prudence to lackadaisical, imprudent Percy and Pete. Like standard damsels in distress, the boys soon require rescue. So when Tempesto yells, "Open up, Pork Chop!" Percy scribbles a panicky plea on a paper airplane, "Help, Save Me," that fortuitously reaches Serafina in time for her to arrive and wafflize the wolf. Moreover, role reversals notwithstanding, some things do not change at all. Her heterosexual progeny marry their fertile porcine sweethearts, for "it wasn't long before Serafina found herself surrounded by dozens of grandchildren," and at one busy corner above this text, a mama bird holds the hand of her cute baby bird.

But this story could be retold otherwise. By overturning (which is to say, by querying and queering) the waffle- or applecart of heterosexual normativity, binary gender roles, and, no less significantly, representations of personhood—signs and cues of identities constructed in a social world—we can keep moving on.

Turning to the flip-up *Three Little Pigs* (2004) produced by Child's Play and illustrated by Richard Johnson, we explore the ways in which this adaptation may be said to exemplify the achievements of third-wave feminism and of queer theory. In the first instance, this version quietly assumes, without beating proverbial drums or using verbal pyrotechnics, that women are competent, autonomous persons (and not vendible or money-making mechanisms at the service of others) and, in the second, that gender is not an inherent, essential, or original category but rather, as a type of masquerade, it can be "worn," acted out, or performed. All gendering, as Judith Butler argues, "is a performance that *produces* the illusion of an inner sex or essence or psychic gender core; it *produces* . . . through the gesture, the move, the gait (that array of corporeal theatrics understood as gender presentation) the illusion of an inner depth" (317). By extrapolation, the flip-up variant uses words and images to undermine the ontological illusions generated by homo-/hetero-sexual and story regimes.

"Once upon a time," this story begins, "there were three little pigs who lived in a fine house with their mother. One day she decided that it was time for them to go out into the world. The pigs were very excited and promised to visit their mother often." Unlike the teary departures from dilapidated hovels shown in numerous versions, these pigs leave a substantial home with hand waves and smiles. But before sending them off, their liberal and literate mother instructs them in the signs of mortal danger. Holding up a book, she presents a picture of a blandly smiling wolf that flips open to disclose the watchful eyes, pointy teeth, and readied tongue behind the act of imposture labeled "smile" (figs. 6.5 and 6.6). Had the siblings been equally attentive to mother's lesson, there would have been no story to tell at all.

In contrast to Kellogg's version, the three little pigs remain unmarked by essentializing names in this adaptation. Nevertheless, one of the pigs evidently feels "like a woman" and assumes the cultural position of "femininity," as indicated visually, at first, through her sartorial preferences: a ponytail and mauve-pink dress. The other two visibly imitate boys and adopt recognizable markings of "masculinity": blue and green T-shirts, with caps perched on short-cut hair. Subsequently, however, personality differences and pronominal categories come into play and further distinguish among the pigs: "[A] farmer walked by with a cart full of straw. 'That straw would be perfect to build a house with,' said the first little pig, who was very lazy. . . . He bought the whole cartful"; then, an old woman appears with a load of sticks, which appeals to the second pig, "who was a little bit lazy. He bought the bundle." Finally, a man with a wheelbarrow full of bricks comes along: "'Those bricks would be perfect to build a house with,' said the third little pig. 'They will be strong and safe. . . .' She bought the whole load there and then." This pig unfurls building designs (fig. 6.7). She plans ahead; she holds a literal blueprint for the future. She is clearly the child of the wise woman in the fine house.

So when the wolf slides down her chimney, he falls headfirst into the pot, whose surface, flipped up, shows his phallic appendages—bowler hat, tie, and tail—sinking fast (fig. 6.8). On the last page, the T-shirted pigs have learned a lesson from their skirted sibling: "Tomorrow, we'll build two more houses—and this time, we'll make them both out of bricks!" This retelling, I propose, redefines what feminism entails and, simultaneously, subverts sex-gender identities in ways that palpably differ from the feminist storybook previously examined. The Child's Play version therefore

Figures 6.5 and 6.6. *Three Little Pigs*. Illustrated by Richard Johnson, *Child's Play*, 2004. Reproduced by kind permission of Child's Play (International) Ltd. *Three Little Pigs* © 2004 Child's Play. First published 2004 by Child's Play. All rights reserved.

Meanwhile, the third little pig came across a man with a wheelbarrow full of bricks. "Those bricks would be perfect to build a house with," said the third little pig. "They will be strong and safe. A strong house is worth spending time on." She bought the whole load there and then.

Figure 6.7. "She bought the whole load there and then." *Three Little Pigs*. Illustrated by Richard Johnson, *Child's Play*, 2004. Reproduced by kind permission of Child's Play (International) Ltd. *Three Little Pigs* © 2004 Child's Play. First published 2004 by Child's Play. All rights reserved.

provides a flippant yet serious introduction to the course segment on queer theory in which we study Michel Foucault's "The Repressive Hypothesis" (1976) and Butler's "Imitation and Gender Insubordination" (1993). Although a detailed account of the sociohistorical grounds for the impact of these texts is beyond the scope of my essay, it is important to note that during the 1980s and early 1990s, second-wave feminism receded, even as many of its legal and cultural gains endured, and gave way to third-wave feminism and postfeminism, which—further contesting gender-role expectations and stereotypes in North America—expanded the notion of

Figure 6.8. *Three Little Pigs*. Illustrated by Richard Johnson. *Child's Play*, 2004. Reproduced by kind permission of Child's Play (International) Ltd. *Three Little Pigs* © 2004 Child's Play. First published 2004 by Child's Play. All rights reserved.

"the female state" to include persons of diverse color, ethnicities, nationalities, and sexualities.

In addition, although ideational continuities may be extended from feminist criticisms of patriarchy, postcolonial analyses of imperialism, and deconstructive critiques of metaphysical binaries (in which the first term, say, male/female or white/nonwhite, is always already superordinate in status) to gay-lesbian studies and queer theory, the significant differences between these contestations of heterosexual hegemony need to be underscored. Whereas gay-lesbian activists would constitute and sustain homosexual identity, queer theorists would destabilize sex and gender identities at large.

Queer theory aims not only at dismantling male/female and masculine/feminine dichotomies but also at deconstructing notions of fixed sex-gender orientation. For queer theorists, to militate for homosexuality as an essential category is to uphold an illusory construction: an imposture or imposition of identity. Where gay-lesbian studies would consolidate the homosexual "nation," granting it the civil and moral legitimation of heterosexuality, queer-theory advocates would nullify not just the oppressive regulatory regimes anatomized in Foucault's *History of Sexuality* but the fabrication of singular, stable identities and sexualities. As Butler writes, "there is no original or primary gender that drag imitates, but [rather] *gender is a kind of imitation for which there is no original*; in fact, it is a kind of imitation that produces the very notion of the original as an *effect* and consequence of the imitation itself" (313).

Back to School

From the coded dress and construction materials that distinguish the pigs in the flip-up version, we can learn about the semiotic systems that (pre)occupy us. At this point, therefore, we return to Saussure's *Course*, and especially to his insight-qua-dictum that linguistic signs, considered separately, have no positive value. Only as part of an interdependent system does each sign acquire its relational significance and value. In and of itself, a thing is nothing. In other words—Saussure's, as transmitted by his devoted students: "The conceptual side of value is made up solely of relations and differences with respect to the other terms of language"; "Signs function, then, not through their intrinsic value but through their relative position"; and "in language there are only differences *without positive terms*. . . . [But] when we consider the sign in its totality, we have something that is positive in its own class" (117–18, 120).

To exemplify Saussure's approach to meaning, as well as his accurate prediction that linguistics would become a part of "semiology"—"[a] *science that studies the life of signs within society*" (16)—we turn to Lévi-Strauss's "The Structural Study of Myth," first published in the *Journal of American Folklore* in 1955. Lévi-Strauss's avowed motivation is the need to introduce law and order or, in a word, structure into the chaotic field of myth studies. With varying degrees of explicitness, however, he also contests the alleged reduction of mythology into an "outlet for repressed feelings." He thus defines his contribution against Freud's and Jung's: "a clever dialectic," the anthropologist warns, "will always find a way to pretend that a meaning has been unraveled" (171).

In the first instance, Lévi-Strauss's quarrel with psychoanalysis, I propose, cannot but demonstrate Saussure's axiom: "only differences *without positive terms*" generate signifying values. The structural study of myths (including fairy tales) is what it is because it is *not* predicated on psychoanalytic interpretations of signification. In the second instance, Lévi-Strauss purposely defines myth in oppositional terms that underscore its difference from other linguistic phenomena: "Its substance does not lie in its style, its original music, or its syntax, but in the *story* it tells"; therefore, mythic singularity consists not in "isolated elements . . . but only in the way those elements are combined" into specific patterns. It is not what Lévi-Strauss designates "*gross constituent units*" but the combinatory arrangement of such units that produce a myth (174).

Illustrator and designer Steven Guarnaccia's adaptation of *The Three Little Pigs*, subtitled *An Architectural Tale* (2010), recasts the tale in a new direction that, presumably, would be recognizable and even welcome to Saussure. Each pig develops a distinctive style of (self-)construction, perhaps because he "lived in a big house in the forest," which is modeled on the landmark Gamble House (1908) designed by the architectural firm Greene and Greene for David and Mary Gamble of the Procter & Gamble Company (fig. 6.9). Guarnaccia's variant is simultaneously oriented toward historic reality—actual people, buildings, and furnishings—and fairy-tale fabrication: "One day the three pigs said good-bye to their mother and went off to make their way in the world." The illustrated page shows them wearing different yet relatedly male-coded suits, carrying implements dissimilarly related to architecture, and setting out in different directions from the same green mansion.

The mother's pictorial and narrative role here is limited to waving good-bye to the threesome from the three-tiered threshold of a three-storied house of fiction. "Three is a Magic Number," as Bob Dorough sings in the animated

Figure 6.9. The Gamble House (1908) designed by Greene and Greene for David and Mary Gamble of the Procter & Gamble Company. Steven Guarnaccia. *The Three Little Pigs: An Architectural Tale*. Illustrated by Steven Guarnaccia, Abrams Books for Young Readers, 2010. Steven Guarnaccia. All rights reserved to Maurizio Corraini s.r.l.

television series, *Multiplication Rock*, and the folkloric rule of three or "third referent," in Lévi-Strauss's phrase ("Structural Study" 173), prevails in the visual and verbal components of Guarnaccia's inventive text. In actuality, however, the Gambles did have three sons who followed distinguished yet distinct career paths.[5] Moreover, in the official family photograph, "The Gambles in Pasadena," Mrs. Gamble and two sons wear eyeglasses as illustrated with the meticulous historical accuracy that characterizes the entire magical, porky, and yet verifiable tale retold here (fig. 6.10).

Thus, reorienting the reader invited to visit a variety of fantastical houses made of scraps ("straw"), glass ("sticks") and, lastly, stone and concrete ("bricks")—all based on functionally similar yet graphically different structures created by world-famous architects and designers—this cunning variant is perhaps best described by its barcoded label: "THREE LITTLE PIGS ARCH TALE." The illustrated houses and objects appear "through reciprocal opposition within a fixed system," in which each item acquires

Figure 6.10. "The Gambles in Pasadena." Greene & Greene Archives, Gamble House. gamblehouse.org/the-gambles-in-pasadena. Greene and Greene Archives, Gamble House.

a value only when perceived against or with other items (Saussure 120). Clearly, a curvy chair is not a linear one, and a curvy armchair by Thonet is not a wiggly side chair by Frank Gehry, as shown on the inner front and back covers of Guarnaccia's book (fig. 6.11). Moreover, the evil wolf, sporting black-leather boots and jacket, does not arrive on his own two feet as in other versions. Possibly saving his breath for huffing and puffing, he rides a Voxan GTV 1200 motorbike designed by Philippe Starck. Structuralism elucidates our ability to get the picture, to apprehend material and nonmaterial phenomena, through the contrastive interplay of systemic elements.

Playtime

Saussurean insights into the linguistic sign pave the way for the study of Derridean deconstruction. This course segment contextualizes deconstruction in historic differential relation to the New Criticism and structuralism

Figure 6.11. Steven Guarnaccia's *The Three Little Pigs: An Architectural Tale.* Illustrated by Steven Guarnaccia, Abrams Books for Young Readers, 2010. Steven Guarnaccia. All rights reserved to Maurizio Corraini s.r.l.

and, then, presents the thematics of *play* and *différance* through passages from Derrida's "Structure, Sign, and Play in the Discourse of the Human Sciences" (1966) and "Différance" (1968). Owing to practical considerations of space, my exposition here will briefly indicate several subjects discussed before proceeding to a text-case: David Wiesner's dazzling, ludic re-vision of the tale of three pigs (2001).

Chronologically, deconstruction was "born" in 1967, a year marked by the publication in France of Derrida's *Of Grammatology*, *Writing and Difference*, and *Speech and Phenomena*. Derrida initially brought deconstruction to Johns Hopkins University, then to Yale, and from there deconstructive thought (or what some regarded as a plague) began to spread. Thus many deconstructionists were first trained as New Critics or American formalists before seeking out the interpretive impasses and irreconcilable contradictions called "aporias." Nonetheless, for the most part, these critics did not discard the techniques of close reading; Derrida, too, who was trained in the tradition of *explication de texte*, continued to rigorously analyze the texts he dismantled. But some topical features seriously changed.

Most immediately, it is no longer only or even mainly literature that is now subject to scrutiny but texts in disciplines as diverse as structural anthropology, linguistics, philosophy, and psychoanalysis. Moreover, Derridean readers employ the tools of formalist criticism and structuralism to expose and subvert the closure of these disciplines, among others, within systems of meaning or truth. Rather than arriving at conclusive significations allegedly *present* within the discursive field of a poem or a myth—conclusions that presuppose a stable epistemological construct, an anchoring center or essence that shores up the entire structure—deconstructionists require close reading to dislocate such illusory centers and to expose the inevitable contradictions, indeterminacies, and aporias that perpetually destabilize truth claims. Deconstruction seeks to open texts, undo their preconstructions, and demonstrate their semantic *dissemination*: that is, how meaning is dispersed or scattered like seeds strewn over a field, or blown away like houses made of straw, sticks, and even bricks.

Thus, while resisting and negating any attempted synthesis of a given system and adopting an intensely quizzical and interrogative stance, Derridean analysis embraces, and celebrates, the infinite play of texts. Play —radically conceived before or beyond the binary alternations of center/margin, inside/outside, presence/absence, et cetera—acknowledges not just "the disruption of presence" but "the joyous affirmation of the play of the world . . . without truth, and without origin which is offered to an active interpretation. *This affirmation then determines the noncenter otherwise than as loss of the center*" ("Structure" 292). The spirit of play again prevails and gains momentum when Derrida coins the neologism *différance* (with an *a*), "which is neither a word nor a concept," and elaborates its dual value as difference *and* deferral of meaning in ways that repeatedly negate—especially through the insistence of his "neither/nor" locutions—or, at least, delay, defer, postpone an arrival at a final designation (*"Différance"* 7). Derrida thereby dramatizes the significance of *différance*, and of deconstruction, while simultaneously avoiding the closure of definition.

Ironically, disruptively, and perhaps with playful aforethought, Derrida presented "Structure, Sign, and Play" at a 1966 conference intended to expound and promote the interdisciplinary scope of structuralism, as well as to consolidate its theoretical traction in the United States. His incisive critique of Lévi-Strauss's structuralist anthropology and privileging of central or key terms presumed to transcend the structurality of differentially produced meaning "left the deepest mark on subsequent American thought. The structuralist 'movement' was no sooner granted an import license than it was pushed aside" (Norris 137). By the early 1970s, deconstruction, or what came to be called "poststructuralism," held sway, and it extends its influence to the present day.

The challenges posed by Derrida, the Big Bad Wolf of modern theory, appear far less threatening when the playfully liberating aspects of his approach to texts and contexts are foregrounded. Wiesner's *The Three Pigs* aptly demonstrates the Derridean undermining of sanctified metaphysical concepts, together with its continual deferrals and qualifications of definitive statement until negation becomes almost, if not quite, an affirmation and occasion for celebration. Possibly because the label "little" no longer describes these protagonists, an originary maternal cause is not required to begin (and be blamed for) their adventures. "Once upon a time," this tale recounts, "there were three pigs who went out into the world to seek their fortune."

Wiesner primarily uses a traditional pictorial style reminiscent of Victorian storybooks that is soon at odds with his text's unconventional content. Empty white borders thus initially frame each illustrated page; however, when Wiesner's wolf arrives at the straw house, his huffing and puffing blow the first pig out of the story and onto its margins. The action then unfolds or, rather, unravels in these framed and liminal spaces until the binarisms of center/margin, inside/outside, and other oppositions visibly collapse or dissolve, and narrative re-formations take shape on every page. On the one hand, as the straw house visibly disintegrates, we read that, predictably, "the wolf . . . ate the pig up"; on the other, with the pig now neither "outside" nor "inside" the storybook page, we see that the wolf has procured no pork dinner in return for his strenuous exhalations. Wiesner portrays a highly perplexed predator raising a fallen wall in search of the prey that got away. His predicament is heightened when, after he blows in the house of sticks, as storytelling convention dictates he must, pig one invites pig two to join him at the story's ostensible margins: "Come on—it's safe out here." Meanwhile, the wolf, deprived again of dinner, gets perceptibly thinner and thinner, even as the text mechanically expounds: "[he] ate the pig up." Pig three springs out of the illustration that shows his fine brick house and asks his brothers, "Why didn't you two get eaten up?" Likewise leaping off the page, a liberated pig replies: "We got away from that wolf . . . for good" (fig. 6.12).

The three pigs literalize the term "deconstruction" as they disassemble the old book that confined them, fold its pages into an airplane, and explore other storylands. From the absurdist rhyming landscape of "Hey diddle diddle, / The cat and the fiddle, / The cow jumped / over the moon," they pick up a musical cat who joins their journeys. No longer rule-bound by story lines or frames, they rescue a treasure-guarding dragon from a greedy king ("he sent his eldest son to slay the dragon and bring back the golden rose") and then decide to reassemble the brick house with playful *différance* and sans closure.

Figure 6.12. "Why didn't you two get eaten up?" "We got away from that wolf . . . for good." David Wiesner. Illustration from *The Three Pigs* by David Wiesner, Clarion Books. Copyright © 2001 by David Wiesner. Reprinted by permission of Clarion Books, an imprint of Houghton Mifflin Harcourt Publishing Company. All rights reserved.

Wiesner concludes with the sociable pigs, fiddler-cat, and dragon pictured contentedly at home, while the lone wolf, faded and framed in a window, stays outside this alternative family (fig. 6.13). Above it all, in unevenly slanted type, we read: "And they all lived happily ever aft"—with neither full stop nor more letters to close off this malleable, multilayered story.

Peace on Earth, Goodwill toward All

To bring this sampling of the uses of enchantment for teaching modern theory, and the uses of modern theory for re-orienting enchantment,

Figure 6.13. David Wiesner. *The Three Pigs*. Illustrated by David Wiesner, Clarion Books. Copyright © 2001 by David Wiesner. Reprinted by permission of Clarion Books, an imprint of Houghton Mifflin Harcourt Publishing Company. All rights reserved.

to something resembling closure, there remains that misanthropic wolf stuck in multiple stories intent on maligning and outsidering him as Not-Me, as rapacious Father, or as dangerous Other. So invoking lessons in postcolonialism, ecocriticism, antispeciesism, and pro-lupine (from the Latin *lupus*, wolf) discourse, I present a dissident tale, "The Three Little Wolves and the Big Bad Pig," in which Eugene Trivizas tells—and Helen Oxenbury shows—us a parable of war and peace. The nonhuman animals are not so much anthropomorphic figures here as allegorical representatives of a populace composed of different races and species. Issues of tolerance and compassion come to the fore, and yet through gently honed verbal and visual wit, this version circumvents the ponderous sermonizing often accompanying traditional allegories and moral tales: "Once upon a time there were three cuddly little wolves with soft fur and fluffy tales. . . . The first was black, the second was grey and the third white." Their mother, who announces "it is time for you to go out into the world," is yellow—but such differences amount to no difference for this familial group. All wolves are equal, and none are more equal than others, say, due to fur color.

Another tacit feature of this revision concerns the nonhuman animal dress code. Unlike many illustrated variants in which the protagonists are anthropomorphized through apparel befitting human animals, all of the creaturely participants—including the kangaroo who freely gives the three wolves lots of bricks; the beaver who donates buckets of concrete after the pig destroys their brick home; the rhinoceros who generously bestows barbed wire, iron bars, and padlocks after the pig smashes their concrete home; and the flamingo who shares a wheelbarrow of flowers after the pig dynamites the strongest, safest shelter imaginable—wear their proper, that is to say, apt and integral skins without material embellishment. Moreover, the various nonhumans share, rather than barter or sell, things; monetary exchanges for goods are not part of their story. Certain animal identity components thus remain intact, and anthropomorphization is partially curtailed, even though the characters necessarily speak and function in some ways like humans, for otherwise this tale could not be recognizably retold.

Other notable features distinguish Trivizas and Oxenbury's contemporary parable. For instance, the big bad pig never says he wants to *eat* the little cuddly wolves; nevertheless, he clearly has a nasty chip on his shoulders and destroys three houses. This mean streak may have formed because he has been long misunderstood and nobody ever invites him to play or visit. On the contrary, he is repeatedly left out: "The three little wolves were playing croquet in the garden. When they saw the big bad pig coming, they ran inside the house and locked the door"; again, "They were playing battledore and shuttlecock in the garden and when they saw the big bad pig coming, they ran inside their house and shut the door"; and so it goes until "sixty-seven padlocks" are closed when he appears. Now how would you feel if your pig-mentation locked all doors against you? In effect, the wolves do not quite see him "coming" but constantly, aggressively "prowling down the road," and often enough, what you see is what you get.

After the pig demolishes the strongholds jointly constructed by the wolves, they wisely conclude something is wrong with their materials and build a house of flowers (fig. 6.14). "It was a rather fragile house... but it was very beautiful," and evidently fragrant, for when the big bad pig arrives at their house, he sniffs the flower-full air and undergoes a conversion experience: "His heart became tender.... He started to sing and to dance the tarantella." He was, I suspect, an Italian (im)migrant into British folklore. Be that as it may, the wolves start including him in games like "pig-pog" and even invite him home for tea (fig. 6.15). Since hostilities are finally suspended and all live "happily together ever after," my own narrative about teaching modern theory with generous help from an oft-transformed tale may also presume or dream beyond its ending that someday the weapons industry will be redeployed to make ploughshares and establish community centers where old stories are recycled.

In the interim between dreaming and waking, however, a question remains: would any frequently retold fairy tale work just as well? Although a candid answer is—you never know until you try, I would hypothesize certain components account for this story's particular efficacy.[6] Unlike rags-to-riches or "rise" tales, "The Three Little Pigs" thematizes an archaic struggle not to obtain a treasure, crown, or peerless marriage but, rather, to retain something vital: life itself. Self-preservation and survival are at stake in this archetypal contestation. Instead of blind luck or magic helpers, only virtue—hard work and savvy responses to the existential menace embodied in the wolf—determines victory. Moreover, this tale differs from other survival stories in two ways: unlike gender-specific tales such as "Little Red Riding Hood" (ATU 333), the pigs' relative neutrality opens their narrative trajectories toward other than sexually oriented ones; and, unlike tales about infantile or juvenile protagonists such as "The Wolf and the Seven Young Kids" (ATU 123), the pigs' comparative maturity (leaving home), initiative (buying materials), ingenuity, and creativity (constructing houses) invite adaptations that build on their foundational story. Lastly but not exhaustively, it seems to me significant that three protagonists, rather than one or two, are involved. Three is the minimum number needed to suggest a *community* and represent a life-threatened group, species, or ethnicity. The proverb "two is company, three's a crowd"

Figure 6.14. Eugene Trivizas and Helen Oxenbury. *The Three Little Wolves and the Big Bad Pig*. Illustrated by Helen Oxenbury. Illustrations copyright © 1993 Helen Oxenbury. Published by Egmont UK Limited and used with permission.

Figure 6.15. Eugene Trivizas and Helen Oxenbury. *The Three Little Wolves and the Big Bad Pig*. Illustrated by Helen Oxenbury. Illustrations copyright © 1993 Helen Oxenbury. Published by Egmont UK Limited and used with permission.

acquires new meaning here. Whether all three survive or not, this story recurrently activates projective processes in its readers-users, who, knowingly and unknowingly, need to retell it for, and re-orient it toward, themselves.

Notes

1. Bruno Bettelheim's often questionable psychoanalytic interpretations notwithstanding, his overall approach to fairy tales persuasively demonstrates their affective significance.

2. George Orwell presciently used the phrase "cold war" in a 1945 article published two months after the United States bombed Hiroshima and Nagasaki. In "You and the Atomic Bomb," Orwell predicts a nuclear stalemate among

"two or three monstrous super-states, each possessed of a weapon by which millions of people can be wiped out in a few seconds."

3. See Alan Elms on the myths surrounding this quotation and its actual source in Princess Marie Bonaparte's journals of her analysis with Freud.

4. Jacobs credits Halliwell as the story's source in his notes (238).

5. Of the three sons, Cecil Huggins Gamble (1884–1956) worked his way up through the ranks of the Procter and Gamble Company, managed the family's financial interests, and was known for his civic, philanthropic, and religious activities; Sidney David Gamble (1890–1968) visited China extensively, doing social work and surveys for the YMCA, and became an outstanding photographer; Clarence James Gamble (1894–1966), a Harvard-trained physician and researcher, was an influential advocate for planned parenthood and the international birth control movement. Further information about the Gamble family and their landmark residence may be found at the Pacific Coast Architecture Database (pcad.lib.washington.edu/building/75) and the Gamble House website (gamblehouse.org).

6. I am indebted to Mayako Murai and Lewis Seifert for articulating this issue and helping me to think through possible explanations.

Works Cited

Bettelheim, Bruno. *The Uses of Enchantment: The Meaning and Importance of Fairy Tales*. Random House, 1976.

Butler, Judith. "Imitation and Gender Insubordination." *The Lesbian and Gay Studies Reader*, edited by Henry Abelove, Michèle Aina Barale, and David M. Halperin, Routledge, 1993, pp. 307–20.

Derrida, Jacques. "Différance." 1968. *Margins of Philosophy*, translated by Alan Bass, University of Chicago Press, 1982, pp. 3–27.

———. "Structure, Sign, and Play in the Discourse of the Human Sciences." 1966. *Writing and Difference*, translated by Alan Bass, University of Chicago Press, 1978, pp. 278–93.

Dorough, Bob. "Three Is a Magic Number." 1973. *Schoolhouse Rock! Multiplication Rock*, season 1, episode 1, www.youtube.com/watch?v=aU4pyiB-kq0.

Elms, Alan C. "Apocryphal Freud: Sigmund Freud's Most Famous 'Quotations' and Their Actual Sources." *Annual of Psychoanalysis*, vol. 29, 2001, pp. 83–104.

Felman, Shoshana. "Women and Madness: The Critical Phallacy." *Diacritics*, vol. 5, no. 4, 1975, pp. 2–10.

Fetto, Funmi, Pandora Sykes, and Eva Wiseman. "Changing Faces: Three Women making their Mark on the Beauty Market." *Guardian*, 3 Sept. 2017, www.theguardian.com/fashion/2017/sep/03/changing-faces-women-making-their-mark-in-the-beauty-market.

Foucault, Michel. "The Repressive Hypothesis." 1976. *The History of Sexuality Volume I: An Introduction*, translated by Robert Hurley, Vintage, 1980, pp. 17–49.

"The Fox and the Geese." 1856. *A Treasury of Pleasure Books for Young People*, edited by J. Cundall, Sampson Low & Son, 12 Oct. 2017, archive.org/stream/treasurypleasure00cundiala/treasurypleasure00cundiala_djvu.txt.

Freud, Sigmund. *The Interpretation of Dreams*. 1900. Vol. 4. *The Standard Edition of the Complete Psychological Works of Sigmund Freud*, edited and translated by James Strachey, 24 vols., Hogarth Press, 1953–74.

———. *Totem and Taboo: Some Points of Agreement Between the Mental Lives of Savages and Neurotics*. 1913. Vol. 13. *The Standard Edition of the Complete Psychological Works of Sigmund Freud*, edited and translated by James Strachey, 24 vols., Hogarth Press, 1953–74.

Frost, Robert. "The Road Not Taken." 1916. *The Mentor Book of Major American Poets*, edited by Oscar Williams and Edwin Honig, New American Library, 1962, p. 250.

"The Gambles in Pasadena." Greene & Greene Archives, Gamble House, University of Southern California, gamblehouse.org/the-gambles-in-pasadena/.

Guarnaccia, Steven. *The Three Little Pigs: An Architectural Tale*. Illustrated by Steven Guarnaccia, Abrams Books for Young Readers, 2010.

Irigaray, Luce. "Women on the Market." 1978. *This Sex Which Is Not One*, translated by Catherine Porter, Cornell University Press, 1985, pp. 170–91.

Jacobs, Joseph. Notes and References. *English Fairy Tales*, 3rd ed., illustrated by John D. Batten, Dover Publications, 1967, pp. 229–61.

———. "The Story of the Three Little Pigs." 1898. *English Fairy Tales*, 3rd ed., illustrated by John D. Batten, Dover Publications, 1967, pp. 68–72.

Jakobson, Roman, and Claude Lévi-Strauss. "Charles Baudelaire's 'Les Chats.'" 1962. *The Structuralists: From Marx to Lévi-Strauss*, edited by Richard T.

de George and Fernande M. de George, translated by F. M de George, Anchor Books, 1972, pp. 124–46.

Kellogg, Steven. *The Three Little Pigs*. Illustrated by Steven Kellogg, HarperCollins, 1997.

Lacan, Jacques. *The Seminar of Jacques Lacan: Book VII The Ethics of Psychoanalysis 1959–1960*. Translated by Dennis Porter, edited by Jacques-Alain Miller, W. W. Norton, 1992.

———. "The Signification of the Phallus." 1966. *Écrits: A Selection*, translated by Alan Sheridan, W. W. Norton, 1977, pp. 281–91.

Lévi-Strauss, Claude. *The Elementary Structures of Kinship*. 1949. Translated by James Harle Bell, John Richard von Sturmer, and Rodney Needham, Beacon Press, 1969.

———. "The Structural Study of Myth." 1955. *The Structuralists: From Marx to Lévi-Strauss*, edited by Richard T. de George and Fernande M. de George, translated by F. M. de George, Anchor Books, 1972, pp. 169–94.

Norris, Christopher. *Contest of Faculties: Philosophy and Theory after Deconstruction*. Methuen, 1985.

Orwell, George. "You and the Atomic Bomb." *Tribune*, 19 Oct. 1945, www.orwellfoundation.com/the-orwell-foundation/orwell/essays-and-other-works/you-and-the-atom-bomb/. Accessed 8 Oct. 2017.

Saussure, Ferdinand de. *Course in General Linguistics.* 1916. Edited by Charles Bally and Albert Sechehaye, translated by Wade Baskin, Fontana/Collins, 1959.

"Sisters Are Doin' It for Themselves." *Eurythmics*. Lyrics by Annie Lennox and Dave Stewart, produced by David A. Stewart, RCA Records, 1985, www.azlyrics.com/lyrics/eurythmics/sistersaredoinitforthemselves.html. Accessed 26 Oct. 2017.

The Three Little Pigs. Illustrated by Paul Galdone, Clarion Books, 1970.

The Three Little Pigs. A Peepshow Book. Illustrated by Karen Acosta, Intervisual Communications, 1977.

Three Little Pigs. Illustrated by Richard Johnson, Child's Play, 2004.

Trivizas, Eugene, and Helen Oxenbury. *The Three Little Wolves and the Big Bad Pig*. Illustrated by Helen Oxenbury, Egmont Books, 2003.

Wiesner, David. *The Three Pigs*. Illustrated by David Wiesner, Clarion Books, 2001.

Wimsatt, William K., and Monroe C. Beardsley. "The Affective Fallacy." 1949. *The Verbal Icon: Studies in the Meaning of Poetry*, University of Kentucky Press, 1954, pp. 21–39.

———. "The Intentional Fallacy." 1946. *The Verbal Icon: Studies in the Meaning of Poetry*, University of Kentucky Press, 1954, pp. 3–18.

World Bank, Food and Agriculture Organization, International Fund for Agricultural Development. *Gender in Agriculture Sourcebook*. The International Bank for Reconstruction and Development/The World Bank, 2009.

7

Adults Reclaiming Fairy Tales through Cinema

Popular Fairy-Tale Movie Adaptations from the Past Decade

Aleksandra Szugajew

PICTURE THE DAZZLING CHARLIZE Theron, draped in gold, face contorted, and captured midscream, with black liquid dripping down from her mouth and flakes of gold dispersing around her. Now try to recall the sharp, intriguing features of Angelina Jolie, but imagine her with blood-red lips, monstrous black horns, and huge, powerful wings. Neither of these actresses nor scenes is likely to be associated with a children's motion picture. Yet both described scenes appear in recent cinematic fairy-tale adaptations (*Snow White and the Huntsman* and *Maleficent*, respectively). Such images are a staple of the clearly emergent trend of fairy-tale movie adaptations aimed at an adult audience, which has been growing in strength over the past decade. These productions are always live-action instead of animated, and are decidedly darker than their cartoon predecessors.

Using the examples of the following American big-production films[1]: *Red Riding Hood* (2011), *Snow White and the Huntsman* (2012), *Hansel and Gretel: Witch Hunters* (2013), *Maleficent* (2014), and *The Huntsman* (2016), which are all (perhaps apart from *Maleficent*) explicitly aimed at an older audience (than most animated fairy tales),[2] I will outline two strategies Hollywood[3] adopts in order to market its product to adults: *the appeal to the origin* and *the appeal to darkness* of the fairy tale. Through an analysis of the patterns of the narrative construction in these films as well as their advertising, I will remark on popular culture's engagement with the fairy tale and its transformation.

What I have termed as the *appeal to the origin* can be seen as either the film referring to the oral origin of a given fairy tale, suggesting that the popularized children's version of the tale is far from the true version of it (e.g., in the film's promotional posters) or as a strategy used in the plot to add a depth[4] to the tale's characters, providing a background story and motivation, moving a character beyond "stereotypes" (Zipes, "Breaking" 352). The *appeal to darkness*, on the other hand, has more to do with the setting of the story and the characters rather than the plot itself. The word *dark*, which in popular culture is often treated as synonymous to adult, is frequently used to signal a return, a re-orientation and contrast to the Disney fairy-tale version. The use of this appeal is closely linked to the use of film genres, which, in turn, often fix the target audience group too. The genres used in fairy-tale movie adaptations are horror, fantasy, and sometimes the history genre. In creating a sense of darkness, a mix of all three is usually applied. I will discuss the uses of film genres later in this chapter.

The presence of fairy tales in cinema has already been critically addressed in *Fairy Tale Films: Visions of Ambiguity*, an important and informative work on the new medium for fairy tales, edited by Pauline Greenhill and Sidney Eve Matrix. The contributors to this volume discuss, among other issues, how by the return to their origin fairy-tale films "manifest the resurrection of the sexual, violent, and supernatural elements of folktale that existed in oral tradition but were censored for children's literature" (8–9). Greenhill and Matrix, in their introduction to *Fairy Tale Films*, propose that what makes a fairy-tale film adult is that it "undoubtedly implicate[s] adult lives and relationships" (4) and, indeed, all of the selected films either introduce new or expand on existing relationships in the adapted fairy tale. The editors of *Fairy Tale Films* also note how "contemporary, sometimes radical, and innovative filmmakers . . . appear to have returned to the roots of folklore's darker elements" (8–9). I developed this "return" and "darker elements" into the two strategies to appeal to the audience in order to showcase their presence in the structure of recent fairy-tale film adaptations.

What this chapter aims to accomplish is to demonstrate through a brief comparative analysis of the selected films how some contemporary fairy-tale film adaptations share certain underlying principles that not only enable them to target an adult audience but, perhaps more importantly, are an expression of the values of modern society and global culture. Examining the structure of a text through the analysis of recurring motifs in multiple texts in order to extract a common pattern is a critical approach that began in the 1920s with the works of Vladimir Propp and later Claude Levi-Strauss. While my analysis of these films was certainly inspired by the work of both Propp and Levi-Strauss, it is not an application of either of their theories. Through the discussion of the two strategies (*appeals*) I proposed and their influence on the narrative of fairy-tale films, I want to reveal how the appeal to the origin (of both fairy tales and individual fairy-tale characters) and the addition of dark elements adapt the classic forms of tales to fit into a modern folk narrative.

Evolution of the Fairy Tale

The fairy tale, as a genre, has over time proven to have incredible adaptive abilities; it has moved from the oral tradition to literature, and in the twentieth century it has progressed to film. Despite the centuries and changes of medium, fairy tales have managed to remain relevant. Jack Zipes, in *Why Fairy Tales Stick,* suggests that fairy tales survived because they are memes: replicable units of information. The creator of the term *meme*, Richard Dawkins, drew comparisons between the survival of a meme and evolution, as did Daniel Dennett. Continuing with this point of view, the evolution of the fairy tale genre could be illustrated with Dennett's bacteria analogy. In *From Bacteria to Bach* Dennett discusses evolution and how improbable it was those four billion years ago for two simple cells to collide and create something better (Kindle loc 241). But they did. This, as he claims, was "the first successful instance of technology transfer, a case of two different sets of competences . . . being united into something bigger and better" (Kindle loc 241). Consider then, for a moment, the fairy tale as a bacterium; a simple prokaryotic cell (fairy tale) through collision was engulfed by another, bigger cell (literature) and through this endosymbiotic union, "this conjoined duo reproduced more successfully" (Kindle loc 253). This analogy portrays the fairy tale's move from the oral tradition to the literary one as adaptation. It ensured the genre's survival. However, what this move also did was establish certain variants of tales as dominant. The tales gathered by Perrault or the Grimm brothers were presumably just a few of the many stories present in the oral tradition, so already by selecting a specific tale variant these collectors contributed to the establishment of a dominant tale variant. Additionally, bearing in mind the literary practices of the times as well as their target readers, these authors edited and rewrote the tales they gathered, recreating a given oral tale for their purposes. For example, "Little Red Riding Hood" according to the oral tradition was significantly less conservative[5] than the versions written by Perrault or the Brothers Grimm (Tatar). Nevertheless, along with the increase in literacy, the popularity of literature instilled the literary version by the Brothers Grimm "Little Red Cap" in people's minds. Literature, in other words, both preserved fairy tales and fixed them.

Within the literary medium, the fairy tale genre evolved further when in the twentieth and the twenty-first centuries authors such as Angela Carter, Robert Coover, Emma Donoghue, and Neil Gaiman published their literary rewritings of fairy tales. These rewritings have spurred on the process of reversion of the fairy tale to its dark, adult origin. Now, returning to the bacteria analogy, these dark and adult motifs in fairy tales have been there all along; they existed in the larger cell of literature. What these postmodern authors have done is access hidden information, expose and elaborate on the social problems present in fairy tales. The re-orientation of the fairy-tale genre toward adults began already during this literary revival of the genre, which was, however, overshadowed by its evolution into a new medium: film.

Fairy Tales on the Screen

Cinema proclaimed itself as "the most significant twentieth-century art form/ form of entertainment" (Bennett et al. 9) and it continues to be one in the twenty-first century. It is quite logical, thus, that the fairy-tale genre progressed to the next dominant cultural art form. Fairy tales have been present in cinema since its very conception and, as Marina Warner states, "the magic of wonder tales and folklore were key inspirations" (Greenhill and Matrix 6). Perhaps it was this characteristic feature of "wonder" that made fairy tales and the moving pictures such a suitable couple. The first moving pictures elicited wonder and amazement from their audience, just as tales of magic would. This aspect of wonder in both cinema and fairy tales is present in fairy-tale film adaptations. These films are visually striking, impressing the audience with carefully constructed images (scenes) as well as action. Walt Disney's first feature film, *Snow White and the Seven Dwarfs* (1937), for example, was at its time an impressive feat of animation. But this visual appeal had the side effect of further fixing certain aspects of fairy tales. Disney's versions, for example, continued to be directed at children (much like the Brothers Grimm's) and promoted the famous "and they lived happily ever after" motif (which, thanks to Disney, became essential for the genre) for a long time. These animated versions also further fixed the fairy-tale canon. Presently, the version of "Snow White" or "Cinderella" with which most people are acquainted is the Disney version. This "fixing" of the tale involves not only the plot but also the elements of the narrative, such as the characters' physical appearance. The influence of the Disney version is apparent in, for example, the TV series *Once Upon a Time* (2011), in which the characters often appear in costumes inspired by the Disney version,[6] as if the recognition of a character was only possible through this visual reference, or the company's own productions, such as *Maleficent*.

As something that over the years has become closely related to the concept of childhood, fairy tales for a long time belonged mainly to the domain of children. The twenty-first century, however, has seen an increase of fairy-tale movies directed toward adults or teenagers and adults (PG-13). There were, of course, fairy-tale-inspired movies aimed at adults in the twentieth century, like the 1997 *Snow White: A Tale of Terror* directed by Michael Cohn or the realistic version of "Little Red Riding Hood," *Freeway* (1996), which struck its viewers by introducing juvenile delinquent Red Riding Hood and a serial-killer and pedophile wolf to the plot. In the early twenty-first century, on the other hand, adults shared fairy tales with children and teenagers: animations such as *Shrek* (2001), are an example of animated films made to be entertaining for both adults and children. *Shrek* is also an example of genre mixing, which I will discuss in the next subchapter. There was also a clear trend of live-action adaptations where fairy-tale plots were cast in real-life situations. For example, *Sydney White* (2007) is a version of "Snow White" set in a U.S. college environment, with all the trappings of a romantic teen comedy. Even *Pretty Woman* (1990) can be considered an adaptation of "Cinderella," despite lacking any fantastical elements (e.g., the Fairy Godmother, evil stepsisters, etc.) or the classic setting (the prince and palace ball). Yet over the past decade the film industry has seen a steady release of live-action fairy-tale adaptations (at least one movie per year) with distinct elements of fantasy or horror, which seem to have become the preferred genres of the fairy-tale film. The movies discussed in this chapter are part of this emergent trend: *Red Riding Hood* (2011), *Snow White and the Huntsman* (2012), *Hansel and Gretel: Witch Hunters* (2013), *Maleficent* (2014),[7] and *The Huntsman* (2016). All of these movies can be classified to the fantasy or fantasy-horror genre.

The Uses of Genre

Genre has a lot of meaning for the film medium. The trappings (elements) of a genre not only build the atmosphere of a film, contributing to and often enhancing the narrative plot, but also suggest a target audience. Knowing a film's genre may influence the viewer's decision to see the movie as well as their experience of it. Ralph Amelio, in an article titled "American Genre Film: Teaching Popular Movies," explains that film genre is "a total of aesthetic devices accessible to the filmmaker and understandable to his audience[:] common ideas, themes, and motifs, typical actions and situations, expressed by characters with a cluster of recognizable attributes in a previously defined setting, all synthesized by a narrative or dramatic structure. The degree of pleasure the audience derives from a genre film depends on the filmmaker's artistic blending of a sense of novelty with a sense of recognition" (47–48). Comparably to the Western fairy-tale canon (Perrault, the Grimms, and Andersen), Hollywood movies have become a staple of Western popular culture, and, over time, viewers have become accustomed to their formulas—for instance, the western or the detective film. Through their experience-based knowledge of the genres (having watched movies), the audience can intuitively and subconsciously respond to these conventions in a movie. Take, for example, the classic romantic comedy plot progression of happy heroine—life turns upside down—happiness is not what she thought it was—happy end.

This well-refined blend of familiarity and novelty is essential for the understanding and enjoyment of fairy-tale films. The audience is expected to identify not only the trappings of the film genre but also the fairy-tale motifs. Filmmakers play on the viewer's expectations, often diverging from or building on the set formulas (Amelio 47–88), and create what Todd Berliner calls "genre breakers and genre benders" (25). Fairy-tale movies are an example of genre breakers, as they often clearly mock or stress their departure from the established style (25), in the sense that they break away from the children's version of the fairy tale. Nevertheless, they can also be perceived as genre benders, due to the fact that they are "using the same old [film] conventions to manipulate audiences in novel ways" (31). Regardless of whether they are genre breaking or bending, both require the use of the mentioned conventions of a given genre in order to manipulate them.

In fairy-tale films, a mix of the fantasy, horror, and historical genres is most often employed, along with a mix of fairy-tale motifs. Cristina Bacchilega in *Fairy Tales Transformed?* remarks on how the film industry hybridizes (Kindle loc 2256) the fairy tale by mixing together different fairy-tale plots and elements and thus creating what she calls a "genre remix" (Kindle loc 2271). This genre remix applies to the hybridity of the cinematic genres used as well. The fairy tale functions dually in a film, in the sense of both a literary genre and a filmic genre. As a result, breaking or bending genre in fairy-tale adaptations may happen on several levels. First is the level of the fairy tale as a genre.[8] Here, breaking or bending the genre involves rewriting, adapting, or expanding the plot while typically retaining the basic structure. It may also involve genre remixing (Bacchilega, *Fairy Tales Transformed?* Kindle loc 2271). An example of such a genre mix is *The Huntsman*, which combines features from the Grimms' "Snow White" with Andersen's tale of the "Snow Queen." Turning (or returning) darkness into a tale, however, is achieved by hybridizing the fairy tale as a movie genre. Within cinema, the fairy tale has been, as Jack Zipes, among others, claims, dominated by Disney (Zipes, "Breaking" 352), and if the Disney fairy tale is to be treated as the model of the fairy-tale movie genre, then the recent fairy-tale movies are a mix of genre breakers and genre benders. It is thus on the level of the fairy tale as a movie, then, that the re-orienting of the tales toward adults actually takes place.

Darkness/Origin Argument

The reason why in recent years fairy-tale adaptations have been set within the fantasy and horror genres has to do with the re-orientation of the genre, or rather, its return to its "dark origin." While *Pretty Woman* may be a reworking of "Cinderella," it does not explicitly attempt to reclaim the tale for adults. Recent fairy-tale adaptations focus on legitimizing adults as the all-along intended audience of fairy tales, and they are aided by lively online discussion (exemplified by the many blog posts, fan sites, and Wikia pages dedicated to fairy tales and their recent movie adaptations) that could be seen as a direct result of the steady release of fairy-tale films directed at adults.

In a 2014 article for the influential fantasy and sci-fi website Tor.com, the writing team Jack Heckel confronts the reappearing question of why people keep coming back to fairy tales. They posit that "the real question is whether this impulse to make these traditionally G-rated stories more PG, or in some cases NC-17, is new or merely a reversion of the fairytale to its original, dark form." A 2015 post on the same subject, for the Act Writer's Center blog by WK Banham also notices a renewed interest in fairy tales: "in the past ten years or more, there's been a resurgence of interest in fairy tales, thanks to movies such as *Ella Enchanted*, *Snow-White and the Huntsman*, *Red Riding Hood*, *Into the Woods* and *Maleficent*. These remind us of stories we heard as children or introduce younger audiences to these timeless tales." Furthermore, Banham supports Heckel's claim about adults reclaiming fairy tales, "especially as many recent retellings are far darker, more adult tales not meant for exclusively for children," not to mention that "many fairy tales were originally written for adults and only later were rewritten for children."

The word *dark* as well as the reference to the beginnings of fairy tales appears in many posts and articles on modern retellings of fairy tales directed at adults. For example, a 2015 post titled "25 Dark And Disturbing Original Versions Of Children's Fairy Tales" by Alex Salamanca lists the more "gruesome and shocking tales." The author claims to have "dug deep with this list to find where our common stories come from and what the original dark (very dark) stories really were" to prove that once upon a time "fairy tales used to be stories aimed at both adult and child alike and the grown-up themes they portray is good evidence of that." Similarly, in a list prepared for the website Culture Trip titled "The Ten Most Dark and Disturbing Fairy Tales," contributor Tara Heuzé stresses the "slightly sinister back stories of ten of our most enduring fairy tales." Yet another list, "The Disturbing Origins of 10 Famous Fairy Tales" by Emily Temple, published in 2012 for Flavorwire.com as part of a review of Philip Pullman's *Grimm Tales for Young and Old*, "take[s] a look at a few terrifying, gruesome, often bizarre early versions of ubiquitous fairy tales after the jump" and marvels at "how much some of the stories have changed along the way—all the blindings and sexual misconduct and death have been mostly scrubbed away."

Blogs and similar sites are not the only ones to proclaim the fairy tale's return to its dark origins. For instance, online versions of well-known periodicals such as *The Atlantic* and the *Los Angeles Times* also attest to this trend. The *Los Angeles Times*, in answer to the spurt of fairy-tale film releases, created their own list of "Fairy Tale Movies for Grown Ups" in which they observe this once-dark aspect of fairy tales: "fairy tales of far-away lands, conquering heroes and mythical beasts are often much darker than the animated, musical movie versions most of us remember from childhood. Hollywood has decided fairy tales will now join 'old TV shows' and 'comic books' as Hollywood's go-to reservoir of material. But unlike the adaptations of yesteryear, the current and upcoming crop of fairy-tale movies is mining those darker elements to make films that have a decidedly adult bent." In this last sentence, the *Los Angeles Times* quite clearly indicates the commercial potential of fairy tales, suggesting this as the reason for Hollywood's recent heavy investment in fairy-tale movies.

Likewise, *The Atlantic* addresses this issue in a 2012 article, "Fairy Tales Started Dark, Got Cute, and Are Now Getting Dark Again" by Scott Meslow. Referring to *Snow White and the Huntsman*, Meslow remarks that contemporary fairy-tale films are "less a subversion of an old story than a return to one," which is in line with the "return to dark origins" discourse outlined earlier. As he explains, "*Snow White & the Huntsman* is, yes, another fairy-tale film adaptation aimed at adults, coming on the heels of . . . dozens of other works in the past decade. They're the latest in the long but accelerating trend that's undoing Disney's twentieth century work of transforming horrifying folk stories into genial animated musicals. While such retellings may seem subversive, they're actually throwbacks, marking a return to what these tales originally were—before, even, the Brothers Grimm got their hands on them" (Meslow). However, Meslow goes further in his investigation than this return to dark and adult origins as the reason for the renewed popularity of fairy tales in film and, like the *Los Angeles Times*, stresses the commercial aspect of this revival in popularity. As he suggests, another possible reason for the genre's popularity is the deliberate targeting of these movies toward the people who grew up on Disney and are now adults (Meslow). In Meslow's view, the film industry did not have to try particularly hard to create adult versions of popular fairy tales, as, "despite the best efforts of the Grimm brothers, Walt Disney, and their contemporaries, fairy tales can never be completely separated from their darker origins."

The Appeal to the Origin and to Darkness

From this brief overview of just a few popular opinion sources it becomes clear that the words *dark* and *origin* hold a special significance to why and how adults are reclaiming fairy tales. In the context of cinema, these two *appeals*, as I call them, could be treated as methods Hollywood employs in its filmic adaptations in order to re-orient the target audience of fairy-tale movies.

The appeal to the origin alludes to the common practice of referring back to the beginnings of the genre as a strategy to support adults as the "historically" intended audience. While fairy-tale scholars are aware of the fact that folk and fairy tales in their oral and early literary form did not have a fixed audience, it is remarkable how well-known this piece of the genre's history has become among the nonacademic public (as evidenced by the many blog posts mentioned earlier). By referring to the origin of fairy tales, it appears, adults are using history to legitimize themselves as the intended audience of fairy tales, thus partially dispelling the strong cultural associations with the realm of the child.

The appeal to darkness, on the other hand, refers to the way recent cinematic fairy-tale adaptations capitalize on the rumored dark side of fairy tales. The word *dark* surfaces in many scholarly articles as well as in popular culture—dark story, dark character, darker traits/elements/side, and so on, and it comes with an imbued meaning people somehow intuitively understand. In popular culture, dark usually stands for danger, evil deeds, terror, fantasy, or horror, but most of all for something despite all its warnings—enticing, dangerously sexy, prohibited, and foreboding but simultaneously awakening our curiosity. It means evil witchcraft and demons as well as elves, fairies, and magic. This understanding of *dark* in contemporary culture has become fetishized and glorified and is certainly in high demand, especially in Hollywood productions, in which this darkness is typically expressed through genre, specifically that of horror and fantasy. Additionally, this appeal is most effective when employed on the level of the fairy-tale movie rather than genre. Much like the genre remix to which Cristina Bacchilega refers, these new fairy-tale adaptations borrow from the fantasy, horror, and history genres and combine them. In practice, this could be seen in, for example, how in *Red Riding Hood* the wolf becomes a werewolf—a fantastical creature often associated with horror, while the setting of the tale appears to be around the time of the witch hunts and the Inquisition. Through the use of historical trappings, plot buildups straight from suspense thrillers, and the "camera in hand" work typical of horror movies (the shots are disrupted when villagers run; the camera focuses on peoples' feet; the movement is disruptive and jumping), not only is "Red Riding Hood" reworked as a tale, but it is also readdressed to a mature audience that is capable of recognizing such genre cues.

Correspondingly, in *Maleficent* the genre mix involves situating the story in a time similar to the Middle Ages, with a faerie kingdom with beings resembling *Lord of the Rings* characters (e.g., tree soldiers and tree ground worms). Maleficent herself is called a spirit, a fairy, or a winged elf, while the other fairies are named pixies. Interestingly, the most terrifying scene of the film does not include the appearance of a terrible beast or picture a supernatural occurrence. Arguably, the most heartbreaking and blood-chilling scene is the betrayal of Maleficent by her beloved, Stephan, when she wakes up to realize her wings have been cut off. The cry of anguish and agony (so masterfully rendered by Jolie) while the camera reverts from the mutilated faerie to Stephan, hiding his face and running away, is the pivotal moment of the movie. Hence, the horror in this scene comes from the cruelty one person can inflict on another, especially loved one to loved one, arguably a scene that adults are better equipped than children to decode.

Both the appeal to the origin and the appeal to darkness attempt to return the romanticized fairy tales of Disney to their *Märchen* form, characterized by, as Kay Stone lists in her article "Märchen to Fairy Tale: An Unmagical Transformation," the struggle to achieve happiness and maturity, overcoming difficulties and violent motifs (233). Using the examples of five following films: *Red Riding Hood* (2011), *Snow White and the Huntsman* (2012), *Hansel and Gretel: Witch Hunters* (2013), *Maleficent* (2014), and *The Huntsman* (2016), I will demonstrate how the two "appealing" strategies are utilized in film production. This should also exhibit the formula Hollywood developed for the modern adult fairy-tale movie.

Establishing a fairy-tale movie as an adult film begins even before its release. Hollywood regularly employs a number of marketing strategies to reel in viewers even before they see the actual movie and stay with them long after they have seen the picture. One way to signal the target adult audience is through posters. This type of promotional activity, alongside trailers, sets the tone for the film, already employing the appeal to the origin and to darkness. For example, the posters for Disney's *Maleficent* used clear signals that this was going to be a genre/tale-breaking experience. The audience could easily recognize the Disney-created villain, Maleficent, by her characteristic costume, but the headline warns: "don't believe the fairy tale"—challenging the potential audience's preconceived notions. Similarly, the poster promoting director Tommy Wirkola's *Hansel and Gretel: Witch Hunters* promises its viewers novelty by adding "witch hunters" to the traditional tale's title, and to further stimulate interest, the following slogan was added: "classic tale new twist." Furthermore, the director's name additionally hints to fans of horror and black comedy that this movie will be within this genre.[9]

    The *Red Riding Hood* poster, on the other hand, appeals to the audience's knowledge of the tale and incites fear with a warning: "Believe the legend. Beware the wolf." The movie's campaign team must have deliberately used the term *legend* and not *fairy tale* here because, while "fairy tales are regarded purely as fiction" (Teverson 25–26), legends imply the possibility of at least partial truth. They are also less culturally tied to the domain of children. With this word choice for the slogan, the PR team for *Red Riding Hood* was clearly attempting to build suspense before release. Nevertheless, the posters for both *Hansel and Gretel: Witch Hunters* and *Red Riding Hood* heavily borrow from the horror genre style. The former portrays the eponymous siblings holding the viewer at gunpoint, posing with their steampunk-like weapons, clad in black leather and clearly meaning business, while the title appears to be written in blood, splashed across the poster. In the case of *Red Riding Hood*, all promotional materials focus on portraying the beautiful actress Amanda Seyfried running or standing in a dark and foreboding forest amid snow, the only intense color on the poster being her blood-red cloak. In one version of the poster, the actress is seated, looking directly at the viewer as her cloak spreads around her, creating the illusion of her sitting in a pool of blood.

    In contrast, the campaign for *Snow White and the Huntsman* and *The Huntsman* (both from Roth Films, who is interestingly also the producer of *Maleficent*, the two *Alice in Wonderland* remakes, and *Oz: The Great and Powerful*) was prepared to closely resemble fantasy or historical film posters. For the first movie, one of the posters portrays the Evil Queen (Charlize Theron) wielding a menacing looking blade positioned in between the person we suppose is the Huntsman, wielding two axes in a battle-like stance, and a young female who must be Snow White, although she is deprived of any of the typical attributes associated for example with the Disney princesses. The three figures are surrounded by black crows, which seem to be emerging from the Evil Queen, and there is a battlefield perceptible in the distant background. The dark colors chosen for this poster and the character's costumes also function as a genre signal. Another poster for this film portrayed Kirsten Stewart (Snow White) as a Joan of Arc, clad in armor with a large shield and sword in hand. Conversely, in the posters heralding the premiere of *The Huntsman: Winter's War*, the subtitle alone guarantees action, while other posters for the film read: "Discover the story before Snow White."

The Huntsman and *Maleficent* posters additionally create a strong connection between the character and the famous actress playing her. In the former the poster quotes: "Emily Blunt is the Ice Queen" while all the *Maleficent* posters include a rather large "Angelina Jolie" sign so that there could be no doubt as to who will be impersonating the villain. Casting is of consequence, as the posters would indicate. Actors and actresses, much like directors, appear frequently in films of a particular genre, and therefore casting decisions further aid filmmakers in creating a certain genre. They also invariably help in building convincing characters. As these movies focus on providing motives, arguably the role of the villain is the more challenging and interesting one to play, which is perhaps why in major feature films like *Snow White and the Huntsman*, *The Huntsman*, and *Maleficent*, top Hollywood actresses are cast as villains. Their names alone will attract people to the cinema, and along with their names, the viewers will come to confront certain expectations they have of them. For instance, Charlize Theron and Angelina Jolie, prior to their roles as, respectively, the Evil Queen Ravenna (*Snow White and the Huntsman*) and wicked faerie Maleficent (*Maleficent*), frequently appeared as strong and often dangerous female characters—as exemplified by Theron's role of a serial killer in *Monster* or Jolie's performance as Lara Croft in *Tomb Raider*. In contrast, Chris Hemsworth, who became the Huntsman in both *Snow White and the Huntsman* and *The Huntsman*, had appeared before these two films as the god of thunder and comic book hero Thor, leading the viewers, even subconsciously, to believe that he would be the good guy, the hero in these movies as well. In consequence, through casting and promotion filmmakers have the possibility to challenge the audience's knowledge of the fairy tale their movie is remaking and to set the story within a certain genre.

Another way these recent fairy-tale adaptations employ the appeal to the origin and the appeal to darkness is in the plot. Nearly all of the promotional slogans and subtitles announce that these movies will not be what the audience is familiar with and promise to satisfy our "postmodern tendency to provide additional commentary and offer the illusion of completeness" (Verstraten 180) through the development of the classic characters' background stories. The plots of all of them make use of the basic formula of fairy tales, or even just selected elements, and build onto the story by fleshing out all of the characters, providing motives for their actions, and moving the presentation of fairy tales to a description level commonly found in novels (Lüthi 50). The use of the *appeal to the origin* in the plot will involve questioning the audience's knowledge of the tale and presenting a different version, one typically providing motives for the villain's actions or reinterpreting the hero. This is clearly visible in both *Snow White and the Huntsman* and *The Huntsman*. In a quite touching scene in *Snow White and the Huntsman* (58 minutes into the film), we see a shaken and teary-eyed Queen Ravenna moments after a flashback to her childhood. Ravenna and her siblings were the children of a sorceress. When their village was attacked, their mother cast a spell on the extremely beautiful Ravenna, preserving her beauty in hopes it would save all of the children. The spell, however, could be undone by the appearance of a different "fairest of them all." This scene follows the burning down of a village inhabited only by women, on Ravenna's orders. Through this addition to the plot, the Evil Queen is cast as a character to be pitied and one who is both an opposite as well as a completion to Snow White. The film portrays the two women as binary opposites—life

(Snow White) and death (Ravenna), innocence (Snow White) and experience (Ravenna)—but ultimately Snow White triumphs as, unlike Ravenna, she accepts this other aspect of herself, and she embraces the fact that she needs to challenge Ravenna personally and even become a killer like her in order to succeed.

Meanwhile, in *The Huntsman*, whose plot both precedes and follows the events of *Snow White and the Huntsman*, the audience not only learns how the Huntsman (Chris Hemsworth) developed such incredible fighting and survival skills and came to be known as the Huntsman but also discovers the story of the Ice Queen. The Evil Queen Ravenna (Charlize Theron), aside from a brother (who appeared in *Snow White*), also had a sister named Freya[10] (Emily Blunt), who, unlike her sister, believed in love and a happy family life, and neither craved power nor strove to become a sorceress. Yet Ravenna, convinced of her sister's hidden potential, set in motion a scheme that resulted in the death of Freya's child, with the father framed as the murderer, which quite literally broke the woman's heart and unleashed her powers, turning Freya into the coldhearted Ice Queen.

A similar origin story is presented in *Maleficent*. The movie begins with a narrator's voice: "Let me tell an old story anew and we'll see how well you know it" (*Maleficent*). Here from the very start we see the story from the villain's perspective, which clearly casts the good king and the kingdom of men as the villains, reversing the roles people know from Disney's animated version of *Sleeping Beauty*. Maleficent is portrayed as the most powerful of the Fae, protector of the moor and the faerie realm, who was gravely wronged by the future king Stephan. Her curse on Aurora as a result becomes a quite justifiable form of revenge, which she later greatly regrets, in contrast to the vengeance-crazed King Stephan. In a (to those familiar with *Kissing the Witch* by Emma Donoghue or *Sleeper and the Spindle* by Neil Gaiman) predictable twist of events, Maleficent becomes the fairy godmother to Aurora, and in the end, it is her true love's kiss that awakens the princess from her sleep.

While *Maleficent*, *Snow White and the Huntsman*, and *The Huntsman* explore origin stories for more than one of the classic tale's characters, *Red Riding Hood* and *Hansel and Gretel: Witch Hunters* focus mainly on providing either an explanation or, in the case of the latter, what happened afterward. Wirkola's *Hansel and Gretel: Witch Hunters* adopts the classic version of the fairy tale as a point of departure, choosing to develop the part after the "happily ever after." In a peculiar mix of action, horror, and fantasy, Wirkola (both director and writer) portrays the siblings as famous witch hunters. Their traumatic experience of nearly dying at the hands of a witch is shown as a turning point in their lives. Hansel and Gretel become hired witch hunters, traveling far and wide to save villages from evil witches. Although at first the movie seems rather simple, it in fact pays a lot of attention to details. For instance, Hansel suffers from diabetes after being force-fed candy by the witch who captured them as children. Through this simple and short expansion on the basic tale plot, the filmmaker introduces depth, a sense of real-life cause and effect, as well as comic relief.

Red Riding Hood, unlike the other fairy-tale movies discussed, focuses on adding description to the events present in the tale. Red Riding Hood, in director Catherine Hardwicke and writer David Leslie Johnson's adaptation, is a young girl approaching sexual maturity and romantically involved with a village "bad boy," while being the love interest of a "Prince Charming"–type character. This love triangle is not very surprising, seeing as Catherine Hardwicke also directed the famous *Twilight* movie, which portrays a love triangle between a human girl, a male vampire, and a male werewolf. In *Red Riding Hood*, the village where Red–called Valerie—lives is plagued by a wolf. When murders begin, the villagers set out to once and for all free themselves from the terror of the wolf. For that purpose, Father Solomon is summoned to the village. This new character, played by Gary Oldman, is a werewolf hunter of sorts, whose entire entourage and methods closely resemble those of the Inquisition. Further in the movie's plot, as a result of Father Solomon's investigation, Valerie is shackled and placed at the center of the village, in an iron wolf mask, as a sacrifice to the werewolf. The horror in *Red Riding Hood* comes more from the behavior of the people than from the werewolf—when Father Solomon suggests that the wolf is, in fact, among the villagers, a man or woman who turns into a werewolf, the film begins to cast suspicion on each of the featured characters, including Valerie's Grandma, Valerie's love interest, and Valerie herself.

Final Remarks

While the comparative analysis of the five selected films could be continued in detail for several more pages, at this point the two questions this volume poses itself need to be addressed. First of all, what insights does such a comparative analysis of fairy-tale film adaptations bring to the explicit and implicit Eurocentric tendencies in current fairy-tale adaptations and scholarship? And what kind of criticisms will be necessary to analyze adaptations of fairy tales and folktales in a globalizing world?

Film, like folklore, can be treated as a description of a society, "a mirror of culture frequently reveal[ing] the areas of special concern" (Dundes 53) for the source culture. Indeed, the return to the origin of fairy tales (*appeal to the origin*), or even the need to repeatedly revisit well-known tales, could be seen as part of the contemporary nostalgia trend. Kayleigh Donaldson, in an opinion piece on "How Nostalgia Became Our Pop Culture Salve During These Dark Times," suggests that society turns to popular culture for relief during hard times. However, as she further explains, "blasts from the past" can also serve a subversive purpose, challenging people's opinions: "Nostalgia provides us with a chance to look inward and to more deeply understand the pop culture that made us who we are. There's a thrill in looking back on the stories you devoured as a kid and being aware enough to understand how influenced you were by them. Nostalgia can subvert our ideas, but it can also reflect them back at us in shiny new ways that ease our sadness. It can show us a sanitized reality that is nonetheless a comfort to us, or it can refresh our worldviews by exposing the stuff we never saw the first time around" (Donaldson). Critics like Mark Fisher (*Ghosts of my Life*, 2015) and Simon Reynolds (*Retromania: Pop Culture's Addiction to Its Own Past*, 2011) also explored the nostalgic direction of popular culture. With this approach, fairy tales, like comic books, are culture products revisited and adapted to reflect contemporary issues or critiques of the previous version(s). These new adaptations of fairy tales often directly challenge the stereotypes that have become the by-product of earlier versions. Popular culture, in other words, creates more popular culture, as well as reflects on itself.

Despite the fact that the films analyzed in this chapter are all American productions of Western tales and therefore could be seen as reflecting not a global, or even Western, but American culture, I believe that the two strategies of appealing to the origin and appealing to the darkness of fairy tales are global phenomena. These two strategies can be used to address stereotypes or issues of earlier versions of fairy tales in order to either critically comment on or redirect them, or both. This could be seen, for example, in the comparison of *Blancanieves* (2012) and *Snow White and the Huntsman* (2012), both inspired by "Snow White" and both released in the same year. In chapter 8, Nieves Moreno Redondo discusses director Pablo Berger's Snow White in the film *Blancanieves* (2012), who is simultaneously the incarnation of the stereotype of Snow White, the innocent princess, and Carmen, a fiery bullfighter (a mix, as Moreno explains, of two well-known Spanish stereotypes). Blancanieves/Carmen undergoes a change from an independent woman to a weaker version of herself due to memory loss. Snow White, in director Rupert Sanders's interpretation, however, goes from innocent to powerful warrior. Like Blancanieves, Snow White in *Snow White and the Huntsman* does not want revenge on the Evil Queen, as she says: "I used to hate her, now I feel only sorrow" (1:25). However, Snow White in Sanders's film realizes (through her death and resurrection, claiming to "have seen what she [Ravenna] sees, I know what she knows, I can kill her" [1:38]) she must be the one to take action against the Evil Queen. The men in the movie are all portrayed as quite cautious in their actions, and it is Snow White who offers herself as the "weapon" for the people to use to rise up against the Evil Queen. It is Snow White who leads the army into battle and Snow White who kills Ravenna in a duel, while the two men at her side (the Huntsman and her love interest, William) are otherwise occupied.

The portrayal of a princess previously seen as a passive witness to the events of her life as a woman who takes matters in her own hands is one recurring in contemporary fairy-tale adaptations around the globe. Creating female characters who are strong and capable of overcoming obstacles, both physical and psychological, I would argue, is a reflection of the goals our global community sets for itself. In all of the five movies discussed in this chapter, women are leading and complex characters. They are presented as individuals with a past, in relation to others, as people who make mistakes, and, most importantly, as people who grow with experience and face their own problems. Similarly, animated movies addressed to children, such as *Brave* and *Moana*, depict strong female leads. The classic romance of Disneyfied fairy tales becomes secondary in both adult live-action films and animations for children, as more diverse types of relationships and more complexity are introduced into the plots, an effect that can be achieved partly through the return-to-the-origin strategy. By elaborating on a character's past, through various methods (flashbacks, prequels, sequels, disrupted timelines, and so on) fairy-tale film adaptations are able to portray emotionally complex female characters (such as Maleficent, the Ice Queen in *The Huntsman*, or even Gretel[11] in *Hansel and Gretel: Witch Hunters*).

The use of the appeal to darkness to readdress or reinterpret fairy tales also appears to be a globally valid phenomenon. In the five Hollywood productions analyzed here, a sense of "darkness" of the reimagined tale was achieved primarily through the distortion of the viewer's expectations. These are no longer "cute," Disney-like fairy tales with wide-eyed animals to join in the chorus but films that make use of fantasy and horror movie conventions to redirect themselves. *Hansel and Gretel: Witch Hunters* is an example of the application of horror and gore trappings to a classic fairy tale. In this adaptation the explanation of both the reason for the abandonment of the children (origin) and what happened after (Hansel and Gretel become professional witch hunters) is used to help develop the two sibling's identity. Outwardly they may seem like fearless fighters, accustomed to beheading, burning, or otherwise killing witches—elements of the plot that are vividly portrayed as part of the "splatter film" genre (a subgenre of horror)—but they harbor unresolved issues with their past. In order to move on and leave their childhood behind, Hansel and Gretel must return home, find out the truth about their parents, and once more find themselves in the candy house, this time killing a witch to end that part of their lives (to close their past).

The tale of "Hansel and Gretel" was also adapted using the horror genre by director Pil-Sung Yim. Michael Brodski analyzes this South Korean film version of the Western tale in chapter 10, with a particular focus on how the body of the child is depicted in this film. Brodski, quoting Sung-Ae Lee, also remarks how the use of the horror genre to adapt fairy tales is a trend in Korea and on the popularity in East Asia of the figure of the ghost-child. Indeed, it is not just Western classics that are adapted to horror. For example, *A Tale of Two Sisters* (2003) directed by Kim Jee-Woon is a psychological horror inspired by a Korean folktale "Janghwa Hongryeon Jeon." Returning, however, to Pil-Sung Yim's version of "Hansel and Gretel," as Michael Brodski writes, the children's chronological development is warped—they search for a "father-figure" yet they are wise beyond their appearance. While in Wirkola's horror movie Hansel and Gretel, despite their adulthood, have an unresolved story in the past (to which they must return in order to move on), the siblings in the Korean version have to accept they present maturity despite their childlike features.

Dark elements and genre mixing in fairy-tale retellings appear in both Western and non-Western tales. This is an approach used in independent films as well as more commercial productions. In the Polish take on Hans Christian Andersen's "The Little Mermaid," *The Lure* (2015), director Agnieszka Smoczyńska deliberately mixes the horror genre with the musical. She places two mermaid sisters within the dance-club scene of the 1980's in Warsaw, Poland. Danger and drama hang in the air to the accompaniment of Polish dance music hits from the 1970s and 1980s. Another example of mixing genres and adopting a dark, eerie approach to folktales is the Estonian *November* (2017), in which director Rainer Sarnet, using black-and-white photography, tells the story of a poor village where folk beliefs, magic, and death run rampant.

The examples mentioned above hopefully demonstrate that the return to the dark aspects of fairy tales and folktales, as well as retelling tales and readdressing them to adult audiences through mixing of film genres (such as horror and fantasy), is not a trend associated with just American culture. These film adaptations engage not only with the retold tale but also with the cultural history of the tale or of the country the film was made in (as in *The Lure* or *Blancanieves*) or cinematic techniques (as in *November*). To fully understand the implications of an analysis of such uses of the fairy tale and folktale in film and their role in a globalizing cultural community, transdisciplinary research projects could be an interesting starting point.

To conclude this chapter, I would like to point to the redirection of fairy tales in cinema. It is not just the fact that these are films directed at adults. I believe they are also a reflection of today's culture. After years of Disney's dominance and countless critiques and challenges of its romanticized fairy-tale formula by academics, critics, and even the public, "a more critical awareness of the fairy tale has taken hold in popular consciousness" (Bacchilega and Rieder 24) that has influenced the production as well as the reception of fairy tales. Fairy tales are produced in near equal number for adults and children, and most of these productions subvert the classic tales to create a tale suitable for contemporary audiences and values. I have compared five fairy-tale-inspired films produced between 2011 and 2016 and proposed a formula that these Hollywood films follow, one that includes the following elements: expanding the tales' narrative to provide motivations and character development; a mix of cinematic genres; (often) a mix of different tales (as in *The Huntsman: Winter's War*); and the use of the appeals to the dark and to the origin. What is interesting is that the appeal to the origin and to darkness can be applied to movie adaptations as well as literary ones (see, for example, the illustrated *The Sleeper and the Spindle* by Neil Gaiman or the graphic novel *Fairest: The Hidden Kingdom* by Lauren Beukes) and they can be used both on older versions of tales and on Disney ones, as in *Maleficent*.

Cinema has approached the topic of fairy tales before the discussed time period, and it will undoubtedly produce many more retellings. The trend of returning to the origin and to the dark may be a reaction to the fast-paced changes occurring everywhere around us. In the face of global problems and a global community, a nostalgic look to the past and a desire to ground oneself in one's roots is understandable. If, however, a global culture is to be created, it will need to be one of both inclusion of old and creation of new tales, one embracing multiculturalism and working toward transcultural narratives. Fairy tales, as a genre, are quite suitable for this global environment, as their most powerful skill and potential lies in their ability to unite people in a shared experience of a different world (but one oddly familiar as well), a skill that they share with cinema, a medium that gathers people together for a shared adventure, and that sparks heated debates as well as touches upon many difficult social subjects. Both fairy tales and film actively engage the audience's imagination and provoke reflection; together they form not only a form of entertainment but also a forum for exhibiting social and other issues.

Notes

1. I take *big production* to mean films with considerable filming budgets, with a wide release in the United States (as opposed to limited release) and worldwide, and having been produced by one of the major American production companies (Paramount, Metro, etc.).

2. All of the selected films have been stamped by the MPAA as above G. *Maleficent* received a PG (Parental Guidance Suggested), while the others (with the exception of *Hansel and Gretel: Witch Hunters*, which is R-rated) are PG-13, deemed appropriate for teenage audiences. Rating movies presents an issue in our times, as it is both an exhibition of how our society perceives and constructs childhood and child-appropriate content and a system that has some definite flaws (see, for example, Scott Mendelson's critical article from November 26, 2013, "Disney's 'Frozen' Proves Failure of PG rating" for *Forbes*).

3. When using the term *Hollywood*, I mean to signify films produced by Hollywood-based film production companies, mainly for commercial purposes, accompanied by marketing campaigns (in the form of posters and trailers) and often identified as a typically Western (North American) product.

4. *Depth* in this chapter will mean going beyond the classic fairy tale formula, characterized by little detail in descriptions (Lüthi 50), and developing the characters by providing motive as well as emotional and historical background.

5. For example, the tale "The Story of Grandmother" from the nineteenth century (collected and published by Paul Delarue in 1951) is considerably more sexual than either Perrault's or the Borthers Grimm's version.

6. See Belle from *Once Upon a Time* season one, episode twelve: "Skin Deep," which aired on February 12, 2012. The TV character was clearly inspired by Disney's 1991 rendition of *Beauty and the Beast*, as evidenced by a nearly identical costume.

7. In 2015 Disney's live-action adaptation of *Cinderella* was released. It will not be discussed here, but it demonstrates that there has been a steady fairy-tale-movie-per-year trend since 2011. In 2017 Disney's live-action *Beauty and the Beast* was released and remakes of *Aladdin* and *Mulan* have been already announced for the following years.

8. Here I mean both oral and literary genre—the genre of the fairy tale in general, as a tale, as opposed, for example, to the crime novel.

9. Wirkola is known for his work in the horror and black comedy genre—for example, *Zombie SS* (2009).

10. For viewers acquainted with Norse mythology this is an interesting choice of name for the Ice Queen, as Freya is the goddess of (among others) fertility and love—things that the Ice Queen renounces and fiercely opposes after her child's death and her presumed betrayal. Yet, true to her name, she yearns for fertility, which in the movie is expressed by her kidnapping children to adopt them and raise them as her huntsmen.

11. Hansel and Gretel in Wirkola's film discover why their parents abandoned them and that their mother was a witch. Both discoveries influence the plot and the characters' development.

Works Cited

Amelio, Ralph J. "American Genre Film: Teaching Popular Movies." *English Journal*, vol. 65, no. 3, Mar. 1976, pp. 47–50. *JSTOR*, doi: 10.2307/814834.

Bacchilega, Cristina. *Fairy Tales Transformed? Twenty-First-Century Adaptations and the Politics of Wonder (Series in Fairy-Tale Studies)*. Wayne State University Press, 2013. Kindle edition.

Bacchilega, Cristina, and John Rieder. "Mixing It Up: Generic Complexity and Gender Ideology in Early Twenty-first Century Fairy Tale Films." *Fairy Tale Films: Visions of Ambiguity*, edited by Pauline Greenhill and Sidney Eve Matrix, University Press of Colorado, 2010, pp. 23–41. *JSTOR*, www.jstor.org/stable/j.ctt4cgn37.6.

Banham, WK. "Why do we keep telling (and retelling) fairy tales?" *Capital Letters by ACT Writers Center*, 8 Sept. 2015, www.actwriters.org.au/2015/09/08/why-do-we-keep-telling-and-retelling-fairy-tales/ Accessed 1 Nov. 2017.

Bennett, Peter, et al. *Film Studies: The Essential Resource*. Edited by Peter Bennett, Andrew Hickman, and Peter Wall, Routledge, 2007.

Berliner, Todd. "The Genre Film as Booby Trap: 1970s Genre Bending and 'The French Connection.'" *Cinema Journal, vol.* 40, no. 3, Spring 2001, pp. 25–46. *JSTOR*, www.jstor.org/stable/1350193.

Dennett, Daniel. *From Bacteria to Bach: The Evolution of Minds*. W. W. Norton, 2017. Kindle edition.

Donaldson, Kayleigh. "How Nostalgia Became Our Pop Culture Salve During These Dark Times," *Syfy.com*, 8 Aug. 2018, www.syfy.com/syfywire/how-nostalgia-became-our-pop-culture-salve-during-these-dark-times. Accessed 17 Mar. 2019.

Dundes, Alan. *The Meaning of Folklore: The Analytical Essays of Alan Dundes*. Edited and introduced by Simon J. Bronner, Utah University Press, 2007.

"Fairy tale movies for grown-ups." *LATimes.com,* 2017, latimes.com/entertainment/la-et-adult-fairy-tales-pictures-photogallery.html. Accessed 24 Mar. 2017.

Greenhill, Pauline, and Sidney Eve Matrix. "Envisioning Ambiguity: Fairy Tale Films." Introduction. *Fairy Tale Films: Visions of Ambiguity,* edited by Pauline Greenhill and Sidney Eve Matrix, University Press of Colorado, 2010, pp. 1–22. *JSTOR*, http://www.jstor.org/stable/j.ctt4cgn37.5.

Heckel, Jack. "Been There, Done That: Why We Keep Retelling Fairy Tales," *Tor.com*, 11 Aug. 2014, www.tor.com/2014/08/11/been-there-done-that-why-we-keep-retelling-fairytales/. Accessed 1 Nov. 2017.

Heuzé, Tara. "The 10 Most Dark and Disturbing Fairy Tales." *The Culture Trip*, 30 Sept. 2016, theculturetrip.com/europe/united-kingdom/articles/the-10-most-dark-and-disturbing-fairy-tales/. Accessed 1 Nov. 2017.

Lüthi, Max. *Once Upon a Time: On the Nature of Fairy Tales*. Indiana University Press, 1976.

Mendelson, Scott. "Disney's 'Frozen' Proves Failure of PG rating." *Forbes*, 26 Nov. 2013, www.forbes.com/sites/scottmendelson/2013/11/26/disneys-frozen

-proves-worthlessness-of-pg-rating/#6217d93c6d35. Accessed 17 Mar. 2019.

Meslow, Scott. "Fairy Tales Started Dark, Got Cute, and Are Now Getting Dark Again." *Atlantic*, 31 May 2012, www.theatlantic.com/entertainment/archive/2012/05/fairy-tales-started-dark-got-cute-and-are-now-getting-dark-again/257934/ Accessed 24 Mar. 2017.

Salamanca, Alex. "25 Dark And Disturbing Original Versions Of Children's Fairy Tales." *List25.com*, 13 Apr. 2015, list25.com/25-dark-and-disturbing-original-versions-of-childrens-fairy-tales/. Accessed 1 Nov. 2017.

Stone, Kay. "Märchen to Fairy Tale: An Unmagical Transformation." *Western Folklore*, vol. 40, no. 3, July 1981, pp. 232–44. *JSTOR*, doi: 10.2307/1499694.

Tatar, Maria. Introduction. *The Classic Fairy Tales (A Norton Critical Edition)*, edited by Maria Tatar, W. W. Norton, 1999, pp. ix–xviii.

Temple, Emily. "The Disturbing Origins of 10 Famous Fairy Tales." *Flavorwire*, 8 Nov. 2012, flavorwire.com/344667/the-disturbing-origins-of-10-famous-fairy-tales. Accessed 1 Nov. 2017.

Teverson, Andrew. *Fairy Tale (Series in The New Critical Idiom)*. Routledge, 2013.

Verstraten, Peter. "Cinema as a Digest of Literature: A Cure for Adaptation Fever." *Between Page and Screen: Remaking Literature Through Cinema and Cyberspace*, edited by Kiene Billenburg Wurth, Fordham University Press, 2012.

Zipes, Jack. "Breaking the Disney Spell." *The Classic Fairy Tales (A Norton Critical Edition)*, edited by Maria Tatar, W. W. Norton, 1999, pp. 332–52.

Zipes, Jack. *Why Fairy Tales Stick: The Evolution and Relevance of a Genre*. Routledge, 2013. Kindle edition.

Filmography

A Tale of Two Sisters. Directed by Kim Jee-woon, B.O.M. Film Productions Co., Malsurpiri Films, 2003.

Blancanieves. Directed by Pablo Berger, Arcadia Motion Pictures, Noodles and Production, 2012.

Hansel and Gretel. Directed by Pil-Sung Yim, Barunson Company, CJ Entertainment, Cineclick Asia, 2007.

Hansel and Gretel: Witch Hunters. Directed by Tommy Wirkola, Paramount Pictures, Metro-Goldwyn-Meyer Pictures, 2013.

The Huntsman: Winter's War. Directed by Cedric Nicolas-Troyan, performances by Emily Blunt, Chris Hemsworth, and Charlize Theron, Universal Pictures, Roth Films, 2016.

The Lure. Directed by Angieszka Smoczyńska, Wytwórnia Filmów Fabularnych i Dokumentalnych, 2015.

Maleficent. Directed by Robert Stromberg, performance by Angelina Jolie, Roth Films, Walt Disney Pictures, 2014.

Moana. John Clements, John Musker, Don Hall, and Chris Williams, Hurwitz Creative, Walt Disney Animation Studios, Walt Disney Pictures, 2016.

November. Directed by Rainer Sarnet, Homeless Bob Production, Opus Film, PRPL, 2017.

Red Riding Hood. Directed by Catherine Hardwicke, performances by Amanda Seyfried and Gary Oldman, Warner Bros., Appian Way, Random Films, 2011.

Snow White and the Huntsman. Directed by Rupert Sanders, performances by Charlize Theron, Kirsten Stewart, and Chris Hemsworth, Roth Films, Universal Pictures, 2012.

8

Trespassing the Boundaries of Fairy Tales

Pablo Berger's Silent Film *Snow White*

Nieves Moreno Redondo

Introduction to Pablo Berger's Film Works

OVER THE YEARS, PABLO Berger has created a brand-new world in the Spanish film panorama by combining elements of dirty realism, Spanishness, popular culture, and cinephilia, and spinning them out into dark comedies, thrillers, and magic tales in up to three of his movies. His first feature film, *Torremolinos 73* (2003), is based on a tragicomic true story of a young working-class couple who are facing economic difficulties during the final years of Francisco Franco's dictatorship in the 1970s and who successfully start making amateur porn movies to sell in Sweden. The film recreates the bright-colored and optimistic 1970s Spanish cinema genre called *landismo* while simultaneously being a satirically gentle movie that criticizes the Spanish clichés born during the so-called economic developmentalism and the tourist boom in the coastal zones of Spain between the 1960s and the 1970s (*Albarrán* 178). These processes of economic and social development, together with the country's timid opening to foreign influence, generated this new subgenre closely related to Spanish stereotypes of passion and traditionalism (Huerta Floriano & Pérez Morán, 5). In the *landismo* genre, for the first time in Spanish film history the hero is not a bullfighter or a soldier; in fact, there are no heroes. In *landismo* comedies we find only middle-class men looking for noncommitted sex, imitating the manners and customs of foreign tourists in order to enjoy the modern life and prove to themselves and the rest of the world that Spanish people are part of the modern world too. In *Torremolinos 73*, Berger twists the basic elements of this subgenre to reveal the weakness and reiteration of the Spanish cinematic stereotypes, and at the same time he uses the subgenre to condemn the social circumstances not represented in *landismo* films. Berger's first steps as a filmmaker criticized this Spanish genre filled with stereotypes inherited from the previous period of dictatorship in Spain.

His second feature film, *Blancanieves* (2012), which is the center of this chapter, is a version of the famous European classic fairy tale "Snow White," first published by the Brothers Grimm in 1812 in its now-dominant form. In this silent black-and-white film, Berger presents his personal views about Spanish film history and combines them with elements of popular culture in order to analyze in depth the roots of Spanish folk images through the narrative of a fairy tale known worldwide, a distant referent for Spanish tradition. In *Blancanieves* Berger juxtaposes his work once again with elements from another well-known popular Spanish genre called *españolada* (Ortega, 101), an earlier version of *landismo*. He does so by contrasting one of the most well-known fairy tales in Western literature, Snow White, with Spanish stereotypes regarding passion, violence, and bullfighting. The darker undertones of the *classic* tale—for instance, the gruesome punishment given to the evil stepmother at the end of the story—serve to contextualize this tragic story about flamenco singers, a troupe of comedian dwarves, and bullfighters. In doing so, the director twists and turns the conventions of both European and Spanish—and more precisely, Andalusian—folklores; Berger's film trespasses the boundaries of all of these influences to create its own story in order to criticize the stereotypes embedded in national tradition.

His last feature film, named *Abracadabra* (2017), pays homage to Pedro Almodóvar's cinematic storytelling. So much so that the characters, the artistic production, the vision of the city, and even the story remind us of those in Almodóvar's films set in the Madrid of the 1980s. The story follows the life of Carmen, a housewife living in a working-class neighborhood. She is married to Carlos, who is a sexist man obsessed with soccer, and together they paint a realistic portrait of an average couple living boring and disappointing lives in an average neighborhood in Madrid. However, things complicate when Carlos is hypnotized and, as a result, he is possessed by the spirit of a serial killer. The film delivers some social satire and comic criticism through the ultimate Spanish stereotype: "almodovarismo." *Abracadabra* is a modern and somewhat eccentric Spanish fairy tale—because of the magic element that triggers the story that presents colorful and vivid images of Madrid—contrasting with a story rooted in the hetero-patriarchal environment usually linked to soccer and grotesque humor portrayed in Spanish *movida* films of the 1980s. When Spanish dictator Francisco Franco died in 1975, a new countercultural movement took place, mainly in Madrid. After a period of forty years of enforced rigid regulations, *movida* films reflected the sense of freedom of the moment by making fun of the former social structures. Once again, Berger intertwines different genres and disparate elements in order to challenge the history of cinema, popular and contemporary perceptions of Spanish culture, and their stereotypes.

All of Berger's films combine magic and reality, drama and comedy, fantasy stories with ordinary and stereotyped characters. Berger's unpredictable filming style deserves our attention and study as one of the most interesting in the panorama of contemporary Spanish filmmakers. The risky enterprise of filming a silent black-and-white movie required Berger to wait more than eight years before he found the necessary funding to start the production of his Carmen and Snow White hybrid in 2011. A year later the movie premiered, and it brought back to life some long-forgotten artistic disciplines for Spanish audiences. This film was the kind of entertainment that had not been seen in Spain for decades, a silent black-and-white movie that pays tribute to the cinematic techniques of Luis Buñuel, Carl Theodor Dreyer, and Pedro Almodóvar and to Spanish artists such as the painter Julio Romero de Torres. At the time of the film's production, in 2011, Michel Hazanavicius appeared at the Cannes Festival with *The Artist* (2011), a silent black-and-white movie remembering the golden years of the Hollywood cinema industry. Berger was utterly devastated. "It was completely out of the blue. I was in my office in Madrid, doing the storyboards for my film, when a producer friend sent me a text message from the festival saying, 'I've just seen *The Artist*, it is black and white and silent and it's going to be huge.' I almost threw my phone against the wall. The high concept was gone" (Matheou). Despite Berger's initial despair, the international success of the French film restored Berger's confidence in his adapted fairy tale. Finally, the film became a success, winning multiple national and international awards.

One of the first intertitles of the movie says: "You never heard the tale quite like this" but, roughly at the same time of Berger's premiere, there were two Hollywood films and an American television drama depicting Snow White. Two of them, *Snow White and the Huntsman* (Rupert Sanders, 2012) and *Once Upon a Time* (ABC, 2011–2017), portrayed Snow White as a woman warrior, and at the same time she is surrounded by magic in a conventional fairy-tale literary context. The third one, *Mirror Mirror* (Tarsem Singh, 2012), is a romantic and classic revisiting of the Grimms' tale. However, the novelty about the Spanish version of this fairy tale lies in its lack of magic and, even more importantly, the lack of a happy ending for Snow White. Berger's version is possibly the first film portraying Snow White without magic or a romantic relationship. The director abandons the main premises of the Brothers Grimms' fairy tale—the magic event being counteracted by love—and instead combines a group of images anchored in better known Spanish stereotypes–that is, Carmen and bullfighting. Berger mixes two cultural referents that could be regarded as difficult to combine: on the one hand, a widely known traditional fairy tale and, on the other hand, the very popular Spanish genre of *españolada*. The analysis of this film generates a lot of questions, mainly related to the artistic choices of the director. Primarily, the questions arise from the visual form in which the movie is narrated, which is essentially similar to the silent works of Buñuel and other expressionist filmmakers. We can, for instance, appreciate traces of the silent era in the exaggerated facial expressions, as in the scene when the grandmother dies and the scene with the assistants to Blancanieves's and the dwarves' first bullfight. Also, some questions arise from the introduction of a fairy tale in an *españolada* story, which shies away from the Spanish literary and popular tradition.

Berger's Use of the *Españolada* Genre

The Royal Spanish Academy states that *españolada*, from the French term *espagnolade,* is "a show or artistic work that exaggerates the Spanish local and cultural practices in a depreciative sense." Regarding cinema, one of the most important Spanish film historians, Roman Gubern says that *españolada* is a "film genre of French origin that intensively exploits the local customs and folklore of the most deprived areas of the rural Spain—such as Andalusia in the south of Spain—from the 19th century onwards. This genre widely represents stories of passion about gipsies, bullfighters and flamenco artists" (157). The romantic imaginary took possession of some of the most durable stereotypes of "Spanishness" that cinema redeveloped and hybridized in the transnational dialogues of mass culture and in a complex game of mirrors between the external and internal viewpoints. Some cinematographies of the twentieth and twenty-first centuries tackle the icons of bullfighters and flamenco dancers to address the difficult functioning of stereotypes in the formation of identity and to criticize basic aspects of popular culture that can be ambiguous or unrecognizable in today's society. Spanish literature from the early twentieth century, particularly Ramón María del Valle Inclán's ironic genre of *esperpento*, analyzed the identity process generated between the internal and external perception of national culture that provided a distorted vision of Spanish culture as led by stereotypes. In *Blancanieves*, Berger is taking an evaluative filmic approach toward the reconsideration of the concepts of identity, stereotype, and cinema. The construction of national stereotypes must be considered from a transnational dimension related to the game of mirrors produced by the crossing of external and internal viewpoints, a combination of different perspectives involved in any process of identity conformation. In this way, cinema can be considered one of the most powerful actors in the formation and dissemination of stereotypes in contemporary societies—a process deeply linked to the creation of film genres. Berger retakes and remakes one of the most histrionic film genres in Spanish film history, the *españolada,* and combines the result with a popular tale known worldwide—the Brothers Grimm's "Snow White"—to stress the process of deformed mirrors that operates in the popular imaginary.

Spain has suffered two big paradigms regarding cultural stereotypes. The first one was named by British scholars "The Black Legend"; the second one matches the exotic and romantic perception of nineteenth-century European artists, specifically the French ones. "The Black Legend" representation of Spanish culture and society, mainly from the sixteenth to the nineteenth centuries, depicts Spain as a violent, religious, and primitive country. This supposed cultural inheritance from the period of the *conquistadores* that represents Spaniards and their customs in a negative light was part of a strategy schemed by European powers against Spain—at that time the strongest colonial power—to intentionally discredit Spain's international image (Marías) Subsequently, the romantic perspective that had originated in French opera and literature over the second half of the nineteenth century transformed the whole country into an exotic place inhabited by passionate women and brave men. The romantic images of flamenco and bullfighting, most of them set in Andalusia, images that persist even as of today, gradually came to represent the country and its culture as a whole. The romantic vision of Spain saw in Andalusia the place where the traditions of the poor and working classes were best represented in opposition to those of the urban bourgeoisie. A mix of the bigotry from the "The Black Legend" and the exotic, popular, and picturesque images created by the French Romantics like Bizet and Mérimée were quickly adopted by Spanish artists like Vicente Blasco Ibáñez, and at the same time criticized by others, like the Spanish writer Pío Baroja and the journalist and women's rights activist Carmen de Burgos, better known as *Colombine*.

Among all these stereotypes, Carmen stands out. This female character deeply connected to Andalusia, bullfighting, and flamenco was born at the hands of French artists but raised and modified in Spain, where it became the image of a passionate and self-sufficient woman. As a result of the positive popular response, Carmen became the ambassador of Spanish women, spreading the powerful and exotic image of Spanish culture (Lema-Hincapie

Figure 8.1. *Carmen* (Ernst Lubitsch, 1918) Source: Courtesy of Filmoteca Nacional de España.

157). If we compare the characteristics of both visions we can appreciate similar concepts represented in different ways. In the Black Legend vision, Spaniards are religious fanatics living in a cruel social environment; in the romantic view, Spanish people respect ancient traditions and live their lives with passion. In Black Legend books, Spain is a country with primitive technology and lazy workers, but the romantic works describe the country as an artistic nation where citizens live with freedom. The *conquistador* or *inquisitor* is the most representative character in Black Legend stories, as Carmen would be for the romantic artists of the nineteenth century. The *españolada* genre elaborates its most popular characters using a combination of both.

In Berger's film the two main female characters, Blancanieves and her mother, are named Carmen. The shared name is an intentional decision from the director in order to link the film to the stereotyped vision of Spain and its culture. Similarly, but on the opposite side of the mirror, Snow White works as a referent of a stereotyped female character. In Berger's project, Carmen and Snow White, once again in this game of deforming mirrors, will work together to show us how a *cliché* operates in our collective imaginary, but they show it to us in a very delicate and visually elegant way.

The genre *españolada* in film, literature, the performing arts, and painting is rooted in these two stereotyped cultural paradigms, becoming the most important consequence of this eccentric game of deforming mirrors between the outside and inside conceptions of Spanish characters and cultural topics over the centuries. However, in the first decades of the twentieth century, Spanish scholars (Camporesi) started debates about the nature of Spanish cinema, including this new genre. *Españolada*, in film and in theater, coexists within the same cultural environment as other artistic *avant-garde* European movements, being led by Pablo Picasso, Luis Buñuel, or Ramón María del Valle-Inclán, to name but a few. Over the first decades of the century, the Spanish national and international image was being built in the narrow space between upper-class culture and popular culture, and between the radical *avant-garde* movement and the conservative *españolada* genre. During the 1920s, both national and international film industries were extensively producing movies about bullfighters, famous and handsome bandits, flamenco dancers, and beautiful and powerful female gypsies.

We can find examples of these stories in the Hollywood industry from the silent era to the present day, as, for example: *Blood and Sand* (Fred Niblo, 1922), based on a Spanish novel, and the animated movie *Ferdinand* (Carlos Saldanha, 2017), a comedy about a nonviolent bull. We can also find the same artistic references in European cinema: from *Carmen* (Ernst Lubitsch, 1918) starring Pola Negri, one of the first *femme fatale* actresses, to *Toreros* (Eric Barbier, 2000), a tragic story about bullfighting and drug dealers. The Spanish film industry itself was spreading the same stereotypes about its own culture with titles like *El embrujo de Sevilla* (Benio Perojo, 1930), a romantic and classic story about flamenco dancers and bullfighters, and the latest version of *Carmen* (Vicente Aranda, 2003).

Berger's visual and narrative conception of the film operates within the same framework. On the one hand, visually *Blancanieves* is a tribute to silent film history, from experimental filmmakers like Luis Buñuel to German expressionists like Robert Wiene and Russian camera pioneers like Dziga Vertov. On the other hand, the story, the characters, the cultural references, and the geographical and social context are an accurate example of the contents of the *españolada* film genre. The whole film acts as an antagonizing story between two worlds, between artistic film texts and popular film texts, between light and darkness, between expressive music and silence. The film questions whether Spanish stereotypes, and Spaniards themselves, offer a truthful image of their culture or rather if they present a deformed reflection of it.

Blancanieves

The film is set in Seville, Andalusia, between 1910 and 1930. Carmencita, performed by the Spanish actress Macarena García, is the daughter of a famous bullfighter and a gorgeous *flamenco* dancer and singer, who is also named Carmen (Inma Cuesta). While Carmencita's mother dies in childbirth, her father Antonio (Daniel Giménez Cacho) is severely injured during a bullfight; Antonio then blames Carmencita for the death of his beloved wife. As a result of these tragic events, the baby's grandmother, performed by the Spanish actress Angela Molina, has to take care of her for years. In the meantime, the disabled torero remarries his nurse, named Encarna (Maribel Verdú), a name related to the term "flesh," appropriate for the character who is an evil fortune hunter greedy for fame, sex, power, and money. When the grandmother dies, Carmencita goes to live with the couple, but her stepmother treats her like a slave—which also echoes Cinderella—and forbids her to meet her father. Due to its cruelty, this episode in Carmencita's life can be also related to one of the first published narrations of Snow White, titled "Little Slave Girl." This story compiled by the Neapolitan Giambattista Basile in a collection of popular tales known as Pentamerone—posthumously published in 1634—offers a cultural context that gently connects Berger's discourse about Spanish stereotypes to a fairy tale that in its dominant and popular form tends to be related mainly to the Grimms' version. However, Carmencita is a fearless child who has inherited her mother's talent and beauty and her father's bravery; while they are together, Carmencita and the stepmother always confront and challenge each other. Eventually, Carmencita creates a bond with her father without Encarna's knowledge, and he teaches her the techniques of bullfighting. Day after day, Carmencita grows into a young woman who is able to dance, sing, and bullfight. When the jealous, greedy, and unfaithful stepmother learns about the rediscovery of father and daughter ties, she kills Antonio and tries to get Carmencita—now Carmen—murdered by the hand of one of her lovers, the family's chauffeur. Running away, Carmen accidentally hits her head and loses her memory and her ability to be self-sufficient; on a deeper level, she has forgotten what it means to be Carmen. A traveling troupe of comic bullfighter dwarves find the confused young woman walking disoriented in the forest. Due to her physical traits—black hair, fair skin, and red lips—they call her Blancanieves, a beautiful teenager alone in the forest who does not even remember her own name. At the precise moment of losing her identity, Blancanieves transforms herself into a delicate and a fearful young lady who needs other people's assistance. Progressively, however, she begins to rediscover her ability to bullfight, and becomes a famous matador supported by the exotic group of six dwarves. As she continues bullfighting, she starts to remember her past, a process that allows her to restart her transformation into Carmen. However, this transformation is interrupted when her stepmother, now a celebrity in the yellow magazines, reads about her in the papers. This time, Encarna tries to kill her with a poisoned apple at the same moment that that she recovers her memory at the bullring. Unfortunately, after eating the apple, she apparently dies. The angry dwarves kill the stepmother but Carmen does not awake from her deadly dream. Finally, the comic group, headed by the greedy manager, exhibits Blancanieves, her artistic name at the time, as part of a freak show in order to obtain profit from the sleeping beauty. There is no magic kiss or happy ending, not for Blancanieves and, of course, not for Carmen either.

Berger's *Blancanieves*	Common references for Snow White
The father is a weak matador	The father is a weak nobleman
The mother is a flamenco artist	The mother is a weak noblewoman
The stepmother is a vamp	The stepmother is a witch
Snow White can be a self-sufficient woman	**Snow White is a dependent woman**
Snow White's best friend is a proud rooster	The docile animals living in the forest help Snow White
The dwarves are six comedian bullfighters	The seven dwarves are miners
There is no prince	**A handsome prince helps Snow White**
There is not a magic episode	**There are several magic episodes**
There is not a happy ending	**There is a happy ending**

This game of contrapositions is shown in the character's development from a powerful woman like Carmen to a weak woman through her transformation into Snow White after losing her memory, and therefore, her identity as Carmen. While Carmen is synonymous with power, Snow White is synonymous with weakness. Snow White is the deformed reflection of Carmen and vice versa. In the same way, *españolada* is the deformed reflection of artistic filmmakers as well as Spanish culture. If we compare Berger's film with the other three versions that appeared in 2012, they have one thing in common: by the end of the stories, Snow White is no longer a naive young lady who needs to be rescued by a prince. Although all versions share this basic approach in order to update a fairy-tale classic character, there exist fundamental differences between them and the Spanish *Blancanieves* that go beyond the formal aspect of Berger's film. Keeping the basic narrative lines of the original story, the filmmaker shows us the character of Snow White contextualized in the Spanish popular tradition, immersed in the *españolada* genre. In contrast to the Snow Whites of the other three versions, the Spanish Snow White is the only one who does not want to take revenge on her stepmother, as happens with the character from the Grimms' story. Blancanieves helps Carmen to find love, kindness, and sympathy; in the same way, Carmen helps Blancanieves to be brave and self-sufficient. Nevertheless, Carmen forgets herself and becomes the fictitious Snow White. The characters in Berger's film are supposedly living in the "real world" and they are not part of a fairy tale; naming Carmen as Blancanieves demonstrates their knowledge about the Grimms' tale. Despite living in a surreal context as a result of the influence of the *españolada* genre, each character in the film has the ability to discriminate between fiction and nonfiction, between the fairy-tale reference and real life. However, neither Carmen nor Blancanieves can have a happy ending because they are deformed images of each other. If Snow White is for all audiences clearly a character without connection to the real world, the distorted version, Carmen, is also unreal. In consequence, Berger cannot afford a happy ending for either of them, since this would prove their existence as an acceptable cultural reference linked to a national or regional cultural reality.

"Snow White" is not the only fairy-tale reference portrayed in the film; we can also appreciate visual and textual influences from "Cinderella," "Sleeping Beauty," "Tom Thumb," and "Little Red Riding Hood." For example, Carmencita is like Cinderella when she sleeps in the basement of the big house surrounded by coal and dirt; when she falls asleep because of the poisoned apple, the dwarves and the manager refer to her as Sleeping Beauty. When Encarna learns that Carmencita is visiting her ill father, the stepmother threatens her with eating her only friend, the rooster, placing herself at the same level as the wolf of Little Red Riding Hood eating the grandmother. Encarna finally fulfils her threat, because she kills and eats the rooster and makes Carmencita eat it too. Finally, when Encarna is murdered at the hands of the dwarves, she insults them, calling them "a band of freak Tom Thumbs." Blancanieves herself knows that the dwarves named her after the classic story but she refuses her new identity because she wants to be a real woman, she wants to be Carmen again. However, Berger does not allow her to choose because the two of them operate in the same fictional context, that of the unreal world of stereotypes. This acknowledgment of fiction places the film in a supposedly real space. The visual narratives regarding cultural references in painting, literature, popular Spanish entertainment, and film history are shared by spectators and characters alike. Berger's film extends its visual possibilities and expands its narrative by working through the space between these two references, *españolada* and fairy tale, and this character with two faces, Carmen and Snow White, in order to stress the veracity of the stereotype against reality.

Characters in *Blancanieves*

Encarna, the evil stepmother, is perhaps one of the most interesting characters in the film. Performed by Maribel Verdú, who usually works with Berger, the character of Encarna is a narrative element directly taken from the French film noir related to the femme fatale, but also a visual reference from the silent film's vamp woman. Encarna is a nurse who takes advantage of the debilitated condition of a famous bullfighter. She takes care of the wounded man until they get married; at that moment she resigns from her job and starts spending money as if she were a rich woman and having sex with other men. Encarna is depicted as an evil character, an unfaithful wife who wants to destroy men. The evil way is the only path that Encarna, the femme fatale, is allowed to follow. In the *españolada* genre, as well as in other film genres and in fairy tales, being an evil woman is the only way to become free and not to rely on men (Doane; Bornay). If we choose to do a feminist reading of the classic tale, we can understand "Snow White" as the story of a powerful woman, the witch, who fights against the traditional representation of female characters in tales. The premise of a sweet and innocent young woman in need of a man seems a futile and tragic effort for the witch. Berger seems to agree with this feminist interpretation of the classic tale but makes the two female characters face each other from the beginning, the archetypical femme fatale against Carmencita. In order to avoid a narrative dead end caused by this strong confrontation of two determined women, the director transforms Carmen into Blancanieves and he makes her look into the deformed mirror of stereotypes.

Historically speaking, cinema has condemned these women of great courage and firm determination to the fate of wickedness. Carmen usually shares the same deadly consequences as a vamp. Berger does not want Blancanieves to succeed either, as Carmen/Encarna and Blancanieves are two sides of the same coin. Many of the film's mirrors, in which the stepmother contemplates herself, reflect the awful image of a terrible fate, and the same happens with her stepdaughter's mirrors—the bull's-eye, the camera lens, the reflection of the light in the moon and in the water's surface; this effect is also visible through the cinema cameras and the photographs published in the tabloids. The function of the magic mirror in the traditional tale is updated to show how contemporary society, specifically mass media, exposes itself, seeking notoriety. At present, reality shows, the Internet, and social networks, among others, are new tools in the formation of stereotypes, as cinema and popular literature were in the past. As Cristina Bacchilega ("Framing" 28) points out, the mirror in fairy tales "refracts what we wish or fear to become." Similarly, Encarna's exhibitionist desire has been captured as a magic mirror by the photo reportage on her dead husband and the huge portraits in which Encarna is painted as a powerful woman. Encarna wishes to see her desires and ambitions reflected in the mirrors that she uses. In contrast, Blancanieves can see herself in photographs and through camera lenses after becoming a female bullfighter and a celebrity in the yellow magazines. She does not want to see the image of what she has become through those mirrors. Each mirror is a future sign of bad things to come. Just a few seconds before Antonio's tragic accident in the bullring, the matador can see his own image reflected in the bull's eye. Years after, when

Blancanieves is bullfighting, the tragic mirror of her fate will be the image of the bull, this time captured by the lens of a camera. For Encarna, the photographs published in the yellow magazines will drive her to poison the apple that will eventually lead her to her untimely demise.

Those mirrors function as a metaphor of the power of the image, as even the six dwarves take profit by exploiting the image of Blancanieves in magazines to become rich and famous as well. The group of six dwarf bullfighters who help Blancanieves is an interesting ensemble related to the classic tale, as well as to popular entertainment in Spain. When the dwarves appear on screen, the visual composition of the movie, until then a traditional narrative and visual construction in terms of melodrama and the *españolada* genre, turns into a grotesque cinematic mixture of European expressionist cinema and the American freak films made by Tod Browning. Following Disney's characterization of the dwarves, Berger uses different attributes to individualize the characters, to make us believe that they can be real. In fact, troupes of dwarf bullfighters have been a usual popular entertainment in local celebrations in Spanish villages. Spanish cinema audiences are used to this kind of entertainment even today. The representation of comic dwarves has been a frequent topic in Spanish pictorial tradition from Velázquez to Goya, but also more recently in the works by Magnum photographer Cristina García Rodero, including her photo essay *España Oculta [Hidden Spain]*. Berger uses this strange and traditional show to exaggerate their behavior and bring them closer to the freak show, as we can appreciate at the end of the film when the sleeping Blancanieves is exhibited in an itinerant freak show designed by the manager and some of the dwarves. For the price of a few coins, people can kiss the beautiful and famous female bullfighter. Some of the members of the troupe and its manager betray the woman who helped them at first. The story of Blancanieves, as the story of Carmen, narrates the continuous betrayal committed by the men around her: her father, the dwarves, the manager, and even the dwarf who is in love with her, who stays by her side in the freak show, taking care of her but allowing her sexual objectification.

The film's male characters represent some aspects of *españolada*: brave men, bullfighters, popular entertainers, passionate lovers, and so on. Yet,

Figure 8.2. Magic mirrors. The images of the bull's eye before Antonio's accident, the camera lens before Blancanieves's accident, and the yellow magazine that triggers Encarna's jealousy. From *Blancanieves* (Berger, 2012).

at the same time, they show us some of the characteristics involved in the fairy-tale tradition: on the one hand, they are weak and submissive men, dominated by powerful and spiteful women, like the father figure in "Snow White" and "Cinderella"; on the other hand, they are greedy and envious men in need of money and power who do not hesitate to take advantage of women in order to fulfil their selfish desires. Berger's Blancanieves is a poor young woman betrayed several times in her short life by different types of men. When she is no more than a newborn she suffers the first rejection from her own father, who, despite having been a brave bullfighter, is now a sick and weak man, unable to protect her from the evil stepmother. All male characters are encompassed in both contexts: *españolada* and fairy tales. Visually, the father, the stepmother's lover, the dwarves, and the manager represent stereotyped depictions in popular Spanish culture related to the *españolada* genre; narratively they epitomize the weak male characters of traditional fairy tales like "Snow White," "Cinderella," or "Sleeping Beauty."

Counterbalancing the power-lacking male characters, female characters inherit the power. We can recognize traits of Carmen in each female character: the grandmother, the mother, and Carmen herself. The three of them are a representation of this stereotype; even the stepmother is portrayed with the courage of this popular character. Unfortunately, all Carmens face the same fate—that is, death. With the exception of the grandmother, who dies dancing and singing while celebrating a traditional religious ceremony, the other two die in one of the most significant places associated with death

Figure 8.3. Image of the poisoned Carmen exhibited in a coffin made of glass in an itinerant show. From *Blancanieves* (Berger, 2012).

in Spanish tradition: the *plaza de toros* or bullring. Carmen's mother dies giving birth to her at the bullring at the same moment that her father is terribly injured by a bull. Some years later, as if it were a cruel joke of fate, the amnesiac Blancanieves is killed by her stepmother at the same spot where she was born, the bullring, just as she is recovering her memory and becoming Carmen again.

Cultural References

Through the recycling and crossing of boundaries of national themes and fairy tales, Berger reconfigures an aesthetic of exhibition. This follows Gaudreault's concept of "monstration," since it is closely related to the exhibition of wonders, film history, popular entertainment, and folk stories, as well as artistic acquisitions. The pictorial references of Berger's film guide us to explore the history of Spanish art, in which stereotypical characters of popular culture and *españolada* topics are reflected. Gypsy women, bulls and bullfighters, people from Andalusia, and flamenco singers and dancers have been widely represented by Spanish painters and filmmakers. Julio Romero

Figure 8.4. From above and left to right: Carmencita's mother and grandmother; Blancanieves the bullfighter; the stepmother, Encarna; the father, Antonio; the troupe of six bullfighter dwarves; and the impresario. From *Blancanieves* (Berger, 2012).

de Torres was a famous Spanish painter included in the so-called Generation of '98 (Azorín), a group of artists and intellectuals active from the last years of the nineteenth century to the first two decades of the twentieth century. Along with writers, essayists, and poets, the group of painters led by Romero de Torres stimulated the debate about the meaning of national identity and the best way to represent it. In 1898 Spain had lost the last colonies in America and in the Pacific area and was defeated in Cuba during the war against the United States. This social and political crisis defined the beginning of the group, who started criticising the traditional ways in politics, the arts, and social practices, which were tightly attached to its imperialist past, the monarchy, religion, and the Black Legend. Disappointed with the upper classes, traditionalist politics, and the bourgeoisie, artists and intellectuals from this artistic and philosophical movement turned their attention toward the lenses of European romantic interpretations of Spanish popular culture in France and Germany, focusing on the working classes and the lowest social strata. Some of the most attractive topics for painters, and later for filmmakers, were popular customs, death, and romantic love. Flamenco and bullfighters best represented this new trend in art and popular entertainment.

Using these cultural referents, Berger develops a post-*españolada* to take control of these inherited clichés to escape from the apparently timeless fairy tales. By deconstructing and mixing two antagonized popular references, Berger is able to exploit several stereotypes and design a visual story to stress the power of the image in the formation of national identities and cultural assumptions. The representations of some characters as well as the paintings that appear in the film replicate perfectly Romero de Torres's most famous paintings. Berger's design of male and female characters, particularly young Carmen, her father, and her stepmother, functions in the same way that Romero de Torres portrayed his sensual men and women, completely idealizing the stereotypical image of Andalusian people. However, when the story turns around and Carmen becomes Blancanieves, the visual aesthetic of the film rapidly changes, and *españolada* topics are abandoned until the end of the movie in order to adopt the romantic images of the fairy tale combined with the representations of freak show entertainment and the dramatic expressions that inhabit silent cinema. Berger's visual conceptions do not respect any of the cultural, narrative, or visual assumptions firmly established by the popular appropriation of these stories and characters. This combination provokes a productive dialogue between the widely known stories of the Grimms' fairy tales and the social satire about Spanish clichés. This exchange is wrapped in the silent film style, where transnational references of avant-garde European filmmakers are mixed with popular and artistic references.

The first part of the movie, until Carmen escapes from the evil stepmother and the chauffeur tries to kill her, is perfectly adjusted to the melodrama style. Its frantic style is noticeable in the acting, the cinematography, and the music choices, but this does not interfere with the narrative as a whole. In this powerful exercise of constant encounters and cultural loans, Berger inserts, in a very smooth way, the Gothic atmosphere of *Rebecca* (Alfred Hitchcock, 1940), Sergei Eisenstein's editing methods, and Dziga Vertov's "Cine-Eye" montage theory, as well as the illumination techniques developed by David Lean and the use of close-ups, reminiscent of *La Passion de Jeanne d'Arc* (C. T. Dreyer, 1928). In spite of the fact that this part of the movie can be seen as a tribute to European and American masters of cinema

Figure 8.5. The first and third image from left to right are the paintings of Julio Romero de Torres, "Machiquito" (1911) and "Diana Cazadora" (1924). The second and the fourth ones are shots from the film. Source: Julio Romero de Torres, "Machiquito" (1911) and "Diana Cazadora" (1924) courtesy of Ceres (Ministry of Culture and Sports of Spain) and screen captures from *Blancanieves* (Berger, 2012).

of the twentieth century, the narrative element is once again provided mainly through the cultural mixing of flamenco music and dancing. The music and dancing, together with the visual techniques mentioned before, work as a perfect narrative engine, specifically in the excessive dance in which Carmencita's grandmother dances until she drops dead while celebrating the First Holy Communion of the child and listening to a song recorded by Carmencita's mother.

In contrast to the melodramatic conception of the film, the structure perfectly accommodates Propp's theory regarding the traditional development of "Snow White." Both in Propp's theories and in Berger's film, the journey is the same for Carmen and Snow White. After a traumatic event a family is dramatically broken and the female main character has to undertake a decisive journey full of challenges in her quest to avoid danger. In Berger's *Blancanieves*, Carmen's journey means the search for her identity.

The second part of the movie, from the moment when Carmen finds the troupe of six dwarves until the end, is full of elements taken from the popular entertainment *vodevil*, the Spanish appropriation of the French vaudeville. The Spanish *vodevil*, existing today mainly in television, is characterized by

Berger's *Blancanieves*	The Grimms' *Snow White*
Limited structure	Limited structure
⇩	⇩
Absence	Absence
⇩	⇩
Transgression	Wickedness
⇩	⇩
Malice	Travel
⇩	⇩
Travel	Magical agent
⇩	⇩
Atavistic agent	Recognition
⇩	⇩
Recognition	Trickery
⇩	⇩
Trickery	Punishment
⇩	⇩
Punishment	Happy ending

the exaggeration of characters who brush against the boundaries of social norms through their sexual and social attitudes. This part of the film also shares formal characteristics in the composition of the frames with film noir, as well as the visual aesthetic of the grotesque typical of Tod Browning. The concluding section of the film certainly provides the best illustration for the freak show influence, as well as for the use of fantasy and magic associated with the tradition of fairy tales. The living corpse of the famous female bullfighter is exhibited in a freak show conceived by Blancanieves's manager in order to continue taking economic advantage of her strange situation. The show, entitled *La feria de lo increíble*, or Show of Wonders, is an itinerant circus with a werewolf, Siamese twins, and the skinniest man in the world, and Blancanieves is the main attraction. Placed in a glass coffin, she can be

Figure 8.6. Influences from popular entertainment and film genres. From left to right: film images from popular comic bullfights, freak show movies, and a classic frame that remind us of the pool scene in *Sunset Boulevard* (Billy Wilder, 1950). From *Blancanieves* (Berger, 2012).

kissed by anyone in exchange for a few coins. The aim seems to be trying to awaken the sleeping beauty. These last scenes inevitably bring to mind the film *Freaks* (1932), due to the eccentric exhibitions of this show, like the ones mentioned before, but also remind us that this is not a traditional fairy-tale happy ending. This film is much more than a work of metamorphosis of the classic tales, it is also is a tribute to the cinematographic art and its power for fascination in the same way that fairy tales were fascinating before the invention of cinema, thanks to their ability to take us to a fantasy world. Berger makes a movie not just to think about the stereotypes and the formation of national identities but also to create a tale about the cinema that Berger himself evaluates as the fairy tale of the twentieth century: "I'm not a film director. I am a story teller. I tell stories. I tell fairy tales" (Susina 165). In this sense, his film works as a visual essay, a critical rereading that invites us to reflect upon it while enjoying its multiple references. Berger's Snow White is the daughter of a fairy-tale heroine but also of a bullfighter and a flamenco singer, as well as a motion picture celebrating the history of cinema and its genres.

Conclusion

Mirror, Mirror, Snow White and the Huntsman, Once upon a Time, and Berger's *Blancanieves* are part of a renewed interest in fairy tales in the entertainment industry. As Kristian Moen (xiii) points out, "cinema is making fairy tales modern." These movies and other later works like *Hansel and Gretel: Witch Hunters* (Tommy Wirkola, 2013) and *Maleficent* (Robert Stromberg, 2014) use fairy tales as a tool to criticize contemporary gender roles. Nowadays, the fairy-tale film genre is using the classic tales to raise questions about gender roles as portrayed in the stories and their validity in the twenty-first century. As Bacchilega ("Mixing It Up" 40) reminds us, fairy-tale films can be addressed as hybrid texts, "to emphasize the competing social uses of the fairy tale in contemporary Western popular culture." Berger uses this hybrid quality as a result of the modern appropriation of fairy tales to delve into female gender roles in the stereotyped Spanish popular culture. Berger's film is a beautiful and critical story about how stereotypes can be uncritically assumed as part of national identity. In the Spanish popular imagination, fairy tales are a distant reference related to North and Central European cultures and not to the Mediterranean. Due to the proximity of magic to fairy tales, the latter are considered children's stories in Spanish culture. Romantic stereotypes about passion and death, like those used in the several adaptations in which Carmen, flamenco dancers, or bullfighters are the main characters, are, again, uncritically adopted by Spanish culture as an actual identity trace. Berger uses a fairy tale in contrast with Carmen to show spectators the irony of their perception of reality and to make them think about the process that lead them either to adopt or to reject a stereotype as an identity trace or as a children's tale. To Berger, Carmen is as far from reality as Snow White is.

The film explores and alters the space that lies within this game of mirrors to invite the spectator to think about believed misconceptions concerning culture and gender roles in contemporary society. At the same time, as a cinephile and filmmaker, Berger narrates this story using silent and classical cinema visual techniques to transport us to a magic world, as fairy tales did centuries before the invention of moving images. The combination of fairy tales and the *españolada* genre allows him the use of clichés to stress national identity from a critical and original perspective and, at the same time, to make us think about the place that women hold in the common belief, artistic or not. Berger's film trespasses the boundaries of all of the cultural references and influences he uses to create his own story in order to criticize the stereotypes embedded in national tradition. As Jack Zipes points out, "George Méliès revolutionized the fairy tale at the beginning of the twentieth century . . . in part due to new technology that enhances cinematic special effects" (5). Berger undergoes a process of immersion, not just from the visual and technical possibilities of this combination but from the synergies created between fairy tales and silent film narrative modes. Early cinema provides a new tool to enjoy, analyze, and make cultural and social use of fairy tales.

As Berger explained at the Roger Ebert Film Festival, *I'm not a film director. I'm a storyteller. I tell stories. I tell fairy tales.* Berger's *Blancanieves* retains the spirit of the Brothers Grimm tale but manages to add the most well-known Spanish stereotypes in a provocative cinematic way in order to make us consider contemporary issues about gender and identity. For the first time in Spanish cinema history, fairy tales are used to explain cultural stereotypes unconnected to the literary and sociocultural environment in which fairy tales developed.

Works Cited

Albarrán, Diego J. "Del 'desarrollismo' al entusiasmo: Notas sobre el arte español en tiempos de *transición*" ["From 'desarrollismo' to Enthusiasm: Notes about Spanish Art in the Transition Era"]. *Foro de Educación,* vol. 6, 2008, pp.167–84.

Azorín. *La Generación del 98* [*The Generation of '98*]. Biblioteca Anaya, 1961.

Bacchilega, Cristina. "The Framing of 'SnowWhite': Narrative and Gender (Re)Production." *Postmodern Fairy Tales: Gender and Narrative Strategies,* University of Pennsylvania Press, 1997, pp. 27–48.

———. "Mixing It Up: Generic Complexity and Gender Ideology in Early Twenty-first Century Fairy Tale Films." *Fairy Tale Films: Visions of Ambiguity,* edited by Pauline Greenhill and Sidney Eve, Utah University Press, 2010, pp. 23–41.

Bornay, Erika. *Las hijas de Lilith* [*The Daughters of Lilith*]. Cátedra, 1990.

Camporesi, Valeria. "La españolada histórica en imágenes" ["The History of 'Españolada' in Images"]. *Historia Contemporánea de España y Cine*, edited by Itor Yraola, Ediciones de la Universidad Autónoma de Madrid, 1997, pp. 25–36.

Doane, Mary Ann. *Femmes Fatales. Feminism, Film Theory, Psycoanalysis*. Routledge, 1991.

"Españolada." *Diccionario de la Lengua Española* [*Dictionary of Spanish Language*]. Real Academia Española de la Lengua, dle.rae.es/?id=GUUlpG2. Accessed 21 July 2017.

García Rodero, Cristina. *La España Oculta* [*Hidden Spain*]. Lunwerg, 1989.

Gaudreault, André. *From Plato to Lumière: Narration and Monstration in Literature and Cinema*. University of Toronto Press, 2009.

Gubern, Román. *Historia del Cine Español* [*Spanish Film History*]. Cátedra. 1995.

Huerta Floriano, M. A., and E. Pérez Morán. "Cine y sociedad: la construcción de los personajes masculinos y femeninos en el 'landismo' tardofranquista" ["Cinema and Society: The Formation of Male and Female Characters in 'Landismo' in the Last Years of Franco's Dictatorship"]. *Arbor: Ciencia, pensamiento y cultura*, vol. 191, no. 773, 2015, pp. 1–13.

Lema-Hincapie, Andrés. "Carlos Saura's Carmen Hybridity and the Inescapable Cliché" *Carmen*, edited by Chris Perriam and Ann Davies, Brill | Rodopi, 2005, pp. 151–65.

Marías, Julián. *España inteligible: Razón histórica de las Españas* [*Intangible Spain: Historical Reasons of the Two Spains*]. Alianza Editorial, 1985.

Metheou, Demetrios. "Pablo Berger: A movie's like a paella, you put all of your obsessions in there." *Guardian. International Edition,* 11 Dec. 2013, www.theguardian.com/film/2013/jul/11/silent-film-blancanieves-pablo-berger-interview. Accessed 9 Dec. 2017.

Moen, Kristian. *Films and Fairy Tales: The Birth of Modern Fantasy*. I.B. Tauris, 2013.

Ortega, M. Luisa. "De la españolada al *fake*. Estereotipos de la españolidad, identidad y diálogos transnacionales" ["From 'Españolada' to Fake. Stereotypes in Transnational Dialogues in Spanishness and Identity"]. *El juego con los estereotipos. La redefinición de la identidad hispánica en la literatura y el cine postnacionales*, edited by Peter Lang, ThéoCrit, vol. 1, 2012, pp. 99–118.

Propp, Vladimir. *Morphology of the Folktale*. 2nd ed., translated by Laurence Scott, revised by Louis A. Wagner, University of Texas Press, 1968.

Susina, Jan. Review of *Blancanieves. Marvels & Tales. Journal of Fairy Tales*, vol. 29, no. 1, 2005, p. 165.

Zipes, Jack. *The Enchanted Screen: The Unknown History of Fairy-Tale Films*. Routledge, 2011.

Filmography

Abracadabra. Directed by Pablo Berger, Arcadia Motion Pictures, Perséfone Films, Noodles Production, Atresmedia Cine, Movistar+ and Scope Pictures, 2017.

Blancanieves. Directed by Pablo Berger, Arcadia Motion Pictures, Noodles and Production, 2012.

Blood and Sand. Directed by Fred Niblo, Paramount Pictures, 1922.

Carmen. Directed by Ernst Lubitsch, Projektions-AG Union and Universum Film, 1918.

Carmen. Directed by Vicente Aranda, Star Line TV Productions, Parallel Pictures, Planet Pictures and TeleMadrid, 2003.

El embrujo de Sevilla. Directed by Benio Perojo, Julio César and UFA, 1930.

Ferdinand. Directed by Carlos Saldanha, Blue Sky Studios, 20th Century Fox Animation and Davis Entertainment, 2017.

Freaks. Directed by Tod Browning, MGM, 1932.

Hansel and Gretel: Witch Hunters. Directed by Tommy Wirkola, MGM, Studio Babelsberg, Gary Sanchez Productions and Paramount Pictures, 2013.

La Passion de Jeanne d'Arc. Directed by C. T. Dreyer, Societé generale de films, 1928.

Maleficient. Directed by Robert Stromberg, Walt Disney Pictures, Moving Picture Company (MPC) and Roth Films, 2014.

Mirror Mirror. Directed by Tarsem Singh, Rat Entertainment, Relativity Studios, Yucaipa Films, Goldmann Pictures and Misha Films, 2012.

Once Upon a Time: The Complete seven seasons. Produced by ABC, 2011–18.

Rebecca. Directed by Alfred Hitchcock, Selznick International Pictures, 1940.

Snow White and the Huntsman. Directed by Rupert Sanders, Roth Films and Universal Pictures, 2012.

Sunset Boulevard. Directed by Billy Wilder, Paramount Pictures, 1950.

The Artist. Directed by Michel Hazanavicius, Wildbunch, La Petite Reine, Studio 37, La Classe Américaine, JD Prod, France3 Cinéma, Jouror Production and uFilms, 2011.

Toreros. Directed by Eric Barbier, Obero Cinematografica, Mallerich Audiovisuales S.L., TPS Cinéma, Annabel Productions, Eurimages, France 2 Cinéma, Vertigo, Canal+ España and Les Films de l'Etang, 2000.

Torremolinos 73. Directed by Pablo Berger, Estudios Picasso, Nimbus Film, Mama Films and Telespan 2000, 2003.

III

Promoting Alternative Ethics and Aesthetics

9

Re-Orienting the Fairy Tale, Revising Age?

Vanessa Joosen

IN WESTERN CULTURE'S MOST popular fairy tales, conflicts between members of different generations abound, from the wicked old witch who threatens to eat the young Hansel and Gretel to the envious stepmother in "Snow White," who cannot bear to be replaced with a member of the younger generation as the most beautiful in the fairy-tale kingdom. Folktales worldwide describe the quest for eternal youth, with *Gilgamesh* as the best known example. With the recent rise of age studies, the construction of age in various cultural discourses has come under scrutiny, and fairy tales have occasionally also been subjected to this type of critique. Age critics such as Sylvia Henneberg have attacked classic fairy tales for conveying ageist discourses to young children, with ageism referring to age-related prejudices (Green 187). Ageism leads to discriminating practices against people on the basis of their age, and it also affects the image that people have of their own past and future selves. Age critics are, of course, not the first to point out that traditional fairy tales hold problematic ideologies. The tales' class and gender bias has been especially scrutinized by various scholars, as well as their heteronormative stance. In addition, and in an intertextual dialogue with the scholarship, postmodern rewritings have also addressed the traditional tales' ideology (Joosen, *Critical*). Authors and illustrators have revised and parodied, among others, the traditional fairy tales' gender and class roles to induce critical reflection on the traditional stories or to make them suited for and appealing to contemporary audiences. But do fairy-tale rewritings also exploit their critical potential when it comes to ideology related to age? In *Fairy Tales Transformed?*, Cristina Bacchilega invites her readers to reflect on the following question: "What are the stakes, and for whom, of adapting fairy tales in the twenty-first century?" (ix). In this chapter, I will raise a plea to include age in the investigation of what Bacchilega calls "the politics of wonder" of the fairy tale and the fairy-tale rewriting, and to draw on the ever-expanding field of age studies to do so. Moreover, when it comes to considering age, Western and Eastern perspectives provide interesting points of comparison and potential mutual enrichment. The chapter opens with a brief survey of the relevance of age studies to the study of traditional fairy tales by referring to three inspirational works. The text then shifts focus to the revision of age in a selection of contemporary fairy-tale rewritings, arguing that current analyses of these can be both problematized by and supplemented with insights from age studies.

Age studies has not been in the picture of cultural studies as much as Marxist, gender, postcolonial or queer studies. In fact, age ideology and casual ageism often go unquestioned—perhaps because aging affects all of us, as a gradual process, and does not concern just one specific group of people. Whatever the case, the cult of youth and the negative discourses around aging are particularly persuasive in Western culture. Some precursors to current age studies, such as Simone de Beauvoir's *La vieillesse* (translated as *The Coming of Age*), already explored age on a systematic basis in the 1970s and also addressed the experience and prejudice against old age. The subsequent decades' critical reflection focused on other markers of identity (race, sexuality, class, and especially gender) occasionally brought age into the picture, but it is especially in the last two decades that age studies as a field has gained attention among researchers in the humanities. The shift in the demographics of many countries in both Asia and the West has led to an increased percentage of old citizens (the so-called old age ratio) and a reported increase in intergenerational conflicts—this gives age studies new urgency. It is currently a booming field that unites researchers from a wide array of disciplines: medicine, law, anthropology, political science, sociology, cultural studies, and also literary studies and children's literature studies. While the focus of many critics working in age studies may lie on old age, the field as whole is engaged in the broader consideration of the role that *any* age plays in human life and reflections on the life course in general.

In current fairy-tale studies, age has already functioned in analyses of individual tales and in reflections on storytelling practices, even if the scholars themselves would not usually identify as age critics or even name age studies as their frame of reference. Three main strands can be distinguished in the analyses of age in traditional fairy tales:

1. The analysis of age leads to new readings of well-known fairy tales.
2. The analysis of age helps us to distinguish between fairy-tale traditions in different countries and to reflect on the cultural context of certain tale types.
3. The analysis of age leads to a critique of ageist stereotypes in fairy tales.

In what follows, I will introduce each strand with reference to inspirational contributions by fairy-tale critics.

Analyzing Age in Traditional Fairy Tales

First, focusing on age and intergenerational relationships can shed new light on well-known fairy tales and yield new interpretations. Shuli Barzilai's "Reading Snow White: The Mother's Story" provides a good example. Although she does not draw on age studies specifically, her interpretation of "Snow White" hinges on a critical examination of the way that the tale constructs the life course and intergenerational relationships. Barzilai starts from the observation that the tale of "Snow White" is marked by the "perspectival dominance" of the daughter and that several critics of the story rely on that perspective for their interpretation of the tale (523). She challenges that point of view and shifts the lens to the mother and her wishes and desires. Rather than a simple tale of female rivalry, "Snow White," in Barzilai's reading, sheds light on a mother's ambivalence as a child grows older and as the parent faces "a fear of being cut off from the child's proximity and dependence" (527). While, for the girl, growing up is a process of ascendance, for the mother, this process is "a passage from ascendence to decline, from omnipotence or, at least, control to a dwindling of authority" (527). As a consequence, Barzilai reads the mother's attempts to kill the girl as ways for her to perpetuate the intimacy with the daughter and stop the clock, halting the process of growing older. Key scenes in the Grimm Brothers' tale gain new potential meanings in this interpretation, and Barzilai's article shows how one tale can address the different feelings and concerns of women from various generations at the same time. Combining her insights with age studies can be fruitful, I argue. The pattern of ascendance and decline that she describes are reminiscent of leading age critic Margaret Morganroth Gullette's critique of the decline narrative: the idea that life goes downhill when we grow older (*Aged by Culture*). Interestingly, Gullette situates the turning point in middle age (*Agewise*). With many popular Western fairy tales' specific focus on marriages, this genre places the turning point at an even earlier stage in life, at least for young women—that is, right after marriage, as Marcia Lieberman (200) has noted, or as Barzilai suggests, when children reach adolescence.

In her influential book *From the Beast to the Blonde*, Marina Warner, too, foregrounds intergenerational relationships in fairy tales. She explores the tradition of telling fairy tales in the light of so-called Old Wives' Tales, foregrounding the figure of the crone as storyteller and pointing out ageist prejudices about old women. "Female old age represented a violation of teleology" (43), Warner writes about the image of old age in early modern times in the West—a tradition that she traces from the medieval period to the nineteenth century. Crones were mocked and scolded for their lust, vanity, outspokenness, and general "lack of compliance" (43, 47). Warner connects the figure of the female storyteller and related ageist prejudices to the vulnerable position of older women in society and the content of a selection of classic fairy tales. Her study sheds an interesting light on, among others, the contrasting figures of the benevolent godmother and the wicked old witch. Warner reads these figures in tandem and interprets them as a plea (or perhaps a threat) to the younger generation to treat the older women in their family circles with due respect: "one can assemble a picture of strain across the three generations, in which the old struggle and plead for the mercy of the young" (230). This is a pattern that is still present in contemporary children's books, where old characters and children have a special connection from which the generation of parents is excluded (Joosen, "Little Girl"). Like Barzilai, Warner shifts attention away from the focus on a young protagonist whose perspective dominates the story, to old, secondary figures in traditional fairy tales, in order to reflect on their potential meaning for both old tellers and young audiences. Her study is, moreover, invested in contextualizing and problematizing ageist stereotypes (without calling them that) and fostering more open-minded intergenerational relationships. In order to take this new perspective on age, it is noteworthy that both Barzilai and Warner treat the tales as being rooted in and reflecting on reality—the former with a stress on the psychology of family relationships, the latter with a stress on social positions.

Second, analyses of age can help scholars distinguish between fairy-tale traditions in different countries and regions, and help them explore and explain what is specific to these traditions. Many Western fairy tales share with "Snow White" the "perspectival dominance" of a young person that Barzilai addresses. When one considers the most reprinted and adapted fairy tales in the West, few have a main character who is not young. In *Connecting Childhood and Old Age in Popular Media*, Mayako Murai makes a revealing comparison of the treatment of old age in Western and Japanese tales. Unlike old people in Western fairy tales, who generally play a supporting role for young characters, old women and men are the protagonists in various popular Japanese tales and, at the end of the narrative, bring the story to a new balance that differs from the usual happy ever after in Western fairy tales. In various stories, such as "The Old Man Who Made Flowers Bloom" and "The Tongue-Cut Sparrow," the aged protagonists undertake adventures and perform difficult tasks. Murai points out that the different tradition of representing old age in fairy tales has also influenced the reception of the Grimms' tales in Japan. "The Bremen Town Musicians" is one of the few

Brothers Grimm tales that does have old characters as protagonists. While many Western fairy-tale collections omit this tale, in Japan, it equaled the popularity of "Snow White" in the late nineteenth century and also merged with the Japanese oral tradition. Murai refers to research by Kayo Kubo, who revealed that the Japanese translations tended to downplay the old animals' victimization and reduced their isolation from society at the end of the tale, thus adapting them to the Japanese expectation that the old are to be respected and still have an active role to play in society. Murai uses this reflection of old age in fairy tales to consider the different position of the old in the West and in Japan. She dismisses the obvious interpretation that the old hold a superior position in Asian families due to Confucian and Taoist influences: "the elderly in Japanese fairy tales are not necessarily any wiser than the young, nor do they possess any supernatural power; there are as many silly, greedy or evil old people as kind, grateful, and humble ones" (Murai 50). Rather, Murai considers old people's social position "outside the social spheres of production and reproduction" (50) a crucial factor in their success as protagonists in Japanese tales. Because of this physical and social position, they are "more suitable characters for the symbolic exploration of the human psyche and human beings' relationship with the world" (50). Murai also points out that the old protagonists take away the focus on beauty and marriage, and thus give storytellers the opportunity to explore other feelings and plots. It is a shame that fairy tales like these are not widely known outside of Asia. In the 1970s, feminists like Angela Carter unearthed tales with female heroines in new anthologies like *The Virago Book of Fairy Tales*. The time would be ripe to do the same for internationally lesser known fairy tales that shed a different light on old age than do the best-known tales of the West. Yet, an anthology may no longer be the best way to do so. Other popular media, such as film and the Internet, and fairy-tale adaptations, are likely to have a better chance of introducing these tales to a wide audience, as I will argue below.

Finally, age has also been central to a number of more critical rejections of the traditional fairy tales. This time, the most vehement critique comes specifically from age critics, although some fairy-tale critics of the 1970s, such as the German Otto Gmelin, already considered the age ideology of the tales problematic for the same reasons mentioned in current attacks: their ageism and their implication in shaping children's worldviews (2–3). According to age critics, the traditional Western fairy tales are implicated in "the narrative of decline" that I have already mentioned briefly: they display and foster a fascination with youth and introduce or reinforce the conviction that life goes downhill as people grow older. In "Moms do badly, but grandmas do worse," Sylvia B. Henneberg takes an intersectional approach to fairy tales. She casts a most negative light on Western fairy tales' views on the female life course and women's old age. She argues that the tales perpetuate ageist stereotypes and negatively influence children's understanding of the life course. The roles of older women are limited, she argues, to "the wicked old witch, the selfless godmother, or the demented hag" (128).

If one casts a critical look at adaptations of fairy tales in popular media, it can be noted that ageist traits are often intensified. Disney's *Tangled* (2010) provides a good example. The movie adds a decline narrative to the Brothers Grimm's "Rapunzel," where Mother Gothel's motives for keeping Rapunzel a prisoner are not linked to age. In *Tangled*, by contrast, the fear of old age is central to the story, the source of all evil: Rapunzel is held prisoner for the magical qualities of her hair, which can restore youth in the ageing Mother Gothel. While Mother Gothel is presented as the antagonist who does not shy away from kidnapping a baby and lying to her for years, her resentment of growing old and ugly is presented as sound. The movie presents old age as particularly undesirable and gruesome. One scene shows the sped-up aging process in which Mother Gothel's body is subject to rapid decay, as Rapunzel's hair is cut off and the natural order is suddenly restored—the scene is reminiscent of Oscar Wilde's *The Picture of Dorian Gray* (1890). In Wilde's novel, the eponymous hero's body is exempt from the effects of time and a hedonistic, immoral lifestyle, while those experiences are captured only in a magical painting, where his image grows older and decays. When he sees his true, old self in the painting, Dorian Gray is abhorred; in his attempt to destroy the painting, he rapidly ages and dies. As Anita Wohlmann points out, similar scenes of rapid aging and decay also appear at the end of two

"Snow White" film adaptations from 2012, *Mirror Mirror* and *Snow White and the Huntsman*, where "old age also implies defeat and is applied with a similarly excessive use of digital effects."

In *Tangled*, the cracked mirror in which Mother Gothel views her old self is significant. On the one hand, it links *Tangled* intertextually with "Snow White," another fairy tale in which old age sets the story into motion. On the other hand, from an age-studies perspective, the cracked mirror can be interpreted as symbolic of what Kathleen Woodward refers to as "The Mirror Stage of Old Age": "As we age we increasingly separate what we take to be our real selves from our bodies. We say that our real selves—that is our youthful selves—are hidden inside our bodies. Our bodies are old, we are not. Old age can thus be described as a state in which the body is in opposition to the self, and we are alienated from our bodies" (Woodward, "Mirror" 104). In "Ageing and Transageing: Transgenerational Hauntings of the Self" (2008), Helene Moglen draws on psychoanalysis and queer theory to suggest an alternative to this split self. She argues that it is more productive to consider "the ageing self as a dynamic multiplicity of innumerable selves" (304) in which identity is seen as diffuse and older and younger versions of the self coexist. While this ideal may be the subtext for the villain who strives for eternal youth, fairy tales and many of their adaptations use the struggle against aging and conflicts between old and young characters as their plots' driving forces. In *Tangled*, Mother Gothel has found a way to stop the aging process of her body. When the spell is broken and the natural, aged state of her body is inevitable, she cannot face her image in the mirror. Yet, it is as if Disney is also trying to protect the *viewer* from seeing her old body: the way the scene is staged, the audience gets to see only glimpses of her, through the cracks in the mirror, and she is immediately withdrawn from view, hidden in a cloak—as if the old body is too repulsive to watch. While one could argue that it is the fear of aging that has set this unnatural, gruesome process in motion, the scenes nevertheless rely on and reinforce the undesirability of signs of aging—the white hair, the wrinkled face, the bony hands, and so forth.

Sylvia Henneberg points out that discourses of femininity evolve over time, and that children's literature now features more empowered heroines than it used to. Disney's *Tangled* is a good example of that: although this movie has been subjected to feminist criticism in its own right, its young heroine appears as more empowered than Rapunzel in the Grimms' tale. Yet Henneberg also notes that this shift toward feminine empowerment does not affect older women as they are represented in narratives for the young: "literary crones . . . are traditionally funneled into a very limited number of static roles located outside such ongoing re-evaluation" ("Moms" 128). Is that also true for those literary rewritings that specifically tackle fairy tales' dated ideologies?

Analyzing Age in Fairy-Tale Rewritings

Henneberg herself mentions Anne Sexton's poetry, referring to, for example, the lines from her "Snow White" poem that describe "Her stepmother / a beauty in her own right / though eaten, of course, by age" (cited in Henneberg, "Moms" 128). Yet Henneberg is not a fairy-tale scholar, and her knowledge of children's books and fairy-tale rewritings can be argued to be limited, as can her readings of certain titles. Is Anne Sexton, in the lines cited here, reproducing ageism, or rather criticizing it? The "of course" suggests a parodic stance. Other fairy-tale rewritings are more extensively and unambiguously engaged in rewriting the age ideology of the traditional fairy tales. In Louise Murphy's "The True Story of Hansel and Gretel" (2003), for example, the wicked witch from "Hansel and Gretel" is recast as an old woman who saves two Polish children fleeing the horrors of the Holocaust, sacrificing her own life. She is compassionate and cunning, hiding the children in her oven to keep them safe. The same qualities can be attributed to the queen in Pat Murphy's rewriting of "Snow White," a short story entitled "The True Story" (1997). Here the queen sends away Snow White to protect her from pedophilia in an ultimately successful instance of female bonding across generations. The same goes for Gillian Cross's *Wolf* (1990), where a grandmother is torn between the love for her son, who is an IRA terrorist, and that for her granddaughter, whom she tries to protect. While the grandmother is at first mainly associated with repression, conservative child-rearing methods, and coldness, at the end of the novel it becomes clear that she has also been brave and cunning—a far stretch from the weak and passive grandmother in Charles Perrault's or the Grimms' "Little Red Riding Hood," on which the story is based. In Hilary McKay's "Chickenpox and Crystal or Snow White and the Seven Dwarves," from her *Fairy Tales* (2017), a grandmother manages to cure her granddaughter of her desire to be the most beautiful in the world. The grandmother tells the teenager the story of "Snow White." As the girl is able to connect the evil queen's obsession with beauty with her own, she admits that she was led by a magical crystal and decides to get rid of it. The old woman is marked by a practical, down-to-earth approach to life. Not only is she attuned to her granddaughter's emotional needs, she is also a creative storyteller who can lead the girl to insight without imposing her ideas. Her story shows that her youthful self is still part of her life narrative, and thus she embodies the ideal of "trans-ageing" that Helene Moglen opposes to the split aged self that is haunted by "the ghostly spectres of youth" (297). In short, fairy-tale rewritings offer interesting new takes on age in fairy tales, and examples can be found in literature both for adults and for children, and in all decades since the 1970s. While an increase in the preoccupation with age in fairy-tale rewritings can be observed since the 1990s, it is too soon to speak of a real trend.

Just as age critics' work may be enriched by an in-depth reflection on age in these more contemporary stories for young readers, it would also be valuable if fairy-tale critics, in turn, engage with age studies when analyzing fairy-tale rewritings. These readings are rarely straightforward. One type of fairy-tale rewriting that frequently replicates the idea that life goes downhill as you grow older, for example, is the so-called fairy-tale sequel. Many of these sequels are written in response to the fairy tale's sugary happy ending, especially the Disneyfied variant of the fairy tale, which they then reveal to be illusionary. Anne Sheldon's "Snow White turns 39" (1996) provides a good example. This sequel to "Snow White" hinges on the concept of the "mid-life crisis." Where once midlife was considered the prime of one's life (as the so-called stages of man illustrate), in more recent Western concepts of the life course, midlife (especially the ages forty to forty-five) is associated with a painful awareness of the loss of beauty, vitality, sexuality, and creativity. This heightened consciousness of the aging process frequently causes moments of reflection on previous achievements, missed opportunities, and lack of time (Green 155). In Sheldon's poem, Snow White can no longer bear to see herself in the mirror, which now mocks her instead of praising her. This comes as no surprise, given that the mirror in "Snow White" favored youth all along. Sheldon's mature Snow White has turned into a reincarnation of her evil stepmother, as she thinks of eating the hearts of virgins and sending out young girls to die. She dreams of a turning point in her life, but from the way she describes it—that "one black dawn" she plans on destroying the mirror and "taking up chess"—it feels unlikely that she ever will. The poem ends on a sad note of unfulfilled longing.

In *Agewise*, Margaret Morganroth Gullette fights the prejudices involved in what she calls "middle ageism." She stresses the negative impact of generalizing narratives about aging, especially if they involve a narrative of decline:

> Whatever happens in the body, and even if nothing happens in the body, aging is a narrative. Each of us tells her own story. But most of us lack an adequate backstory. Not only my own physiology and my personal life experience but societal influences determine my age autobiography. (Gullette, *Agewise* 5)

While Sheldon's poem challenges the traditional narrative and romance of "Snow White," it does not question the establishment of midlife as a time of crisis, unhappiness, and dissatisfaction. In destroying one myth, Sheldon seems to reinforce another. But does she? The fact that Snow White's midlife crisis is so intense and complies with many stereotypical associations of the midlife, and the combination with the fairy-tale context and the references to popular culture all together produce a mixture that points toward parody—not just of the fairy tale, but also of the midlife as it is constructed in popular culture. Reading the poem this way opens up its potential for a critique of middle ageism rather than a reproduction of ageist discourse. To be able to do so, however, a reader needs to be what Gullette calls "agewise": aware and critical of the discourses and stereotypes around age.

While Sheldon's poem gives a rather short and pointed view on age and the fairy tale, Emma Donoghue's *Kissing the Witch* responds to traditional fairy tales more extensively. First published in 1997, *Kissing the Witch* has become one of the most praised and analyzed fairy-tale rewritings. It has gained this status mostly because of its innovative composition and its queering of gender roles and heteronormative plots. Donoghue offers the reader a succession of rewritten fairy tales. In each of these, a woman encounters either another woman or an animal, and all of these are then invited to tell their own life stories, producing a retrospective chain of female narratives. As in the traditional fairy tales that Donoghue retells, women from different generations play a part in her stories: young princesses and common girls, but also women in middle adulthood and older women. She sets out to revise their parts in the stories in various ways, creating plot twists and adding psychological depth.

In an article from 2010, Ann Martin highlights the "generational collaborations" in Donoghue's short story collection. She argues that "Donoghue figures the complexity of gendered and sexed identities . . . through her depiction of interactions between younger and older women" (7). Martin positively values the discourse about intergenerational relationships that Donoghue's collection produces, but does not draw on any age criticism to do so. Before I was interested in age studies, I would have agreed with her assessment, with some reservations. In *Critical and Creative Perspectives on Fairy Tales*, I argue that I find *Kissing the Witch* problematic in producing what Anna Altmann has called a "seesaw" effect: while the female figures are raised to more favorable, active roles in the rewritten tales, the male figures are invariably brought down—they are reduced to incestuous fathers, tyrannous husbands, sexual predators, and weak rulers. This seesaw affects both the young and older male figures in Donoghue's text. As Jeff Hearn (1995) reminds us, age critics in literary studies have mostly focused on female rather than male characters, and it is also important to take the old male figures into account when reflecting on the intergenerational ties in Donoghue's stories.

Yet, even if one focuses on only the female figures, age studies helps to see the intergenerational relationships in Donoghue's book in a somewhat different light. Ann Martin, for example, praises Donoghue's collection for emphasizing "the differences between women's experiences" (7). This claim is certainly true when one considers the younger female characters, who indeed comprise a diverse cast, and the relationships between the different generations. If one isolates the old females as a group, however, the variation is far more limited. All of the older women in Donoghue's tale can be ranged under the archetypical figure of the "wise old mentor." The "Tale of the Shoe," a rewriting of "Cinderella" and the first story in the collection, sets the tone. Here, we see a young girl who is plagued by the voices in her head and who debases herself after her mother's death. In the course of the story, she is visited by a woman whose "eyebrows were silvered with ash" (3). As in various other instances, Donoghue uses grey hair as a shorthand, metonymic indication that a character is old. In what follows, the girl describes her "transformation" under the influence of this woman: "My dusty self was spun new. This woman sheathed my limbs in blue velvet. I was dancing on points of clear glass" (3). The older woman is experienced, understanding, and nurturing. Yet, it can be argued that she can play this role only because she puts herself entirely at the service of the girl, effacing herself.

Sylvia Henneberg sees three problems with the "benevolent godmother" in the traditional fairy tales—some of which Donoghue resolves, some of which she reproduces. The first aspect that Henneberg criticizes is the idea that "all beauty comes at a cost and that its acquisition is imperative" ("Moms" 129). Donoghue's tale avoids that message and gives the godmother a different role. In "The Tale of the Shoe," all the measurements that the girl takes to acquire beauty stem from her own initiatives. The godmother assists her only reluctantly and in order to teach her a lesson. Likewise, Donoghue amends another stereotype that Henneberg criticizes: that of the weak and "ineffectual crone" (129). Like all of the female figures in Donoghue's stories, the old women here are cunning and ultimately successful, and not subject to a simple decline narrative. The third issue that Henneberg raises, however, is linked to the stereotype of the wise old mentor. She argues:

> All too often, fictional benefactresses are ultimately self-sacrificing lambs in disguise. At first sight, they seem like

important leaders, but upon consideration, they are relegated to the margins, existing only to develop other characters and plot lines rather than their own . . . the female elder is tolerated if she has the will and ability to boost, support, guide, and serve the young. (Henneberg, "Moms" 129)

Once that task has been fulfilled, the wise old mentor becomes invisible.

In her analysis of *Kissing the Witch*, Martin calls the older female figures "catalysts" for change (8)—displaying what Henneberg calls the "ability to boost" the young ("Moms" 129). Yet it must be stressed that Donoghue's stories remain focused on younger women. To be fair to the fairy, not all the godmothers in Donoghue's rewritings are self-sacrificing figures. For one, at the end of "The Tale of the Shoe," after serving the young girl for a long time, the godmother is truly noticed by the young girl, and her gaze also directs the reader's: "How could I not have noticed she was beautiful?" (7). After being acknowledged, the old woman dares to demand something for herself: "What about me? she asked very low. I'm old enough to be your mother. Her finger was spelling on the back of my neck. You're not my mother, I said. I'm old enough to know that" (8). An awareness of age studies and the trope of the wise old mentor reveals how significant this moment in the story is: an old woman who demands something for herself and who is not just satisfied to function as the younger woman's helper. To use Nick Lee's terminology, the godmother at this point in the story is no longer a human being, but a "human becoming" (5)—a human who is experiencing change and growth. This kind of change and growth is possible at every age, age critics stress. Although Donoghue's structure is intriguing and challenging, this moment of self-assertion and growth in the old woman is limited to just that line, and then left to the imagination of the reader, as the next story immediately returns to the focus on a younger protagonist. The same thing happens at the end of the book, in "The Tale of the Kiss," where an older woman expresses desire for a younger one, but we never see that desire materialized. The imagination of the reader may fall short in imagining the older woman as "human becoming" rather than as human being, especially when that process of becoming is not a narrative of decline but one of positive change. After all, our cultural products offer little to feed the imagination when it comes to so-called progress narratives about old age.

According to Martin's analysis of *Kissing the Witch*, "the conflicts of the stories often revolve around the gaps between these perspectives, particularly in tales where the protagonist cannot acknowledge the wisdom of the older woman" (7–8). Here, age studies may inform an interesting different perspective. First of all, the intergenerational conflicts that Martin mentions are rare, if they exist at all in Donoghue's book. The old female characters are sometimes frustrated by the younger women's reliance on male figures and heteronormative patterns, but they do not challenge that reliance to the point of conflict. Rather, they stand by, offer advice, and wait until the younger female figures come to their senses. In "Against Wisdom: The Social Politics of Anger and Aging," Kathleen Woodward highlights the limitations that the trope of the "wise old mentor" sets on the kind of behavior that is tolerated from the old. According to Woodward, wisdom is "almost always understood as a capacity for balanced reflection and judgment that can only accrue with long experience," and usually involves "a lack of certain kinds of feelings—the passions, for instance, including anger" ("Against Wisdom" 187). Woodward is concerned that because of the ideal of wisdom, intense emotions, especially anger, that old people also experience are not tolerated or are dismissed as trifling and even pathological, as signs of illness or dementia. Marina Warner underscores this interpretation of the wise old woman, arguing that "wise" functioned as an adjective to control women (34). When read in that perspective, Donoghue's lack of angry old women becomes frustrating in its own right. In "The Tale of the Rose," for example, we learn from the young protagonist that it took her a long time to get used to the idea that what she presumed to be a male Beast was actually an older woman: "After months of looking, I saw that beauty was infinitely various, and found it behind her white face" (Donoghue 40). The older woman, it is assumed, has patiently granted her the time to find out. In "The Tale of the Hair," the senior woman is described by the young protagonist as "my store of knowledge, my cache of wisdom" (85). In "The Tale of the Skin," too, the older woman is a helper who waits in the margins, always ready with advice and assistance. In "The Tale of the Voice" the old witch "sighs" at the protagonist's foolishness, laughs, and turns her palms to the sky in a small gesture of resignation, but never gets angry. She yawns, smiles, and uses irony, but never seems upset. That being said, "The Tale of the Voice" is an interesting tale because the protagonist (a Little Mermaid figure) here is not as young as the female leads in the other tales—she mentions having "ripped out" her "first gray hair" (185) before falling in love. Donoghue challenges what Elizabeth Freeman calls the "chrononormativity" of the life course, pointing at alternative, queer paths of personal development that deviate from the life stages with which certain experiences are typically associated. Donoghue shows that women with grey hair are not necessarily wise, but can still fall in love and even resign their agency to win the love of a man. This middle-aged woman is a dynamic human becoming, to use Nick Lee's words. Yet, this woman, too, meets a woman who is older still, a feminist witch, who does act as a patient source of wisdom until the mermaid figure comes to her senses and reclaims her voice.

Conclusion

Age plays a significant part in both fairy tales and fairy-tale rewritings, and is as of yet relatively unexplored territory. In *Critical and Creative Perspectives on Fairy Tales*, I have argued that both fiction and criticism can contribute to the critical exploration of ideology in fairy tales. That also holds for age. As I have shown in this chapter, various rewritings indeed revise the way that age is constructed by Grimm or Perrault. Age studies provide a rich framework to study both the traditional tales and the rewritings, yet the way this field has so far approached children's literature is reminiscent of some of the issues that were raised against the so-called images of women studies in the 1970s (see Joosen, *Critical* 84–86). To do justice to how narratives shape, sustain, and challenge discourses about age, analyses have to take into account the very means by which fiction operates, including character construction, parody, irony, gaps, and contradictions. From the development of gender studies, we must also keep in mind that identity markers always intersect, and that critics need to be attentive to the way age operates at cross-sections with gender, race, class, ability, and sexual preference. Finally, national and cultural differences need to be further introduced and explored in the analysis of age in literature, and this is especially true for the rich international context in which fairy tales function. In our glocalized world, various geographical spheres do not operate separately but also interact (think, for example, of the adaptations of German fairy tales in the United States and Japan; see Joosen and Lathey). While in this chapter I have focused on literature, other media come into play here, using their own—often visual means—to produce age narratives and norms: film, television, and the Internet (YouTube videos, fan fiction), in particular, are popular and powerful media in which fairy tales have frequently been revised in the first two decades of the twenty-first century and provide interesting material for analyses focused on age (see, among others, Wohlmann; Greenhill and Rudy). Finally, more research is also needed in how audiences respond to these age norms. Fairy tales and their rewritings are, after all, received by readers and viewers of all ages, who do not just consume but also coproduce discourses about age, drawing on their experiences and views of life.

Works Cited

Altmann, Anna E. "Parody and Poesis in Feminist Fairy Tales." *CCL: Canadian Children's Literature,* vol. 73, 1994, pp. 22–31.

Bacchilega, Cristina. *Fairy Tales Transformed? Twenty-First-Century Adaptations and the Politics of Wonder.* Wayne State University Press, 2014.

Barzilai, Shuli. "Reading 'Snow White': The Mother's Story." *Signs,* vol. 15, no. 3, 1990, pp. 515–34.

Cross, Gillian. *Wolf.* Puffin, 1990.

De Beauvoir, Simone. *The Coming of Age.* 1977. Translated by P. O'Brian, Norton, 1996.

Donoghue, Emma. *Kissing the Witch: Old Tales in New Skins.* Harper, 1997.

Freeman, Elizabeth. *Time Binds: Queer Temporalities, Queer Histories.* Duke University Press, 2010.

Green, Lorraine. *Understanding the Life Course: Sociological and Psychological Perspectives.* Polity, 2010.

Gmelin, Otto F. "Worüber man heute nachdenken muß, wenn man seinem Kind ein *Grimmsches Märchen* vorliest." *Gmelin—Märchen Venus—Schwänke [Fibel 2]*. Ifez, 1977.

Greenhill, Pauline, and Jill Terry Rudy, editors. *Channeling Wonder: Fairy Tales on Television*. Wayne State University Press, 2014.

Gullette, Margaret Morganroth. *Aged by Culture*. University of Chicago Press, 2004.

———. *Agewise: Fighting the New Ageism in America*. University of Chicago Press, 2011.

Hearn, Jeff. "Imaging the Aging of Men." *Images of Aging: Cultural Representations of Later Life*, edited by M. Featherstone and A. Werknick. Routledge, 1995, 97–115.

Henneberg, Sylvia B. "Moms Do Badly, but Grandmas Do Worse: The Nexus of Sexism and Ageism in Children's Classics." *Journal of Aging Studies*, vol. 24, 2010, pp. 125–34.

———. "Of Creative Crones and Poetry: Developing Age Studies Through Literature." *NWSA Journal*, vol. 18, no. 1, 2006, pp. 106–25.

Joosen, Vanessa. "'As If She Were a Little Girl': Young and Old Children in the Works of Lucy M. Boston, Eleanor Farjeon, and Philippa Pearce." *Interjuli: Internationale Kinder- und Jugendliteraturforschung*, vol. 1, 2013, pp. 21–34.

———. *Critical and Creative Perspectives on Fairy Tales: An Intertextual Dialogue Between Fairy-Tale Scholarship and Postmodern Retellings*. Wayne State University Press, 2011.

Joosen, Vanessa, and Gillian Lathey, editors. *Grimms' Tales around the Globe: The Dynamics of Their International Reception*. Wayne State University Press, 2014.

Lee, Nick. *Childhood and Society: Growing Up in an Age of Uncertainty*. Open University Press, 2001.

Lieberman, Marcia K. 1972. "'Some Day My Prince Will Come': Female Acculturation through the Fairy Tale." *Don't Bet on the Prince: Contemporary Feminist Fairy Tales in North America and England*, edited by Jack Zipes, Routledge, 1989, pp. 185–200.

Martin, Ann. "Generational Collaboration in Emma Donoghue's *Kissing the Witch: Old Tales in New Skins*." *Children's Literature Association Quarterly*, vol. 35, no. 1, 2010, pp. 4–25.

McKay, Hilary. *Fairy Tales*. Illustrated by Sarah Gibb, Macmillan, 2017.

Moglen, Helene. "Ageing and Transageing: Transgenerational Hauntings of the Self." *Studies in Gender and Sexuality*, vol. 9, 2008, pp. 297–311.

Murai, Mayako. "Happily Ever After for the Old in Japanese Fairy Tales." *Connecting Childhood and Old Age in Popular Media*, University of Mississippi Press, 2018, pp. 43–60.

Murphy, Louise. *The True Story of Hansel and Gretel*. Puffin, 2003.

Murphy, Pat. "The True Story." *Black Swan, White Raven*, edited by Ellen Datlow and Terry Windling, Avon, 1997, pp. 278–87.

Sheldon, Anne. "Snow White Turns 39." 1996/97. *The Poets' Grimm: 20th Century Poems from Grimm Fairy Tales*, edited by Jeanne Marie Beaumont and Claudia Carlson, Story Line Press, 2003, p. 109.

Warner, Marina. *From the Beast to the Blonde*. 1994. Vintage, 1995.

Wilde, Oscar. 1890. *The Picture of Dorian Gray*. Penguin, 1980.

Wohlmann, Anita. "Of Young/Old Queens and Giant Dwarfs: A Critical Reading of Age and Aging in *Snow White and the Huntsman* and *Mirror Mirror*." *Age Culture Humanities,* vol. 2, 2015, //ageculturehumanities.org/WP/of-youngold-queens-and-giant-dwarfs-a-critical-reading-of-age-and-aging-in-snow-white-and-the-huntsman-and-mirror-mirror. Accessed 18 Jan. 2018.

Woodward, Kathleen. "Against Wisdom: The Social Politics of Anger and Aging." *Cultural Critique,* vol. 51, 2002, pp. 186–218.

———. "The Mirror Stage of Old Age." *Memory and Desire: Aging—Literature—Psychoanalysis*, edited by Kathleen Woodward and Murray M. Schwartz, Indiana University Press, 1986, pp. 97–113.

10

Re-Orienting Fairy-Tale Childhood

Child Protagonists as Critical Signifiers of Fairy-Tale Tropes in Transnational Contemporary Cinema

Michael Brodski

Introduction

THE AIM OF THIS chapter is to relocate the potential impact of contemporary fairy-tale adaptations within a wide but at the same time quite specific interdisciplinary context, namely the heterogeneous field of childhood studies. Especially since the 1990s, a growing body of contributions from the fields of sociology, cultural history, and also literature, film, and media studies have developed various concepts and depictions of children and childhood ranging from portrayals of their social role, to their changing historical figurations, to their medial representations.[1] Following predominantly a social constructivist paradigm, the notion of childhood is thus primarily regarded as a cultural idea with inscribed meanings constituted from an exclusively adult position of "cultural needs and fears" (Kincaid, *Child-Loving* 78). Considering children as being placed inside a regressive matrix of socialization or developmental psychology, such approaches unravel Western society's thinking by classifying them as a being lacking in relation to the adult as well as mostly dependent on the latter's guidance and protection.

Besides, they are constructed predominantly by the signifiers of innocence and purity,[2] thereby functioning as a powerful cultural myth in a Barthesian sense that legitimizes such passive definitions as supposedly being natural (see Jenkins, *Children's Culture Reader* 15). The fairy tale seems to be a privileged site for such considerations, especially given its status as a popular children's literature subgenre for a juvenile audience and its tendency to feature child protagonists in many of its canonical texts. Therefore, this chapter follows two corresponding aims. On the one hand, it will demonstrate how traditional literary fairy-tale texts[3] can be approached from a revisionist and critical angle due to their depictions of children and childhood, therefore functioning as not yet fully explored research objects for childhood studies. At the same time—and even more significantly with regard to the overall aim of this volume—it sets out to analyze how contemporary fairy-tale adaptations can function as creative approaches epistemologically similar to the methods used in childhood studies, thus staging the child's figure as a critical signifier that concretely or at least implicitly comments upon the normative childhood discourses as they are expressed in the traditional texts to which they refer. In this regard, modern adaptations can contribute to the scholarly debate on childhood studies. Additionally, they can have an impact upon the increase in the academic relevance of the fairy tale in relation to other interdisciplinary dimensions beyond scholars with a primarily folklorist and fairy-tale studies background. Therefore, they offer many new possibilities of methodological reflections originating from multidisciplinary approaches to childhood.

From the fairy-tale scholar's perspective, it is accordingly important to enter into a continuous and dynamic dialogue on the traditional fairy tale (see Joosen 3) with its contemporary adaptations, which Vanessa Joosen convincingly identifies as a historico-critical practice between retellings and academic approaches. In which way is there an equivalent critical awareness in contemporary fairy-tale adaptations to be detected, given the possibilities of academic criticism? Or, to put it differently, how is such a kind of childhood study–related criticism articulated artistically? Accordingly, this chapter will comparatively juxtapose methodological examinations of traditional fairy-tale texts with similar observations articulated by means of the aesthetic and narrative strategies of contemporary retellings. Besides, considered from a perspective rooted in reception and participation studies, the sociocultural use of contemporary fairy-tale retellings can importantly be regarded as actively contributing to a progressive awareness and understanding of childhood. This can be especially achieved by adaptations with an inherent reworking of clichéd tropes in earlier versions of a fairy-tale text that are entrenched in their audiences' collective memory.

Drawing upon Henry Jenkins's proclaimed "critical utopianism" prevalent in today's convergence culture, which serves as a complex globalized web undercutting the clear demarcations between old and new media as well as producer's aesthetic decisions and receiver's participatory agency (see Jenkins, *Convergence*), Cristina Bacchilega fittingly observes a "new economy of knowledge, whereby today's young adult and adult public has acquired or has the potential to access a more complex and expansive sense of the 'fairy tale' than what was generally available some thirty years ago" (76). The contemporary media-literate audience's "immediate recognition of the fairy-tale icons of popular cultural memory gives rise to ambivalence, a double take that is not feeding simply into nostalgia, but moving outward to multiple links in the fairy-tale web" (76). As will be shown in the further subchapters, the specific backtrack of such various links can also reveal a truly critical potential in a comparative juxtaposition between older and more contemporary motifs, thereby contributing to the audience's rather ambivalent stance toward the universally important notion of childhood.

Similar to Bacchilega's case studies, this approach also highlights the importance of film as a suitable medium for effective retellings. Its key role in contemporary global mass productions, distributions, and receptions of fairy tales will also be further exposed by underlining its ontological specificity as an audiovisual art. It is therefore not surprising that Jack Zipes aptly notes: "Fairy-tale films have been swamping big and small screens throughout the world ever since the beginning of the twenty-first century, seeking to overwhelm audiences with innovative and spectacular adaptations in a kind of globalized cultural tsunami" ("Tsunami" 1). Such a globalizing and unifying importance of contemporary retellings is also relevant to explaining the rather scattered analytic spectrum of this chapter. The adaptations chosen for the following analysis seem to be quite heterogeneous at first glance: namely, the Hollywood production *A.I. Artificial Intelligence* (directed by Steven Spielberg, USA, 2001), which contains plot-relevant allusions to Carlo Collodi's *The Adventures of Pinocchio* (1883); the Korean horror movie *Hansel and Gretel* (directed by Pil-Sung Yim, Korea, 2007), which echoes the title of the Brothers Grimm's canonical text (1812); as well as the Ukrainian art film *Melody of a Street Organ* (directed by Kira Muratova, Ukraine, 2009), which is loosely based on "The Little Match Girl" (1845) by Hans Christian Andersen. However, given their national production backgrounds, they all seem to have the shared aim of "reworking familiar tropes and revitalizing critical interest in this area" (Short 20), especially in the contexts and depictions of childhood. Thus, what unites all of these contemporary Western and non-Western adaptations is a reflection upon children that transcends predominantly European and Anglophone stereotypes such as the stated innocence, passivity, and purity. In addition to *Hansel and Gretel*, which also serves as a case study in Bacchilega's own analysis (99), *A.I. Artificial Intelligence* likewise contains an important transmedia aspect: both works portray the motif of the child protagonist reading a supposedly traditional fairy-tale version. In this way, they not only integrate the medium of literature into film but they also self-reflectively envision an awareness of the mentioned participatory potential of audiences via a cinematic "mise-en-scène of 'reading'" (Bacchilega 76) constructed around the child protagonist.

The further analysis will try to elaborate potential additional meanings of this important motif. One of the leading analytical questions will be, for instance, how the diegetically reproduced traditional literary text, as well as the figure of the child, is mimicked in an uncanny and almost parodic way by the retelling, thereby revealing the problematic inscriptions of childhood in the original tale. Apart from predominantly Freudian notions, this chapter defines "uncanny" simply as a violation of primarily physical norms of the child's body in relation to the audience's expectations. Initially, however, a methodological fundament shall be introduced, which will constitute further important intersections between fairy-tale studies, childhood studies, and film studies, particularly in relation to adaptation strategies.

Interdisciplinary Inscriptions and the Child's Body

Given the highly ambiguous nature of the subject, a too diffused, heterogeneous approach should be avoided. Thus, it is important to ask, how can the cinematic depiction of the child protagonist in contemporary fairy-tale retellings offer significant audiovisual references for the audience? To which ideas of childhood in the traditional urtexts are they more or less explicitly referring, and which of these ideas shared in the viewer's cultural memories are radically subverted? A promising possibility implies consideration of children's bodies, as it highlights a significant overlap of the different mentioned research fields. At first, by incorporating the social constructivist paradigm in childhood studies, discourses on the child's body can productively be applied to the analysis of the emergence of canonical literary fairy-tale texts. The metamorphosis from the oral folktale into a literary adaptation made specifically for the target audience of children took place predominantly during the nineteenth century. In this way, the originally rather both adult- and child-intended contents turned into something that, according to Zipes, can be explained by the influence of the civilizing process. Borrowing his description from the German sociologist Norbert Elias, Zipes shows how literary fairy tales "appropriated the oral folktale and converted it into a type of literary discourse about morals, values, and manners so that children . . . would become civilized according to the social code of that time" (Zipes, *Fairy Tale* 3). The historical domestication of folktales from a genre for a formerly mixed audience into primarily a literary subgenre of children's literature can be also regarded as part of a physically connoted agenda of child rearing. Many discourses of corporeal discipline and passivizing contemplation were inscribed into the tales in order to offer role models of infant protagonists with appropriate bodily manners for the implied child reader. Traditional nineteenth-century fairy tales, including the key examples selected in this chapter, *The Adventures of Pinocchio*, "Hansel and Gretel," and "The Little Match Girl," can be regarded as being shaped by such rather problematic corporeal discourses in the dominant rise of a bourgeois social class and a corresponding "literary 'bourgeoisification' of oral tales" (Zipes, *Fairy Tale* 61). Such discourses self-explanatorily outlasted their historical appearance and are accordingly sustained in later adaptations, especially due to the "Walt Disney cinematic fairy tale of the culture industry" (Zipes, *Breaking* 34). An important critical perspective also implied in the following analysis will therefore reflect upon "how powerful discursive formations can be in shaping how children's bodies are perceived, understood, worked upon and produced" (Prout 6).

However, to highlight the subversive possibilities of cinematic representation of contemporary fairy-tale retellings, the methodological spectrum needs to be enhanced. Therefore, one should consider an important shift to additional concepts and sociological approaches to the child's body in childhood studies. In the addressed discipline, another paradigm emerged, which alarmingly highlighted the analytical lack of children's corporeality in many purely social constructivist methodologies. In the introduction to *The Body, Childhood and Society* (2000), Alan Prout importantly remarks in this regard that the child's body should not be exclusively analyzed as being rendered passive by cultural discourses. Instead, it must also be considered from the perspective of constituting agential and expressive potentials as well as being regarded not solely as representational but also as a pure *material* entity parallel to social life. Such an alternative consideration of corporeal presence also corresponds with the materiality of the moving image itself. In comparison to the abstract nature of language, film thus offers a quite different potential of representing the body. Because film has the idiosyncratic ability of audiovisual media to "impart characters with physical concreteness in image and sound" (Eder 26), the cognitive film scholar Jens Eder importantly explains that "some characters are predominantly *body-centered* because of their shape, attractiveness, and physical abilities" (36). Eder therefore highlights that some film figures can be merely defined by their corporeal, that is, material qualities.

This observation can be referred convincingly to the bodily status of cinematic children being tendentially contrastive in their physiognomy and size from the adult. Also especially fruitful for considerations about the child's bodily analysis, Vicky Lebeau states that because cinema therefore "offers privileged access to the perceptual, its visual and aural richness, would seem to have the advantage [over words]" because as "[c]loser to perception it can be closer to the child" (Lebeau 18). This corporeal difference can, of course, be neglected in cinematic representations, or—in analogy to the social constructivist paradigm—even rendered as being completely shaped by adult normative discourses, as, for instance, in the aforementioned Disney examples. But used in a consciously subversive way, it opens up possibilities to even highlight the difference and material presence of the bodies in order to render them strange and uncanny. Differentiating between the notions of children as concrete bodily entities and childhood as an abstract and performative concept carrying the stated social constructivist traits, Robin Bernstein nevertheless interestingly describes that the latter is determined by a "legible pattern of behaviors that comes into being through bodies of all ages" (24) as adults can also perform traits of childhood. This eventually results in an uncanny effect when being performed either by an adult or by a child's body that does not represent the normative figurations of childhood. Although her research examples are African American children depicted by racist-connoted photographs that simply do not intend to present them as conventionally innocent children, this concept can also be positively recoded to be applied as a superordinate aesthetic strategy. In the cinematic fairy-tale retellings that have been selected for the following analysis, such an approach can also be interesting, as they all feature a child figure with an uncannily made body to implicitly refer to and subvert the normative corporeal discourses of the child protagonist in the traditional fairy tales. By this means, contemporary cinematic adaptations such as *A.I. Artificial Intelligence*, *Hansel and Gretel*, and *Melody of the Street Organ* can generate the effect of a strongly alienating parody of corporeal discourses on the traditional fairy-tale texts to which they are openly or implicitly referring. By comparing the modern retellings with the original texts, the viewer can develop new kinds of critical distance to certain aspects and motifs of childhood that previously have been taken for granted. The following subchapters will portray this via a close reading of the films in comparison to their source texts.

Steven Spielberg's Reference to Carlo Collodi

By highlighting the interdependencies between traditional fairy tales and their retellings, the following analysis will show how cultural policies of children's bodily determinations can be potentially reworked. In this way, earlier definitions and demarcations of the corporeal anthropology of the child in fairy-tale texts can be altered, thus highlighting the re-oriented position of many contemporary fairy tales as revisionist critiques of the discourses in their templates. One of the previously mentioned corporeal discourses to be further considered is the educational practice of bodily discipline and punishment. As I will show, *The Adventures of Pinocchio*, as well as its famous adaptation by the Walt Disney Company, *Pinocchio* (directed by Norman Ferguson et al., USA, 1940), can be considered a fairy-tale text paradigmatically representing such discourse. At the same time, its contemporary semi-adaptation, *A. I. Artificial Intelligence*, reveals and criticizes exactly such an implicit ideological orientation by deviating from, while at the same time metacritically commenting upon, its source text.

To analyze the discourses of child discipline that shape Collodi's most important and referred to literary source of this fairy tale, it is first important to locate it in the epoch of its publication. Referring to Michel Foucault's seminal work *Discipline and Punish: The Birth of the Prison* (1975), the social geographer Gil Valentine describes the development of particular disciplinary spaces constructed especially for children, such as the school and the controlled home environment, as being the most salient ones since the nineteenth century. Such spaces did not only serve as culmination points for discourses of corporeal punishment and restriction functioning as a disciplining method to achieve behavior typical of normative expectations of childhood. Importantly, these spaces also marked the beginning of a discourse of maturation through corporeal advice and restriction. Thus, the "process of 'civilising' the body has become fundamental to the process through which children in contemporary societies make the transition from childhood to adulthood" (Valentine 24). However, at the same time, Western methods of child socialization in the nineteenth century underwent a paradigm shift in abolishing too-harsh corporeal discipline methods such as caning for a gentler and less haptic form of punishment (Bell 94). But as Sophie Bell interestingly argues in relation to Harriett Beecher Stowe's American classic *Uncle Tom's Cabin* (1852), its author introduces the black child as being located inside an "experimental space." Therein, apart from gentle punishment, raced African American children are still affected by a corporeal chastisement by their parents for being naughty (94). Their implicitly exposed *otherness* therefore provides a fictional and thus experimentally flexible possibility to still allow the reader to imagine corporeal punishment as being effective and appropriate.

Such a praxis of legitimizing bodily castigation by simply employing an othered protagonist also can be noted in *The Adventures of Pinocchio*. Given the boy's status as a nonhuman wooden puppet, aberrations in his development are explicitly marked as heavily influencing his physiognomy. The most apparent moments in which disciplining is achieved through corporeal restriction consist of the immediate growth of his nose when he is lying, and the temporary transformation into a donkey after deciding to visit a theme park instead of the supposed disciplinary space of the school. The tale's ultimate moral is to become a real human being and overcome the permanent bodily restrictive punishment of being made of wood.[4] This is achieved by doing good deeds and being gentle, docile, or simply a "good boy." Thus, the fairy tale's structure implicitly strengthens the interconnectedness of child rearing and corporeal punishment. A similar observation can be made in relation to the Disney adaptation: as Zipes remarks, Disney copied the main intention of the original text in order to uphold a conservative ideology through plots that exemplified a traditional civilizing process (*Fairy Tale* 208). As I will argue below, *A.I.* partly revises and even ridicules the portrayed discourses of the original text and its Disneyficated adaptation. Its story is centered on the android David (played by Haley Joel Osment). He is artificially constructed to be a perfectly good boy and loves his female owner, whom he is programmed to consider his mother. Shortly after having read Collodi's version of *Pinocchio*, he is simply thrown away as the real son of his owner awakes from a coma and therefore he is no longer needed. He then believes that he can reclaim her love by becoming a real boy—like Pinocchio, who succeeds in making his dreams come true—and starts an odyssey to find the blue fairy who will transform him. Interestingly, in Collodi's version, which is read to David, a "Blue Fairy" is explicitly mentioned. However, this figure is only referred to this way in the Disney version, while she is called "the Fairy with Turquoise Hair" in Collodi's work. By this means, Spielberg subtly refers to the inseparable connection between these source materials and contemporary media-socialized audiences. Besides, David's artificial physiognomy in connotation with his programmed behavior as a perfectly gentle and loving child turns the narrative structure of the original text upside down: David's desire canalized by the fairy tale exposes its logic as a fictional and highly adultist discourse as it simply becomes paradoxical in relation to the android boy. Whereas Collodi's text suggests how normative childlike behavior leads to an overcoming of the corporeal restriction in relation to the transition from childhood to adulthood through discipline as proclaimed by Valentine, David's body is instead marked by the simultaneous permanence of both the corporeal restrictive punishment and the rightful adult-expected attitude. Furthermore, David's longing to become "real" results only from the automated need of being loved by his former owner, for whom he no longer has any use. Thus, it seems to have a cynical implication when his inventor, Professor Hobby (William Hurt), assures him that he can actually become an authentic boy. Having been inspired by a fairy tale, he "set out on a journey to make it real," trying to achieve his personal dreams.[5] However, David is actually only following the tale's prescribed normative narrative. Referring to Bernstein's already stated significant distinction, the quality of David's wish in relation to the original tale is therefore accidentally only to meet adult expectations of children by embodying norms of childhood. However, while the traditional text uses Pinocchio's physical otherness as a possibility for inscribing discourses of disciplining in order to highlight the notion of growing up and becoming real, David's permanently *othered* corporeality instead automatically resists such adult-motivated teleology. Thus, corresponding to Prout's considerations, *A.I.'s* retelling strategy comments on its inspirational source material by reversing the significance of the child's body from an adult inscription and exposing its material ambivalence and even paradoxical nature in comparison to the obvious developmental idea of Collodi's work. This ambivalent nature is further highlighted in a scene where an uncanny visual reversion of the originally intended developmental process is created. Instead of turning into a real boy, David is damaged by an engine overload, whereupon his facial expression—emphasized by a close-up—seems to liquidate and melt all over his face. By employing a parodic technique that is often typical of retellings (see Joosen 47) and then inverting it into an uncanny alienation, the child's body is re-oriented as a notion of ideological revelation of its predecessor's power relations. Accordingly, the inscribed necessity of exemplary behavior and a normal bodily appearance is thus resolved. David's body becomes a permanent symbolic surrogate for revealing the idea of rightful upbringing through corporeal restriction to be an adultist discourse.

Two Perspectives on *Hansel and Gretel*

Traces of the rise of a bourgeois society with accentuated norms of socialization in the nineteenth century can be also detected in the works of the Brothers Grimm. The original folktales they incorporated into their literary versions were mixed with normative middle-class values, given the definition of childhood as an unstable and vulnerable stage in need of adult care. One paradigmatic example can be detected in "Hansel and Gretel," which in a significant and complex way establishes a narrative that sociologist Michael Honig describes as the "answer to the question of the child, in terms of a deficit" (Honig 62) in relation to adults. Thus, the latter are regarded as stable, and adulthood in general as a fixed point in development that legitimizes social agency. In contrast, children are categorized as primarily unfinished and still in the making and therefore are regarded as dependent upon the adult's care and experience. In the Grimms' "Hansel and Gretel," this discourse is especially visible, given the significant opposition between the fairy tale's main narrative and its circular ending. Firstly, the predominant plot of the story shows the two eponymous siblings emancipating themselves from adult control by first surviving in the woods without their parents and afterward outwitting and killing the evil witch. However, this impression is completely undermined by the resolution of the tale's main conflict in the end. Significantly, it is stated: "The man had not had even one happy hour since he had left the children in the woods. However, the woman had died. . . . Now all their cares were at an end, and they lived happily together" (Hunt 245). Although previously portrayed as morally weak and unreliable, the father seems inevitably in need of being rehabilitated in order to achieve the closure of a happy ending as well as the restoration of the familial status quo established in the beginning. Thus, the notion of childhood agency is abruptly replaced by the necessity of adult (patriarchal) dependence on a safe development, restoring and highlighting the seemingly inevitable hierarchical relationship between agentic adults and passive children.[6] Therefore, the inscribed discourse of the child as a deficit being automatically implies a definition of development as situated within a strictly chronological and a coercively adult-oriented context. Unlike *The Adventures of Pinocchio*, "Hansel and Gretel" does not stress the necessity of corporeal punishment. Instead, it underscores the sheer need of placing the child's body in a one-way time line in order for that child to grow up in a normatively regulated way. To underline this, the agentic qualities the children seem to have acquired during their journey are simply not mentioned at all; their purpose is only that the children have brought back material

Figure 10.1. David's (Haley Joel Osment's) melting face in *A. I. Artificial Intelligence* (2001).

goods that are now handed over to the father, who is also in this way restored in the role of the caregiver.

It is exactly this discursively constructed correspondence between child development and straightforward time that is implicitly emphasized and challenged in the South Korean retelling of *Hansel and Gretel*.[7] Partly following the contemporary Korean "trend to turn [Western] fairy tales into horror films" (Lee, "Fairy-Tale" 209), the retelling can also be considered a complex and subversive meditation on the child's body being subjected to a linear and unfinished becoming. Accordingly, such depictions use tropes of the horror genre to interrogate the normative idea of child development as both physically and mentally successive. Although many South Korean fairy-tale films can be analyzed from a primarily national stance as serving "cultural conservation and sociopolitical allegory" (209) to both preserve traditions in aesthetical representation of South Korean art history and react to contemporary societal contexts of the South Korean status quo—thus creatively combining the past and future of the country's culture—it is also possible to contextualize *Hansel and Gretel* within a more general East-Asian cinematic figure of the ghost child: Hye Seung Chung fittingly remarks that in "contemporary Japanese and Korean cinema, the motif of the child ghost or demon has emerged as a response to the social crisis triggered by the pan-Asian financial meltdown in the late 1990s" (90). In this regard, Karen Lury's observations about ontological interconnection between ghosts and children in J-horror films like *Ringu* (directed by Hideo Nakata, Japan, 1998) or *The Grudge* (directed by Takashi Shimizu, Japan, 2004) shall be taken into comparison. Lury relates the mentioned economic instability to a crumbling of an idealized notion of the child as a perfect national image of a promising future. Similar to the characters in these works, the child figures in *Hansel and Gretel* have not grown up, although they are technically much older than their appearance would suggest.

Hansel and Gretel tells the story of three siblings, the boy, Kim Man-bok (Eun-Won Jae), and his two sisters, Shim Eun-Kyung (Kim Young-hee) and Kim-Jung Soon (Jin Ji-hee), who live in an orphanage whose very cruel director beats and rapes them regularly. But on Christmas Eve, a mysterious entity embues them with supernatural powers and the ability not to age physically. Moreover, it provides them with a copy of the Grimms' "Hansel and Gretel." The children interpret the story as a model that they should follow. Thus, they assume they have to force the unsuspecting protagonist, the young man Eun-soo (Chun Jung-myung), who accidently got lost in the woods and wandered into the orphanage the children are still living in, to eternally adopt the role of their father. While also integrating the reading of the traditional fairy tale into its diegesis, the Korean retelling implicitly deconstructs the inscribed hegemony of chronological development with adult support. In a manner quite similar to *A.I.*, this is achieved by simultaneously staging a further discrepancy between the bodily consistencies of the child protagonists and the discourse of the traditional fairy tale itself. Lury describes the paradoxical quality of the ghost child as subverting both normative meanings of childhood and, interestingly, the perception of time:

> At once childlike in terms of their physique but not children in terms of their behaviour and knowledge, they enter the category of the freak. . . . The temporal disorder associated with and represented by these threatening child-ghosts not only challenges the category of childhood, but inevitably and palpably disturbs the supposedly coherent, stable, homogenous and empty time of modernity. (40)

The break in experiencing time in a modern way[8] can also effectively be equated with the deconstruction of chronological time of the child's development. Additionally, in the given case, the ontology of the eternal ghost child who stands outside this discourse shatters the developmental moral of the Grimms' "Hansel and Gretel" and eventually the child protagonists' belief in it. The film's conflict is consequentially resolved when Eun-soo convinces the children that they do not need him as a father in their eternal life at all, as they are mentally already grown up and can look after themselves. The three siblings therefore embody a different conception of uncannily unstable childhood as a discrepancy between the constant childlike appearance and the actual age, which subverts the discourse of development. Drawing on the original fairy tale by the Brothers Grimm, its logic of the inevitability of a father figure is undermined so that Eun-soo finally can return to his pregnant fiancé.

Figure 10.2. The uncanniness of the three ghost siblings in *Hansel and Gretel* (2007).

Additionally, the stated connections between the children's bodies and a distortion of chronological time are occasionally staged and interpreted in a genuinely cinematic way, creating an uncanny effect around the children. As the children kill a serial murderer who finds shelter in their house through their supernatural powers, scenes depicting their murder of the orphanage director are interrelated via a flashback with the present situation. The result is a merging of different time levels through a cross-cutting technique as a temporal discontinuity attached to the child's perspective. Thus, the children's ontology—unlike that of their infant counterparts in the original text they were reading—is again defined to be outside of the linear time of adult-supported development. Instead, it represents a temporal disorder deconstructing normative views of linear childhood.

Kira Muratova's Deconstruction of "The Little Match Girl"

The last bodily connoted discourse on childhood arising from the nineteenth century, predominantly the Victorian era, can be classified as a form of aesthetical sentimentalism, which manifests itself in several visual ways. One of its main motivations can be located in preserving the bodily condition and its seemingly childish physiognomic traits to evoke an effect of cuteness. Medially speaking, such an intention manifests itself in paintings as well as in the Victorian obsession with child photography, as in the works of Julia Margaret Cameron, which show children ornamented with angelic wings to underline the ideas of purity and innocence ascribed to them. James Kincaid identifies the effect of motionlessness as being most important for such a presentation of the child: "Adoration always seems to be a plunge into a psychic deep freeze, which is why children are especially adorable when they are still: the sleeping child or, for the Victorians, the child in the coffin, stilled forever" (*Erotic* 114).

In literary fairy tales, this possibility of an idealized description of childhood can be prominently found in the work of Hans Christian Andersen, who synthesized such an approach with a highly religious predisposition. Zipes importantly remarks that "when one compares Andersen to other fairy-tale writers of his time, how he constantly appeals to God and the Protestant Ethic to justify and sanction the actions and results of his tales" (*Fairy Tale* 81). "The Little Match Girl" combines a sentimentalist notion with his belief in Christianity (e.g., the idea of redemption) as a dominant structure of childhood. The work's ending, especially, can be effectively analyzed in regard to aesthetic tropes of the child's sentimental stillness:

> She took the little girl in her arms, and both of them flew in brightness and joy above the earth, very, very high, and up there was neither cold, nor hunger, nor fear—they were with God. But in the corner, leaning against the wall, sat the little girl with *red cheeks and smiling mouth*, frozen to death on the last evening of the old year. The New Year's sun rose upon a little pathetic figure. The child sat there, *stiff and cold*, holding the matches, of which one bundle was almost burned. (Pinkney 45; my emphasis)

The theme of redemption seems to be crucial in Andersen's work and especially in "The Little Match Girl," as death is portrayed as the only escape to God and from the strife of everyday life. Childhood takes a key role in this concept; being a phenomenon marked by change, it can be preserved through dying, thus aesthetically marking a comforting idea of afterlife eternity. Also, in this context, it appears significant how the girl's body is described as being marked by the death's tragic causes of frostbite, but it is nevertheless leaving her in an aesthetically appealing shape by highlighting the face's childish appeal. In earlier film adaptations, like *The Little Match Girl* (directed by Jean Renoir, France, 1928), this anesthetized approach to the girl's death also legitimized by her seemingly redeemed soul is transposed into cinematic imagery by overflowing her body with extreme front lighting, evoking a sacralizing aura and in this way also encouraging the audience to feel sentimental affection for the child's stilled body.

Like the two examples discussed above, the Ukrainian retelling *Melody of the Street Organ* by Kira Muratova also seems to implicitly highlight and subvert the bodily discourse of childhood by staging the corporeality of its infant actors in an uncannily alternative way. The story is about two siblings, Alijona (Lena Kostyuk) and Nikita (Roma Burlaka), who travel to contemporary Moscow to find their father after their mother's death. Muratova constructs her story out of a bricolage of different fairy-tale tropes, also including the aforementioned "Hansel and Gretel" but primarily focusing on the main motif in "The Little Match Girl" of being outside in the deadly cold at Christmas, thereby also mirroring Fyodor Dostoyevsky's Russian adaptation of Andersen's fairy tale, "The Beggar Boy at Christ's Christmas Tree" (1876).[9] Thus, the discourse of sentimentalism is challenged by the director's specific style of character staging. As in most of her other works, Muratova uses a Brechtian approach of distancing effects to prevent the audience's emotional engagement by making her actors play in a non-naturalistic way, such as pronouncing single words too excessively and applying improper mimic (Taubman 1).

In *Melody of a Street Organ* she employs such a highly stylized way of expression regarding the two children's unnatural look and highly artificial acting. This is also accentuated by means of anti-aestheticizing makeup, including unnaturally dark eyeshadow. Especially in contrast to the aesthetics of sentimentalism of the original text, this overall prevents the audience

Figure 10.3. The anti-aestheticizing effect of the siblings contradicting sentimentalism in *Melody of a Street Organ* (2009).

from feeling a maudlin sympathy and pity for the two protagonists who, contrary to the mentioned bodily discourse of Andersen's story, are not visualized as cute and adorable. Besides, the two infants occasionally tend to lapse into sudden blank facial expressions. On the one hand, this decision in actor staging mimics the representations of sentimental stillness in the original text in a parodic way. Moreover, the fluent transition from the moving image to a photograph-like stilled expression evokes a rather uncanny effect. In *Childhood and Cinema* (2008), Lebeau identifies such a way of transmedia staging as a central possibility to represent child figures in cinema in general: "Sometimes, of course, cinema behaves like a photograph, appearing to halt the flow of images to diverse, but often staggering effect. . . . [There is] an uncanny domain of the photograph that threatens to bring the illusion of the moving image to a halt" (137). This uncanniness of the suddenly stilled child in film seems both to return to the idea of motionless staging of children's bodies for sentimental purposes and to subvert it by referring to its disturbing effect. A similar impact is also achieved during the film's last scene, which highly resembles the ending of Andersen's tale quoted above: a few workers cleaning up an attic at last find one of the siblings, the little boy, frozen to death. Unlike in Andersen's description, the boy's hands cover his face, once again preventing a final sentimental affection for the audience. Moreover, the whole image, with all of its participants, freezes to an uncanny *tableau vivant*. In this way, a shift from the sentimentalized body of the child in Andersen's version to the role of the surrounding observers[10] is achieved, thereby turning the main statement of the fairy tale from the child's redemption to the role of the adults as guilty participants. Thus, Muratova reshapes Andersen's role of childhood. Accordingly, it is preserved in the afterlife, turning the child's death into something to deal with in the contemporary world and thus becoming a focus for societal problems.

Conclusion

As this chapter intended to show, traditional fairy-tale texts can be effectively approached via new ways of critical analysis and interpretation constituted by different perspectives of the interdisciplinary field of childhood studies. Furthermore, contemporary fairy-tale films have a significant adaptive and re-orienting function in relation to their source texts. As the portrayal of three complex interconnections between earlier fairy-tale source texts and their cinematic retellings has demonstrated, cinema can be a powerful tool to induce its audience, which, in turn, in our time is socialized with endless recreations of classic literary fairy tales, to critically challenge the inherent discourses surrounding bodily inscriptions of the child. Staging the child's body in an uncanny, unusual, and unexpected manner visually deconstructs its earlier depictions by adult normative expectations. In this way, contemporary film adaptations can themselves function as cinematic approaches to childhood studies that stage the child as an epistemological culmination point for indirectly commenting on the normative childhood discourses in the original texts. As this chapter has endeavoured to demonstrate, an enlargement of fairy-tale criticism through the field of childhood studies can be quite fruitful. It is particularly insightful when analyzing fairy-tale retellings from the background of a globalized world, since—as has been underscored by the different examples—fairy-tale motifs and the notion of childhood seem to be constructed in a similar way in films emanating from different cultural backgrounds. Despite their different cultural origins, these films ultimately show in a transnational way how childhood may be obscured by cultural myths constructing it as a universal notion in traditional fairy-tale texts and how contemporary adaptations can deconstruct these texts. As there are many different examples where a child protagonist is portrayed in contemporary fairy-tale adaptations, and equally many ways of cinematically staging the child's body in a quite revealing way, this chapter's approach offers further possibilities to highlight such a specific use of contemporary fairy tales to contribute to the fast-expanding research field of childhood studies. Such a comparative analysis of transnational adaptations in relation to childhood can also fill a blind spot in fairy-tale criticism in another important way. By means of a more nuanced fairy-tale criticism approach to the motif of childhood, the dominant Eurocentric tendency toward always accepting the Western models embedded in many traditional texts could be also revealed. This is also true, for example, in the case of contemporary adaptations, such as in mainstream cinema (e.g., Disney). Thus, not only progressive reinterpretations of childhood, as stated in this chapter, but also the numerous reactionary views articulated in both old and new fairy tales could be reconsidered.

Notes

1. Exemplary cornerstones can be located within the so-called new sociology of childhood with representatives such as Allison James, Alan Prout, William A. Corsaro, Michael Wyness, and Nick Lee (see James and Prout 1990, Corsaro 1997, 2003, Wyness 2000, 2006, and Lee 2001), cultural historians like James Kincaid (1992, 1998) and Robin Bernstein (2011) and particularly children's literature criticism with Jacqueline Rose's *The Case of Peter Pan, or the Impossibility of Children's Fiction* (1994) as an important landmark text in constructivist thinking, and film scholarly work of Vicky Lebeau (2008) and Karen Lury (2010).

2. James Kincaid convincingly locates the origins of these key motifs of a culturally constructed notion of childhood in the Victorian era, which, following

the more ambivalent romantic age, stripped the child of any active traits (see Kincaid, *Erotic*).

3. For my definition of the relation between traditional fairy-tale texts and contemporary fairy-tale retellings, I am referring to Vanessa Joosen's distinction between the traditional text as one well-known version and a retelling supposedly referring to such a most well-known text or at least one potential version of the latter (see Joosen 9).

4. Being made of wood can most of all be considered as a restriction to both the movement and the flexibility of a human body and thus be equated to similar disciplining punishment where children are restricted in, for instance, not being allowed to leave their room.

5. Spielberg's narrative of the scientist Hobby, who created David as a replacement for his dead son, seems to be notably influenced by the Japanese manga series *Astro Boy* (Osamu Tezuka, 1952–68), where likewise an inventor creates an artificial boy to compensate for his own loss.

6. A progressive alternative use of such a motif can be observed in E.T.A. Hoffmann's fairy tale *The Strange Child* (1816), where the father dies in the end and the two sibling protagonists must instead find the inner strength to live without his help.

7. As Aleksandra Szugajew and Nieves Moreno Redondo refer to in this volume, the recent *Hansel and Gretel: Witch Hunters* (Tommy Wirkola, 2013) also subverts the traditional version by criticizing contemporary gender roles as well as adding depth and humor by introducing a time after its presumably happy ending.

8. Lury interprets the idea of modernity as an experience marked by (industrial and societal) progress and expansion, which is therefore associated with a straightforward, chronological definition of time similar to the chronological growth of children.

9. Although Dostoyevsky was inspired by a wider range of sources, it is almost certain that he also read Andersen's tale (see Feuer Miller 55).

10. On a national level it also seems to be a metaphorical critique of contemporary Russian society that Muratova continuously presents in her works (see Taubman 1).

Works Cited

Bacchilega, Cristina. *Fairy Tales Transformed? Twenty-First-Century Adaptations and the Politics of Wonder*. Wayne State University Press, 2013.

Bell, Sophie. "'So Wicked': Revisiting Uncle Tom's Cabin's Sentimental Racism through the Lens of the Child." *The Children's Table: Childhood Studies and the Humanities*, edited by Anna Mae Duane, University of Georgia Press, 2013, pp. 89–104.

Bernstein, Robin. *Racial Innocence: Performing American Childhood from Slavery to Civil Rights*. New York University Press, 2011.

Chung, Hye Seung. "Acacia and Adoption Anxiety in Korean Horror Cinema." *Korean Horror Cinema*, edited by Alison Peirse and Daniel Martin, Edinburgh, 2013, pp. 87–100.

Corsaro, William A. *The Sociology of Childhood*. Pine Forge Press, 1997.

———. *We're Friends Right? Inside Kids' Culture*. Joseph Henry Press, 2003.

Eder, Jens. "Understanding Characters." *Projections*, vol. 4, no. 1, Berghan Books, 2010.

Feuer Miller, Robin. "A Childhood's Garden of Despair: Dostoevsky and 'A Boy at Christ's Christmas Party'" *Russian Writers and the Fin de Siècle*, edited by Katherine Bowers and Ani Kokobobo, Cambridge University Press, 2015, pp. 52–68.

Foucault, Michel. *Discipline and Punish: The Birth of the Prison*. 1975. Translated by Alan Sheridan, Vintage Books, 1995.

Honig, Michael-Sebastian. "How is the Child Constituted in Childhood Studies?" *The Palgrave Handbook of Childhood Studies*, edited by Jens Qvortrup, William A. Corsaro, and Michael-Sebastian Honig, Palgrave Macmillan, 2009, pp. 62–77.

Hunt, Margarete. *Grimm's Complete Fairy Tales*. Canterbury Classics, 2011.

James, Allison, and Alan Prout. *Constructing and Reconstructing Childhood: New Directions in the Sociological Study of Childhood*. 1990, Routledge, 2011.

Jenkins, Henry. *Convergence Culture: Where Old and New Media Collide*. New York University Press, 2006.

———. "Introduction: Childhood Innocence and Other Modern Myths." *The Children's Culture Reader*, edited by Henry Jenkins, New York University Press, 1998, pp. 1–40.

Joosen, Vanessa. *Critical and Creative Perspectives on Fairy Tales: An Intertextual Dialogue between Fairy-Tale Scholarship and Postmodern Retellings*. Wayne State University Press, 2011.

Kincaid, James Russell. *Child-Loving: The Erotic Child and Victorian Culture.* Routledge, Chapman and Hall, Inc., 1992.

——. *Erotic Innocence: The Culture of Child Molesting.* Duke University Press, 1998.

Lebeau, Vicky. *Childhood and Cinema.* Reaktion Books, 2008.

Lee, Nick. *Childhood and Society.* Open University Press, 2001.

Lee, Sung-Ae. "The Fairy-Tale Film in Korea." *Fairy-Tale Films beyond Disney: International Perspectives*, edited by Jack Zipes, Pauline Greenhill, and Kendra Magnus-Johnston, Routledge, 2015, pp. 207–21.

Lury, Karen. *The Child in Film: Tears, Fears and Fairy Tales.* IB Tauris & Co. Ltd, 2010.

Pinkney, Jerry, Andersen, Hans Christian. *The Little Match Girl.* Puffin Books, 2002.

Prout, Alan. "Childhood Bodies: Construction, Agency and Hybridity." *The Body, Childhood and Society*, edited by Alan Prout, Palgrave Macmillan, 2000, pp. 1–18.

Rose, Jacqueline. *The Case of Peter Pan, or the Impossibility of Children's Fiction.* University of Pennsylvania Press, 1994.

Short, Sue. *Fairy Tale and Film: Old Tales with a New Spin.* Palgrave Macmillan, 2008.

Taubman, Jane A. *Kira Muratova.* I.B. Tauris, 2015.

Valentine, Gil. "Children's Bodies: An Absent Presence." *Contested Bodies of Childhood and Youth*, edited by Kathrin Hörschelmann and Rachel Colls, Palgrave Macmillan, 2010, pp. 22–40.

Wyness, Michael. *Childhood and Society: An Introduction to the Sociology of Childhood.* Palgrave Macmillan, 2006.

——. *Contesting Childhood.* Routledge, 2000.

Zipes, Jack. *Breaking the Magic Spell: Radical Theories of Folk and Fairy Tales.* 2nd ed., University Press of Kentucky, 2002.

Zipes, Jack. *Fairy Tale and the Art of Subversion: The Classic Genre for Children and the Process of Civilization.* 2nd ed., Routledge, 2006.

Zipes, Jack. "The Great Cultural Tsunami of Fairy-Tale Films." *Fairy-Tale Films beyond Disney: International Perspectives*, edited by Jack Zipes, Pauline Greenhill, and Kendra Magnus-Johnston, Routledge, 2016, no. 1–17.

Filmography

A.I. Artificial Intelligence (directed by Steven Spielberg, USA, 2001)
The Grudge (directed by Takashi Shimizu, Japan, 2004)
Hansel and Gretel (directed by Pil-Sung Yim, Korea, 2007)
Little Match Girl (directed by Jean Renoir, France, 1928)
Melody of a Street Organ (directed by Kira Muratova, Ukraine, 2009)
Pinocchio (directed by Norman Ferguson et al., USA, 1940)
Ringu (directed by Hideo Nakata, Japan, 1998)

11

Alice on the Edge

Girls' Culture and "Western" Fairy Tales in Japan

Lucy Fraser

DESPITE NATIONAL CLAIMS TO narratives, the idea of "ownership" of any text is dubious, but particularly so for fairy tales, with their oral, transcultural origins and unpredictable movement across geographical and chronological lines. Through the proliferation and sharing of fantastical tales, singled-authored stories also soon spiral out beyond their original, authoritative editions. This is the case for Lewis Carroll's *Alice's Adventures in Wonderland* (1865) and *Through the Looking Glass and What Alice Found There* (1871), those much-loved English books that may be described as literary fairy tales, or as fairy-tale-like children's literature. Carroll's stories themselves appear in several versions: based on "Alice's Adventures Under Ground" (told in 1862 and written in 1864), and then later rewritten as *The Nursery "Alice"* (1890), they have since continued to take new forms.

Alice and her associates have enjoyed a long and varied career in Japan since their introduction at the end of the nineteenth century. In addition to being retold on page and screen, the stories are reimagined in wonderlands of trinkets and goods, fashion, and even in Alice-themed restaurants with lavish storybook interiors, where menus offer dishes such as the "Queen of Hearts' Jewelry Box Mixed Berry Parfait,"[1] or the "Cheshire Cat Cheese

Omelette" with the food arranged into the cat's smiling face.[2] In the Alice-themed restaurants, Carroll's work is thus quite literally "devoured" by diners, many of whom are female. Indeed, the character Alice and the stories she appears in enjoy a particularly close association with girls in Japan. In 2015, the prominent Japanese cultural journal *Eureka* published a special issue, edited by Hiroshi Takayama, celebrating the 150th anniversary of *Alice's Adventures in Wonderland*—one of the latest in a large number of Lewis Carroll or Alice-themed critical and creative anthologies. This collection of essays, poetry, and artwork is presented within a girlish cover taken from Yūko Higuchi's print for female fashion label Emily Temple Cute: against a pink background, stars twinkle around a monochrome Alice, who, wearing a spotty dress with puffed sleeves, tumbles upside-down among iconic objects such as the white rabbit, a glass bottle, a teacup, and books (see fig. 11.1). The volume features a cluster of "girl"-themed entries, including a discussion of "Alices of the Twenty-first Century" by five women collectively described as "Gakuma Gāruzu Kenkyūtai."[3] The discussants muse on the huge popularity of *Alice* in Japan, especially with girls, touching on the network of stories and objects that have generated from Carroll's book: the Disney film, goods, and even body modification, fashion, and costume.

In this way, foreign literary fairy tales are appropriated into Japan and themselves become a series of "conversations" across national borders and about gender, as Mayako Murai shows in *From Dog Bridegroom to Wolf Girl: Contemporary Japanese Fairy-Tale Adaptations in Conversation with the West*. Japanese appropriations of foreign texts also forge connections with and reveal disconnects between genres and across media. As such, they call for criticism that acknowledges this dialogic process; they also call for a critical perspective that is embedded in the Japanese context without essentializing and "re-marginalizing" Japan in relation to a dominant West (Murai 141–42). Here I explore some permutations of Japanese "possession" of foreign fairy tales, with a focus on "Arisu to iu namae" ["The Name Alice"], a tale included in author Yōko Ogawa (1962–) and illustrator Kumiko Higami's (1963–) fantastical collection aptly titled *Lost Property Fairy Tales* (*Otogibanashi no wasuremono*, 2006). "The Name Alice" exemplifies the ways in which, in her many different iterations, the character of Alice stands

Figure 11.1. Special issue of *Eureka* journal on Alice (edited by Takayama, March 2015, vol. 47, no. 3).

at the intersections of different spheres, both marking and unmaking their "edges." That is, the story presents an image of girls' imaginative relationships with foreign objects and texts that recollects the evolution of the *Alice* tales upon their introduction to Japan, particularly within girl culture. It is also an example of works in which Alice and her wonderland act as conduits between girls' stories and what may be viewed as more "serious" literature written by adult women. Ogawa and Higami's appropriation embodies some of the ways that new *Alice* stories enliven and re-orient "Western" fairy tales, and the relationships of these tales with girls' culture in Japan.

Japanese Girls Devour Ants, *Alice*, and Other Foreign Objects

> One day, while holding my observation notes and peering into the glass tank, in the instant I took a quick breath in, I inhaled one of the ants. The ant flew straight through the inside of my nose, and fell sliding down my bronchial tube. The ant, like me, was unable to understand what was happening to its body, and half-unconscious it arrived at my lungs. (Ogawa, *Otogibanashi* 69)

Ogawa's story "The Name Alice" combines much of the spirit of Carroll's famous books with some of the motifs of Japanese girls' culture; as such it recalls some of the surprising ways in which the *Alice* books have been translated and reimagined in Japan. In the episode cited above, where the girl narrator unwittingly inhales an ant, which goes on a rabbit-hole journey down her bronchial tube, Ogawa presents a cross-species relationship of intimate devouring and destruction, as well as one of unexpected reconstruction. Just as Carroll's Alice imbibes strangely powerful foods and drinks that transform her, just as Ogawa's Alice figure inhales ants that build a new home inside her, so Japanese girls' culture has blossomed through the devouring of stories from beyond Japan. Indeed, girls' culture in Japan has embraced and expanded foreign visual and textual objects with much less horror and much more imaginative agency than that with which Ogawa's despairing narrator absorbs the ants.

Alice reached Japan as part of the extensive adoption and adaptation of foreign and especially "Western" works that took off during the Meiji period of rapid, intense sociocultural change from 1868 to 1912. Educational reform, such as compulsory schooling, established newly recognized periods of childhood and adolescence, and new works of children's literature, in Japanese or translated from English and some European languages, were mobilized to shape young generations into state-sanctioned ideals. The early Japanese translations of Carroll's *Alice* books are chronicled by Kimie Kusumoto in *Hon'yaku no kuni no Arisu: Ruisu Kyaroru hon'yakushi, hon'yaku ron* [*Alice in Translationland: Lewis Carroll Translation History and Theory*] (2001). The first is credited to eight installments appearing in *Shōnen sekai* (*Boys' world*) magazine in 1899: "Kagami sekai: Seiyō otogibanashi" ("Mirror World: A Western Fairy Tale"), by literary critic Tenkei Hasegawa, is described by Kusumoto as somewhere between a translation and adaptation of *Through the Looking-Glass* (21), with the heroine now a Japanese girl named Miyo (cutely nicknamed Mii-chan).

Boys' World, launched in 1895 by fairy-tale author and translator Sazanami Iwaya, was one of several boys' magazines established in the 1890s. Delineation of the "boy" identity during this period necessitated a separate "girl" identity and this, combined with more schooling and higher literacy rates for girls, is evident in the establishment of girls' magazines in the early 1900s. These magazines included *Shōjo sekai* (*Girls' World*, 1906) and *Shōjo no tomo* (*Girls' Friend*, 1908).

The word *shōjo*, used in these titles, has come to refer to a figure of the girl that is particularly resonant of Alice. Different from other words for "girl" that more straightforwardly denote sex or gender, *shōjo* can describe an idea and a genre, works with a special sensibility that in the first half of the twentieth century nearly always featured girl characters and were consumed by actual girls. Multiple definitions circulate around the contested and complex figure of the *shōjo*. Here I follow the shape sketched by child studies scholar Masuko Honda, focused on the girl as genre and text, but also her interiority as a reader. Honda describes the ephemeral, intangible figure of the *shōjo* through "the 'signs' of the girl," a cluster of "'colours, fragrances and sounds' that resonate uniquely with the aesthetics of the girl" across different decades (27), from 1920s Japanese novels to 1970s *manga* and more. Of such "signs," the most illustrative for Honda are "ribbons and frills" (28) and their fluttering movement, which is replicated in the text: "verbal images that 'flutter and drift,' girls' fiction and lyric poetry secretly narrates the same characteristics that are represented by an excess of 'ribbons and frills'" (31). Honda describes girls' liminal world as both dreamlike and a private space in which girls dream (33). Honda, through this analysis of fragmented, meandering text and images of wide-eyed, beribboned girls, narrates in a nostalgic and poetic register a *shōjo* who, like Alice, is a girl within her own Wonderland, on the edge of change, so absorbed in her story that she is unaware of the adult audience observing her in its pages.

Girls' Friend magazine featured the next iteration of Alice: "The Tale of Alice" ["Arisu monogatari"], published in 1908 under the (female) penname of Sumako, by the (male) journalist Shizuo Nagayo. The episodes of this work, Kusumoto notes, begin with a translation of *Wonderland* but later become Sumako's own original story about a girl called Arisu (29–30). Sumako's translation was soon followed by the first book edition, *Ai-chan yume monogatari* (*The Tale of Ai-chan's Dream*), translated by Eikan Maruyama and published in 1910. This is a much closer translation (Kusumoto 38), though it names its heroine "Ai" (the character for "love"), adding the affectionate "-chan." As was common, early versions were often closer to adaptations, made culturally accessible and meeting the educational purposes of the time, then growing efforts were made to accurately represent the source text.

By the 1920s, girls' magazines were joyfully embracing the foreign. Translated novels from overseas that now form a canon of girls' classics included Frances Hodgson Burnett's *Little Lord Fauntleroy* (first translated in the girls' column of *Shōnen sekai*, 1890–92), Louisa May Alcott's *Little Women* (first abridged translation in 1906), and L. M. Montgomery's *Anne of Green Gables* (first translated in 1952). A penchant for the exotic is also particularly evident in the work of Nobuko Yoshiya (1896–1973), the Japanese author of the popular collection of *Hanamonogatari* [*Flower Tales*] (first episode in 1916 in *Shōjo gahō* [*Girls' Pictorial*]). *Flower Tales* is characterized by close, sometimes romantic friendships between its young heroines, a lack of concrete detail and an ornate descriptive style, and the romanticized use of Western imagery and "exotic foreign words scattered across the pages" (Honda 21). Aesthetic appropriation of the "West" is evident in images as much as text in girls' culture of this period. Another *Alice* translation, attributed to Yoshiko Tamura (then later Yōko Tamura), serialized through 1926 in *Girls' Friend*, has story and illustrations switching Alice into more "active" Western clothing rather than the kimono of previous translations (Kusumoto 94). The magazines also featured illustrations of beautiful *shōjo* to aspire to, such as Jun'ichi Nakahara's pale, wide-eyed girls, innocent, petite, and often elegantly posed in the latest fashions, appearing from the 1930s to the 1960s.

From the mid-twentieth century, text and images within girls' culture intersect even more closely in the form of *manga* (comics), also serialized in periodicals. Osamu Tezuka's trail-blazing *shōjo manga*, *Ribon no kishi* [*Princess Knight*] (serialized in *Shōjo kurabu* [*Girls' Club*] from 1953 through 1956, then adapted into an animated television series from 1960 through 1968), has Princess Sapphire and other noble characters dressed in vaguely medieval costumes, in a vaguely European, Disneyesque setting of forests and castles. The 1970s saw the "Golden Age" of *shōjo manga*, with hugely successful female *manga* artists creating artistic, complex works. Foreign settings abound, as in Riyoko Ikeda's *Berusaiyu no bara* [*The Rose of Versailles*] (1972–73), set in the French court hurtling toward revolution, complete with an extravagantly costumed Marie Antoinette. *Shōjo manga* with clearer fairy-tale connections include those featuring "magical girls," such as the early *Mahō tsukai Sarī* [*Sally the Witch*] (Mitsuteru Yokoyama, 1966–67), and, for example, *Akazukin Chacha* [*Red Riding Hood Chacha*] (Min Ayahana, 1991–2000). Successful *manga* serials such as these become even better known through publication in stand-alone volumes, animated adaptations, and further transformation. After the experimental and spectacular *manga* of the 1970s, more works with realistic Japanese settings emerged, though we may observe a recent resurgence of foreign fairy-tale backdrops in girls' anime, such as *Princess Tutu* (see Monden, this volume). Concurrent to *manga*, girls' novels continued in the form of juvenile or "junior" novels of the 1960s and 1970s, from the 1980s often known as "Cobalt" novels, after the famous imprint published by Shūeisha. The latter wave includes *Alice* retellings, notably Ryō Nakahara's *Alice Series* of 34 novels (1987–2000): the girl protagonist Alice must navigate trials and puzzles in different "lands" from *benkyō no kuni* (studyland) to *kyōryū no kuni* (dinosaurland).

The 1970s also saw *Alice* flourish in Japan's popular as well as intellectual and artistic culture. This boom is discernible in a flurry of anthologies, including special periodical issues on Lewis Carroll[4] in *Bessatsu gendaishi techō* [*Special Issue of Modern Poetry Notebook*] (1972), *Bokushin* [*Pan*] (1973, on Alice and Carroll), and the aforementioned *Eureka* (December 1978, then another in April 1992).[5] Photographs and illustrations were often included in such anthologies and special issues, and visual art seems to have played an important role in the uptake of Alice at the time. In particular, artist Kuniyoshi Kaneko illustrated a 1974 picture book edition of *Alice*, then exhibited and published a set of somewhat surreal and disturbing works, "Arisu no yume" ["Dream of Alice"] in 1978, seen in an art book of his *Alice* works in 1979 (*Arisu no garō*, Gallery of Alice; see a 2005 painting featured as a *Eureka* cover in Fig. 11.2) (see Knighton 56). In the popular realm, *Alice* was even retold in an episode of the classic children's television series *Manga sekai mukashibanashi* (*Manga World Folktales*) in December 1976.

Kusumoto analyzes fourteen translations of the two *Alice* books appearing from 1899 to 1948, but cites a study that counts 102 complete and abridged translations published up until 1975 in book format alone.[6] If retellings, adaptations, parodies, and other transformations were added, the number would surely exceed one thousand.[7] Ogawa and Higami's illustrated *Lost Property Fairy Tales* belongs to a long line of girlish works that reimagine *Alice* in a marriage of image and text. From the glimpses at girls' culture we are already beginning to see that a narrative yearning for the "foreign," such as the world of *Alice*, does not result in simple reproduction or mimicry of the "original" story. Instead, the imaginary, exotic Europe, England, or elsewhere of imported fairy tales and children's literature is transformed, set to work in the construction of new tales.

Figure 11.2. Special issue of *Eureka* journal on Kuniyoshi Kaneko, featuring a 2005 Alice artwork (edited by Nishidate, July 2015, vol. 47, no. 9).

The Edge of Girlhood: Alice Grows Up

> "It was much pleasanter at home," thought poor Alice, "when one wasn't always growing larger and smaller, and being ordered about by mice and rabbits. I almost wish I hadn't gone down that rabbit-hole—and yet—and yet—it's rather curious, you know, this sort of life! I do wonder what *can* have happened to me! When I used to read fairy-tales, I fancied that kind of thing never happened, and now here I am in the middle of one! There ought to be a book written about me, that there ought! And when I grow up, I'll write one—but I'm grown up now," she added in a sorrowful tone; "at least there's no room to grow up any more here." (Carroll, *Alice's Adventures in Wonderland*, 52)

The author of *Lost Property Fairy Tales*, Yōko Ogawa, is a writer of "serious" literature for adults, well respected and recognized, with over thirty works of fiction to her name. Among her many accolades, one of her early works, *Ninshin karendā* [*Pregnancy Diary*] (1991) was awarded the prestigious Akutagawa Prize, and Ogawa has sat on the judging committee for this prize since 2007. The slim illustrated volume of *Lost Property Fairy Tales* is an obscure piece within her oeuvre. Yet, there is a sense of the timeless and the fantastic to much of Ogawa's writing, and it is this book that makes more explicit the characteristics of fairy tales that have contributed to this atmosphere.[8] As such, the collection exemplifies another juncture of Japanese girls' culture with Western fairy tales: the role works such as *Alice* play in literary writing by women, for adults. As Carroll's Alice herself plans in the epigraph to this section, grown-up Alices have continued to write the stories that girls' fairy-tale experiences demand.

The character Alice, and Carroll's *Alice* books, form links for several women writers whose work resonates with both fairy-tale and girl culture. Foremost is Sumiko Yagawa (1930–2002), one of the most popular translators of Carroll's work: *Alice's Adventures in Wonderland* in 1990, and *Through the Looking Glass* in 1991. Yagawa translated an incredible amount of literature from both English and German; the *Alice* books number among her many translations of children's literature and fairy tales, including the

Grimm's fairy tales,[9] *Tales from Mother Goose* [*Mazā gūsu fantajī*] (translated in 1977), and classic girls' novels such as Johanna Spyri's *Heidi* (translated in 1974) and Louisa May Alcott's *Little Women* (translated in 1985). Yagawa was a poet, essayist, and author in her own right and used the figure of Alice to reflect on girlhood, an identity that remained close to her heart and shaped her public image for her entire life. *Shōjo* and Arisu are key, recurring terms in writing by and about Yagawa, such that the special issue of *Eureka* ("Yagawa Sumiko") published after her death at the age of seventy-one dubs her *Fumetsu no shōjo* (Everlasting shōjo), the title of Yagawa's own 1972 essay about Alice, as well as one of her poems.

Yagawa's approach to *Alice* is both sympathetic and challenging. Before her translation, she had engaged with Alice in her own creative work at the forefront of the 1970s craze. Two of her early poetry collections are *Kotoba no kuni no Arisu* [*Alice in the Wordland*] (1974) and *Arisu kanginshū* [*Alice's Song Collection*] (1980). The use of Alice in these poems is emblematic of the character's escape from Carroll's book and her journeys in Japanese girl culture: as Tomoko Aoyama demonstrates, "In this Wordland, Yagawa's Alice repeatedly transforms and multiplies herself" ("'Girl' Critic" 42), through linguistic play and intertextual invocations and leaps. The 1994 paperback edition of Yagawa's *Wonderland* translation is illustrated by the aforementioned Kuniyoshi Kaneko and includes a translator's afterword. Here, Yagawa describes the way Alice's journey through the rabbit hole into wonderland isolates her:

> In *Wonderland* and in *Through the Looking Glass*, Alice is spectacularly solitary. . . . Of the multitude of characters who appear, Alice is the only properly human one, and encounters no one the same type as herself. Those she does encounter are insects, or beasts, all of some different species, every one of them an odd creature, on a different wavelength. (*Fushigi* 180)

The loneliness of this girl, Yagawa says, has appeal for all readers, "So," she invites, "please do join us, do not take your kindly gaze from this *shōjo*, watch over her to the very end of her solitary travels" (*Fushigi* 181). As we shall see, this same girlish isolation is expressed by Ogawa's narrator Arisu, who yearns for female friendship but instead is forced into an intimate association with ants.

Another example of a woman author drawing upon the *shōjo* figure of Alice is poet, novelist, and essayist Mieko Kanai (1947–). In one of her many erudite and far-reaching essays, Kanai recalls that the lack of a clear plot or drama in *Alice* dissatisfied her as a girl. But her aunt had told her that Kanai resembled some of the "clever, precocious, appealing" heroines of classic girls' novels; while this "is not a characteristic limited to me, and probably describes all girls," this made Kanai feel that she must read the books from the perspective of Alice herself ("Arisu no ehon" ["Picture Book of Alice"] 98–99). Like Yagawa, Kanai described her adult self as a *shōjo* at times, and in her early career she was dubbed as such by others. Kanai weaves this irrepressible girl identity into the male-dominated realm of literary fiction—for example, in her novel *Indian Summer* (1988) (see Aoyama "Transgendering *Shōjo Shōsetsu*"). Mary Knighton sees Kanai at the forefront of the 1970s Alice trend, tracing the influence of her 1967 Humpty Dumpty poem[10] on important (male) poets. Kanai's wicked, parodic imagining of *shōjo* and Alice emerges in her 1972 short story "Rabbits." Here, the emblematic image of the white rabbit is quite literally dissected when a girl protagonist gains from her father a love of slaughtering, skinning, and cooking rabbits. The girl descends along a dark, bloody path; already isolated from her peers, she eventually loses nearly all human contact, dressing in furs and "becoming" a rabbit herself, before reaching her own gory end. Knighton speculates

> whether or not the force behind Kanai's revision of innocent Alices into violent *shōjo* with minds of their own is completely unrelated to the simultaneous praise and paternalistic treatment she received in her early years, when she was determined to be a successful writer in the male-dominated *bundan* (literary establishment). (55)

As noted in the next section, Kanai's subtle, clever story leads the way for a number of works by female writers and creators that recast the innocent young Alice as a more independent young woman. But this potential for change seems inherent in Alice herself. Honda's theory of the textual figure of *shōjo* describes an ability to subvert adult patriarchal norms, or at the very least, avoid conforming to them: "Girls' culture . . . never associates itself with the establishment. For it perpetually sways and drifts, rejecting the intervention of everyday logic" (36).

Any number of other fiction writers and academics embody some aspect of the deep-rooted interconnections between girls' novels or *manga*, *Alice*, and Western fairy tales.[11] For example, Akiko Waki (1948–) is both a translator of Carroll's *Alice* and a researcher of Anglo-European children's literature. Her book *Shōjo-tachi no 19seiki: Ningyo-hime kara Arisu made* [*The Girls' Nineteenth Century: From The Little Mermaid to Alice*] (2013) examines the two works of children's literature in their social and literary contexts. The blurb uses *Alice* as a drawcard: "The lively group of the new girl figures who appeared in nineteenth century European tales: a different look on the history of children's literature that investigates the mystery of the birth of *Alice*."

Carroll's *Alice* books and other foreign fairy tales and children's literature were available in Japanese translation to all of the women authors discussed here. Those growing up in the 1970s onward had the added influence of the "Golden Age" of *shōjo manga*. This includes late 1980s through 1990s literary fiction superstar Yoshimoto Banana (1964–), who acknowledged the influence of *shōjo manga* on her work and also takes up fairy tales such as "The Little Mermaid" in *Utakata* [*Bubbles*] (1988). Kazuki Sakuraba (1971–) writes novels for adults as well as popular fiction for younger readers; her writing demonstrates a nuanced view of the *shōjo* identity and often has fairy-tale themes. Sakuraba's "light novel" series for young readers, *GOSICK* (13 vols, 2003–11, followed by sequel series and cross-media adaptations), set in the *shōjo* mode in an imagined Francophone country in Europe, includes an epigraph from *Wonderland* and Alice-themed elements from rabbits to Victorian fashions (see King and Fraser). The girl figure Alice has in this way offered women authors—and their readers—a kind of imaginative bridge from *shōjo* culture into literary fiction.

Renaming and Reviewing Alice

> Having an Agatha or an Agnes in the class would be great. . . .
> I would give Agatha an Agatha Christie murder mystery, and I would give Agnes Anne Brontë's *Agnes Grey,* and of course in return I would receive *Alice's Adventures in Wonderland.* Together the three of us, Alice, Agatha, and Agnes, would form a secret gang of "3A" girls, and we would carry those books as membership cards wherever we went.
>
> [. . .]
>
> The Gang of the 3A Girls would be feared by everyone.
>
> [. . .]
>
> To keep on our good side, the other students would present us with gifts of chocolates, and moisturizers, and baby chicks. (Ogawa, *Otogibanashi* 62–63)

Ogawa and Higami's volume of *Lost Property Fairy Tales* exemplifies the entangled nature of foreign fairy tales and girls' culture in Japan, as well as taking up the tradition of adult women rewriting girlish Alices. Carroll's Alice endlessly imbibes mysterious substances that affect her size and her relationship with the topography and creatures of the wondrous world in which she finds herself. Ogawa's tale "The Name Alice" plays on the name of Carroll's girl protagonist, which in Japanese pronunciation is rendered *Arisu.* This girl narrator bemoans the fate her name bestows on her: since it begins with "A," in the alphabetical order used at school she must stand at the front whenever the class lines up. She is always forced to be the first one to face the vaccination needle, the first to try jumping over the vaulting horse (65). Arisu longs for some fellow girls with "A" names, dreaming of the friendships she would form if an Agnes and an Agatha joined her class. But her name instead brings about another fate. Arisu receives a birthday present from her father in the form of an ant farm. Though she would have preferred a "puffed-sleeve dress" (68) or some other girlish item, she cares for her new pets dutifully. However, one day Arisu accidentally inhales one of the ants. The ant, which was carrying eggs, lays them in the mucous membrane of her lungs. In Japanese, the word for ant is *ari*; the ants that are born from the eggs build a nest—*ari-no-su*—within the body of Ari-su (69); in other words, in a Carroll-esque tradition of wordplay that was carried on by women authors such as Yagawa and Kanai, Ogawa's entire plot depends on a pun.

Shōjo associations with Alice and fairy tales come together in *Lost Property Fairy Tales*, where *Alice's Adventures in Wonderland* is retold alongside classics from Andersen and the Grimms. Carroll's nonsensical adventure tale differs from the imaginative literary fairy tales of Andersen, and again from the Grimms' compact rewritings of folktales. But in any case, academic distinctions between folktales, (literary) fairy tales, and children's literature are less relevant in this context. Rather, certain labels invoke a girlish aesthetic and a dreamy atmosphere: the word *otogibanashi* (fairy tales), used in the title of the book and in some early *Alice* translations,[12] and the word *shōjo*, used widely and routinely to refer to Carroll's Alice, and in this book used by both the author and the illustrator in their afterwords (116 and 117, respectively) to refer to themselves, as well as to the girls in the pictures. Other key invocations could include *dōwa* (children's story); the loanword *meruhen* (*märchen*) and, perhaps *ohime-sama* and *purinsesu* (the native and the loanword used for "princess"). In this book, Ogawa's four fairy-tale transformations were composed in response to illustrations of girls by Higami. The involvement of Higami herself situates Ogawa's "Alice" story in closer connection to both girls' culture and fairy tales. Higami, who majored in German literature at university, depicts many heroines from the Grimms' and other fairy tales. Higami's style is reminiscent of earlier illustrations for girls' periodicals and storybooks: it recalls the vivid colors and tiny, closed mouths of the girls painted by Yumeji Takehisa from the early 1900s to the early 1930s, and the huge eyes, rosebud mouths, and lovely dresses of girls depicted by the aforementioned Jun'ichi Nakahara in subsequent decades. The darker side of Higami's work may also owe something to Kuniyoshi Kaneko's Alice artwork first appearing in the 1970s.[13]

More concretely, this book's sustained interest in physical *things* such as frilly clothing and sparkling jewelry exemplifies another link between

Japanese girls' culture and fairy tales. The "classic" fairy tales tend to revolve around memorable solid objects: the long hair of an imprisoned princess, a cursed spinning wheel, a glass coffin, a magic bean, a gingerbread cottage. Here, Higami's illustrations and Ogawa's stories translate the trembling, transient "signs of the girl" into the solidity of fairy tale objects. A frame story takes place in a candy store—sweet, colorful foods being another "sign" of the girl—and it describes the collected fairy tales as physical items that were discovered in the "lost property" rooms of train stations and such anonymous venues around the world. The first tale revisits the Grimms' "Little Red Riding Hood," and the illustrations and the story focus on clothing, featuring Red Riding Hood in a plush wolf-skin coat, and a modern-day society for dedicated fans of hoods. Next, in a response to Andersen's "The Little Mermaid," illustrations show girl mermaids adorned with sparkling jewels, and the accompanying story tells of a merman jewelry maker. In the five illustrations for "The Name Alice," objects associated with metamorphosis and change emphasize the theme of girlhood and growing up with Alice's dramatic physical transformations: for example, in "Niwa" ["Garden"], tiger lilies in progressive states of budding, blooming, and wilting (Ogawa, *Otogibanashi* 54–55), and in "Haru" ["Spring"], uprooted flowers and bulbs floating with a strange lack of gravity that suggests Alice's fall down the rabbit hole (Ogawa, *Otogibanashi* 56). Another, titled "Heya" ["Room"] (Ogawa, *Otogibanashi* 58; Fig. 11.3), gathers the most recognizable *Alice* and fairy-tale goods: on a chessboard floor are an egg, a key, a cup of tea, and some chess pieces, and on the walls are a clock and some framed paintings (or mirrors, or windows), one featuring a single leg with a red shoe. Finally, drawing from stories such as *Swan Lake* and Andersen's "The Wild Swans," illustrated swan princesses are also gorgeously frilled and beribboned, and the story tells of a swan drowned in a lake when it is weighed down by too much candy.

Higami thus adorns her illustrations with fairy-tale objects, "signs of the girl" that collectively capture a culture. Responding to this visual framework, it is no coincidence that Ogawa's narrator, Arisu, expresses her dreams of female friendship through an eccentric catalog of girlish items: "books," "chocolates, and moisturizers, and baby chicks" (63). Similarly, Arisu's

Figure 11.3. Higami Kumiko's Alice illustration, "Heya" ["Room"] in Ogawa, *Otogibanashi* 58. Courtesy of Poplar.

birthday gift wish list was "red shoes or a puffed-sleeve dress" (68). Within *shōjo* culture, girl protagonists and their girl readers seem to yearn for that romantic, fairy-tale atmosphere of fluttering princess frocks, tea parties with cakes and fine porcelain, and stately gardens laden with flowers. This type of girls' yearning is a driving force in many fairy tales: Cinderella's desire to attend the royal ball is met, in memorable detail, with beautiful gowns and glass slippers; in Andersen's "The Red Shoes," Karen's obsession with her beloved footwear leads to her downfall (and Christian salvation). So these potent desires are perhaps girlish manifestations of the phenomenon of "wishing" that is at the heart of fairy-tale plots.

In Japanese girls' stories, the objects of yearning often appear to be associated with Western or perhaps "old-fashioned" European lifestyles. A penchant for European settings and characters is often seen in *shōjo manga*, and has been theorized as expressing girl readers' *akogare* or aspiring to "the West." Honda refers to "girls' yearning for the exotic and the privileged" (32), and in a recent volume of *shōjo* research, *Girls' Manga Wonderland*,[14] Dollase states that in 1970s popular *shōjo manga*, "the use of worlds removed from reality such as foreign or historical settings made the creation of grand dramas possible, and fulfilled girls' cravings for romantic tales" (15). Fusami Ōgi, scholar of *manga* and graphic novels, points out that the beloved use of Western figures and locales in *shōjo manga* can tend to be critiqued as a kind of cultural colonization: "othered" Japanese girls are seen to aspire to the desirable Western subject in the "center." However, Ōgi believes that this aspiration forms part of a more positive identification process. She argues that "*shōjo manga* is a genre that has developed with a deep-seated connection to women's agency"; she ties the "Golden Age" of *shōjo manga*, when the genre was claimed by women and grew more artistically sophisticated and gender radical, to global feminist movements of the 1960s and 1970s (111). Indeed, the genre crosses the borders not only of nation but also of gender: it frequently features foreign intertexts, settings, and people, as well as cross-dressed, gender ambiguous, or highly feminized characters with large eyes, elegant, long-limbed bodies, and flowing, voluminous hair. If "the West" is a glamorous, romanticized escape from reality, equally important for Ōgi is the converse effect that "men" and "Japan" are omitted from this narrative world; this erasure has been an effective strategy for women to claim the space to explore and express their own agency (112).

But the *Alice* books are by no means the exclusive property of Japanese girls' culture. *Lost Property Fairy Tales* itself is not published by a "girl"-specific label but rather pitches its *shōjo* themes at adults or women, though it may certainly interest younger readers.[15] Indeed, the striking juxtapositions of eerie, dark, sexual, and sweet in Higami's illustrations find their match in Ogawa's writing style. "The Name Alice" pivots on a dramatic switch from a girl's yearning to her grotesque or paranoid ending of a body overrun by ants from the inside. Accompanying the obsessive wordplay is some sense of an ordinary world gone mad, or alternatively an ordinary, imaginative girl gone mad. That is, the story plays with *Alice's Adventures in Wonderland* but it is also a subtle parody of the *shōjo* herself, lovingly ridiculing her desires and dreams, her wild emotions and imaginings. As such, the tale continues the work done by Kanai in her 1972 story "Rabbits," treating the innocent Alice to a critical revisioning.

Girl Alices rebel in linguistic but also visual realms. In Higami's five illustrations for "The Name Alice," each girl's ensemble somehow recalls Alice. In "Aki" ["Autumn"] (Ogawa, *Otogibanashi* 50–51), for example, a naked girl reclines on a spotted toadstool wearing the striped stockings from John Tenniel's illustrations for *Through the Looking Glass*. Girls' and women's fashions play a significant role in Alice's popularity in Japan. As elsewhere, Tenniel's iconic illustrations and the 1951 Disney film *Alice in Wonderland* are the main visual referents. In an exploration of Alice-inspired fashions, Masafumi Monden notes lines and looks by brands such as Jane Marple and Emily Temple Cute (of the 2015 *Eureka* cover), but also Alice costumes worn in music videos by female pop singers Alisa Mizuki, Tomoko Kawase, and Kaela Kimura. Monden emphasizes that the multifaceted *shōjo* identity makes it possible for these singers to mount what he terms a "delicate kind of revolt" (100). They express a sweet, naive, "cute" (*kawaii*) aesthetic, wearing asexual and "infantile"-looking, Victorian-era-inspired, chaste Alice ensembles (94), while simultaneously parodying the doll-like passivity demanded of them as pop idols by portraying more active roles in their music videos and—increasingly for each singer across time—asserting their own independence and creative control over their musical careers (100). Conversely, Higami's sexualized girls might cause discomfort for the viewer; in her afterword to *Lost Property Fairy Tales*, Ogawa interprets the girls as keeping their own counsel (116), but others may find the images disturbingly objectified. The eroticism of the semi-naked figures is perhaps somehow repressed by the flat, unyielding expressions on the girls' faces, so that "a delicate kind of revolt" on their part may well be imagined. In this way, the dreamy space of Japanese girls' culture, built around exoticized versions of the West and Western (literary) fairy tales such as the *Alice* stories, reaches into adult women's writing and visual art, creating lively, critical fictions.

Conclusion

In Ogawa and Higami's "The Name Alice," the girl Alice stands at the intersections and overlaps of *shōjo* culture, fairy tales, and literary fiction by women. Then, testing the structures that surround them all, Alice once again changes form and escapes our proprietary grasp. In fact, these are only some of the intersections Alice represents, and some of the realms she inhabits, and she does not belong exclusively to any. Though Carroll himself and other such "non-girls" are not examined here, of course they also overlap with girls' spheres through the *Alice* books and their retellings. Moreover, this analysis relegates crossings between languages, cultures, and nations to the background, but given the appeal of Japanese reimaginings of Alice, and the widespread enjoyment of Japanese popular culture in other countries, many Japanese versions of *Alice* are making their way back into English.

To note just a few instances of multiple border crossings, Alice-themed *shōjo manga* such as Yū Watase's *Arisu Naintīnsu* ([*Alice 19th*] 2001–3) and Kaori Yuki's *Kakei no Arisu* ([*Alice in Murderland*], 2014–) are translated into English. The latter is one of many "dark" retellings, which is a defining aspect of both Kaneko's and Higami's artwork; such retellings are also found in *manga* outside of *shōjo* genres, such as Peach-Pit's gothic doll story *Rōzen Meiden* ([*Rozen Maiden*] 2002–7), also available in translation and animated versions. Other examples of work from beyond the girls' realm include the internationally successful Japanese-developed *Kingdom Hearts* roleplay videogame series (2002–), which introduces Disney characters, including Alice, to Japanese figures from *Final Fantasy*, a flagship series by the same game developer, Square (now Square Enix). Also, the well-known works of prominent "superflat" artists such as Takashi Murakami and Yoshitomo Nara manipulate the possibilities of the kinds of girlish objects and figures described in this chapter[16] and have some links to Alice stories.[17] One final example of Alice returning from Japan is the edition of *Alice's Adventures in Wonderland* cited here, featuring Carroll's 1865 English text illustrated by contemporary Japanese artist Yayoi Kusama (1929–), the pages scattered with her trademark brightly colored spots. These contrasting samples bring us to yet more "edges" that Alice unmakes, crossing the lines between children's literature classics, popular screen culture, and contemporary visual art.

Much "Western" fairy-tale scholarship debunks ongoing notions of fairy tales as national property, critiques the use of fairy tales to nationalist ends, and uncovers the influence of foreign literary versions on tales that have been romanticized as belonging entirely to local "folk" traditions. Examinations of the global movements of fairy tales can continue and broaden this scholarly work. When stories such as the *Alice* books flourish in a new location, such as Japan, their reception demands a detailed analysis in context, avoiding tired Orientalist notions of mimicry and mere aspiration to the West. In this case, the changes made to *Alice* in Japan show how romantic notions of the West in Japanese girls' culture in fact lovingly appropriate Western fairy tales and children's literature as entertainment and means for self-expression. This wholehearted appropriation, in turn, has informed complex literary productions from beyond the realm of girls' culture. Critics and readers can only imagine what "foreign" fare global girl-Alices will gobble next, and the stories that will grow up from their wild dreams.

Notes

1. All translations of Japanese are my own, unless otherwise indicated.

2. These examples are taken from the Alice in Fantasy Land restaurant, one of six different Alice-themed restaurants across Tokyo, Nagoya, and Osaka, belonging to the Alice's Fantasy Restaurant chain owned by Diamond Dining. See www.alice-restaurant.com/.

3. "The Academia Demon Girls' Research Squad": Kozue Hayashida, Iori Morita, Shōko Komine, Moemi Niiro, and Arisu Onodera. The five women are presumably students or associates of Hiroshi Takayama, nicknamed "Gakuma" (Academia Demon). Takayama, the editor who contributes several pieces to this special issue, has published literary and interdisciplinary criticism on Carroll and Alice, including *Arisu-gari* [*The Hunting of Alice*] (1981) and translations of the *Alice* books, as well as Martin Gardner's 1990 *More Annotated Alice* (translated in 1994).

4. The phantom of Lewis Carroll hovers over the girl figure of Alice and, as elsewhere, in Japan discussions of *Alice* muse on the author, his photography and relationship with Alice Liddell, and so on. Commentators also compare the Japanese idea of the "Lolita complex" with Carroll and his writing (see Knighton for an example). However, an examination of Carroll in Japan is beyond the scope of this chapter.

5. A list with the contents of each special issue is available at *The Rabbit Hole*, an encyclopedic website on Alice in Japan created by Shin'ichi Kinoshita, apparently an amateur enthusiast whose profile states he works for a pharmaceutical company.

6. Miyuki Narita and Makiko Fujiwara, cited in Kusumoto (6).

7. Kinoshita's website *The Rabbit Hole* offers reviews of over fifty Japanese translations of *Wonderland* and twenty-five of *Through the Looking Glass*. It also catalogs over one hundred Japanese books and over seventy *manga* influenced by Carroll or Alice.

8. Mayako Murai identifies "Bluebeard" connections in three of Ogawa's stories for adults, "Domitorī" ["Dormitory"] (1990), "Kusuriyubi no hyōhon" ["Specimen of a Ring Finger"] (1992), and *Hoteru Airisu* [*Hotel Iris*] (1996), and also analyzes the "Red Riding Hood" retelling that appears in *Lost Property Fairy Tales*. See also Fraser on the retelling of "The Little Mermaid" in *Lost Property Fairy Tales*.

9. Yagawa translated some of the Grimms' tales for picture books and anthologies, as well as those included in Jungian psychoanalyst Hayao Kawai's *Mukashibanashi no shinsō* [*The Deep Layers of Folk Tales*] (1977).

10. "Humpty ni katarikakeru kotoba ni tsuite no omoimegurashi" ["Turning Over in My Mind the Words to Say to Humpty"] (Knighton 53).

11. Ogawa, Yoshimoto, and Sakuraba are all cited in Hasegawa's entry on "Women's Literature and Representations of Shōjo" in *Shōjo shōsetsu jiten* [*Encyclopedia of Girls' Novels*] (2015); their fairy-tale retellings are examined in Fraser.

12. For example, the first known translation, "Kagami sekai: Seiyō otogibanashi" ["Mirror World: A Western Fairy Tale"] (translated by Tenkei Hasegawa, 1899), as well as *Kodomo no yume: chōhen otogibanashi* [*A Child's Dream: Long-Form Fairy Tale*] (translated by Gorō Niwa, 1911) (Kusumoto 44).

13. Higami's illustrations inspired a spirited discussion following the presentation this chapter is based on. I thank James Welker, Barbara Hartley, and other participants for their comments.

14. Two academic anthologies, *Shōjo shōsetsu wandārando* [*Girls' Novel Wonderland*] (edited by Satoko Kan, 2008) and *Shōjo manga wandārando* [*Girls' Manga Wonderland*] (edited by Satoko Kan, Hiromi Tsuchiya Dollase, and Kayo

Takeuchi, 2012), trace the development of Japanese girl culture. These volumes, which build on a growing body of *shōjo* scholarship, use the loanword *wandārando* in their titles, highlighting the importance of foreign—especially English—fairy-tale-like stories in the *shōjo* sphere (though this is by no means limited to stories for girls).

15. Originally published for general readers by Hōmu-sha, the current publisher, Popura bunko, also lists it for a general audience, though Popura bunko as a whole is described as targeting "intellectual women in their 20s to 30s who are brimming with curiosity" (editor Kenjirō Yoshikawa, "Popura bunko"). However, the swan-themed fairy tale, "Aisaresugita hakuchō" ["The Swan That Was Loved Too Much"] and one of Higami's illustrations was recently included in a Japanese language textbook for high school students (Ogawa 2017).

16. Marilyn Ivy writes that Nara's works "incorporate a thoroughly disciplined syntax of dreamlike associations, fairytale motifs from European sources, American and Japanese comic-book styles, and naïve figurations of young girls and animals" (5). Ivy's description of Nara's "archetypical scene" of "a solitary child" (7) also resonates with Sumiko Yagawa's musings on the lonely Alice.

17. See, for example, David Surman on Murakami's short film *Superflat Monogram*.

Works Cited

Alice's Fantasy Restaurant. *Alice in Fantasy Land*. www.alice-restaurant.com/genso. Accessed 14 Nov. 2017.

Aoyama, Tomoko. "The Genealogy of the 'Girl' Critic Reading Girl." *Girl Reading Girl in Japan*, edited by Tomoko Aoyama and Barbara Hartley, Routledge, 2010, pp. 38–49.

———. "Transgendering *Shōjo Shōsetsu*: Girls' Inter-text/sex-uality." *Genders, Transgenders and Sexualities in Japan*, edited by Mark McLelland and Romit Dasgupta, Routledge, 2005, pp. 49–64.

Carroll, Lewis. *Alice's Adventures in Wonderland*. 1865. Illusrated by Yayoi Kusama, Penguin Books, 2012.

———. *Through the Looking Glass and What Alice Found There*. 1871. Illustrated by John Tenniel, Puffin Books, 2010.

Dollase, Hiromi Tsuchiya. "Shōjo manga no rekishi o furikaeru: nanajū nendai hana hiraku shōjo manga" ["Looking Back at the History of Shōjo Manga: The Blossoming of Shōjo Manga in the 1970s"]. *Shōjo manga wandārando/Girls' Manga Wonderland*, edited by Satoko Kan, Hiromi Tsuchiya Dollase, and Kayo Takeuchi, Meiji shoin, 2012, pp. 12–16.

Fraser, Lucy. *The Pleasures of Metamorphosis: Japanese and English Fairy Tale Transformations of "The Little Mermaid."* Wayne State University Press, 2017.

Gakuma Gāruzu Kenkyūtai. "21seki no Arisu-tachi" ["Alices of the Twenty-First Century"]. *Yurīka: 150nenme no* Fushigi no kuni no Arisu [*Eureka: The 150th Year of Alice in Wonderland*], vol. 47, no. 3, 2015, p. 336–43.

Hasegawa, Kei. "Josei bungaku to shōjo hyōshō" ["Women's Literature and Representations of Girls"]. *Shōjo shōsetsu jiten* [*Encyclopedia of Girls' Novels*], edited by Hiroko Iwabuchi, Satoko Kan, Yoriko Kume, and Kei Hasegawa, Tokyodō *shuppan*, 2015, pp. 356–58.

Honda, Masuko. "The Genealogy of *Hirahira*: Liminality and the Girl." *Girl Reading Girl in Japan*, translated by Tomoko Aoyama and Barbara Hartley, edited by Tomoko Aoyama and Barbara Hartley, Routledge, 2010, pp. 19–37.

Ivy, Marilyn. "The Art of Cute Little Things: Nara Yoshitomo's Parapolitics." *Mechademia 5: Fanthropologies*, 2010, pp. 3–29.

Kan, Satoko, and Megumi Fujimoto. "'Shōjo shōsetsu' no rekishi o furikaeru" ["Looking Back at the History of Girls' Novels"]. *Shōjo shōsetsu wandārando/ Girls' Novels Wonderland*, edited by Satoko Kan, Meiji shoin, 2008, pp. 5–23.

Kaneko, Kuniyoshi. *Arisu no garō*. Bijutsu shuppansha, 1979.

Kanai, Mieko. "Arisu no ehon" ["Picture Book of Alice"]. *Shōsetsu o yomu, kotoba o kaku* [*Reading Novels, Writing Words*], *Kanai Mieko essei korekushon 1964-2013* [*Kanai Mieko Essay Collection 1964-2013*], vol. 3, Heibonsha, 2013, pp. 98–100.

———. "Rabbits." 1972. *Rabbits, Crabs, Etc.: Stories by Japanese Women*, translated by Phyllis Birnbaum. University of Hawai'i Press, 1982, pp. 1–16.

Kawabata, Ariko. "Hon'yaku shōjo shōsetu" ["Translated Girls' Novels"]. *Shōjo shōsetsu jiten* [*Encyclopedia of Girls' Novels*], edited by Iwabuchi Hiroko, Kan Satoko, Kume Yoriko, and Hasegawa Kei, Tokyodō shuppan, 2015, pp. 338–41.

Kinoshita, Shin'ichi. *The Rabbit Hole*. www.hp-alice.com/index. Accessed 16 Nov. 2017.

King, Emerald, and Lucy Fraser. "Girls in Lace Dresses—The Intersections of Gothic in Japanese Youth Fiction and Fashion." *New Directions in Children's Gothic: Debatable Lands*, edited by Anna Jackson, Routledge, 2017.

Knighton, Mary A. "Down the Rabbit Hole: In Pursuit of Shōjo Alices, from Lewis Carroll to Kanai Mieko." *U.S.-Japan Women's Journal*, vol. 40, 2011, pp. 49–89.

Kusumoto, Kimie. *Hon'yaku no kuni no Arisu: Ruisu Kyaroru hon'yakushi, hon'yaku ron* [*Alice in Translationland: Lewis Carroll Translation History and Theory*]. Michitani, 2001.

Monden, Masafumi. *Japanese Fashion Culture: Dress and Gender in Contemporary Japan*. Bloomsbury, 2015.

Murai, Mayako. *From Dog Bridegroom to Wolf Girl: Contemporary Japanese Fairy-Tale Adaptations in Conversation with the West*. Wayne State University Press, 2015.

Nishidate, Ichirō, editor. *Yurīka: Kaneko Kuniyoshi no sekai* [*Eureka: The World of Kuniyoshi Kaneko*], vol. 47, no. 9, 2015.

Ogawa, Yōko. "Aisaresugita hakuchō." *Seisen kokugo sōgō gendaibunhen*, edited by Hideo Suzuki, et al., Chikumashobō, 2017, pp. 46–54.

———. *Otogibanashi no wasuremono* [*Lost Property Fairy Tales*]. Illustrated by Kumiko Higami, Shūeisha, 2006.

Ōgi, Fusami. "Ekkyō suru shōjo manga to jendā" ["Gender and Shōjo Manga beyond Borders"]. *Manga wa ekkyō suru! / Beyond Borders: The Transnational Power of Manga*, edited by Fusami Ōgi, Masashi Ichiki, and Hideko Motohama, Sekai Shinshōsha, 2010, no. 110–34.

"Popura bunko 6shūnen de 'teiban' fea" ["Popura bunko 'Staples' Fair on Sixth Anniversary"]. *Sankei News*, 23 March 2014, https://www.sankei.com/life/news/140323/lif1403230026-n1.html. Accessed 23 Jan. 2018.

Surman, David. "A Networked Daydream." *Australian Centre for the Moving Image*, 2018, www.acmi.net.au/ideas/read/networked-daydream. Accessed 18 Feb. 2019.

Takayama, Hiroshi, editor. *Yurīka: 150nenme no Fushigi no kuni no Arisu* [*Eureka: The 150th Year of Alice in Wonderland*], vol. 47, no. 3, 2015.

Waki, Akiko. *Shōjo-tachi no 19seiki: Ningyo-hime kara Arisu made* [*The Girls' Nineteenth Century: From The Little Mermaid to Alice*]. Iwanami shoten, 2013.

"Yagawa Sumiko: Fumetsu no shōjo" ["Yagawa Sumiko: Everlasting Girl"]. *Yuriika* [*Eureka*], vol. 34, no. 13, 2002.

Yagawa, Sumiko, translator. *Fushigi no kuni no Arisu* [*Alice in Wonderland*]. 1990. Illustrated by Kuniyoshi Kaneko, Shinchō bunko, 1994.

12

Magical Bird Maidens

Reconsidering Romantic Fairy Tales in Japanese Popular Culture

Masafumi Monden

Introduction

EVEN FOR SCHOLARS OF popular culture, it is sometimes easy to forget how bleak and terrifying the fairy tales of today were in their early forms. Often originating in feudal societies where women were considered property, tales such as "Little Red Riding Hood" were frequently told as cautionary morality tales (Murai, "Ōkami shōjo" 243; Zipes 1). Victorian society, with its nostalgia for medieval chivalry and Arthurian legend, removed some of the sexual violence—Red Riding Hood is not raped and Rapunzel no longer becomes pregnant (Warner 133, 135). Similarly, the figure of the water spirit—a predecessor of the little mermaid—has transformed from a powerfully erotic and dangerous siren to a "charmingly girlish" and naive water nymph in the long nineteenth century (Fraser 18). And in the twentieth century, the stories were transformed again, most famously by Walt Disney, whose last name is now synonymous with the process of cultural sanitizing. Thus, today it is probably no wonder that the stories we regard as "classic" fairy tales have been criticized for portraying women in passive roles.

However, the changing and reimagination of these stories is an ongoing process, and the Japanese anime series *Princess Tutu* (2002–3), remixes aspects of fairy-tale texts. Utilizing the conventions of *shōjo manga* (girls' comic), magical girl anime, and ballet, *Princess Tutu* avoids some of the clichés and reimagines fairy tales as modern stories of girls confronting and challenging their own fates. As well as the simple inversion of gendered agency between the princess and the prince/hero in the anime series, *Princess Tutu* introduces complexity and moral nuance in the relationship between the two main female characters. In this chapter, I show how Japanese popular culture offers different interpretations of the romantic fairy-tale genre, in some cases subverting it. I will first explore the modern views of female figures in the romantic fairy-tale genre, which can frequently be negative, and the relationship with classical ballet and "princess culture." Then, I will examine two aspects of *Princess Tutu*: its treatment of the two main girl characters and its attempt to reimagine some of the conventions of the romantic fairy-tale genre. I argue that the narrative and visual images of *Princess Tutu* offer one way to reevaluate and assign new meanings to modern interpretations of fairy tales. The theory of "format" and "product," as articulated by sociologist Keiko Okamura (137–49), seems important here. This theory allows a cultural form to be seen as a "format" when becoming transculturally accepted. This standardized "format" becomes a carrier of a local culture, making its qualities visible and hence comparable with those of other cultures. In this sense, *Princess Tutu* is an example of cultural syncretism where fairy-tale texts become "format" that is ready to create a "product" that reflects further processes of cultural commingling, interaction, and appropriation (Okamura). In this sense, the idea of cultural globalization is crucial in understanding fairy-tale adaptations in a globalizing world.

Femininity and Fairy Tales

Fairy tales have been reimagined and reinterpreted from a modern and feminist perspective since the 1970s, perhaps the most influential works being Angela Carter's retelling of fairy tales, revealing their often concealed and controversial contents, as in her *The Bloody Chamber* (1979). Despite, or because of, that, the "conventional" femininity of heroines such as "Snow White," "Cinderella," and "Sleeping Beauty" is regarded by some scholars and critics as too obedient, passive, and timid. Snow White, for example, has been seen as "the passive, personality-free princess swept off by a prince (who is enchanted solely by her beauty) to live in a happily-ever-after that he ultimately controls" (Orenstein 12). A series of Disney's famous fairy-tale animations—*Snow White and the Seven Dwarfs* (1937), *Cinderella* (1950), and *Sleeping Beauty* (1959)—have also been accused of "solidifying their definition of the princess as helpless, hyper-feminine trope" (Whelan 170). Susan Hopkins, in her book *Girl Heroes,* claims that the young female audience of "the post-feminist 1990s" would reject such "modest, sweet, and softly spoken" heroines (141). This claim is debatable, considering the enduring popularity of Disney princesses even today—and not just the modern ones with a semblance of agency from *Frozen* (2013), *Beauty and the Beast* (1991), and *Enchanted* (2007) but also *Cinderella* and *Snow White*.

Why are classic fairy-tale princesses perceived as undesirably passive? Such criticism indicates an assumption of a compatibility between lived reality and the aesthetic depiction of these princesses. For example, linking "princess-hood" as depicted in these fairy-tale fictions to contemporary concepts of ideal girlhood has been a common practice, that "conform[s] to societal convention regarding girls and their place in society," who are "trapped in a tower and waiting rescue by an exotic prince from a foreign land–[the] image of stillness and passivity" (Whelan 169).

In Japan, Midori Wakakuwa argues that popular romantic fairy tales impose a particular ideology of romance upon girls and women, which operates to sustain their passivity and dependence, and results in asymmetrical gender relations (43). According to this logic, these fairy tales indoctrinate women from an early age into believing that their goal in life is marriage, and prevent them from imagining or planning their life after their happily-ever-after life. In contrast, men and boys are continuously taught to follow their "achievable" goals and are encouraged to develop a sense of agency. Masculinity is a liberated, active, and above all positive attribute, whereas femininity is seen as a restricted, passive, and negative one. These gendered roles in fairy tales have, according to some, been strengthened by Disney, which has taken this aspiration of prince/princess and assigned specific characteristics to young male and female fantasies:

> Prince-hood remains linked with notions of power, freedom, and exploration, as exemplified by Disney heroes like Aladdin, Simba, and Tarzan, whereas princess-hood is now rigidly bound to concepts like dutifulness, self-sacrifice, and desire for and subservience to males—all character traits shared by both first- and second-wave Disney princesses (Whelan 176).[1]

The negative stereotype associated with fairy-tale princesses also shapes how they are perceived in experienced reality. Samantha Holland, in relation to the fairy-tale princess, also articulates the ambivalence attached to the figure of the normatively beautiful, apparently passive fairy-tale princess. Her female research participants, who perceive themselves as "alternative," declare their admiration for the figure of the beautiful princess. But Holland also points out that "they also contradicted themselves and made statements to place themselves in opposition to her—they liked how she looked but they did not like the fact that she stood for complicity and passivity" (58). Thus, while they appreciated the looks of such figures as Snow White, they articulated their preference for the evil queen. This is because "she was strong, intelligent, wicked, had black hair and looked like a goth with her white face, red lips and black clothes—that is, someone [who] looked more like them" (Holland 58).

The archetype of such feminine passivity in fairy tales is without doubt the clichéd image of the damsel in distress. Be it Sleeping Beauty, Snow White, Rapunzel, or Brunnhilde, or even Florine in Madame d'Aulnoy's "L'Oiseau bleu" ["The Blue Bird"] (1697), they are destined to dream, sing, contemplate, or in extreme cases lie in an enchanted sleep, in a confined space until their rescue by a man, generally, a man with whom the heroine then becomes romantically involved. The heroines' physical beauty and sometimes their wealth or social rank is the motivation for these heroes to come to the rescue.

This is not a surprise, given the feudal origins of many of the tales; the physical submissiveness and psychological dependence of these female figures was deliberate. But while many other elements of these tales have evolved over time, the passive female archetype has persisted.

According to Rebecca-Anne Do Rozario, the more recently created Disney fairy-tale princesses such as Belle, Ariel in *The Little Mermaid* (1989), and Pocahontas (1995) show how "heroism, egalitarianism and autonomy are slipped into the conventions of Disney princesshood" (Do Rozario 47), even though these characters are not, strictly speaking, "princesses" (Orr 16; Do Rozario 46). But for most "classic" Disney princesses that do manage to escape domestic confinement and carve out the semblance of adventure, "that 'adventure' often still revolves solely around marriage and romance" (Whelan 179).

While ideas like the one presented by Wakakuwa indicate the possible acceptance of such a negative stereotype of fairy-tale princesses in contemporary Japan, the idea of the fairy-tale princess and her apparently passive condition seem to have been understood differently in Japan. In her essay, Sumiko Yagawa, a translator and a famous literary figure contributing to the development of the *shōjo* (*girls* in Japanese) genre, presents her view that these imprisoned maidens and princesses do not necessarily have to be understood only in terms of their passivity. For Yagawa, being imprisoned in fairy tales equates with the idea of being chosen (among many other young women) (134). This implies two things: first, that the young woman is chosen because of a special quality that is unique to her, be it her physical beauty or her lineage, differentiating her from other (more "ordinary") individuals. Second, the status of imprisonment in fairy tales inevitably makes the young woman an object of the gaze. With the narrative being centered around the object of the gaze, this allows the young woman to monopolize attention and give principality to her presence. Therefore, the passive position can sometimes, apparently, be more powerful and pleasurable than that of the subject (male) gaze in these stories.

Moreover, in contrast to Euro-American cultural perceptions of fairy-tale narratives, which are strongly tied to a hetero-romantic narrative that "begins and ends with the princesses' romantic involvement with men" (Whelan 177) and demands a woman to be a dependent, fragile feminine ideal (princess) ascending a throne (Fabos 191), some popular portrayals of fairy-tale princesses in Japan offer the possibility of detachment from such narratives. In the Japanese context, a degree of independence is attached to the concept of princess.

Princesses in Contemporary Japanese Culture

The subtle inversion of the "passivity" of the princess into her individual agency is evident in contemporary Japanese culture. For example, the fairy tale of *Cinderella*, which has become popularized through Disney's film and has frequently been coded as symbolic of passive and obedient femininity in Anglophone culture, is instead interpreted as "a strong message of self-transformation and individual achievement in the Japanese setting" (Miller 393). Using the examples of the aesthetic salon industry, Miller, for example, writes that Cinderella is frequently used to praise these women who have achieved the improvement of their physical appearance without the immediacy of cosmetic surgeries. This connotes a magical transformation, perhaps aided by the industry and beauty therapists, but ultimately it is with these women's will, determination, and diligence that Cinderella is most strongly associated. Appeals that lie in the Cinderella narrative, in this sense, are "self-development and discipline" (Miller 397), which "denote individual agency to overcome obstacles or to achieve one's dreams, thus reconfiguring her message in a manner that appeals to a wide range of consumers" (Miller 394). In this sense, self-actualization, determination, and diligence have been added to Cinderella as symbols of success in Japanese culture.

The aspirational place that the idea of "princess" holds in contemporary Japanese culture is largely constructed by the imagery of the princess herself, not by her position achieved through her fairy-tale marriage to the prince. This point is reinforced by how the figure of Marie Antoinette of France is represented in Japanese girls' culture, especially in Riyoko Ikeda's girls' comics *The Rose of Versailles* (1972–73), which have undoubtedly contributed to the popularity of the tragic French queen in Japan. Ikeda portrays the young Marie Antoinette as a born princess—girlish, sympathetic, mischievous, yet dignified—to whom marriage (to the dauphin/prince) means not so much the elevation of her social status but rather a "setting" to glamourize her tragic image as a "fallen princess" struggling between her duty and forbidden true love. Here the importance lies in the fact that Marie Antoinette was born an archduchess and a princess, whose privileged social origin is further highlighted by her confrontation with Madame du Barry, a woman who climbed the social ladder from position of illegitimate daughter of a seamstress to the last *Maîtresse-en-titre* of King Louis XV through her sexuality and relationship with men.

This tendency is also visible in *manga* works that center on the heroine who is placed at the opposite end of the born-princesses: ambitious social climbers. There is a series of *shōjo manga* works, especially in the 1970s and 1980s, in which the main character is typically an adolescent girl with "ultra-feminine" appearance, whose ambition and desire to escape from a miserable life leads her to perpetrate lies, deceptions, betrayals, and murders. Whether it is set in contemporary Europe (Masako Watanabe's *Glass Castle*, 1969–70) or contemporary Japan (Suzue Miuchi's *A Canary of Peacock Colour*, 1973; Mihoko Koiwa's *Midnight Cinderella*, 1981; Akiko Miyawaki's *Canon of Gold and Silver*, 1984), the motivation of these girls in such a darkened narrative of rags-to-riches fairy tales is never to climb the ladder by marrying a prince. Instead, their motivation and activities are predominantly predicated on their desire for the fairy-tale life itself, wearing opulent dresses and living in princesses' bedrooms. And the solution is to rob such a life from "born-princesses." The princesses and the ambitious social climbers in these *shōjo manga* are two sides of the same coin. This further endorses the idea that the imagery of the princess herself—through her dresses and opulent lifestyles—holds the aspirational place as the idea of "princess," and her fairy-tale marriage to the prince, if it exists, is only periphery.

This is not to say that romance is unnecessary for those who appreciate fairy tales in Japan. But what is significant is the apparent separation of the imagination of the princess from the romantic object of the prince. The princess and the qualities of extravagantly opulent girlish aesthetics associated with her, such as feminine dresses and princessly bedroom, have been playing a large part in feminist criticism of princess culture. This is because feminine fashion and look has been interpreted as a "requirement" imposed by a patriarchal society to make woman an erotic object (e.g., de Beauvoir, 543). This is different in Japan. In separating the imagination of the princess and her romantic, girlish aesthetics from a hetero-romantic narrative, they are assigned a sense of independence and autonomy, and not necessarily always read as symbolic of female oppression in Japanese culture. Classical ballet is often talked about in a similar way.

Ballet, Fairy Tales, and Princess Culture

The ballerina's tutu and beribboned slippers have profoundly feminine, more precisely girlish, connotations in modern culture. As Marina Warner points out, many famous classical ballets, which crystallized "various elements from national folklore (Russian folk tales) and literary classics (Perrault, E. T. A. Hoffmann)," are:

> also essentially fairy tales, composed by bricolage with features that define the genre; supernatural and mysterious beings, a prevailing atmosphere of enchantment and vulnerability to destiny, and opening onto another, imaginary world that is only accessible through the work of art. (159)

Many of the heroines in classical ballet repertoires, from *La Sylphide* (1832) and *Swan Lake* (1877) through to *The Sleeping Beauty* (1890), *Cinderella* (1945), and *Ondine* (1843, 1958), are, moreover, innocent maidens, free-spirited fairies and princesses, often based on well-known fairy tales.

The aesthetic symbolism of the light, gauzy tutu has a strong connotation of ethereal femininity. By the early twentieth century, as more middle-class girls in Europe studied and performed ballet, the tutu became increasingly associated with "girl culture" and with idealized femininity; couth and graceful, yet disciplined and regulated (Peers 73). In reality, the tutu is a marriage of aesthetics and functionality; its lightness liberated women dancers to engage in more acrobatic, athletic movement (Chazin-Bennahum).

Contrary to the image of female ballet dancers as light, ethereal beings, "the emphasis placed on technical prowess and virtuosity of the ballerina counteracts the stereotyped images of gender. Female dancers know from experience that the 'feminine' grace that ballet connotes goes together with a feeling of strength and stretch in the muscles" (Aalten 272).

Despite this physical reality, ballet's association with girl culture is often perceived as endorsing antiquated, coded passive, ideals of femininity. Mariko Turk, for example, points out that classical ballet is often tangled up with consumer-oriented "princess culture," and thus can theorize it as obscuring "recognition of the varied ways that ballet as an art form, rather than as a mode of dress, informs girls' culture" and therefore superficiality (484). According to these authors, the prevalence of ballerina Barbie dolls and hybrid fairy/princess/ballerina costumes in the girls' toy section indicates that both ballet and the tutu have been appropriated broadly by "princess culture."

Started in around 2001, the ultra-girly marketing strategy of "princess culture" is supported by "a vast array of material objects and media representations" (Orr 9), which capitalize on heteronormative, materially extravagant, and appearance-focused messages (Orenstein 14). With its "emphasis on beauty and play-sexiness," the prevalence of princess culture is also causing moral panic in parents over girls' vulnerability to depression, eating disorders, distorted body image, and risky sexual behavior (Turk 482). In such a political view, the cultural image of the "ballerina" in a ballet based on a fairy tale is most likely seen as endorsing hetero-romantic ideologies together with asymmetrical gender roles and concepts to primarily female consumers.

We can ask a question here: since fairy-tale princesses are coded differently in contemporary Japanese culture as a more independent figure, does Japanese material culture offer us some potentially different readings of fairy tales, princesses, and ballet, and the relationship between them? In order to examine this possibility, I use Ikuko Itō's celebrated anime series *Princess Tutu*. The anime is set in a fictional country whose architecture resembles Europe in the romantic past (Germany in particular, the home of the Brothers Grimm), images that strongly evoke an association with Western fairy tales in Japan. Not only that, the anime is "a *bricolage* of motifs and formulas

Figure 12.1. Princess Tutu and Princess Kraehi representing the White-Black Swan Maiden binary in *Princess Tutu* (2002), episode 13, directed by Jun'ichi Satō, written by Michiko Yokote. Hal Film Maker.

from available traditional and folk-influenced literary sources" (Ellis 231), making it an ideal text to analyze the adaptations of Western folktales and fairy tales in the non-Western culture of Japan.

Princess Tutu's Retelling of Fairy Tales

Princess Tutu was originally aired in two seasons on Kids Station, a Japanese children's television channel showing anime and other cartoon material. The first season ("Chapter of the Egg"), consisted of thirteen half-hour episodes. The second season ("Chapter of the Chick"), was aired as twenty-five quarter-hour episodes and one half-hour episode. The DVDs of *Princess Tutu* have been subtitled or dubbed in other languages, such as English, French, and Italian, and are available outside Japan.

The series tells the story of a girl ballerina named Ahiru (literally a duck in Japanese) who transforms herself from—quite literally—an ugly duck into the magical heroine Princess Tutu, who fights evil and attempts to save a beautiful yet troubled boy called Mytho. Tutu's rival, Princess Kraehe, the Raven's daughter, attempts to taint him with evil to make him hers. *Princess Tutu* references a number of popular European fairy tales and folktales, which include, quite obviously, Hans Christian Andersen's "The Ugly Duckling" (1843); "The Little Mermaid" (1837), as Princess Tutu will perish if she declares her love for Mytho; "The Snow Queen" (1845), as the boy, Mytho, loses his heart and becomes emotionless; "The Red Shoes" (1845), as Princess Kraehe's black pointe shoes are a symbol of her curse; Tchaikovsky's *Swan Lake* (1875–76), as two bird maidens, like Odette and Odile, dressed in white and black, fight over the love of Prince Siegfried; and Drosselmeyer, who gives Ahiru a magical power to transform into the magical ballerina, a direct reference to the magical character with the power to bring toys to life from *The Nutcracker*, Tchaikovsky's ballet adaptation of E. T. A. Hoffmann's story (1892). Music from the ballet is featured extensively in the anime. Toward the end of the second series, Mytho's heart is tainted with the Raven's blood, which turns him into the beastly figure of a were-raven (in episode 24). Rue, a human girl, attempts to nurse the suffering were-raven Mytho in a reference to Gabrielle-Suzanne Barbot de Villeneuve's "Beauty and the Beast" (1740). In this sense, *Princess Tutu* is about "the ongoing tradition of generating new versions of old tales and inventing entirely new tales out of bits and pieces of existing ones" (Ellis 231). This also endorses the idea of fairy tales themselves, for they "have never been exclusively verbal," and the history of fairy tales as a narrative genre "result[s] as much from the stories' constant reincarnations" (Warner 159) in various other fictional texts.

As a narrative that passes through time and cultures, fairy tales often involve transformation, and this process can involve "its relation to other genres" (Bacchilega 3). In terms of *Princess Tutu*, the most obvious combination of genres is fairy-tale and the magical girl anime subgenres. The series is often considered as part of the *Mahō shōjo* (magical girl) anime subgenre, perhaps a Japanese predecent of "princess culture" in terms of marketing strategy, with the active sales of toys that resemble the magical items in the anime.[2] *Princess Tutu*'s association with the magical girl anime is significant because it is a subgenre that combines and negotiates femininity and power

Figure 12.2. Tormented Rue dances with were-raven Mytho in a fashion resembling "Beauty and the Beast." *Princess Tutu* (2002), episode 24, directed by Jun'ichi Satō, written by Michiko Yokote. Hal Film Maker.

and gives principality to girls as both the protagonist and the primary target viewer.

Princess Tutu and a Magical Girl Subgenre

According to Akiko Sugawa-Shimada, an expert in "magical girl" culture, the subgenre of "magical girl" anime has enjoyed lasting popularity in Japan for more than forty years since the introduction of *Mahōtsukai Sarī* [*Sally the Witch*] (1966–68) (2). In this subgenre, a girl protagonist, usually a (pre)teen girl, is given supernatural powers that defeat boys, while at the same time magically transform her into more beautiful and attractive self (Sugawa-Shimada 4). Magical girl anime frequently shows Euro-American cultural references, as in the case of *Sally*, which was inspired by the American sitcom *Bewitched* (1964–72, first aired in Japan, 1966–70). The magical items via which the girl summons her magical powers—an essential device in the subgenre—often take the shape of accessories, such as a tiara, a pendant, a compact mirror, or a bracelet (Sugawa-Shimada 5). The inclusion of such accessories as an essential device signals the idea that (girlish) femininity equals, rather than negates, power (Sugawa-Shimada 84)—as well as providing a good marketing opportunity to sell collectable toys of these magical devices. The magical anime often involves the combination of fairies, a magical kingdom, and princesses with an ordinary contemporary society, which makes the subgenre a perfect platform to adapt elements of fairy tales.

Princess Tutu continues the motifs of the subgenre set by two of the most famous magical girl anime, *Mahō no purinsesu Minkī Momo* [*Magical Princess Minky Momo*] (1982–83) and *Mahō no tenshi Kurīmī Mami* [*Creamy Mami, the Magic Angel*] (1983–84). These motifs include the heroine's balletic, choreographed transformation sequence and the idea of a girl transforming into her older, idealized, and more glamorous self. In addition, *Princess Tutu* follows a number of other traditions of the "magical girl" subgenre: a (preteen) girl protagonist who is skinny, average-height, and possessing ballet skills that are average to inferior, creating a more striking contrast between the heroine in her ordinary girl form and her transformed, more accomplished self (Sugawa-Shimada 77). The heroine is given a necklace (a bird-shaped pendant with a tear-drop ruby-red gemstone) that transforms her into the magical heroine and marks her power as feminine. In addition, the story is largely set in the sphere of everyday school life (Sugawa-Shimada 78–79), rather than in the space or technology-governed worlds that are often associated with the male superhero genre. There are many ways that this series has the potential to offer more positive interpretations of ballet, girlish femininity, and fairy tales. In the following sections, I will focus on two: the treatment of girl characters and agency; and a sometimes brutal degree of narrative realism.

Two Princesses

At first glance, *Princess Tutu* appears to be merely another hetero-romantic fairy tale where the actions of a prince and a maiden are predicated on romance. What makes the anime different is its emphasis on the complexity of the female characters, especially in comparison to a Euro-American retelling of fairy tales. The anime has two main girl characters, Ahiru and Rue. At the beginning of the series, Ahiru is actually a duck who is given the magic power to turn herself into a human by Drosselmeyer, the author of an unfinished, tragic fairy tale called *The Prince and The Raven*. Ahiru undergoes two transformations: one from a duckling to a human girl who is a mediocre ballet student, and then from a human girl to Princess Tutu, a magical heroine with exceptional ballet skills. Rue, the other main character, is a human girl who was abducted and raised by the evil character of the Raven. Rue feeds upon the Raven's blood, which gives her the ability to transform into Princess Kraehe, the dark opponent of Princess Tutu.

Princess Tutu and Princess Kraehe fight over the heart of Mytho. In Drosselmeyer's unfinished fairy tale, the Raven was defeated and imprisoned by Prince Siegfried. In order to do this, the prince shattered his own heart with his sword, causing him to lose all of his memories and emotions and become Mytho, a commoner. Princess Tutu and Princess Kraehe fight over the pieces of Mytho's heart, which are both the key to the resurrection of the Raven and the way of restoring Mytho to his rightful identity, Prince Siegfried.

As I mentioned earlier, the role of the female figure in romantic fairy tales is often to wait in a confined space until her rescue by a man she will marry, and this has led to the criticism of such fairy tales and their modern adaptations, especially by feminist critics and scholars (Warner 132). Here, the two main characters are female and have considerable agency. This seems to correspond with contemporary fairy-tale adaptations, especially but not limited to, those in Japan. As Murai rightly points out:

> As in the West, fairy-tale adaptations in contemporary Japan tend to feature female characters with a more independent spirit and display a more female-oriented perspective than traditional tales... revise the stereotype of passive heroines in fairy tales and depict the adventures of strong-minded, intelligent, and imaginative women. (*From Dog Bridegroom to Wolf Girl* 2)

Ahiru/Princess Tutu is the protagonist, who propels the narrative. While this is good, a gendered reading is still not without some problems in *Princess Tutu*.

Gendered Reading of *Princess Tutu*

The ultimate narrative power in the anime is still held by two male characters: the mad-scientist-like Drosselmeyer, who has the power to make what he writes a reality, and his descendant, Fakir, a nihilistic boy who goes to the same arts academy as Ahiru. The female protagonists, Ahiru and Rue, are ultimately characters in Drosselmeyer's fairy tale. But Princess Tutu and Princess Kraehe are not damsels in distress. In an inversion of the "normal" gender roles, they are the ones who fight over the passive and softly spoken Mytho, to restore him to Prince Siegfried or doom him to eternity as a commoner. Indeed, the principal male characters in *Princess Tutu* are not typically strong and "masculine" in a conventional sense. Until the second final episode of season 2, where he is fully restored to his power as Prince Siegfried, Mytho is portrayed rather as a weak, fragile, and beautiful prince in distress who needs protection and care by Ahiru, Rue, and Fakir. Graphically, this is portrayed through Mytho's large round eyes with narrow, roundly arched eyebrows, long eyelashes, and a round face, drawing him closer to the female characters of Ahiru and Rue.

Contrast these graphic attributes of Mytho to another male character, Fakir. Fakir has a considerably sharper face with thicker eyebrows as well as narrower and more rectangular shaped eyes, all of which signal masculine qualities in the tradition of *shōjo* graphic styles (Fraser & Monden 555). Takahiro Sakurai, who voiced Fakir, has a distinctly deeper and stronger voice than Naoki Yanagi's Mytho, who almost always whispers. Fakir, though, does not completely fit conventional masculinity—he is a "useless" knight who is no good at fighting with a sword, and gradually accepts this fact, exchanging his sword for a pen to play his role in the battle against the Raven and hence, Drosselmeyer. These "flaws" in the principal male

Figure 12.3. The soft-sharp comparison of male characters Mytho and Fakir in *Princess Tutu* (2002), directed by Jun'ichi Satō, written by Michiko Yokote. Hal Film Maker.

characters' masculinity serve to blur the traditional gender separation between the *Princess Tutu* characters.

The white (and pale pink) and black (and crimson) color coding of their outfits provide a binary separation between Princess Tutu and Princess Kraehe, referencing the Odette/Swan maiden-Odile/Black Swan pairing, further emphasized by the feather headpiece of Princess Tutu. In girls' comics or *shōjo manga*, an important cultural form for girls and young women in Japan, the binary of girl characters with fair and black hair tends to signal the opposing qualities of two different girls who are nonetheless (often) equally important, as Fusami Ogi argues (121). *Princess Tutu* follows this convention: Ahiru has lighter hair, while Rue's is black.

In *shōjo* culture the binary of good and evil is often represented via two female characters, but the evil one, rather than being a one-dimensional monster "other," is frequently a more psychologically complex and nuanced figure. This tradition is also visible in the "magical girl" subgenre, from Meg and Non in *Majokko meguchan* [*Little Meg the Witch Girl*] (1974–75) through to Chocolat and Vanilla in *Sugar Sugar Rune* (2005–6; based on Moyoko Anno's girls' comic of the same title, 2003–7). According to this tradition, Ahiru and Rue are both friends and rivals. Due to her tragic upbringing, Rue is initially portrayed as an aloof and enigmatic girl who does not mingle with others in the academy other than Mytho. Ahiru, with her simplistic yet friendly and meddlesome nature, wishes to be friends with Rue. In episode 9, for example, Ahiru candidly initiates a chat with Rue after her ballet class in the studio. Rue, whom we have seen in the previous scene as being tormented over her fear of losing Mytho due to his increased interest in Princess Tutu, replies that she has never had such a casual chat with other girls but she does not hate it. In this sequence Ahiru and Rue are both seen from the side, in a long shot, standing apart from each other. Their physical distance connotes their emotional space. As Ahiru replys to Rue's comment by saying "I'm glad. We can be even better friends, can't we?" she rushes toward Rue and taps her shoulder with smile. As their distance diminishes, so does their emotional distance. Ahiru's attitude toward Rue dose not change even after she learns that Rue is actually Princess Kraehe, her enemy.

This opposite-yet-almost-equal portrayal of the relationship between the two princess figures is significant in terms of gender and fairy tales. Peggy Orenstein articulates that one of the issues that has contributed to the negative perception of "princess culture" is the lack of a bond between

Figure 12.4. The heroines Ahiru and Rue representing the binary of girl characters with fair and black hair in *shōjo manga* (girls' comics) tradition. *Princess Tutu* (2002), episode 2, directed by Jun'ichi Satō, written by Michiko Yokote. Hal Film Maker.

princesses. As Orenstein writes, "Among other things, princesses tend to be rather isolated in their singularity ... princesses avoid female bonding. Their goals are to be saved by a prince, get married ... and be taken care of for the rest of their lives" (23). Also, despite numerous revisions and sanitization of violence and sexual depictions in fairy tales, what has been left untouched is the good/bad women binary. The "deep malice of the witches and evil stepmothers, the unrelieved spite of some sisters, and the murderous jealousy between mothers and daughters were left to stand, unchallenged," writes Warner (133). This asymmetrical binary divides women against one another and leaves them vulnerable. This lack of female/girl friendship in fairy tales in general, and contemporary "princess culture" in particular, contributes to the dominance of heterosexual romance and hence the affirmation of the idea that female figures are defined primarily in relation to their relationship to male figures. *Princess Tutu*, like many other Japanese girls' comics and magical girl anime, treats female/girl bonding as one source of the heroine's power. Likewise, rather than through the highly asymmetrical binary of evil-ugly/good-beautiful women in conventional fairy tales, *Princess Tutu* portrays the two princesses as of equal importance and character depth. This all offers a new contemporary interpretation of the princess in fairy tales: a girl with agency, relationships, and character nuances.

The use of ballet, and especially the ballet skirt and ribbon pointe shoes as a fighting uniform, effectively reinterprets the stereotypically "masculine" activity of fighting as positively girlish. The history of ballet in Japan is relatively recent, being introduced to the culture only around 1910. Despite that, Japanese popular culture, and especially *shōjo manga*, has a subgenre of ballet *manga* featuring ballerina heroines (Monden "Layers of the Ethereal"). As Sugawa-Shimada argues, representations of girlish femininity in "magical girl" anime through dress and accessories can be interpreted as a device to articulate the power, confidence, and social responsibilities of these characters as girlish empowerment (141). Ahiru is a timid ballet student, but when transformed into the graceful Princess Tutu, with her ballet skirt and pink pointe shoes, she becomes powerful and confident. Using a similar example of Usagi in the anime adaptation of Naoko Takeuchi's *Sailor Moon*, Sugawa-Shimada reads this in a fashion similar to Joan Riviere's "Womanliness as a Masquerade" (1929), in which a display of emphasized femininity allows women to claim power in environments of male-dominated activity, where girls who engage in fighting need feminine dress, makeup, and accessories as a mask to prevent criticism for deviating from conventional feminine roles. But it is also possible to read that in Japanese popular culture, displays of girlishness and what are conventionally coded as masculine concepts, such as fighting and a sense of agency, can be combined (Monden, *Japanese Fashion Cultures* 117). The platform and length of serialized anime has also provided room for *Princess Tutu* to further enhance this point, by adding complexity and nuance to the characters of the two princesses.

Rue is introduced in the story as a perfect princess in the ballet division of the academy that Ahiru, Mytho, and Fakir also attend. As the story progesses, she is torn between her identity as the dark princess and her love for the prince. Ahiru learns that she herself is only a sidekick in Drosselmeyer's tale as, after all, she is just a duck—there is no miraculous permanent transformation in her future. The dark Rue is revealed as the true princess of Drosselmeyer's tale, and is incorporated into the hetero-romantic narrative. These complexities in *Princess Tutu* challenge some of the clichés of the conventional romantic fairy-tale genre where victimized maidens are cursed into imprisonment, instead reimagining the genre as a story of girls confronting and challenging their own fates. As I will argue below, *Princess Tutu* also offers some serious critiques of fairy-tale conventions and plots.

Serious Critique of Fairy Tales in *Princess Tutu*

Despite its origin as an anime program primarily targeted at children, what makes *Princess Tutu* differ from Anglophone adaptations of fairy tales such as the Disney princesses is its embrace of darker, serious themes.[3] This seems to reflect a tendency in modern Japanese culture itself. According to Murai, "The first tendency stems from the belief that beneath traditional European fairy tales lie meanings darker—more violent and more sexual—than appear on the surface" (*From Dog Bridegroom to Wolf Girl* 9). While it may not emphasize sexuality, *Princess Tutu* surely gives insight into these darker readings of fairy tales. In the second series, a piece of Mytho's heart has been dipped into the Raven's blood before it was restored to him, which has caused him to transform into the Prince Raven, dressed in black feathers like Rothbart in *Swan Lake*, lusting after young and beautiful hearts. He, like Rue, suffers conflict between his good and evil selves. Rue and Mytho, two "good" characters in the fairy tale, are now vacillating between innocence and brutality, which resonates with the sometimes brutal nature of "good" characters in the original forms of fairy tales, which are filled with "the graphic descriptions of murder, mutilation, cannibalism, infanticide, and incest" (Tatar 3). Often ruthless acts of retribution are committed by "good" characters, such as Snow White allowing the evil queen to dance in heated iron shoes until her death, or Cinderella having her stepsisters' eyes pecked out at their weddings. In referencing these ideas, *Princess Tutu* critiques and challenges the diluted, picture-perfect modern view of fairy tales, adding complexity and multidimensionality to the characters and the story.

Princess Tutu explores this brutality in several ways. In the second season, we learn that Drosselmeyer is much less pleasant than his Nutcracker namesake. The population of Gold Crown Town in *Princess Tutu* fear Drosselmeyer's power to turn what he writes into reality, and cut off his hands to prevent him from writing more. Drosselmeyer wants to write a fairy tale that never ends, and to do this he believes it must be a tragedy—because, of course, popular fairy tales end happily ever after. This is a reflection of our common desire as readers (and viewers) to want a good story to continue without ending. The principal characters' attempt to rewrite and retell the fairy tale, to alter the tragic and chaotic plot that the author (Drosselmeyer) has intended, is a metaphor for the process of retelling and transformation. As Cristina Bacchilega writes in relation to the transformative and adaptive practices of fairy tales, "we are not passive consumers, and this is but one scene in the tale; we can imagine different choices and endings, and we do" (3). If, as Bacchilega proposes, "fairy tales come in many versions and are in turn interpreted in varied ways that speak to specific social concerns, struggles, and dreams" (3), *Princess Tutu*'s darker and more intricate tale with psychologically complex characters indicates a more general tendency in Japanese popular culture where a story, even if targeted at a young audience, does not necessarily have to follow a stereotypical happy ending where the distinction between good and evil is never blurred. This tendency is already evident in the apparently tragic endings of Japanese animal bride tales such as "The Crane Wife." This makes Japanese popular culture an ideal platform from which to examine and nurture the transformation of fairy tales through "reproduction, adaptation, and translation" (Bacchilega 3) that might result in offering a different perspective on those fairy tales.

Princess Tutu, moreover, successfully increases the complexity of the narrative by playing with the fundamental structure and traditions of fairy tales—its plurality (Bacchilega 3) as a tale that is told and retold to the audience. The anime has three major, nested layers of story—the story the narrator (voiced by renowned actress Kyōko Kishida) reads to the viewer as an introduction to each episode, always starting with "once upon a time [*mukashi mukashi*] . . ."; the tale that Drosselmeyer has created and retells (the anime's general framework); and the main story where Ahiru and her friends live and take action. The presence of these layers lends the content of the *anime* a considerable depth. Also, characters in different layers—notably Drosselmeyer—frequently address characters in other layers of story, such as Ahiru, and sometimes us, the viewer (e.g., after the ending credit of episode 26). In turn, Ahiru speaks to (and thus is conscious of) Drosselmeyer, who no longer lives in the layer of her world. This series of breaking "the fourth wall," a practice commonly found in *shōjo manga* tradition and embodied in the anime by one of Drosselmeyer's last lines in the final episode, directed to the viewer: "I never dreamt a character inside a tale would change the story . . . ," augments the fictionality in the anime, at the same time adding reflexivity and multideminsionality to the characters and the story, resulting in the increase of a sense of realism. In such a treatment of fairy tales, the characters, like Ahiru and Fakir, become self-aware and rebel against the restrictions of their genre (most obviously represented by Drosselmeyer's intentions) to alter expectations in their "tale."

To complete the tale, Ahiru has to return the last piece of his heart to Mytho. This is the precious magic stone in the necklace that allows her to remain a human girl. This sacrifice means that Ahiru loses her magical powers and has to return to her original animal form. This creates a sense of realism within an otherwise fantastical story—Ahiru does not get the prince, or even a transformation to a beautiful swan—she goes back to being an ordinary duck. Rue, Ahiru's dark antagonist, on the other hand, does get the prince in the end. Although arguably Rue does conform to some of the conventions of the traditional heroine—a beautiful human maiden who was entrapped and cursed by the Raven—this brutal reality subverts the expected denouement. The anime ends with Ahiru, now forgotten by her human school friends, swimming on the lake, with Fakir sitting on the deck chair nearby, perhaps writing a new story of the gentle duck girl. While conforming to the tradition of Japanese folktales, where the female bird, after taking human form, returns to her original form at the end (Ellis 223), it does not lead to a conventional narrative closure. Literary studies scholar Bill Ellis, in his analysis of *Princess Tutu*, interprets this ending as a "queered" one that challenges traditional gender identities (224). A more nuanced reading is possible; that the anime leaves it vague, leaving the audience with an ambivalent feeling. *Princess Tutu*, in this sense, offers fairy-tale retellings that never end, albeit in a significantly different and more positive fashion than Drosselmeyer intended.

Conclusion

The narrative of *Princess Tutu* offers one way to reevaluate and assign new meanings to modern interpretations of fairy tales. In addition to the simple inversion of gendered agency between the cursed princesses and the knight/hero, it introduces complexity and moral nuance in the relationship between the two main female characters. Utilizing the conventions of *shōjo manga*, magical girl anime, and classical ballet, *Princess Tutu* avoids some of the clichés and reimagines fairy tales as modern stories of girls (and a boy, too) confronting and challenging their own fates.

The adaptation and bricolage of European fairy tales in *Princess Tutu*, and its (re)export to outside Japan as an anime dubbed or subtitled in other languages, outlines the ideas of cultural globalization and fluidity in the flow of culture against the increased disruption of center-periphery binary in the global cultural economy (Appadurai 275). The absence of a center in the concept of cultural globalization, along with disjuncture and fluidity in the flow of culture, suggests the potential for what Jan Nederveen Pieterse has called the countercurrents, or "reverse" flows of culture: the notion that cultural forms circulate in more than singular way. When a "Western" culture is accepted and understood in a non-Western cultural context, the adopted cultural format makes local characteristics visible rather than eclipsing them (Okamura 137–49). The process of countercurrents stands for "the impact non-western cultures have been making on the West," and "the role of local reception of western culture" (Nederveen Pieterse 69). This idea of cultural flow operating in more than a singular way questions and possibly problematizes the idea that "globalization is constituted as a monolithic one-way flow from the west-to-the rest" (Barker 42). Likewise, it questions the power dynamic between European fairy tales and other cultures, Japanese popular culture in the case of *Princess Tutu*, that adapt and reimagine them.

The gendered analysis of *Princess Tutu* also highlights implicit Eurocentric tendencies and limitations in current fairy-tale scholarship. Authors like Hopkins and Whelan, whose focus is solely on contemporary Euro-American culture (and Disney films in particular), nonetheless present their analyses as universal, and hence present a danger of falling into the Eurocentric. Whelan (179–80), for example, argues that a fairy-tale princess figure with stronger senses of agency and free will whose activity are not wholly predicated on hetero-romantic desires is a recent, more precisely a twenty-first-century, phenomenon. As *Princess Tutu* and its intertexual reference to other, more established genres in Japanese *shōjo manga* and anime cultures indicates, such a portrayal of fairy-tale princess and social climber characters who would do anything to attain a "princess life" enjoyed popularity long before Anglo-American culture "realized" their potential. The analysis of *Princess Tutu* thus adds more depth and wider scope to current fairy-tale scholarship with the emphasis on representations of gender and princess narrative.

In conclusion, *Princess Tutu*'s (re)introduction of a harsh, almost brutal reality to the story subverts more modern conventions of the genre, offering a clever alternative to the common criticism of fairy tales as primarily reinforcing heteronormative, patriarchal, and anthropocentric romantic ideologies where the passive good girl is always rewarded with a happy ending. The real story, as *Princess Tutu* shows us, is sometimes more complicated, but no less fascinating for that.

Notes

I am very grateful to David Jellings for his careful reading and editing of this chapter. I wish to thank Mayako Murai and Luciana Cardi for their poised guidance and suggestions. Thank you also to Greg Ralph and anonymous reviewers for their constructive comments.

1. Whelan groups Disney's fairy-tale animations that were produced during Walt Disney's lifetime (i.e., *Snow White and the Seven Dwarfs*, *Cinderella*, and *Sleeping Beauty*) as the first-wave Disney princess films, and those produced after his death (i.e., *The Little Mermaid* and everything after) as second-wave Disney princess films.
2. Despite its categorization as a magical girl anime, there was no such marketing of toys with *Princess Tutu*.
3. It needs to be noted that non-Japanese culture, such as Disney and Hollywood films, have also started reevaluations of darker heroines in fairy-tale themed works, such as *Maleficent* (2014) and *Frozen*.

Works Cited

Aalten, Anna. "'The Moment When it All Comes Together': Embodied Experiences in Ballet." *European Journal of Women's Studies*, vol. 11, no. 3, 2004, pp. 263–76.

Appadurai, Arjun. "Disjuncture and Difference in the Global Cultural Economy." *The Phantom Public Sphere*, edited by Bruce Robbins, University of Minnesota Press, 1993, pp. 269–95.

Bacchilega, Cristina. *Fairy Tales Transformed? Twenty-First-Century Adaptations and the Politics of Wonder*. Wayne State University Press, 2013.

Barker, Chris. *Television, Globalization and Cultural Identities*. Open University Press, 1999.

Carter, Angela. *The Bloody Chamber and Other Stories*. Penguin, 1979.
Chazin-Bennahum, Judith. *The Lure of Perfection: Fashion and Ballet 1780–1830*. Routledge, 2005.
de Beauvoir, Simone. *The Second Sex*. 1949. Penguin, 1975.
Do Rozario, Rebecca-Anne C. "The Princess and the Magic Kingdom: Beyond Nostalgia, the Function of the Disney Princess." *Women's Studies in Communication*, vol. 27, no. 1, 2004, pp. 34–59.
Ellis, Bill. "The Fairy-telling Craft of Princess Tutu." *The Folkloresque: Reframing Folklore in a Popular Culture World*, edited by Michael Dylan Foster and Jeffrey A. Tolbert, University Press of Colorado, 2016, pp. 221–40.
Fabos, Bettina. "Forcing the Fairytale: Narrative Strategies in Figure Skating Competition Coverage." *Culture, Sport, Society*, vol. 4, no. 2, 2001, pp. 185–212.
Fraser, Lucy. *The Pleasures of Metamorphosis: Japanese and English Fairy Tale Transformations of "The Little Mermaid."* Wayne State University Press, 2017.
Fraser, Lucy, and Masafumi Monden. "The Maiden Switch: New Possibilities for Understanding Japanese Shōjo Manga (Girls' Comics)." *Asian Studies Review*, vol. 41, no. 4, 2017, pp. 544–61.
Holland, Samantha. *Alternative Femininities: Body, Age and Identity*. Berg, 2004.
Hopkins, Susan. *Girl Heroes: The New Force in Popular Culture*. Pluto Press, 2002.
Miller, Laura. "Japan's Cinderella Motif: Beauty Industry and Mass Culture Interpretations of a Popular Icon." *Asian Studies Association of Australia*, vol. 32, no. 3, 2008, pp. 393–409.
Monden, Masafumi. *Japanese Fashion Cultures: Dress and Gender in Contemporary Japan*. Bloomsbury, 2015.
———. "Layers of the Ethereal: A Cultural Investigation of Beauty, Girlhood, and Ballet in Japanese Shōjo Manga." *Fashion Theory*, vol. 18, no. 3, 2014, pp. 251–95.
Murai, Mayako. *From Dog Bridegroom to Wolf Girl: Contemporary Japanese Fairy-Tale Adaptations in Conversation with the West*. Wayne State University Press, 2015.
———. "Ōkami shōjo no keifu" ["The Genealogy of Werewolf Girl"]. *"Akujo" to "ryōjo" no shintai no shintai hyōshō* [*Corporeal Representations of Good and Bad Women*], edited by Chinami Kasama. Seikyu-sha, 2012, pp. 243–66.
Nederveen Pieterse, Jan. *Globalization and Culture: Global Mélange*. Roman & Littlefield Publishers, 2004.

Ogi, Fusami. "<Ekkyō> suru shōjo manga to jendā" ["Shōjo Manga and Gender That 'Transgress'"]. *Manga wa ekkyō suru* [*Comics Transgress*], edited by F. Ogi and M. Ichiki, Sekai shisō-sha, 2010, pp. 110–34.

Okamura, Keiko. *Gurohbaru shakai no ibunka-ron* [*Cross-Cultural Theory in Global Societies*]. Sekaishiso, 2003.

Orenstein, Peggy. *Cinderella Ate My Daughter: Dispatches From the Front Lines of the New Girlie-Girl Culture.* HarperCollins, 2011.

Orr, Lisa. "'Difference That Is Actually Sameness Mass-Reproduced': Barbie Joins the Princess Convergence." *Jeunesse: Young People, Texts, Cultures*, vol. 1, no. 1, 2009, pp. 9–30.

Peers, Juliette. "Ballet and Girl Culture." *Girl Culture: An EncyclopediaI*, Vol. 1, edited by M. Mitchell and J. Reid-Walsh, Greenwood, 73–84.

Princess Tutu Complete Collection. DVD. Australia: Madman Entertainment, 2007.

Riviere, Joan. "Womanliness as Masquerade." 1929. *The Inner World and Joan Riviere: Collected Papers: 1920–58*, edited by A. Hughes, Karnac Books, 1991.

Sugawa-Shimada, Akiko. *Shōjo to mahō* [*Girls and Magic: Representations of Magical Girls and Japanese Female Viewership*]. NTT Publishing, 2013.

Tatar, Maria. *The Hard Facts of the Grimms' Fairy Tales.* Princeton University Press, 2003.

Turk, Mariko. "Girlhood, Ballet, and the Cult of the Tutu." *Children's Literature Association Quarterly*, vol. 39, no. 4, 2014, pp. 482–505.

Wakakuwa, Midori. *Ohime-sama to jendā* [*Gender and the Princess*]. ChikumaShobō, 2003.

Warner, Marina. *Once Upon a Time: A Short History of Fairy Tale.* Oxford University Press, 2014.

Whelan, Bridget. "Power to the Princess: Disney and the Creation of the Twentieth-Century Princess Narrative." *Kidding Around: The Child in Film and Media*, edited by Alexander N. Howe and Wynn Yarbrough, Bloomsbury, 2014, pp. 167–88.

Yagawa, Sumiko. "Toraware no shōjo samazama" ["A Variety of Imprisoned Girls"]. 1978. *Han-shōjo no haizara* [*An Ashtray for an Anti-Girl*], Shinchō-sha, 1981, pp. 129–36.

Zipes, Jack. *The Trials & Tribulations of Little Red Riding Hood: Versions of the Tale in Sociocultural Context.* Bergin & Garvey Publishers, 1983.

13

When Princess(es) Will Sing

Girls Rock and Alternative Queer Interpretation

Katsuhiko Suganuma

WITH THE PHENOMENAL COMMERCIAL success of the 2013 Disney motion picture *Frozen*, "Let It Go," the song from the film, became ubiquitous across all media. Having trained in feminist studies and gender studies, however, I resisted watching *Frozen* on the assumption that Disney's animated films can be problematic in their representations of gender, race, and ethnicity. Yet, in the end, I surrendered, unable to ignore the fact that some perceive the film to be queer, especially in its representation of the character of Princess Elsa.

Frozen, of course, is not perfect in a feminist sense. At the same time, there are several elements of the film that are indeed queer. This is particularly apparent in the presence of a female protagonist singing about and trying to come to terms with her own identity against powerful societal forces working to undermine her. Even more interesting is the fact that Elsa's search does not culminate with Prince Charming, a confirmation by a male authority found in many fairy-tale stories, such as *Snow White* and *Sleeping Beauty*. Instead, because the society in which she lives is not equipped with the ideas necessary to make her subjectivity possible, Elsa's quest takes its own course without relying on preexisting means. For this reason Elsa is queer.

In my encounter with a female figure whose singing voiced her concerns in a manner that involved queer strategies and gender subversion, I had a strong moment of déjà vu. This takes us to the princess(es) with whom this chapter is mainly concerned, the members of the Japanese female band, Princess Princess.

I first encountered Princess Princess while only in the third grade of elementary school. My older sister, who was in middle school and had heard one of the most popular songs in the Princess Princess repertoire, called "Diamonds," introduced me to the music of the band. I have been continuously drawn to Princess Princess since that time. Growing up as a queer boy, confused, in the midsize regional city of Okayama, my upbringing made it difficult for me to regard my sexual orientation in any positive light. The music of Princess Princess gave space for me to dwell on and explore who I was, or who I could become. I was never bookish, nor did I show interest then in the boy toys that my male friends became excited about. Princess Princess, however, was a fairy tale in which I could immerse myself.

I begin the chapter with this anecdotal account of my experience with Princess Princess not to privilege one particular subjective view but to acknowledge the fact that popular music can be a useful medium through which to analyze the adaptation and re-orientation of fairy-tale studies. Furthermore, as I demonstrate below, new interpretations or adaptations of ostensibly heteronormative tales can be found from an alternative and personally situated queer point of view. Adale Sholock aptly summarizes this point by stating that "the autobiographical within queer studies provides a locus from which we can address the difference that sexual difference makes in the discursive production of academic knowledge" (130). Following this lead, I take an anecdotal approach in this chapter, in the hope of creating an intermingling of fairy-tale studies, popular music studies, and queer studies.

In her critical review essay, Jodie Taylor emphasizes a need for us to further investigate, through an approach that is as interdisciplinary as possible, the close relations that subversive queer cultures may have with popular music (202–3). Cristina Bacchilega gives an equal weight to the importance of "divergent social projects that fairy-tale adaptations imagine . . . [and] their participation and competition in multiple genre and media systems"

(16). In pursuit of interdisciplinary analysis, this chapter also refers to the approach of popular musicology. Relative to orthodox musicology that looks at music through its forms and compositions, popular musicology places emphasis not only on the content of music but also on their "embodied" meanings, such as performances and receptions (Taylor 201). In order to conduct interdisciplinary analysis of a popular song by Princess Princess, this chapter necessarily sidesteps into areas including intercultural critique and popular literature, which relate to the discussion of female agency within material or consumerist culture.

This chapter also contributes to the growing body of work concerned with the feminist adaptations of fairy tales in Japan. Mayako Murai observes that feminist fairy-tale adaptations began to appear in Japan only in the 1990s, mainly in the forms of novels and short stories (24, 29–30). While a productive dialogue between fairy-tale retellings and formal critical studies developed in Japan from that time, intertextual analysis of fairy tales in relation to popular music is far from adequate. By examining the tale of Princess Princess, whose popularity peaked in the late 1980s and early 1990s, this chapter sheds new light on the intersection of fairy-tale studies, popular music, and queer studies.

The Princess Princess Fairy Tale

Princess Princess is often hailed as the most successful female band, both commercially and symbolically, in the history of Japan's music industry. The band's official website gives a third-person narrative that portrays Princess Princess as the "pioneer . . . girls band" ("Profile").[1] This journey to unprecedented commercial success as a female band meets the conditions necessary for their narrative to be read as a fairy tale.

Princess Princess debuted in the mid-1980s under the name Akasaka Komachi. Five young teenage women—Atsuko Watanabe, Kanako Nakayama, Kyoko Tomita, Tomoko Konno, and Kaori Okui—came together to form the group following an entertainment agency audition. The name of the band came from the fact that the agency was located in Akasaka, Tokyo, while "komachi" evokes beautiful woman in Japanese. The way in which the agency packaged Akasaka Komachi was a far cry from the Princess Princess that I encountered a few years later. As a band leader and bass-guitarist, Atsuko Watanabe recalls, in retrospect, Akasaka Komachi was an invention of the production agency with the obvious intention of creating a girl band that people would respond to as "the Candies with instruments" ("Whether it speaks to the heart is the importance of music"). The Candies were a wildly popular female idol trio from mid-1970s Japan.

Like the Candies and other so-called female idol groups of that time, Akasaka Komachi was strictly directed and produced by the male-centered music industry. Despite each member's musical talent, they were treated as pretty dolls for the stage, and often required to lip-synch and mime instruments to music written by male composers.

Like Elsa in *Frozen*, members of the band quickly became dissatisfied with not being able to express their talents and identities. As a consequence, they transferred to a different agent and re-debuted as Princess Princess. We might refer to this second debut as the band's "Let It Go" moment. Following that, the true colors of Princess Princess emerged as they fulfilled their aspirations to release albums and singles written and composed by members of the band. Within a couple of years, the band's popularity had commensurately increased. Assisted by the late-1980s boom in band music, which coincided with the final commercially heated years of Japan's bubble economy, Princess Princess became the first all-girl band to have million-selling singles and albums. They were also the first ever female group to hold a live concert at Nippon Budōkan, the venue of the 1966 concert by The Beatles. Since that performance by the legendary British band, the Budōkan has been considered the Mecca of rock music in Japan.

Princess Princess's transformation from Akasaka Komachi to Japan's most commercially successful girl band follows the familiar narrative of the traditional fairy tale. Despite many initial adversities, the heroine(s) finally emerge as a butterfly. What separates Princess Princess from traditional fairy-tale princess narratives, however, is suggested by the name of the band itself. In its literal juxtaposition of princesses, the name Princess Princess, doubles the effect of the term, thereby blurring the significance of what it means to be a princess while simultaneously creating an uncanny space for fluidity and experimentation. Rather than reproducing an all-too-familiar heteronormative discourse of a princess whose identity is often substituted by her male counterpart, namely a prince, the figure of heroine depicted by the music of Princess Princess departs from such a binary configuration. A repetition of the meaning of princess with modification each time leads to a rejection of its singular definition, hence calling into question the premise of simple gender dualism—princess/prince, female/male, and weak/powerful. We will now turn to an analysis of the song "Diamonds," the first ever million-selling single by Princess Princess, in order to present an instance of the re-orientation of the fairy tale at the intersection of popular music, gender subversion, and queer interpretation.

Material Princess

In the popular imagination, Princess Princess has often been hailed as a symbol of the consumption culture that operated at the pinnacle of Japan's bubble economy. Numerous nostalgic commentaries that echo this evaluation have been made in response to some clips, posted on YouTube and similar sites, of Princess Princess's music and performances from the late 1980s. This popular discourse is, however, not entirely accurate. The optimism that came from Japan's ever-inflating bubble was on the verge of evaporation before the end of the 1980s. In terms of Japan's music industry, however, the 1990s peak of CD sales had yet to be reached. And while the Princess Princess hit "Diamonds" became the first single CD ever to sell over a million copies, it was not until the latter half of the 1990s that CD sales records were reached. As Kyohei Miyairi observes, the fact that the so-called CD bubble took until 1998 to reach its height resulted from the success of the comprehensive marketing strategies of the "J-Pop" industry in Japan (65, 72). Considering such intricate socioeconomic situations, the enormous popularity of "Diamonds" is best regarded as a social phenomenon that reflects the residual sentiment of the hyperconsumerist culture of the 1980s. Furthermore, the sentiment echoed widely among the youth by coinciding with the initial period of the maturing CD-based music industry in Japan. It is for this reason that later in this chapter I contextualize my analysis of "Diamonds" in relation to popular literature and youth culture from the 1980s, and its effect on the public discourse about female agency in consumerist culture.

The song "Diamonds" was first conceived as a score composition by Princess Princess vocalist Kaori Okui. Okui gave the tune the provisional title of "Otoshidama," a Japanese term meaning a New Year's gift of money. In a repertoire of nearly 120 original songs, ranging through rock, pop-rock, and pop, "Diamonds" exemplifies the more pop-like quality of the band's music. Accompanied by E major chords and an upbeat tempo, the lyrics present the narrative of a heroine—although the gender remains unspecified—who expresses her desire and quotidian mode of living through reference to romance and consumer culture. Written by lead guitarist Kanako Nakayama, the lyrics begin by portraying a heroine who asserts willful agency in seeking her own joy and fun in everyday life.

> Dipping my bare foot in cool water, I look up at skyscrapers
> Wearing whatever clothes I choose, I am not doing anything wrong
> Driving around with a golden steering wheel in my hands, I am absorbed with the chance to have fun
> I want to see things that I cannot see on a television screen.
>
> (Princess Princess, "Diamonds" [1989])

Evoked in this opening verse is the unapologetic attitude of a heroine who expresses her sense of entitlement to forms of joy and fun that are incongruent with social norms. The reference to "skyscrapers" confirms the urban setting in which the heroine resides. The fact that she cools her feet by removing her footwear may imply that the heroine's shoes are indeed binding and painful to wear. The narrative of painful footwear for women may evoke "glass slippers" in *Cinderella*. And yet, unlike Cinderella, who is given a pair of slippers by her fairy godmother in the hopes of winning the heart of a prince, the heroine's choice of fashion in "Diamonds" is no one's business but her own. A frank celebration of the freedom of girls and their enjoyment of life is the undeniable undertone of the song.

To audiences familiar with American 1980s pop music, the undertone of "Diamonds" is reminiscent of Cyndi Lauper's 1983 single, "Girls Just Want to Have Fun." Although originally created by Robert Hazard a few years earlier, the revised rendition by Lauper was widely hailed as a feminist anthem. In the opening frames of Lauper's music video, viewers see a woman in eccentric dress, played by Lauper herself, freely dancing and walking along an urban street as she makes her way home after a night out. Defying the controlling parents who are shocked at their daughter's behavior, the heroine sends the straightforward message that "girls just want to have fun."

There is a close correlation between the Princess Princess song "Diamonds" and Lauper's music that becomes particularly apparent in the middle segment of the music video. There, the woman (Lauper) makes a mockery of the scene of a film being screened on a television set, which portrays long-standing misogynist discourses about women in the media—women as possessions of men. The heroine in "Diamonds" echoes this critique by seeking out, as the lyrics quoted above suggest, alternative discourses about women that cannot normally be found "on a television screen."

Recalling the television screen, the sheet of glass has been a familiar object in traditional fairy tales as well as contemporary adaptations. Drawing on *The Mad Woman in the Attic* (1979), the influential feminist critique by Sandra M. Gilbert and Susan Gubar, Vanessa Joosen observes that a mirror, most notably the magic mirror in *Snow White*, functions as a tool to pit women again each other in competition for marketability and appeal to the male gaze (17). The television screen was one of the most applicable manifestations of this "magic mirror" in the visual media–oriented consumerist society of the 1980s. In the world of traditional fairy tales, however, the "magic mirror" normally functions as an instructive tool of male wisdom through which to indoctrinate women. Furthermore, women are often trapped in the spell of magic. While the television screen in consumerist culture has a similar effect, women with newly gained economic power possess their own agency of not purchasing the screen. Women can switch off misogynist shows screened on TV and look elsewhere by expressing their independent preferences. Both Princess Princess's "Diamonds" and Lauper's "Girls Just Want to Have Fun" express the strength of women's will to resist submitting to the male authority that a sheet of glass normally suggests.

As "Otoshidama," the provisional title of the song "Diamonds," implies, material sentiment is the prominent theme foregrounded in Nakayama's lyrics. This certainly sums up the heroine's desire to acquire material goods and experience the hedonistic feelings that these bring. In terms of an unapologetically materialist heroine in popular music, this Princess Princess hit cannot help but recall Madonna's 1984 hit "Material Girl." It further comes as no surprise to find that, while the narrative of ascendancy from a girl of limited means to a princess who is chosen by a royal male is a common formula in traditional Cinderella-like fairy tales, the financial gain and pragmatic benefits that accompany this rise are carefully concealed by the charm of romantic love and innocence. In this sense, Madonna's music video of "Material Girl," which portrays a heroine who is desired by numerous high-caliber men and yet is unapologetically materialist, captures not only the atmosphere of US consumerist culture in the 1980s, but also breaches long-standing fairy-tale convention.

While it is useful to discuss the Princess Princess hit, "Diamonds," in relation to US popular music, I am aware that this methodology runs the risk of reinforcing US- and Euro-centric paradigms of adapting fairy-tale studies to the so-called "elsewhere." James Stanlaw, for example, specifically identifies Princess Princess's "Diamonds" as the most obvious instance of Japan's music industry being influenced by a tide of consumerist culture from the West (80). In order for this chapter to avoid the assumption that popular culture in Japan is merely a passive receptor of cross-cultural communication flows, I will now tease out the complexities involved in the music of Princess Princess by discussing "Diamonds" in reference to two Japanese literary narratives from the 1980s that also portray the intersection of female identity and consumerist culture. As noted earlier, discussing the meanings of the song "Diamonds" in reference to these two key literary texts is of vital importance in terms of understanding the music of Princesss Princess, not solely within the terms of musicology but within the broader context of popular consumption culture.

From *Somewhat, Crystal* to "Diamonds"

The eponymous "diamond" appears in the main chorus of the Princes Princess hit in the following context:

> All those moments and scenes are diamonds
> Though I cannot describe them very well, they are precious
>   to me
> The sense that I felt then was real
> That keeps me carrying on
>
>   (Princess Princess, "Diamonds" [1989])

The term "diamond" is used in the song as a figurative object by which to reflect upon the importance of the full range, good or bad, of the quotidian activities that make up the heroine's life. Rather than perceiving these as superficial and without substance, or only skin deep, the heroine finds meaning in these experiences in terms of how they shed new light upon and enrich her as a person. These elements do not accumulate into a foam of bubbles that simply burst. Rather, each feeling and each experience contributes to defining who she is or whom she might become. Her "real" sense of identity is experiential rather than something being determined by someone else.

The diamond is the gemstone that most strongly implies heteronormativity in our time. In part for the purpose of sustaining a billion-dollar industry, the diamond has been commercialized in conjunction with a narrative of modern romance and love. The use of the gemstone for engagement rings is the obvious example. The prismatic radiance of the diamond is the crystallization of a symbol of every bride-to-be at her supposed prime of beauty. In this way, the rays of the diamond illuminate the heteronormative terrain, fully in sync with the capitalist system that sustains it. In contrast, the diamonds of Princess Princess shine in an autonomous light. Because there is no other word available just yet to identify this sentiment, the heroine refers to the things she constructs as "diamonds," in the plural. The more she experiences, the brighter the light that radiates from the prism that her "diamonds" create.

This use of a gemstone as a metaphor for the heroine's sentiment in consumerist-driven Japanese society immediately reminds us of a few key texts from the 1980s. The most obvious is the 1980 novel *Somewhat, Crystal* (*Nantonaku, kurisutaru*) by Yasuo Tanaka. First published in a literary quarterly, the phenomenal commercial success of the book form of this narrative resulted at the time in the so-called crystal phenomenon. In its sharp commentary on the connection between urban consumption culture and youth in the early 1980s, the novel features in an unconventional manner over four hundred footnotes. Part of "the source of [the novel's] popularity" lies in the fact that the majority of these footnotes relentlessly catalog the consumer items and the "brand-name goods favored by the affluent youth" of Tokyo (Field 171). The college-girl heroine of the novel is one of many young women of that era who works, as Norma Field observes, "in order to acquire money to ensure their freedom—in this case, freedom to purchase the commodities that produce the 'atmosphere' defining their identity" (174). Rather than assuming an omnipresent identity core, however, the heroine relies on her quotidian "atmospheric feeling" (*nantonaku no kibun*) to make sense of herself (Tanaka 30). At one point in the novel, the heroine goes so far as to say: "Our daily living is like crystal. No distress whatsoever can cloud it" (87). The heroine's freedom to collect and purchase is perhaps driven by the abundance of crystal-clear space to be filled in her life. The numerous consumer items that are detailed in the novel's footnotes assist in augmenting the heroine's "atmospheric feeling" of wanting to give meaning to that transparent crystal space.

It is important to note, however, that the ostensible active female agency demonstrated by the heroine of *Somewhat, Crystal* is undermined by a masculinist narrative. Rather than expressing the heroine's thoughts, the novel's footnotes are more or less narrated by the male author Tanaka in a tone that, far from remaining objective, is often cynical and judgmental. The footnote for the pastry shop, "Laurie," located in Tokyo's Harajuku area, for example, reads as follows: "Laurie—a shop frequented only by people who really know about Harajuku. Therefore, it is best not to go. In fact, you are not permitted to go" (163). The assumed addressee of this subjective view of the male-identified narrator is the novel's reader, with the footnote exemplifying the narrator's dismissive tone toward the consumer activities of women. Connoted in this tone is a critique of the idea that material abundance or the acquisition of this can lead to anything meaningful. Norma Field observes that "[t]he persistence" of this "mocking tone transforms the narrator of the notes into a controlling presence" (177).

This intervention of male authority in the heroine's quotidian "crystal" lifestyle is further developed by the novel's plot line. While the "crystal" feeling pervades her mode of living, the heroine reminds herself that it is sex with Jun'ichi, her musician boyfriend, that in fact provides her with substance. She further muses that Jun'ichi gives her something that no other man has been able to during sex. Field appositely summarizes a heteronormative narrative that accompanies the plot structure of the novel.

> The moral, we conclude, is that orgasm has no brand name. . . . That physical loss of freedom singly experienced in sexual surrender to the man to whom one is spiritually bound is priceless and therefore threatens to overwhelm the values guaranteed by the freedom-to-buy. (175)

We see here that the heroine's gesture toward the autonomy of her agency through consumption is ultimately undermined by an androcentric authority. As previously noted, the idea that the happiness of the heroine can be guaranteed only through the promise of love by a male partner is a perennial theme of traditional fairy tales. Tanaka's *Somewhat, Crystal* also resorts to this pattern, despite its effort to portray the construction of female agency in a materialist culture. After all, the novel's "crystal" remains only "somewhat" transparent until fully illuminated by beams of male light.

In contrast to the heroine from *Somewhat, Crystal*, the heroine of Princess Princess's "Diamonds" refuses to surrender to a male authority. In the second pre-chorus verse of the song, she sings the following:

> Lock in the sweet nothings that would otherwise melt in
> your ear

> Love is not for sale, you may give it to me, but I won't sell mine
> Fasten the seatbelt, spin the propeller, kick the ground, and fly high
>
> (Princess Princess, "Diamonds" [1989])

Here we see the heroine of "Diamonds" reject any invitation to submit herself to "Mr. Right" at the expense of the freedom to enjoy her mode of life. As the second line suggests, rather than the interpersonal, her affection tends toward the self-referential. Accordingly, the counter-reference of a male figure is in no way mandatory for her existential purpose. The last line can furthermore be interpreted as the heroine's intention to be willful. This line expresses in spatial terms a headstrong attitude that goes against the purported direction of her gender and sexuality in terms of the expectations of the heteronormative society. In traditional fairy tales, most clearly *Sleeping Beauty* and *Snow White*, the princess often falls asleep or lies down horizontally as she passively waits for the moment of rescue by a true "male" love. In contrast, the "Diamonds" heroine willfully chooses to ascend vertically and thereby dismisses the passivity connoted in the act of horizontal waiting. I am here drawing on Sara Ahmed's *Queer Phenomenology* (2006), which theorizes the importance of understanding our gender and sexuality through spatial narratives. Unlike the heroine from *Somewhat, Crystal*, who is ultimately orientated toward heteronormative space, the young woman in "Diamonds" succeeds in re-orienting that very space.

The Prism of *Shōjo* and Queer Doings

The association between consumption culture and the questioning of heteronormative gender roles as presented by the heroine of "Diamonds" can also be observed in *Kitchen*, a 1987 novel by Banana Yoshimoto that enjoyed phenomenal commercial success. Debuting with this work, Banana Yoshimoto, the daughter of prominent intellectual Takaaki Yoshimoto, became one of the top-selling authors of late-1980s Japan. Like Tanaka's *Somewhat,*

Crystal, Yoshimoto's *Kitchen* played a substantive role in constructing discourses around women's identity in the consumerist culture of Japan at that time. The fact that *Kitchen* and "Diamonds" by Princess Princess were released only a few years apart naturally suggests that a comparative analysis will yield valuable insights.

As Amanda C. Seaman observes, readers of Yoshimoto's novel can immerse themselves in the quotidian domestic space of a kitchen filled with consumer goods, especially modern appliances (51). Mikage, the heroine of the novel, is an orphan who experiments with a new living arrangement involving her male friend and classmate, Yūichi, and the transsexual mother who was once Yūichi's father. Notwithstanding that a sense of nostalgia for family—a longing for membership in a certain social unit—runs through Yoshimoto's works, the heroine of *Kitchen* illuminates the possibility of alternative gender roles in a domestic space. In fact, as John Whittier Treat points out, "[c]ontrary to what we might have expected to find in fiction directed towards an audience of adolescent women, there are no stereotypically perfect families in any of Banana's stories" (287). In this sense *Kitchen* recalls "Diamonds," in that neither portray the conventional life course expected of a female heroine in heteronormative society.

In the same year that "Diamonds" was released, Princess Princess had another hit single called "The Hottest Summer on Earth" ["Sekai de ichiban atsui natsu"]. In lyrics written by the band's drummer, Kyoko Tomita, the heroine here sings about her active and emotional infatuation with her partner using the superlative of "sekai de ichiban," the best in the world. At a cursory look, this song seems to represent the hopelessly tedious narrative of an adolescent love affair. However, the discourse of "sekai de ichiban," which the heroine declares with conviction, can be considered as yet another stance by a female figure who wishes to ascend vertically. This wish does not necessarily express a need to feel superior to others but merely to depart from the horizontal gender role that a woman is often required to play in relation to the male. In other words, the superlative of "sekai de ichiban" here suggests the woman's state of narcissistic infatuation with her own inner concerns rather than a desperate desire to be other-oriented.

As the name "Princess Princess" tellingly suggests, the heroines of their hit singles released at the end of the 1980s can be read as being homosocial and intrapersonal. Rather than succumbing to the force of the heteronormalization of their gender and sexuality, these heroines engage in modes of consumption that permit the exploration of alternative space—a discursive gender-scape that is yet to be recognized by social norms. For want of fitting terminology, the heroine describes this constellation of various momentary gender-scapes as "diamonds."

In reference to Banana Yoshimoto's work, John Whittier Treat finds a similar quality of narcissism represented by heroines who refuse to participate in a logocentric capitalist system (283). Paradoxically, it is precisely this inward tendency and resistance that permits the readers of Yoshimoto's novels to experiment with the possibility of alternative gender identities (281). Treat builds his argument upon girls-studies theories that emerged in the late 1980s. Numerous critics and scholars have written about the potential power of *shōjo*, who embody a liminal space between childhood and adulthood. In *Shōjoron* (1988), Masuko Honda, for example, characterizes *shōjo* as figures who are devoid of conventional genders and sexes and are hence resistant to a labor of economy.[2] This aestheticization of *shōjo* or girls' culture, of course, runs the risk of essentializing the gender binary and thus reinforcing the infantilized images of female youth in Japan (Ueno 90–91). For one thing, Honda forecloses the potential of the future-oriented subversive *shōjo*-scape by stating that "Sooner or later, the swaying moment will subside.... While it may express the expansion of the body or the yearning for freedom, it is, after all, but a 'momentary dream,' a 'vanity'" ("The Genealogy of *hirahira*" 35). Rather than diminishing the values of shōjo-scape itself, Honda, as I understand it, attests to the incompatibility of accommodating such a minority culture on the part of male-centered society. Honda's conceptualization of *shōjo* culture can, nonetheless, be useful in helping us to understand how certain communities in society resist the forces of gender normalization by various means. Rather than nostalgic aestheticization of childhood's past, *shōjo*-scapes can be read as a temporary suspension of the co-option of the girl into heteronormative systems.

What separates the heroine of Princess Princess's "Diamonds" from Honda's *shōjo*, however, is the heroine's will to retain her *shōjo*-scapes into the future.

> Some nights I wonder whether I could redo my life
> Like going back to being a child free of all I have done
> But the emotion that I felt then was real
> Diamonds that keep me carrying on
>
> (Princess Princess, "Diamonds" [1989])

In this final chorus, despite being frank about the lure of childhood nostalgia, the heroine ends the song by embracing "diamonds" of both past and present that will continue to make meaning of her life to come. In the context of gender subversion, this treatment of the "now" as a simultaneous embodiment of both shortcoming and future potential reminds us of the critical concept of "queer futurity" put forth by José Esteban Muñoz. In his critique of heteronormative reproductive futurity, Muñoz emphasizes the effects of "queer futurity" as follows:

> Queer cultural production is both an acknowledgement of the lack that is endemic to any heteronormative rendering of the world.... Queer utopian practice is about "building" and "doing" in response to that status of nothing assigned to us by the heteronormative world. (18)

Some may feel that "Diamonds" is just another popular cultural text of the consumer culture of the late 1980s, devoid of any deep meaning. However, as I hope this essay has demonstrated, the song exemplifies a cultural artifact that represents an uncanny moment and precarious space for the many youth, regardless of gender or sexual orientation, who seek to imagine their gender and sexual identities in ways that are not necessarily congruent with contemporary heteronormativity.

The Heroine Returns

Princess Princess disbanded in 1996. By the mid-1990s, the popularity of the "band music" genre had long gone, and the entire Japanese music industry was being re-oriented toward so-called J-Pop, an umbrella genre encompassing different types of preexisting music. Because its popularity and wide reception meant that J-Pop was accommodating the needs of the masses, it remained relatively undefined and less political than earlier popular music forms (Miyairi 124–25, 152). While, as previously mentioned, net sales of music CDs in Japan continued to rise until 1998, during the last few years of their career, Princess Princess never repeated the phenomenal success of earlier hits such as "Diamonds." Although the band's popularity had declined, news of its retirement was widely reported in the Japanese media. In fact, the band's very last concert at Nippon Budōkan was broadcast live through the premier cable TV channel, WOWOW. There was, however, a twist to the finale of the Princess Princess fairy tale.

In many traditional Western fairy tales, the concept of aging is taboo. With intergenerational competition among women prominent, the young heroine must work to preserve her youth and beauty (Joosen 13). In order to conform to this pattern, a number of fairy tales finish abruptly and thus refuse, in effect, to tell the story of how the heroine subsequently grows and ages. The Princess Princess fairy tale was, however, revitalized in 2012 when the band reunited to raise funds to assist with the reconstruction of the Tohoku regions affected by the 2011 Great East Japan earthquake and tsunami, and also by nuclear radiation. Within a year, mainly by the sales of tickets for live concerts and associated merchandise, Princess Princess raised and donated approximately five million US dollars to this cause.

At an average age of just under fifty, the members of Princess Princess once again created the magic wonder of their music. In order to promote their fund-raising activities, the band members appeared in numerous TV shows and music programs, and there is no doubt that the song that they performed most frequently was "Diamonds." Foretold in the first pre-chorus of the song, "I will not stop doing it . . . even if I am old" (Princess Princess, "Diamonds" [1989]), the heroine of "Diamonds" returned nearly a quarter of a century after the first release of the song. At the time that they first retired, each band member was single. When the band reunited, however, they were variously married, had children, were divorced, or had long formed marital partnerships without children. The heroines of the postmillennium "Diamonds" presented different life courses that could not be restrained by the single formula for heteronormative happiness.

Furthermore, although the band awoke from a long period of sleep and inaction, each member's cumulative experience over that period became part of the new "diamond" prism of the band. In commentary on the collection of testimonies from band members during the period of reunion, Makoto Hasegawa suggests that the song "Diamonds" itself has grown and continues to reflect the diversity of each member's personality (103). The fact that "Diamonds" has been repeatedly performed by Princess Princess and repeatedly appreciated by both past and present fans suggests the capacity and breadth of this song to accommodate as many diverse emotions and feelings today as in the late 1980s. Discussion of the emotions and feelings that might be accommodated by the radiance of postmillennium "diamonds," however, merits a chapter of its own.

Coda—Ode to Re-Orienting Fairy-Tale Studies

I wish to return to my opening anecdotal account to conclude this chapter. It has taken me nearly thirty years to make sense of what the song "Diamonds" means to me. Like any reader of fairy tales, my first moment of fascination with the narrative came in my childhood. With the 2012 Princess Princess reunion, however, I had the unexpected opportunity to revisit this tale as an adult. By that time, my academic training in feminism, queer studies, and cultural studies, together with my long-standing interest in Japanese popular music, enabled me to use a fairy-tale studies approach to understand the meaning of the song. What a long time it took me to arrive at this productive intermingling of these disciplines.

Donald Haase, on various occasions, has argued that there is no origin as such for any fairy tale. Notwithstanding the numerous adaptations of fairy tales, rather than having a single meaning benchmarked against certain lineages and hierarchies, each should be treated as an intertextual entity ("Yours, Mine, or Ours?"; "Hypertextual Gutenberg"). I wish to emphasize that this concept of fairy tales as intertextual is imperative for our methodology of re-orienting fairy-tales studies itself. As I hope this chapter has demonstrated, the reading of queer elements and gender subversions embedded in Princess Princess's "Diamonds" would not be possible without considering the intertextuality of the song. Each of the references made—from the relevant socioeconomic background through music culture, feminism, cross-cultural communication, literary analyses and queer theory—has been necessary to the practice of fairy-tale studies adopted in this chapter. This is not to say that fairy-tale studies is amenable to every single situation or concern. Instead, fairy-tale studies continues to re-orient itself as a useful analytical means through acknowledging its shortcomings and strengths in conversation with an array of relevant disciplines.

In my adolescence, Princess Princess was both soundtrack and guiding queer fairy tale. As my experience with the Japanese female band exemplifies, popular music has much to tell us about the adaptations of fairy tales. Popular music is incessantly replayed and widely consumed in order to become popular. Similar to fairy tales, however, popular music is not limited to a singular interpretation among its many audiences. In the analysis of popular music, Michael K. Bourdaghs argues that an important question for us to ask is "what people *do* with the songs in a specific situation" rather than how they are intended (8, emphasis is in original). In order for us to tease out those specific experiences and personal accounts of consuming popular music, the employment of queer studies is useful, as the field has been attentive to views that are always cutting edge, non-normative, and undefined. Queer studies, furthermore, situates analyses of popular music in critical dialogue with fairy-tale studies, as the latter has also developed out of its concerns for the constructions of gender and sexuality in society. The intermingling of these fields, as this chapter has advanced, is vital for ongoing refinements of fairy-tale studies.

The project of re-orienting fairy-tale studies is still in its own making. Being attentive to cross-cultural adaptations of fairy tales in multivalent forms will be a useful way to further develop this process. Around the world, there are numerous contemporary as well as historical diamond-tales still waiting for us to discover. Let us project the diverse rays of light needed in order to make these shine.

Acknowledgments

I would like to thank my academic mentors and friends Mayako Murai, Barbara Hartley, and Matthew Kirkcaldie, who patiently read this chapter at different stages and gave me invaluable advice and feedback.

Notes

1. Unless otherwise stated, all of the English translations of Japanese texts are mine, including the lyrics of songs.

2. Also see Kinsella (118) for an overview of the *shōjo* discussions that took place in the late 1980s.

Works Cited

Ahmed, Sara. *Queer Phenomenology: Orientations, Objects, Others*. Duke University Press, 2006.
Bacchilega, Cristina. *Fairy Tales Transformed? Twenty-First-Century Adaptations and the Politics of Wonder*. Wayne State University Press, 2013.
Bourdaghs, Michael K. *Sayonara Amerika, Sayonara Nippon: A Geopolitical Prehistory of J-POP*. Columbia University Press, 2012.
Field, Norma, "Somehow: The Postmodern as Atmosphere." *Postmodernism and Japan*, edited by Masao Miyoshi and H. D. Harootunian, Duke University Press, 1989, pp. 169–88.
Gilbert, Sandra M., and Susan Gubar. *Madwoman in the Attic: The Woman Writer and the Nineteenth-Century Literary Imagination*. Yale University Press, 1979.

Haase, Donald. "Hypertextual Gutenberg: The Textual and Hypertextual Life of Folktales and Fairy Tales in English-Language Popular Print Editions." *Fabula*, vol. 47, nos. 3–4, 2006, pp. 222–30.

———. "Yours, Mine, or Ours? Perrault, the Brothers Grimm, and the Ownership of Fairy Tales." *Merveilles & Contes*, vol. 7, no. 2, 1993, pp. 383–402.

Hasegawa, Makoto. *Diamonds: Princess Princess*. Shinko Music Entertainment, 2013.

Honda, Masuko. "The Genealogy of *hirahira*: Liminality and the Girl." *Girl Reading Girl in Japan*, edited by Tomoko Aoyama and Barbara Hartley, Routledge, 2010, pp. 19–37.

———. *Shōjoron* [*Theory of girls*]. Seikyūsha, 1988.

Joosen, Vanessa. *Critical and Creative Perspectives on Fairy Tales: Intertextual Dialogue Between Fairy-Tale Scholarship and Postmodern Retellings*. Wayne State University Press, 2011.

Kinsella, Sharon. *Schoolgirls, Money and Rebellion in Japan*. Routledge, 2014.

Miyairi, Kyohei. *J-POP bunka ron* [*On J-POP culture*]. Sairyū sha, 2015.

Muñoz, José E. *Cruising Utopia: The Then and There of Queer Futurity*. New York University Press, 2009.

Murai, Mayako. *From Dog Bridegroom to Wolf Girl: Contemporary Japanese Fairy-Tale Adaptations in Conversation with the West*. Wayne State University Press, 2015.

Princess Princess. "Diamonds." Written by Kanako Nakayama, composed by Kaori Okui, CBS Sony, 1989.

"Profile." [Purofīru] *Princess Princess*, www.princess2.net/profile/. Accessed 13 Oct. 2017.

Seaman, Amanda C. *Bodies of Evidence: Women, Society, and Detective Fiction in 1990s Japan*. University of Hawaii Press, 2004.

Sholock, Adale. "Queer Theory in the First Person Academic Autobiography and the Authoritative Contingencies of Visibility." *Cultural Critique*, vol. 66, 2007, pp. 127–52.

Stanlaw, James. "Open Your File, Open Your Mind: Women, English, and Changing Roles and Voices in Japanese Pop Music." *Japan Pop! Inside the World of Japanese Popular Culture*, edited by Timothy J. Craig, M.E. Sharpe, 2000, pp. 75–100.

Tanaka, Yasuo. *Nantonaku, kurisutaru* [*Somewhat, Crystal*]. Kawade shobō shinsha, 1981.

Taylor, Jodie. "Claiming Queer Territory in the Study of Subcultures and Popular Music." *Sociology Compass*, vol. 7, no. 3, 2013, pp. 194–207.

Treat, John W. "Yoshimoto Banana Writes Home: The Shōjo in Japanese Popular Culture." *Contemporary Japan and Popular Culture*, edited by John W. Treat, Curzon, 1996, pp. 275–308.

Ueno, Chizuko. *Onna asobi* [*Woman Play*]. Gakuyō shobō, 1988.

"'Whether it speaks to the heart is the importance of music' Atsuko Watanabe from Princess Princess." ["ongaku wa kokoro ni todoku ka ga taisetsu" puri puri Watanabe Atsuko san]. *Asahi.com*, 21 Jan. 2015, www.asahi.com/articles/ASH1K7KC9H1KUTIL023.html?iref=comtop_list_edu_f01. Accessed 21 Jan. 2015.

14

The Plantation, the Garden, and the Forest

Biocultural Borderlands in Angela Carter's "Penetrating to the Heart of the Forest"

Daniela Kato

1. Introduction: Unruly Edges and Biocultural Borderlands in the Modern Fairy Tale

> Outside the house, between the forests and fields, bounty is not yet exhausted.
>
> Anna Tsing, "Unruly Edges"

THIS ESSAY IS ABOUT unruly, bounteous edges and their import for an ecologically inflected re-orientation of the fairy tale. Perhaps to a greater extent than any other genre, the fairy tale, especially in its most subversive modern forms, can be a privileged site for rethinking such edges. Through all its metamorphoses, adaptations, and transculturations, the genre remains deeply enmeshed in worlds that connect humans with other life forms in an array of material and affective configurations, crossing manifold boundaries. Animals and plants often display wondrous forms of agency: wolves and birds speak and seduce; trees and flowers shift from one shape to another and crucially influence the course of events by producing either miraculous gifts or poisonous curses. Even life forms such as fungi "repeatedly form the context or substance of tales; they comprise the beds, tables, seats or umbrellas of elfin or fairy royalty" (Dugan 58). Moreover, as Marina Warner notes, in fairy tales, "animate forces keep circulating regardless of individual bodies and their misadventures" in ways that defy boundaries we ordinarily take for granted: "even when a tree has been cut down into a table or a spindle, its wood is still alive with the currents of power that charge the forest where it came from" (*Once Upon a Time* 21). Fairy-tale worlds are thus composed of "vibrant matter," to use philosopher Jane Bennett's felicitous expression. By critically engaging with the animate materiality of these lifeworlds, I wish to reframe the politics of wonder through a new ecological sensibility, and thereby to contribute to the ongoing conversation on how best to steer the challenge of truly comparative fairy-tale studies in a *worldly* direction, along the lines proposed by Cristina Bacchilega in her book *Fairy Tales Transformed? Twenty-First-Century Adaptations and the Politics of Wonder* (2013). The worldly direction I envision crucially takes into account the complex workings of capitalism and the coloniality of what is taken for *nature* in the modern configurations of the genre.

Anthropologist Anna Tsing's insights regarding "unruly edges" provide a suitable doorway into this ecological reframing of the fairy tale. Unruly edges are, for Tsing, the margins that confound our habitually rigid boundaries cordoning nature from culture: the landscapes where we can no longer ignore the "interspecies interdependencies that give us life on earth" ("Unruly Edges" 141). These ideas inform the emergent transdisciplinary field of multispecies ethnography and carry far-reaching eco-political implications. Not all spaces "where species meet"—henceforth defined as "biocultural borderlands" (Kirskey, Schuetze, and Helmreich 13)[1]—are equally hospitable to the idea of multispecies livability on earth. They often configure highly asymmetrical forms of species companionship: "domination, domestication, and love are deeply entangled," Tsing reminds us ("Unruly Edges" 141). And it is so because these are the very strings with which imperial conquest, capitalist penetration, and colonization have historically woven their webs around the globe, by entangling species and genders together in multiple material and affective arrangements. Consider the relationship between women and plants: women were the first plant domesticators (Howard xvi), and yet throughout history they have been recurrently brought together by men for domestication purposes. The transformation of intricate humid forest ecosystems into monocultural landscapes ruled by rigid species and gender hierarchies, as happened through the spread of colonial plantations, is a notorious example of the workings of domestication. The vast repository of Edenic fantasies that were inflicted on New-World rainforests by first-world explorers, builders of empire, and romantic naturalists is another example.

It is the purpose of this essay to tease out some of these webs of species interdependence and domestication in the modern fairy tale, with reference to three biocultural borderlands: the plantation, the garden, and the forest. It must be said, however, at the outset that such borderlands do not form watertight compartments; rather, they have porous, unstable boundaries, thus opening up the imagination to competing stories and alternative arts of living. Implicit in this way of seeing is Arjun Appadurai's definition of the work of the imagination as "neither purely emancipatory nor entirely disciplined but [as] a space of contestation" (4).

Reverting to the fairy tale, what scholars and creative writers make of the material and affective configurations of the interspecies relationalities outlined above has changed substantially in recent years. Let me thus begin with a brief overview of the most relevant scholarly studies and creative works in this regard. In line with the radical decentering of human subjectivity and the concomitant breakdown of the human/animal boundary that have been taking place across the sciences and the humanities, scholars and creative writers have been actively reimagining alternative contact zones for human-animal exchanges. These imagined sites of interspecies encounter often revise traditional fairy-tale representations, which have tended to reduce animals to mere ciphers symbolizing human experiences. Instead, contemporary reimaginings posit animals as beings that manifest their own forms of agency, creativity, and resistance. Thus Lewis Seifert has drawn attention to the frequent motif of metamorphosis (animal to human, and vice versa) in fairy tales as a way of challenging the divide between the human and the nonhuman: "tales of metamorphosis necessarily delineate what it means to be human and nonhuman through the experience of hybridity, whereby a character finds himself or herself between species" (245). Much in the same vein, Lucile Desblache has argued that contemporary fairy-tale re-creations offer new constructions of nature-culture and "introduce literary beasts as powerful agents of intra- and interspecies relationships [that] whisper in our ear imaginative ways of relating to different beings in non-hierarchical ways" (85).

No less importantly, fairy-tale scholars have begun turning their attention to the significant gender ramifications of these interspecies entanglements. In her study *From Dog Bridegroom to Wolf Girl* (2015), Mayako Murai shows how contemporary women artists such as Tomoko Kōnoike address the human-animal boundary by boldly reappropriating for women an animality that goes beyond the male-oriented, overly eroticized (and often misogynistic) images that have characterized such interface in many fairy-tale traditions and in mainstream cultural products at large (121–40). Hence these gender-inflected creative reappropriations challenge not just normative sexualities and their often rigid dualisms but also the very boundaries between species.

And yet, the wide-ranging ecological and gender implications of interspecies relationalities have been barely extended to the consideration of plants—vegetation, flowers, bushes, trees, and their various conglomerations—in the fairy tale. In fact, critical analyses in the field remain firmly zoocentric (that is, animal-centered). Such lack of attention to plant life is unsurprising, in a way. As Carla Hustak and Natasha Myers point out, we tend to privilege "'the encounter value' of organisms that humans can 'hold in regard,' that is, those animals with whom we can lock eyes." Plants patently lack a center; their "extensive, distributed, and entangling" bodies unsettle us, they add (81). Thus to human eyes the individuated activity of animal beings takes precedence over the unindividuated passivity of vegetal beings, with the consequent relegation of plants "to the background against which the real action of the world plays out" (80).

The research gap becomes somewhat more surprising when we consider that anxieties surrounding the behavior of plants have been around since time immemorial and have found a variety of creative expressions across the ages. In her introduction to the edited book *Plant Horror* (2016), Dawn Keetley writes:

> At its most basic, plant horror marks humans' dread of the "wildness" of vegetal nature—its untameability, its pointless excess, its uncontrollable growth. Plants embody an inscrutable silence, an implacable strangeness, which human culture has, from the beginning, set out to tame. (1)

The vegetal's evasion of categories instils horror. Keetley singles out the Green Man as one of the most enduring figures of plant horror in Western culture. Despite its roots in pre-Christian antiquity, this foliate figure became integral to Christian iconography between the eleventh and sixteenth centuries, variously etched in stone on the roofs, bosses, and doorways of cathedrals and churches throughout Europe. Typically a face with vegetation protruding from—or perhaps penetrating into—the nose or mouth, the Green Man embodies a rupture of the familiar, by suggesting an unsettling entwining of human and plant (Keetley 2).

A new phase of vegetal horror began when Charles Darwin revealed the astonishing devices that plants (particularly orchids) use to lure and conscript insect pollinators. The disconcerting discovery gave birth to what Jim Endersby has identified as a distinct literary subgenre concerned with seductive, deceptive, and ultimately rapacious plants that always get the upper hand (215–29). These vegetal monsters go about indifferently destroying human beings, striving only to reproduce and survive. Catriona Sandilands even claims that such plant horror stories form a whole tradition "in which botanical monstrosities of one sort or another invert the accustomed EuroWestern hierarchies of life to wreak havoc on the human beings who are supposed to be safely at the top of the cosmic pile" (421). It is also significant that in these stories plants were sexualized as distinctly *feminine*; the overpowering scents they used as tools of seduction were "loosely linked to the heavily perfumed prostitutes and other women of 'loose morals' who embodied the alluring dangers and freedoms that came with the anonymous life of the great cities or of distant colonies" (Endersby 218–19).

These woman-plant associations found their way into countless artistic depictions, many of which draw on fairy-tale imagery. Such associations figure prominently, for example, in the paintings of the Pre-Raphaelites, as Bram Dijkstra colorfully demonstrates in his study *Idols of Perversity* (1986). Of the fantasy of woman as flower, Dijkstra writes: it "became a nightmare vision of woman as a palpitating mass of petals reaching for the male in order to encompass him, calling to him to be drained by her pistils yearning for fertilization" (241). A case in point is Edward Burne-Jones's take on the *Sleeping Beauty* story by the Grimms, in a series of paintings titled *The Legend of Briar Rose* (1885–90). The images of the fabled slumbering Princess awaiting liberation from the Prince, while her flowery emissaries stealthily exterminate the wrong suitors but eventually let in Mr. Right, indicate how ingrained this woman-plant association, with its double suggestion of seductive passivity and perversity, was in the classic fairy-tale tradition.[2] Here I am reminded as well of the Grimms' *Rapunzel*, whose very name, *rapunzel*, or *rampion*, was that of an autogamous plant—that is, a plant that can fertilize itself. Maria Tatar remarks that this lurid plant "has a column that splits in two if not fertilized, and the halves will curl like braids or coils on a maiden's head, and this will bring the female stigmatic tissue into contact with the male pollen on the exterior surface of the column." Tatar cautions, however, that "most versions of the story give the girl the name of a savory herb" (105). This illustrates the lengths to which the classic fairy-tale tradition has gone to subdue plants' resistance to a normative, binarized either/or gender and sex, and it has done so by channeling the excesses of vegetal proliferation through more acceptable symbolic figurations—in the case of Rapunzel, through the "language of hair," to use Marina Warner's suggestive phrasing (*From the Beast to the Blonde* 374–75).

A more recent and politically subversive take on plant horror in the fairy tale is Jan Svankmajer's *Otésanek* (*Little Otik*, 2000). This film, based on a Czech folktale of the same name, tells the story of an anguished childless couple who are unexpectedly rewarded with a baby in the shape of a tree root. As the baby-root, Otik, grows at an alarming pace, its appetites become so ravenous that it ends up devouring everything and everyone around it, including its own parents. The film has been interpreted as a harrowing critique of the excessive appetites of neoliberalism and global capitalism (Zipes, *The Enchanted Screen* 352–53). Sandilands has queered this critique, suggesting that Otik's breaching of the line between vegetal and mammal provides "an important queer comment on the relations between heteronormativity, capitalism, and biopolitics" (421).

But what larger ecological implications have been drawn from these vegetal associations in the fairy tale? Not many as yet. To be sure, much has been written on the significance of forests and woods as privileged settings and theme setters for fairy stories. In *Gossip from the Forest*, Sara Maitland discusses the manifold ways in which forests have shaped our fairy-tale imaginary, by evoking "a sense of enchantment and magic, which is at the same time fraught with fear" (10). Yet, Maitland's analysis is ultimately anthropocentric, in that it focuses mostly on the forest as a wild backdrop against which to test human conduct and disclose the human self. The nonhuman inhabitants of the forest appear as little more than providers of magical assistance, far removed from "our" world. Everything revolves around human nature, with other "natures" orbiting it in more or less distant ellipses, to paraphrase plant philosopher Michael Marder (241).

Zipes's study of the enchanted forest in the Grimms' fairy tales provides a far more historically grounded and nuanced analysis. He acknowledges the forest as "always large, immense, great, and mysterious"; it is "the supreme authority on earth and often the great provider," possessing "the power to change lives and alter destinies" (*Brothers Grimm* 65). Remarkably, his analysis resists the tendency of cultural historians such as Robert Pogue Harrison and Simon Schama to define forests as "the shadow of civilization," that is, the spaces of nonsocial nature that haunted European sociality, particularly the nationalist imaginations of its elites. In Zipes's view, the forest is not an empty, wild space outside the bounds of history and civility and thereby utterly available for elite manipulation.[3] Though never a "home," it has a social nature that allows for positive transformation, as long as certain conditions are met: "the heroes of the Grimms' tales customarily march or drift into the forest and they are rarely the same people when they leave it. The forest provides them with all they will need, if they know how to interpret the signs" (89). Still, this forest is a place of hopelessly asymmetrical encounters, where the normative behaviors of male heroes are rewarded—and, of course, "heroines are generally portrayed as domestic figures who need domestication" (84). There is not much scope here for resisting or contesting such asymmetries through other forms of companionship within and across species and genders.

In what follows I want to explore the alternative idea of a fairy-tale forest that is located on neither side of the natural/social dichotomy. It has the contours of a multilayered biocultural landscape: to find it, we need to tap into its symbols and representations as well as into its histories of travel and colonialism, without nevertheless losing sight of the intricate multispecies interactions it enables or constrains, as human and nonhuman histories interpenetrate there. Informing my discussion will be Tsing's statement that "human nature is an interspecies relationship" ("Unruly Edges" 144). This stance rejects the belief in a supposedly autonomous and universal human nature, which has undergirded egregious masculinist narratives at the service of imperial and colonial projects, thereby perpetuating the idea that "dominance hierarchies, patriarchy, and violence are fixed in our nature" (Kirskey, Schuetze, and Helmreich 2). In contrast, a multispecies approach asks us to imagine a human nature that shifted historically and together with multiple webs of interspecies dependence. This involves "a mapping exercise through mindscapes and landscapes of what may count as nature in certain global/local struggles" (Haraway, "The Promises of Monsters" 295). And inasmuch as the physical and the imagined are inextricably entangled here, in what Haraway calls "a relentless artifactualism that forbids any direct si(gh)tings of nature," such mapping assumes the form of an allegorical journey (295). Its ultimate purpose is to create not effects of distance "but effects of connection, of embodiment, and of responsibility for an imagined elsewhere that we may learn to see and build here" (295).

Due to their gender, ecological, and decolonizing concerns, many modern fairy tales offer us plenty of journeys through biocultural borderlands to think with *artifactually*. The complex entanglements of humans and nonhumans across their magical terrains bring our attention to problematic interspecies arrangements that are often taken for granted in established Western narratives of history, empire, masculinity, and femininity. By unsettling such narratives, fairy tales may offer glimpses into alternative forms of livability "in multispecies alliance, across the killing divisions of nature [and] culture" (Haraway, *Staying with the Trouble* 118). In the next section I shall illustrate the potentialities of this approach through the discussion of a modern fairy tale by Angela Carter.

2. Vegetable Transmutations: Multispecies Entanglements in Angela Carter's "Penetrating to the Heart of the Forest"

> I never believe that I'm writing about the search for self. I've never believed that the self is like a mythical beast which has to be trapped and returned, so that you can become whole again. I'm talking about the negotiations we have to make to discover any kind of reality. I tend to think it's the world we're looking for in the forest.
>
> Angela Carter, Interview, 1992 (qtd. in Gordon xiii)

"Penetrating to the Heart of the Forest," published in the 1974 short-fiction collection *Fireworks* (though likely written some years earlier, between 1970 and 1973), is not among Carter's most celebrated tales. Unlike the majority of the stories collected in *The Bloody Chamber*, it does not re-create any immediately recognizable classical fairy tale, though it is composed of an array of fragments that allude to fairy-tale themes, motifs, settings, and symbols, alongside many other intertexts. The theme of abandoned, neglected children and the journeys they undertake for survival figures prominently and evokes classic fairy tales such as "Ninnillo and Nennella," "The Juniper Tree," and, most notably, "Hansel and Gretel." Hence, "Penetrating to the Heart of the Forest" fits Cristina Bacchilega's comprehensive definition of the fairy-tale adaptation as a weaving together of multiple texts across a range of genres, languages, critical discourses, and cultural practices in an intertextual dialogue that becomes part of an ever-expanding "fairy-tale web" (*Fairy Tales Transformed?* 18).

In their introduction to *Angela Carter and the Fairy Tale* (2001), editors Danielle Roemer and Cristina Bacchilega usefully summarize "Penetrating to the Heart of the Forest" as "a tale of inverted biblical allusion and dark wonder in which Hansel- and Gretel-like children journey into a marvel-filled forest with mystery/knowledge/danger at its center" (9). This is one of Carter's tales, it could be argued, that most explicitly revolves around the forest as the liminal place where her protagonists go when they leave home in order to be radically challenged and transformed, and from whence they emerge—or where they decide to stay—with a new perception of the world. "The Werewolf" and its companion piece "The Company of Wolves" (both included in *The Bloody Chamber*) readily spring to mind as two other notable examples in Carter's short fiction. In these tales, the child protagonist enters the forest and eventually chooses to stay there, in her grandmother's house, seemingly content with her newfound feral identity. It is my contention, however, that the relevant genealogy of "Penetrating to the Heart of the Forest" can be traced back to Carter's 1969 novel *Heroes and Villains*, in which the domestic setting is radically rejected in favor of a fearless entry into "the unguessable forest" by the protagonist Marianne (6). Indeed, the novel seems to have provided a testing ground for Carter to explore ideas that she would resume and develop in her forest tale: "she conceived it as another version of the Fall (for a while, she flirted with calling it *Adam and Eve at the End of the World*) as well as an attempt to cross-fertilise Jean-Jacques Rousseau & Henri Rousseau," as Edmund Gordon explains in his recent biography of Carter (119). She researched the novel painstakingly, Gordon adds, "anchoring the fantasy to solid facts: . . . [she] read books about tribal societies, snakebites, midwifery and witchcraft" (120). It is thus no small wonder that the novel is permeated by uncannily lush vegetal imagery that will resurface, with a vengeance, in "Penetrating to the Heart of the Forest."

With these ideas in mind, I would now like to pursue the worldly implications of leaving home for the forest in the direction of the multispecies concerns outlined in the previous section. Accordingly, my discussion will draw on anthropological perspectives that highlight how the multiple linkages among men, women, and plants often work as "mechanisms to conceive of and structure social relations" (Dove 2011), with a view to understanding the ecological import of such relations for Carter's fairy-tale adaptation. Against the grain of dominant readings that tend to foreground the ironic and parodic dimensions of Carter's intertextuality, I shall argue that "Penetrating to the Heart of the Forest" can be read as an allegorical narrative of ecological recuperation from the damages of a colonial history, taking the shape of a journey through three biocultural borderlands: the plantation, the garden, and the forest. This narrative arc compels us to consider the different modes of interspecies entanglement that each borderland entails and interrogates, as well their ultimate significance for reimagining less damaging forms of livability through the power of enchantment. In my reading, I will alternate passages from Carter's tale with critical commentary.

The Plantation

The tale opens with an idyllic community whose verdant isolation stems from past tribulations:

> The region was like an abandoned flower bowl, filled to overflowing with green, living things; and protected on all sides by the ferocious barricades of the mountains, those lovely reaches of the forest lay so far inland the inhabitants believed the name, Ocean, that of a man in another country.... They built neither roads nor towns; in every respect like Candide, especially that of past ill-fortune, all they did now was to cultivate their gardens. (Carter, *Burning Your Boats* 58)

History enters the narrative when we learn that the region's inhabitants are the descendants of runaway plantation slaves, who, vowing never to relive the insults of their masters, had rebuilt a village in the groves skirting a forest. Forbidding themselves any dreams of exploration, they conjured a taboo in the shape of "a mythic and malign tree within the forest, a tree the image of the Upas Tree of Java whose very shadow was murderous, a tree that exuded a virulent sweat of poison from its moist bark and whose fruits could have nourished with death an entire tribe." This reassured the woodlanders "it was safest to be stay-at-home," even though they knew well that "such a tree did not exist" (59).

It is worth unraveling the colonial intertext at work here, for it suggests, in my view, the true source of the woodlanders' anxiety—the "ghost" of the plantation and the toxic natural-cultural assemblages it had bred:

> They had brought with them as a relic of their former life only the French their former owners had branded on their tongues, though certain residual, birdlike flutings of forgotten African dialects put unexpected cadences in their speech and, with the years, they had fashioned an arboreal argot of their own. . . . But such bloodstained ghosts could not survive in sunshine and fresh air and emigrated from the village in a body, to live only the ambiguous lie of horned rumours in the woods, becoming at last no more than shapes with undefinable outlines who lurked, perhaps, in the green deeps, until, at last, one of the shadows modulated imperceptibly into the actual shape of a tree. (Carter, *Burning Your Boats* 58)

The poisonous tree embodies, then, the human rapacious relationships with the forest that unfold in plantation contact zones. The slave plantation system was, Donna Haraway reminds us, "the model and motor for the carbon-greedy machine-based factory system that is often cited as an inflection point for the Anthropocene." And its nefarious interspecies entanglements continue, with ever-greater ferocity, "in globalized meat production, monocrop agribusiness, and immense substitutions of crops like oil palm for multispecies forests and their products that sustain human and nonhuman critters alike" ("Anthropocene, Capitalocene, Plantationocene, Cthulucene" 162).

As the ghosts of the colonial plantation continue to haunt so many of our contemporary landscapes and ways of living, it is important to understand in more depth its manifold eco-political entanglements. Plantations are, according to Anna Tsing, those ecological simplifications through which plants and humans are transformed into resources and future assets, by being forcefully removed from their lifeworlds: plants are disentangled from the intricate webs that connect them to other species and put at the service of monocultures, thus opening the door to the proliferation of virulent fungal pathogens. Humans, in turn, are disentangled from their local social ties through slavery, indenture, and conquest, leaving them with no routes for escape ("A Feminist Approach" 00:09:40–00:10:40). Plantations are therefore machines of replication devoted to purification and the production of the same. They fueled European conquest and development, making navies, science, and industrialization possible, but also inducing a cascade of changes that would have momentous ecological and social consequences. Tsing points to the proliferation of sugar cane plantations between the seventeenth and the nineteenth centuries as a paradigmatic example:

> Slaves were sent from West Africa to the New World. Contracted coolie labour from India and China moved into the Pacific. Peasants were conquered and coerced in the Indies. And in forging a new antagonism to plantation plants, humans changed the very nature of species being. Elites entrenched their sense of autonomy from other species; they were masters not lovers of nonhuman beings, the species Others who came to define human self-making. But for planters this was only possible to the extent that human subspecies were formulated and enforced: Someone had to work the cane. Biology came to signify the difference between free owners and coerced labour. Coloured people worked the cane; white people owned and managed it. No racial laws or ideals could stop miscegenation, but they could guarantee that only those of the white race could inherit property. Racial divisions were produced and reproduced in each dowered marriage and inheritance. ("Unruly Edges" 148–49)

By dividing us firmly into races, plantations also remade the very nature of human species being. And the gender consequences of this were no less momentous, with women assuming a central role in the home as agents of racial hygiene. Again, Tsing's commentary deserves ample citation:

> In the plantation zones, with their unsettled mixtures of native and foreign, free, bound, and enslaved, wild and tame, disease and plenty, things could so easily go awry. Here white women became responsible for maintaining the boundaries of homes, families, species, and the white race. . . . They became models of species and subspecies alienation. ("Unruly Edges" 149–50)

With the fetishization of the home as a space of purity and interdependence, the expected boundaries of affect became circumscribed by the domestic; extradomestic intimacies, whether within or between species, would increasingly appear as archaic fantasies or passing affairs, Tsing adds. Such are the affective webs of domestication and alienation in which humans have entangled themselves: "love is just not expected outside family walls. Within the family, other species can be accepted; pets are models for family devotion. But the model of the loving and beloved pet does not spread love; it holds it tight inside the family" (Tsing, "Unruly Edges" 150). Indeed, the bourgeois home may not be the best idea for multispecies life on earth.

It is no wonder that disaffected humans have striven to find alternative modes of livability ever since—and such appears to be the case with the woodlanders in Carter's tale. In stark opposition to what they perceive as the brutally rapacious, malevolent nature of the forest linked to the human desire for exploitation, they find a more hospitable bountifulness at its margins, where "a profusion of flowers grew all around them, so many flowers that the straw-thatched villages looked like inhabited gardens" (*Burning Your Boats* 59). They cultivate just enough vegetables to fulfil their simple dietary needs, and grow fruits that they dry, candy, and preserve in honey; they then sell this produce to passing travelers in exchange for the colorful fabrics with which they make their clothes.

This *locus amoenus* seems far removed from the hyperdomesticated world of the colonial plantation. The woodlanders are careful to avoid domesticating their plants too forcefully: "they needed nothing more than a few flowers before they felt their graceful toilets were complete" (59). One day, however, a voyaging botanist with his own dream of plenty brings a new layer of domestication to this vegetal bountifulness.

The Garden

> The soil was of such amazing richness and the flora proliferated in such luxuriance that when Dubois the botanist came over the pass on his donkey, he looked down on that paradisial landscape and exclaimed: "Dear God! It is as if Adam had opened to the public!" (Carter, *Burning Your Boats* 59)

Voyaging botanists like Dubois were liminal figures in the imperial scheme of things. On the one hand, "their inventories, classifications, and transplantations were the vanguard and in some cases the 'instruments' of European order" (Schiebinger 11), laying their own peculiar grid of reason over nature. Through these tools, they appropriated nature's vegetal exuberance to the benefit of Europe's capitalist and industrialist projects. On the other hand, a different order of dreams stirred in botanists: the search for relics of worlds on the verge of disappearance, which they saw as the last remaining outposts of Eden. As Hecht and Cockburn explain, many botanists' dreams corresponded to "Rousseau's view of the noble savage in harmonious relation with his brethren and nature in a world of primal innocence beyond the taint of commerce, industry and history," and in which "tropical exuberance [honored] moral perfection" (10–11).

Jean-Jacques Rousseau himself had been a keen botanist in the final years of his life. During his persecution and exile, he sought solace in the flowers and plants that inhabited his immediate surroundings, and wrote what was to become one of the most widely read eighteenth-century texts on botany, *Lettres élementaires sur la botanique* (George 5). Published posthumously in 1782, this little book is based on a series of letters that Rousseau had written to his friend Madelaine Catherine Delessert, the owner of a famous herbarium and botanical library. When Rousseau was in exile, Delessert had asked for his help in introducing her daughter, Marguerite-Madelaine, to botany. Theresa Kelley shrewdly remarks that the book's "rhetorical structure implies a clear hierarchy in which men teach botany, women learn it and then (at best) teach their children" (93). Kelley adds a further intriguing note: "Sophie, the intended spouse for Rousseau's *Émile*, is taught only enough to make her dependent on his greater understanding" (94).

All of these colonial, scientific, and romantic intertexts are at work in the outlook that Dubois brings on the woodlanders' community. He, too, seeks solace "in a return to the flowering wilderness" (*Burning Your Boats* 59). The frail, dark-eyed Portuguese wife he had married in a colonial outpost of "awesome respectability" in Brazil died young, giving him "two children at one birth before she died" (59). With his children, Dubois is intent on the Rousseauist eco-pedagogical project of becoming "'*homo silvester*, men of the woods," which he considers "'by far superior to the precocious and destructive species *homo sapiens*—knowing man. Knowing man, indeed; what more than nature does man need to know?'" (61).

But Dubois's vision of a nature freed entirely from man's despoiling hand turns out to be no mode of livability either. It symbolizes a double impulse that was to have tremendous consequences for the tropical world: a desire to turn its nature into a therapeutic "Eden under glass," on one side, and a pure scientific outlook that treated it as an unsullied laboratory for taxonomic classification, on the other side. Hecht and Cockburn pithily summarize those consequences: "pillage at one extreme and at the other a pastoralism that can be as anti-human as any bulldozer" (15). The garden conceived in this way is, not unlike the plantation, a figure of domestication, wrestling things from their entanglements with the living world and turning them into inert matter available for colonial appropriation—be it scientific or aesthetic.[4] The margins of the forest, for the sake of which Dubois had "closed the doors of his heart," "were to him a remarkable book it would take all the years that remained to him to learn to read" (*Burning Your Boats* 60).

In *Storming the Gates of Paradise*, Rebecca Solnit elaborates on why the very notion of Eden is the problem here:

> Eden stands as the idea of nature as it should be rather than as it is, and in an attempt to make a garden resemble Eden, the gardener wrestles the garden away from resembling nature—nature, that is, as the uncultivated expanses around it, the patterns that would assert themselves without interference. (254)

Hence Dubois's Garden of Eden is definitely not a viable form of multispecies livability. The woodland critters that gather around him appear as rather too gentle and tamed: "the birds and beasts showed no fear of him. Painted magpies perched reflectively on his shoulder . . . while fox cubs rolled in play around his feet and even learned to nose in his capacious pockets for cookies" (*Burning Your Boats* 60). The narrator describes this in terms of "a certain radiant inhumanity which sprang from a benign indifference towards by far the greatest part of mankind—towards all those who were not beautiful, gentle and, by nature, kind" (60–61). This model of interspecies relationality does not spread affect either, instead holding it tight inside the confines of the garden.

Dubois's children, left to their own devices by their emotionally remote father, immerse themselves in "the green world [that] took them for its own" (61), in a state of undifferentiated sexual innocence: "they resembled one another so closely each could have used the other as a mirror and almost seemed to be different aspects of the same person" (61). But the bonds they are forming with the green world are radically different from their father's "erudite botanizing" (63)—from his intellectual conquest and ordering of the natural world. As the children's knowledge of the environment grows in awareness and intimacy, they become discontented with the idea of home Dubois had inculcated in them: "they found out their home did not lie at the heart of the forest but only somewhere in its green suburbs" (62). In reality, as the children begin their journey into the heart of the forest, the very word *home* becomes tainted with a "faint, warm claustrophobia" (63). We can already foresee here a very different ending from that of most versions of "Hansel and Gretel," in which the children return home to live with their father, despite what appears to be his outrageous neglect.

The Forest

> In their father's books they found references to the Antiar or Antshar of the Indo-Malay archipelago, the *antiaris toxicaria* whose milky juice contains a most potent poison, like the quintessence of belladonna. But their reason told them that not even the most intrepid migratory bird could have brought the sticky seeds on its feet to cast them down here in these land-locked valleys far from Java. They did not believe the wicked tree could exist in this hemisphere; and yet they were curious. But they were not afraid. (*Burning Your Boats* 62)

A cascade of metamorphoses unfolds as Madeline and Emile—we now learn their names—proceed on their sylvan journey. The forest increasingly teems with myriads of animal and vegetal life forms that are unabashedly sexual: the trees grow "in shapes of a feminine slightness and grace" (63); a water lily unfurls "its close circle of petals with an audible snap," to display "a set of white, perfect fangs" (63–64), biting Madeline. The children's perception of themselves undergoes a corresponding sexual shift: "this new awareness of one another's shapes and outlines had made them less twinned, less indistinguishable from one another" (65). Feminist readings have persuasively approached these transformations through psychoanalytical lenses. Hope Jennings, for example, reads in the children's metamorphosis an overturning of the Fall myth and the phallogocentric order that provides an alternative discourse of sexual difference predicated on a reciprocal relationship between the sexes (305–31). Here, however, I want to explore a non-identitarian, nonpsychoanalytic interpretation; a *worldly* reading open to other ways of imagining that do not necessarily hinge on the hierarchy-free critical imaginary that has dominated Eurocentric approaches.

One motif that runs through "Penetrating into the Heart of the Forest" is the characters' changing perception of the nature—toxic or beneficial—of the tree at the center of the forest. If the imagined toxic tree can be read as an embodiment of a particularly problematic set of social relations, it can also be read at a more cosmological level. The notion that the physical shape of a plant is a clue to its likely impact on humans was one of the key principles informing prescientific medicine—including the medicinal culture of many indigenous peoples—as well as an array of plant mythology and folklore. The naturalist Richard Mabey argues that such a system, known as "sympathetic magic:"[5]

> is really part of a more complex view of natural creation, in which all components are connected and have resonances with other components of a similar form or seasonal rhythm or position in a cosmological hierarchy. If you see the world as a connected whole, then exterior resemblances may indicate similarity in internal processes and effects. (144–45)

This system and its hierarchies of sentient matter permeate the classic European fairy-tale tradition, whose magic, in Marina Warner's phrasing, "works along lines closer to magnetism and the pull of the tides or the silence of eclipse because it reflects a vision of correspondences that developed in early modern society" (*Once Upon a Time* 23).

Richard Mabey's aim, however, is to take sympathetic magic and the intense awareness of the physical environment it involves in a distinctly non-Eurocentric direction. Understanding it requires yet another brief detour, but one that ultimately illuminates the point I am attempting to make in relation to Carter's tale. Drawing on the research by Gerardo Reichel-Dolmatoff, an anthropologist who spent much of his life working with the Tukano Indians in north-west Amazonia, Mabey draws attention to the way in which the Tukano find vegetal cures for minor illnesses "by simply entering the forest, while concentrating acutely on sounds, odour, colours, the behaviour of insects and the temperatures of different layers of vegetation" (153). According to Reichel-Dolmatoff's findings, the Tukano see themselves as participating in the cosmos and their immediate forest environment through an energy circuit that includes all plants and animals, alongside all sense data. Thus, in their worldview, "the literal and the metaphorical are inseparable," and so they are able to see "the forest [as] a memory device in which all sensory perceptions are registered and trigger associations, awaken memories which help solve personal conflicts" (qtd. in Mabey 153).

This is an instantiation of what Eduardo Kohn, another anthropologist who spent years working with the Runa people in the Ecuadorian Amazonia, calls "enchantment." Among the Runa, Kohn found a forest "ecology of selves"—an entanglement of human and nonhuman *souls* configuring an enchanted realm that is reducible neither to the forest nor to the cultures and histories of the humans who relate to it (217). In this way of seeing, "souls emerge relationally in interaction with other selves in ways that blur the boundaries we normally recognize among kinds of being." And beings possess souls, Kohn explains, "because of their abilities 'to become aware of,' to notice those beings that stand in relation to them," including in a relation of predation (106). An enchanted forest is therefore an animate world "that reaches well beyond the human but which also catches up in its tendrils the detritus of so many all-too-human pasts" (23).

Such, too, is the forest to whose heart Madeline and Emile finally penetrate, through an ever-growing attention to the sights, scents, sounds, and rhythms of the myriad critters dwelling there—discrete critters who fully reciprocate their attention:

> Ferns uncurled as they watched, revealing fronded fringes containing innumerable, tiny, shining eyes glittering like brilliants where the ranks of seeds should have been. A vine was covered with slumbrous, purple flowers that, as they passed, sang out in a rich contralto with all the voluptuous wildness of flamenco—and then fell silent. (*Burning Your Boats* 66)

The progression through the forest is described in terms of a "vegetable transmutation, for it contained nothing that was not marvellous" (65).

The culminating marvel of this forest is the vision of a flower- and fruit-bearing tree whose magic contours evoke the "tree of life" or "world tree" at the center of many creation myths and models of the universe, from the Buddhist Tree of Wisdom to the Norse Yggdrasil. But it is a tree that is also rooted in the real ecology of the forest: a focal point of transmutation of the sun's energy—"all the unripe suns in the world were sleeping on the tree until a multiple, universal dawning should wake them all in splendour"

(*Burning Your Boats* 66)—and of multiple reciprocal entanglements with other sylvan beings. And yet, this tree bears as well in its fruit the marks of previous appropriative human histories: "in the rind, set squarely in the middle of each faintly flushed cheek, was a curious formation—a round set of serrated indentations exactly resembling the marks of a bite made by the teeth of a hungry man" (66). It is a riddle, a rainforest Sphinx of sorts.

The children's response to the presence of the tree—Madeline/Eve eating its fruit first then offering it to Emile/Adam—leads to a rather too predictable and ecologically grim conclusion for the tale if we read it only in relation to its biblical intertext. Indeed, the Genesis story bodes ill not just for women and plants but for multispecies livability in general, as God decrees plants as being in existence solely as food for animals and humans, thereby reiterating a natural hierarchy of value in the world that was already at work in the philosophies of Plato and Aristotle (Hall 61). For Anne Primavesi, it is this very drive toward hierarchical value-ordering that undergirds "the Christian binary codes of heavenly/earthly; sacred/secular; human/animal; male/female" (129)—and, I should add, the binaries animal/plant and human/plant. Searching for another intertextual path out of this conundrum is thus in order:

> [Madeline] sprang towards the exquisite, odoriferous tree which, at that moment, suffused in a failing yet hallucinatory light the tone and intensity of liquefied amber, seemed to her brother a perfect equivalent of his sister's amazing beauty.... The dark pool reflected her darkly, like an antique mirror. She raised her hand to part the leaves in search of a ripe fruit but the greenish skin seemed to warm and glow under her fingers.... Her enormous eyes were lit like nocturnal flowers that had been waiting only for this special night to open.... (*Burning Your Boats* 66–67)

Multispecies ethnographer Deborah Bird Rose comes to my aid for a more ecologically grounded interpretation of this intriguing passage, in which woman and tree lure each other in a dance of reciprocal capture. Inspired by her long-term research with Aboriginal peoples in Australia, Rose sees in such acts of reciprocal capture, of encounter and transformation, an aesthetic of "shimmer"—that is, "things that appeal to the senses, things that evoke or capture feelings and responses . . . lures that both entice one's attention and offer rewards." It is a brilliance—or enchantment, as a fairy-tale scholar would perhaps rephrase it—that allows us, or brings us, "into the experience of being part of a vibrant and vibrating world" (G53). Most importantly, it reminds us that enchantment is not a uniquely human trait. The orchestration of desire, the impulse to attract through elaborate aesthetic display, Rose suggests, is the way of life in all its forms—and this cannot but dislodge humans from their pedestal, over and above the natural world.

To be sure, since the nineteenth century these interspecies intimacies have been explained away by Darwinian and neo-Darwinian hardliners as nothing but biological deception and exploitation of the insect by the plant. And as I discussed at length in the previous section, such misconceptions came to underpin numerous artistic representations of plant horror associating rapacious plants and feminine behavior, with some striking ramifications reaching fairy-tale landscapes. In recent years, however, as more feminist theorists have turned to biology—and, notably, to a revised Darwin—in order to theorize difference and materiality, as well the kinship among humans, animals, plants, bacteria, and other organisms, far more nuanced ecological perspectives attuned to affect and creativity have begun to emerge. This essay has discussed their import for an ecological reorientation of fairy-tale scholarship, by engaging the insights of multispecies feminist theorists such as Anna Tsing and Donna Haraway in a reading of Angela Carter's "Penetrating to the Heart of the Forest."

Regrettably, Carter herself did not pursue the eco-political possibilities opened up by this tale, so as to impart a viable shape to the feminist historical materialism she endorsed (Dimovitz 9). In the novel *The Infernal Desires Machines of Doctor Hoffman* (1972), as well as in the subsequent book-length essay *The Sadeian Woman* (1979), Carter turns to Sade and surrealism to tear apart, with gusto, a vast and disturbing parade of images of woman-plant horror, without nevertheless offering "an alternative vision of how to live" outside the patriarchal logic whence such imagery emanates, as Scott Dimovitz remarks (136). And if this substantiates Camille Paglia's polemical dictum, in *Sexual Personae*, that "every road from Rousseau leads to Sade" (14), at least in "Penetrating to the Heart of the Forest" Carter may have momentarily entertained the possibility of another road leading from there to a more hopeful elsewhere.

Environmental degradation fueled by industrial engineering, militaristic and neocolonial projects continues to spread around the world with increasing virulence, threatening the continuing multispecies livability of the earth. In this climate, it does matter indeed "what stories tell stories" (Haraway, *Staying with the Trouble* 35). By teasing out some of the complex entanglements of capitalism, coloniality, and ideational domesticities that twine together the biocultural borderlands where humans and nonhumans meet in the modern fairy tale, I hope to have illustrated the potentialities of an ecologically oriented reading to bring to the fore alternative stories and arts of living on our damaged planet that do not hinge on too avid an ideal of domestication of women, plants, and other living beings.

Acknowledgments

The author would like to thank Martine Hennard Dutheil de la Rochère, Cristina Bacchilega, and the editors for their excellent comments on earlier versions of this manuscript.

Notes

1. The definition of "biocultural borderlands" as "places where species meet" has been proposed by multispecies ethnographers Kirskey, Schuetze, and Helmreich (13), and draws on the thinking of two feminist cultural theorists, Gloria Anzaldúa and Donna Haraway. Anzaldúa defines "borderlands" as the critical spaces that arise when divergent discourses of dominance intersect and compete in a contested hierarchy; they have no typical citizens, and the experiences there undermine the safe grounds of cultural certainty and essential identity. For Haraway, the meeting of species refers to those "lively knottings"

that tie together the world we inhabit, including the entwining of human and nonhuman critters (*When Species Meet* vii), which she calls "companion species:" those life forms with whom we are in an "ongoing becoming with" (16). Haraway's notion of "contact zones" as "world-making entanglements" (4) is akin to that of "biocultural borderlands."

2. Disney fairy-tale film productions have relentlessly exploited these woman-plant associations to spectacular effect. A striking example is the haunted forest scene in *Snow White and the Seven Dwarfs* (1937), in which gnarled trees with the hands and faces of old witches assail a panic-stricken Snow White. Another example is the thorns scene in *Sleeping Beauty* (1959), in which Maleficent conjures a formidable wall of thorns to prevent the Prince from reaching the castle where the slumbering Princess lies. This wall of thorns acquires even more spectacular contours in Disney's most recent take on the tale, *Maleficent* (2014).

3. In *Friction*, Anna Tsing remarks that this notion of forests as empty and wild, and available for elite manipulation, was also an integral part of the repertoire of colonial scientists in their quest to understand the environment at the peripheries of European empire. Such forests "were a key component of the discovery of this environmental form of 'nature,' which, these scientists learned, could be used for European profit but also destroyed beyond repair" (*Friction* 201).

4. The colonial plantation and the imperial botanical garden as biocultural borderlands partake of what postcolonial critics call "the coloniality of nature." Arturo Escobar has usefully summarized its main features in the following terms:

> Classification into hierarchies ("ethnological reason"), with nonmoderns, primitives, and nature at the bottom of the scale; essentialized views of nature as being outside the human domain; the subordination of the body and nature to the mind (Judeo-Christian traditions; mechanistic science; modern phallogocentrism); seeing the products of the earth as the products of labor only, hence subordinating nature to human-driven markets; locating certain natures (colonial and third world natures, women's bodies, dark bodies) outside of the totality of the male Eurocentric world; the subalternization of all other articulations of biology and history to modern regimes, particularly those that enact a continuity between the natural, human, and supernatural worlds—or between being, knowing, and doing. (121)

5. The concept of sympathetic magic was first introduced in the West by Marcel Mauss in 1902 and subsequently developed by James Frazer in *The Golden Bough* in 1922. It rests on the idea that "things act on each other at a distance through a secret sympathy, the impulse being transmitted from one to the other by means of what we may conceive as a kind of invisible ether" (Frazer 12). Mauss emphasized, however, that "magical contagion is not only an ideal which is limited to the invisible world. It may be concrete, material, and in every way similar to physical contagion" (82).

Works Cited

Anzaldúa, Gloria. *Borderlands/La Frontera: The New Mestiza*. Aunt Lute Books, 1987.

Appadurai, Arjun. *Modernity at Large: Cultural Dimensions of Globalization*. Minnesota University Press, 1996.

Bacchilega, Cristina. *Fairy Tales Transformed? Twenty-First-Century Adaptations and the Politics of Wonder*. Wayne State University Press, 2013.

Bennett, Jane. *Vibrant Matter: A Political Ecology of Things*. Duke University Press, 2010.

Carter, Angela. *Burning Your Boats: The Collected Short Stories*. Penguin, 1995.

———. *Heroes and Villains*. 1969. Penguin, 2011.

———. *The Infernal Desire Machines of Doctor Hoffman*. 1972. Penguin, 1994.

———. *The Sadeian Woman: An Exercise in Cultural History*. Virago, 1979.

Desblache, Lucile. "Animal Leaders and Helpers: From the Classical Tales of Charles Perrault to the Postmodern Fables of Angela Carter and Patrick Chamoiseau." *Journal of Romance Studies*, vol. 11, no. 2, Summer 2011, pp. 75–87.

Dijkstra, Bram. *Idols of Perversity: Fantasies of Feminine Evil in Fin-de-Siècle Culture*. Oxford University Press, 1986.

Dimovitz, Scott A. *Angela Carter: Surrealist, Psychologist, Moral Pornographer*. Routledge, 2016.

Dove, Michael R. *The Banana Tree at the Gate: A History of Marginal Peoples and Global Markets in Borneo*. Yale University Press, 2011.

Dugan, Frank M. "Fungi, Folkways and Fairy Tales: Mushrooms & Mildews in Stories, Remedies & Rituals, from Oberon to the Internet." *North American Fungi*, vol. 3, no. 7, 2008, pp. 23–72.

Endersby, Jim. "Deceived by Orchids: Sex, Science, Fiction, and Darwin." *British Journal for the History of Science*, vol. 49, no. 2, 2016, pp. 205–29.

Escobar, Arturo. *Territories of Difference: Place, Movements, Life, Redes*. Duke University Press, 2008.

Frazer, James George. *The Golden Bough: A Study in Magic and Religion*. 1922. Palgrave Macmillan, 1990.

George, Sam. *Botany, Sexuality and Women's Writing 1760–1830*. Manchester University Press, 2007.

Gordon, Edmund. *The Invention of Angela Carter: A Biography*. Chatto & Windus, 2016.

Hall, Matthew. *Plants as Persons: A Philosophical Botany*. State University of New York Press, 2011.

Haraway, Donna J. "Anthropocene, Capitalocene, Plantationocene, Chthulucene: Making Kin." *Environmental Humanities*, vol. 6, 2015, pp. 159–65.

———. "The Promises of Monsters: A Regenerative Politics for Inappropriate/d Others." *Cultural Studies*, edited by Lawrence Grossberg and Paula A. Treichler, Routledge, 1992, pp. 295–337.

———. *Staying with the Trouble: Making Kin in the Cthulucene*. Duke University Press, 2016.

———. *When Species Meet*. University of Minnesota Press, 2008.

Harrison, Robert Pogue. *Forests: The Shadow of Civilization*. University of Chicago Press, 1992.

Hecht, Susanna, and Alexander Cockburn. *The Fate of the Forest: Developers, Destroyers, and Defenders of the Amazon*. Updated ed., University of Chicago Press, 2010.

Howard, Patricia L. Preface. *Women & Plants: Gender Relations in Biodiversity Management and Conservation*, edited by Patricia L. Howard, Zed Books, pp. xvi–xx.

Hustak, Carla, and Natasha Myers. "Involuntary Momentum: Affective Ecologies and the Sciences of Plant/Insect Encounters." *difference: A Journal of Feminist Cultural Studies*, vol. 15, no. 3, 2012, pp. 74–118.

Jennings, Hope. "Genesis and Gender: The Word, the Flesh, and the Fortunate Fall in 'Peter and the Wolf' and 'Penetrating to the Heart of the Forest.'" *Angela Carter: New Critical Readings*, edited by Sonya Andermahr and Lawrence Philips, Continuum, 2012, pp. 315–21.

Keetley, Dawn. "Introduction: Six Theses on Plant Horror; or, Why are Plants Horrifying?" *Plant Horror: Approaches to the Monstrous Vegetal in Fiction and Film*, edited by Dawn Keetley and Angela Tenga, Palgrave Macmillan, 2016, pp. 1–30.

Kelley, Theresa M. *Clandestine Marriage: Botany and Romantic Culture*. John Hopkins University Press, 2012.

Kirskey, Eben, Craig Schuetze, and Stefan Helmreich. "Introduction: Tactics of Multispecies Ethnography." *The Multispecies Salon*, edited by Eben Kirskey, Duke University Press, 2014, pp. 1–24.

Kohn, Eduardo. *How Forests Think: Toward an Anthropology beyond the Human*. University of California Press, 2013.

Mabey, Richard. *The Cabaret of Plants: Forty Thousand Years of Plant Life and the Human Imagination*. 2015. W. W. Norton, 2016.

Maitland, Sara. *Gossip from the Forest: The Tangled Roots of Our Forests and Fairy Tales*. Granta, 2012.

Marder, Michael. "For a Phytocentrism to Come" *Environmental Philosophy*, vol. 11, no. 2, Fall 2014, pp. 237–52.

Mauss, Marcel. *A General Theory of Magic*. 1902. Routledge, 1972.

Murai, Mayako. *From Dog Bridegroom to Wolf Girl: Contemporary Fairy-Tale Adaptations in Conversation with the West*. Wayne State University Press, 2015.

Paglia, Camille. *Sexual Personae: Art and Decadence from Nefertiti to Emily Dickinson*. Yale University Press, 1990.

Primavesi, Anne. "Ecology and Christian Hierarchy." *Women as Sacred Custodians of the Earth? Women Spirituality and the Environment*, edited by Alaine Low and Soraya Tremayne, Berghahn, 2001, pp. 121–41.

Roemer, Danielle M., and Cristina Bacchilega. Introduction. *Angela Carter and the Fairy Tale*, edited by Danielle M. Roemer and Cristina Bacchilega, Wayne State University Press, 2001, pp. 7–25.

Rose, Deborah Bird. "Shimmer: When All You Love Is Being Trashed." *Arts of Living on a Damaged Planet,* edited by Anna Tsing, Heather Swanson, Elaine Gan, and Nils Bubandt, Minnesota University Press, 2017, G51–G61.

Sandilands, Catriona. "Fear of a Queer Plant?" *GLQ: A Journal of Lesbian and Gay Studies*, vol. 23, no. 3, 2017, pp. 419–29.

Schama, Simon. *Landscape and Memory*. HarperCollins, 1995.

Schiebinger, Lorna. *Plants and Empire: Colonial Bioprospecting in the Atlantic World*. Harvard University Press, 2004.

Seifert, Lewis. "Animal-Human Hybridity in d'Aulnoy's 'Babiole' and 'Prince Wild Boar.'" *Marvels & Tales*, vol. 25, no. 2, 2011, pp. 244–60.

Solnit, Rebecca. *Storming the Gates of Paradise: Landscapes for Politics*. University of California Press, 2007.

Tatar, Maria, editor. *The Annotated Classic Fairy Tales*. W. W. Norton, 2002.

Tsing, Anna Lowenhaupt. "A Feminist Approach to the Anthropocene: Earth Stalked by Man." *YouTube*, uploaded by Barnard Center for Research on Women, 18 Dec. 2015, youtube.com/watch?v=ps8J6a7g_BA.

———. *Friction: An Ethnography of Global Connection*. Princeton University Press, 2004.

———. "Unruly Edges: Mushrooms as Companion Species." *Environmental Humanities*, vol. 1, 2012, pp. 141–54.

Warner, Marina. *From the Beast to the Blonde: On Fairy Tales and their Tellers*. 1994. Vintage, 1995.

———. *Once upon a Time: A Short History of Fairy Tale*. Oxford University Press, 2014.

Zipes, Jack. *The Brothers Grimm: From Enchanted Forests to the Modern World*. 2nd ed. Palgrave Macmillan, 2002.

———. *The Enchanted Screen: The Unknown History of Fairy-Tale Films*. Routledge, 2011.

Contributors

CRISTINA BACCHILEGA is professor of English at the University of Hawaiʻi at Mānoa. She is the author of *Fairy Tales Transformed? Twenty-First-Century Adaptations and the Politics of Wonder* (2013), *Legendary Hawaii and the Politics of Place* (2007), and *Postmodern Fairy Tales: Gender and Narrative Strategies* (1997) and coeditor with Marie Alohalani Brown of *The Penguin Book of Mermaids* (2019). With Anne E. Duggan, she coedits *Marvels & Tales: Journal of Fairy-Tale Studies*.

SHULI BARZILAI is professor emerita of English at the Hebrew University of Jerusalem. Author of *Lacan and the Matter of Origins* and *Tales of Bluebeard and His Wives from Late Antiquity to Postmodern Times*, she has published essays in many journals and edited collections, including *Marvels & Tales* and *The Cambridge Companion to Fairy Tales*.

MICHAEL BRODSKI is currently working on his PhD thesis on intermedial representations of childhood and child figures at the Institute of Film, Theatre and Empirical Cultural Studies at the University of Mainz, Germany, where he also works as an associate lecturer. His main research interests include cognitive film theory, Soviet and Russian cinema and culture, children's film, and intermedial representations of childhood and children's culture, as well as cinematic portrayals of remembrance.

LUCIANA CARDI is lecturer in Japanese studies and Italian language and culture at Osaka University, Japan. Her research interests include contemporary Japanese narrative, Asian American literature, fairy-tale studies, and gender studies. She has published in journals and edited volumes such as *Marvels & Tales* and *Folktales and Fairy Tales: Traditions and Texts from* *around the World* (2016). She is currently working on a book about modern and contemporary adaptations of Japanese folktales in American fiction.

LUCY FRASER is lecturer in Japanese at the University of Queensland, Australia. She teaches Japanese language and culture and researches literary and popular culture fairy-tale retellings. She is the author of *The Pleasures of Metamorphosis: Japanese and English Fairy Tale Transformations of 'The Little Mermaid'* (2017).

KUʻUALOHA HOʻOMANAWANUI is associate professor of Hawaiian literature, English Department, University of Hawaiʻi at Mānoa. She is a Native Hawaiian scholar who works extensively with nineteenth-century Hawaiian language archives and translation of traditional *moʻolelo* (stories, history, literature).

ROXANE HUGHES is an independent scholar specializing in ethnic American studies and immigrant literatures. She is the author of "Cinderella from a Cross-Cultural Perspective: Connecting East and West in Donna Jo Napoli's *Bound*," published in *Cinderella Across Cultures* (2016).

NATSUMI IKOMA (PhD, Durham) is professor at the International Christian University, Japan. Her research covers women's writing and representation of monstrous body with comparative perspectives. She recently translated Sōzō Araki's memoir of Angela Carter into English. Her current project deals with Japanese influences on gender performativity in Carter's writing.

VANESSA JOOSEN is professor of English literature and children's literature at the University of Antwerp. She is the author of *Critical and Creative Perspectives on Fairy Tales* (2011), which was given a Choice Award for Outstanding Academic Research by the American Library Association, and coeditor of *Grimms' Tales around the Globe* (together with Gillian Lathey, 2014), which won the Children's Literature Association Honor Award for Edited Book 2014.

DANIELA KATO is associate professor at the Kyoto Institute of Technology, Japan. Her research interests and publications are intermedial in orientation and revolve around landscape aesthetics, travel, and ecotranslation from gendered perspectives. She is particularly interested in exploring the interface between contemporary literature, the visual arts, and anthropology regarding multispecies ecojustice and feminist practices of creativity.

MASAFUMI MONDEN is lecturer in Japanese Studies at the University of Western Australia, specializing in Japanese fashion and culture. His first book, *Japanese Fashion Cultures* (2015), is an interdisciplinary study analyzing the relationship between fashion, culture, and identity within contemporary Japan. He is currently researching the cultural history of male fashion icons in Japan and *shōjo* culture.

NIEVES MORENO REDONDO is a research fellow in film history at the Autonomous University of Madrid. She obtained her PhD in artistic, literary and cultural studies at the Autonomous University of Madrid. She graduated in drama studies from the University of Madrid (RESAD) and in Japanese studies from the Autonomous University of Madrid, where she also holds a Master's in film history. She was a research fellow at Waseda University.

MAYAKO MURAI is professor at Kanagawa University, Japan. She is the author of *From Dog Bridegroom to Wolf Girl: Contemporary Japanese Fairy-Tale Adaptations in Conversation with the West* (2015) and is currently writing a book on fairy-tale animals in contemporary art and picture-book illustrations.

HATSUE NAKAWAKI is an award-winning Japanese novelist and an accomplished storyteller. She has also edited and retold Japanese *mukashibanashi* in *Onnanoko no mukashibanashi* (2012) and *Chā-chan no mukashibanashi* (2016). She began publishing her retellings of fairy tales in the eighty-volume series *Hajimete no sekai meisaku ehon* [Picture Book Classics: A Child's First Collection] (2018–). Her most recent novel is *Kami no shima no kodomotachi* [Children on the Island of Gods] (2019).

Katsuhiko Suganuma is lecturer in the School of Humanities at the University of Tasmania. He is the author of *Contact Moments: The Politics of Intercultural Desire in Japanese Male-Queer Cultures* (2012), and coeditor of *Queer Voices from Japan* (2007) and *Boys Love Manga and Beyond* (2015).

Aleksandra Szugajew is a PhD candidate at the University of Warsaw. Currently she is working on her thesis in the field of medical humanities, analyzing autobiographical texts written by doctors. Her research interests also include bioethical issues in contemporary literature, fairy-tale rewritings, and the role of music in popular culture.

Index

Abracadabra, 236–37
Adichie, Chimamanda Ngozi, 102n3
Adieu (Balzac), 180–81
adults, fairy-tale movie adaptations marketed to. *See* movie adaptations, fairy-tale
Adventures of Pinocchio, The (Collodi), 292, 293–95
aesthetical sentimentalism, 299–303
African American tradition, 27–29
age, 265–67, 280–81
  analysis in fairy-tale rewritings, 273–80
  analysis in traditional fairy tales, 267–73
  and reunion of Princess Princess, 376
age critics, 265, 270–71
ageism, 265, 266, 275
age studies, 266–71, 276–77, 279, 280
Ahmed, Sara, 372
A. I. Artificial Intelligence, 288, 292–95, 305n5
"Ain't Joking" photographs (Weems), 28
Akasaka Komachi, 363–64. *See also* Princess Princess
Alice's Adventures in Wonderland, Japanese appropriation of, 309–12, 327–29
  and devouring of foreign objects, 312–16
  and link between girls' culture and fairy tales, 322–27
  and women's literary writing for adults, 318–21
Alice Series (Nakahara), 316
Almodóvar, Pedro, 236–37
almodovarismo, 237
Altmann, Anna, 276

Amazing Asian Americans (Louie), 103n15
Amelio, Ralph, 212–13
Americanization, 27, 48. *See also* assimilation
Amewakahiko zōshi, 152
Andersen, Hans Christian, 300–301, 302–3
animal bride and bridegroom tales, 146–53
Annotated African American Folktales, The (Gates and Tatar), 27
Anzaldúa, Gloria, 405n1
Aoyama, Tomoko, 319
Appadurai, Arjun, 385
Arabic tales
  Samatar on unwittingly reproducing tropes of, 34n8
  Samatar's "The Tale of Mahliya and Mauhub and the White-Footed Gazelle," 17–22
Arab world, re-orientation to present-day horrors and wonders in, 21
Araki, Sōzō, 125, 129–31
Arisu kanginshū [*Alice's Song Collection*] (Yagawa), 319
"Arisu to iu namae" ["The Name Alice"] (Ogawa), 310–16, 322–28
Artist, The, 237–38
"Aschenputtel" (Grimm), 90
assimilation. *See also* Americanization
  hegemonic fairy tale as tool of, 30
  mo'olelo kamaha'o and resistance to, 44
Austen, Jane, 34n9

Bacchilega, Cristina
  on adapting fairy tales, 266
  on boundaries of fairy-tale genre, 2–3

on Carter's "Penetrating to the Heart of the Forest," 392
  on contemporary media literacy, 287
  on divergent social projects imagined by fairy tales, 362
  on fairy-tale films as hybrid texts, 257
  on genre mixing in fairy-tale movie adaptations, 217
  on Hawaiian fairy tales, 41
  on hybridization of fairy tale in film industry, 213
  on mirror in fairy tales, 248
  on transformative and adaptive practices of fairy tales, 353
bacterium, fairy tale compared to, 209–10
Baker, Chris Kaliko, 51–53, 54–56
Baker, Tammy Haili'ōpua, 51–53, 54–56
Ball, Katherine M., 106n30
ballet, 342–44, 352–53
Balzac, Honoré de, 180–81
Banham, WK, 214–15
Barthes, Roland, 121
Barzilai, Shuli, 267–68
Beazley, Del, 47–49, 52–54
Bell, Sophie, 293
Bennett, Jane, 384
Berger, Pablo, 256–58
  characters in *Blancanieves*, 247–51
  cultural references in *Blancanieves*, 251–56
  introduction to works of, 235–39
  overview of *Blancanieves*, 225
  plot of *Blancanieves*, 243–47
  use of *españolada* genre, 239–43
Berliner, Todd, 213

Bernstein, Robin, 291
Berusaiyu no bara [*The Rose of Versailles*] (Ikeda), 315, 340–41
Bettelheim, Bruno, 202n1
biocultural borderlands, 383–91
　defined, 384, 405–6n1
　and forest in Carter's "Penetrating to the Heart of the Forest," 400–405
　and garden in Carter's "Penetrating to the Heart of the Forest," 397–99
　and multispecies entanglements in Carter's "Penetrating to the Heart of the Forest," 391–93
　and plantation in Carter's "Penetrating to the Heart of the Forest," 393–97
black, in Māori culture, 68–69
"Black Legend, The," 240, 242
Black Lives Matter, 31
Blackwell, Su, 22–23, 25f
Blancanieves, 256–58
　Berger's approach to, 239
　characters in, 247–51
　cultural references in, 251–56
　other fairy-tale influences on, 246–47
　overview of, 225, 236
　plot of, 243–47
"Bloody Chamber, The" (Carter), 115
"Blowing the House In" tale type. *See also* "Three Little Pigs"
　Kellogg's adaptation of, 182–84
　old English ballad following, 171–72
　and teaching Modern Literary Theory course, 169–70
　and teaching poetry, 170–73
borderlands. *See* biocultural borderlands
botany, 397–98
Bourdaghs, Michael K., 378
Boy, Snow, Bird (Oyeyemi), 27, 35n11
Boys' World, 313
"Bremen Town Musicians, The" (Grimm), 269–70
Brown, Marie Alohalani, 75n2
bunraku, 120–24, 125, 133n7

Burne-Jones, Edward, 388
Butler, Judith, 184, 189

Cambridge Companion to Fairy Tales, The (Tatar), 2
Cameron, Julia Margaret, 300
capitalism, 24, 389
Carmen (Spanish stereotype), 240–42, 250–51, 257
carps, 92, 95, 105n24
Carroll, Lewis. *See Alice's Adventures in Wonderland*, Japanese appropriation of
Carter, Angela. *See also* "Loves of Lady Purple, The" (Carter); "Penetrating to the Heart of the Forest" (Carter)
　"The Bloody Chamber," 115
　"The Company of Wolves," 392
　and femininity in fairy tales, 336–37
　and feminist counter-narratives with defiant heroines, 114–15
　Heroes and Villains, 392
　on heroic optimism, 36n17
　The Infernal Desire Machines of Doctor Hoffman, 404–5
　knowledge of, concerning *bunraku* and *kabuki*, 125
　on prostitutes, 117–18
　The Sadeian Woman, 117–18, 122, 132–33n2, 404–5
　"A Souvenir of Japan," 130
　on *The Tale of Genji*, 127
　"The Tiger's Bride," 115
　"The Werewolf," 392
"Celestial Maiden, The," 152
"Cendrillon ou la petite pantoufle de verre" (Perrault), 88–89, 90, 104n16
"Charcoal Burner *Choja*, The," 157
Chavarria, Tony, 69
Chesler, Phyllis, 180
"Chickenpox and Crystal or Snow White and the Seven Dwarves" (McKay), 274
childhood studies, 285–86, 290, 303
children and childhood, 285–89, 303–4
　and bodily discipline in *A. I. Artificial Intelligence*, 292–95

　bodily status of cinematic, 289–91
　child development and chronological time in *Hansel and Gretel*, 297–99
　child development in Grimms' "Hansel and Gretel," 295–97
　as cultural idea, 285–86
　preservation of bodily condition of, in "The Little Match Girl" and *Melody of the Street Organ*, 299–303
Child's Play, 184–87, 188f
"Chinese Cinderella Story, The" (Waley), 88
chirimen-bon Japanese Fairy Tale Series, 141, 144, 163n9
chuanqi tales, 86–87, 103nn10–11
Chung, Hye Seung, 297
"Cinderella"
　evoked in Princess Princess's "Diamonds," 366–67
　exchangeability of gender of protagonist of, 161–62
　as heroine tale, 145
　in Japanese popular culture, 340
　Perrault's "Cendrillon ou la petite pantoufle de verre," 88–89, 90, 104n16
　as stepdaughter tale, 146, 149–50
Cinderella (Disney live action), 230n7
"Cinderella in China" (Jameson), 88
cinema. *See* movie adaptations, fairy-tale
Cobalt novels, 316
Cockburn, Alexander, 397, 398
Cold War, 171, 173, 202–3n2
Collodi, Carlo, 292, 293–95
colonialism, 24, 393–97, 406nn3–4. *See also* settler colonial storytelling
corporeal discipline, 292–95
Course in General Linguistics (Saussure), 173–74, 189
"Crane Wife, The," 144–45
Cross, Gillian, 273–74
cross-dressing, and Japanese theater tradition, 124–25
cultural flow, 357

416 • Index

Daphne, 112–13
darkness
  appeal to, in fairy-tale movie adaptations, 208–9, 216–23, 225, 226, 228
  and origins of fairy tales, 214–16
Darwin, Charles, 387, 404
Dawkins, Richard, 209
Dawson, Brian, 70–71
death, and preservation of children's bodily condition, 300–303
deconstruction, 193–97
Delessert, Madelaine Catherine, 397–98
Dennett, Daniel, 209–10
Derrida, Jacques, 193–97
Desblache, Lucile, 386
Deso, Gaëtan, 58, 60, 62
"Diamonds" (Princess Princess)
  intertextuality of, 378
  and Japanese consumer culture, 365–68
  in reference to Tanaka's *Somewhat, Crystal*, 369–72
  in reference to Yoshimoto's *Kitchen*, 372–75
  and re-orientation of fairy-tale studies, 377–79
  and reunion of Princess Princess, 376–77
différance, and deconstruction, 193–97
Dijkstra, Bram, 388
Dimovitz, Scott, 405
discipline, corporeal, 292–95
Disney
  and evolution of fairy tale, 335
  fairy-tale cinema as dominated by, 214
  Frozen, 361
  and gendered roles in fairy tales, 338, 339
  influence of, 211, 230n5
  live-action films of, 230n7
  looking beyond, 72
  Maleficent, 207, 218, 219, 220, 222
  Moana, 42, 70–71, 73
  Pinocchio, 292, 293
  portrayal of Māui, 70–71
  Sleeping Beauty, 406n2
  Snow White and the Seven Dwarfs, 211, 406n2
  Tangled, 271, 272–73
  woman-plant associations in, 406n2
Disneyland, 27

Dollase, Hiromi Tsuchiya, 325–26
doll narratives. *See also* "Loves of Lady Purple, The" (Carter)
  counter-narratives with defiant heroines, 114–15
  genealogy of, 112–14
  "House of the Sleeping Beauties" as, 127–29
  Japanese, 133–34n9
  prostitution and, 116–20, 131–32
  The Tale of Genji as, 126–27
Doll's House, A (Ibsen), 114
Donaldson, Kayleigh, 224
Donoghue, Emma, 276–80
Do Rozario, Rebecca-Anne, 339
Dragon Gate, legend of, 95
Duan Chengshi, 81–82. *See also Yeh-Shen: A Cinderella Story from China* (Louie)
  Yexian tale, 88–96, 104–5nn20–21
  Youyang Zazu, 83–85, 86–87, 89, 102–3nn6–8
Dugan, Frank M., 384
Dvaravati, 85–86
dwarves, 249

Eden, 398–99
Eder, Jens, 290
E Ho'omau series, 65–66
Eisenstein, Sergei, 253
Elementary Structures of Kinship (Lévi-Strauss), 181
Ellis, Bill, 356
Endersby, Jim, 387
English Fairy Tales (Jacobs), 175–76
envious sister motif, 152
Escobar, Arturo, 406n4
españolada genre, 236, 238–43, 245, 246, 247, 249, 250, 257. *See also* post-*españolada*
Eureka, 310, 311f, 317f, 319, 329n3
Eurocentrism, challenging, in fairy-tale studies, 26–27
exhibition, aesthetic of, in *Blancanieves*, 251

fairy and folk tale(s). *See also* located wonder tales; *mo'olelo kamaha'o*; movie adaptations, fairy-tale; romantic fairy tales; wonder tales
  appeal of, 159–60

  appeal to origin and darkness of, in movie adaptations, 208–9, 216–23, 225, 226
  ballet as, 342
  boundaries of genre, 2–3
  class and gender bias in, 265–66
  critiques in *Princess Tutu*, 353–56
  darkness of origins of, 214–16
  dismissed as children's stories, 32
  disorienting and re-orienting, 2
  European, translated into Japanese, 141
  evolution of, 209–10, 335–36
  femininity in, 336–40
  function of magic mirror in, 248
  God Help the Child presented as, 29–32, 35n12
  as memes, 209–10
  metamorphosis from oral, into literary adaptation, 289
  mo'olelo kamaha'o versus, 74
  versus *mukashibanashi*, 140, 142–43
  ownership of, 309
  plurality of, 24
  as polyvalent genre, 1
  published in Hawaiian language, 75n8
  renewed interest in, 256–57
  re-orientation of, 6–7
  as tool of assimilation, 30
  twentieth-century evolution of, 210
Fairy Tale Films: Visions of Ambiguity (Greenhill and Matrix), 208–9
fairy-tale meme, 16
fairy-tale sequels, 274–75
fairy-tale studies
  challenging Eurocentrism in, 26–27
  decentering approaches to, 4
  decolonization of, 3
  disorienting, 3–4
  expansion of, 1–2
  re-orientation of, 2
  social themes structuring, 24
Fairy Tale World, The (Teverson), 2, 7
"False Bride, The" motif, 165n22

Index • 417

fantasy (genre), as Eurocentric genre, 35n13
"Farting Bride, The," 145, 155
"Farting Guardian, The," 153–55
father, feared, and fearful sons paradigm, 174–76
Felman, Shoshana, 179–81
femininity. *See also* feminism; women
  and ballet in Japanese popular culture, 342–44
  as image of other in "A Souvenir of Japan," 130
  in Japanese theater tradition, 120–21, 122–23, 125
  prostitution and performance of, 122, 131–32
  in romantic fairy-tale genre, 336–40
feminism. *See also* femininity; women
  and ageist stereotypes in fairy tales, 268–69, 271, 272–73
  and Carter's empowering storylines, 111
  and doll counter-narratives with defiant heroines, 114–15
  and femininity in fairy tales, 336–40
  and feminist and queer retellings of "Three Little Pigs," 182–89
  and masculinist bias of "Three Little Pigs," 178–83
  and prostitution in "The Loves of Lady Purple," 118–20
Field, Norma, 370, 371
fish
  as Asian cultural symbol, 90, 95
  in Buddhist tradition, 105–6n30
  carps, 92, 95, 105n24
  koi, 92
  in "Yeh-Shen: A Cinderella Story from China" TV adaptation, 98–99
  in Young's illustrations of *Yeh-Shen*, 92–96
Fisher, Mark, 224
"Flatulent Girl, The" tale type, 154–55
folk tales. *See* fairy and folk tale(s)
forest
  alternative idea of fairy-tale, 390

in Carter's "Penetrating to the Heart of the Forest," 400–405
  colonial conception of, 406n3
  impact on fairy-tale imaginary, 389–90
"format," 336
four, significance of, in *moʻolelo kamahaʻo*, 54, 55
Frazer, James, 407n5
Freaks, 256
Freeway, 212
Freud, Sigmund, 173, 174–76
"Frog Sister, The" (Samatar), 24
Frozen (Disney), 361
Fukutō, Sanae, 123

Gaiman, Neil, 26, 34–35n10
Galdone, Paul, 176, 177*f*, 178*f*, 179*f*
Gamble, Cecil Huggins, 203n5
Gamble, Clarence James, 203n5
Gamble, Sarah, 132–33n2
Gamble, Sidney David, 203n5
Gamble House, 190, 191*f*
Gambles, 190–92
garden, in Carter's "Penetrating to the Heart of the Forest," 397–99
Garden of Eden, 398–99
Gates, Henry Louis Jr., 27
Gaudreault, André, 251
gender binarism, as structuring fairy-tale mapping and journeying, 24
gender-crossing, and Japanese theater tradition, 124–25
gendering, 184, 189. *See also* queer theory
gender studies, 280–81
generational conflicts, 265, 268–69. *See also* age
Generation of '98, 252
genre benders, 213, 214
genre breakers, 213, 214, 219
genre mixing, 212–14, 217–18, 227
ghost child, 297–98
Girls' Friend, 314
"Girls Just Want to Have Fun" (Lauper), 367–68
Global Gender Gap Index, 155–56
God Help the Child (Morrison), 27, 28–32, 35nn12, 15–16
Gordon, Edmund, 392

GOSICK (Sakuraba), 321
graphic novels, 65–70. *See also manga; shōjo manga*
Greenhill, Pauline, 208–9
Green Man, 387
Grimm, Jacob and Wilhelm
  allusions to "Aschenputtel" in *Yeh-Shen*, 90
  "The Bremen Town Musicians," 269–70
  forest in tales of, 389–90
  "Hansel and Gretel," 295–97
  introduction in Japan, 162n2
  Lüthi on protagonists of, 151
  reception in Japan, 269–70
  Snow White, 254, 255, 267–68
Grimms' Tales around the Globe (Joosen and Lathey), 2
Guarnaccia, Steven, 190–93
Gubern, Roman, 239
Gullette, Margaret Morganroth, 268, 275

Haase, Donald, 3, 7, 377
"habits of whiteness," 35n13
hair
  of Māui and Hina, 60, 63
  of Polynesians, 61
Hakone gongen emaki, 150
Halliwell, James Orchard, 175
Hanabe, Hideo, 158, 164n13
Hanamonogatari [*Flower Tales*] (Yoshiya), 314–15
"Hansel and Gretel" (Grimm), 295–97
Hansel and Gretel (Korean film), 288, 297–99
Hansel and Gretel: Witch Hunters, 219, 222–23, 226, 230n11, 305n7
Haraway, Donna, 390, 394, 405–6n1
Hardwicke, Catherine, 223
Harrison, Robert Pogue, 389
Hasegawa, Makoto, 377
Hasegawa, Takejirō, 163n9
Hauʻofa, ʻEpeli, 42, 73
Hawaiʻi. *See moʻolelo kamahaʻo*; Oceania
Hawaiian Creole English (HCE), 52–54
"Hawaiian Sup'pah Man" (Beazley), 47–49, 52–54
Hayashida, Kozue, 329n3
Hazanavicius, Michel, 237–38
Hearn, Jeff, 276
Hearn, Lafcadio, 133n9
Hecht, Susanna, 397, 398
Heckel, Jack, 214

He Kōrero mo Māui, pukapuka 1 (*The Legend of Māui book 1*) (Te Puia), 69–70
heliaki, 71
Hemsworth, Chris, 221
Hennard, Martine Dutheil de la Rochère, 100, 105nn22–23
Henneberg, Sylvia B., 271, 272–73, 277, 278
Hereniko, Vilsoni, 73
Heroes and Villains (Carter), 392
heroic optimism, 32, 36n17
Heuzé, Tara, 215
Higami, Kumiko, 310–16, 322–28
Hina
  plays and hula dramas celebrating, 49–57
  visual depictions of, 57–62
  wonder tales of, 45–46
Hitchcock, Alfred, 253
Hoffmann, E. T. A.
  "The Sandman," 113–14
  The Strange Child, 305n6
Hōkūle'a, 64
Holcomb, Bobby, 57–62, 64, 76n9
Holland, Samantha, 338
home, fairy tales' relation to, 22–26
Honda, Masuko, 313–14, 321, 325, 374
Honig, Michael, 295
Hopkins, Susan, 337
horror genre, and adaptation of fairy tales, 217–19, 223, 226–27
"Hottest Summer on Earth, The" (Princess Princess), 373
"House of the Sleeping Beauties" (Kawabata), 127–29
hula dramas, 49–54
human becoming, 278–79, 280
Huntsman, The, 214, 219–22, 230n10
Hustak, Carla, 386

Ibsen, Henrik, 114
Ikeda, Riyoko, 315, 340–41
Inada, Kōji, 140, 143, 155, 164nn12–13, 165n22
Indigenous people
  and digital storytelling techniques, 66
  misrepresentation of, 42–43
  re-orientation of, back to ancestral knowledge, 43–44
Infernal Desire Machines of Doctor Hoffman, The (Carter), 404–5
intergenerational relationships, 265, 268–69. See also age
Interpretation of Dreams, The (Freud), 173
interspecies relationalities
  in Carter's "Penetrating to the Heart of the Forest," 391–93
  and forest in Carter's "Penetrating to the Heart of the Forest," 400–405
  and garden in Carter's "Penetrating to the Heart of the Forest," 397–99
  and plantation in Carter's "Penetrating to the Heart of the Forest," 393–97
  scholarship on, 385–87
Irigaray, Luce
  Speculum of the Other Woman, 180
  "Women on the Market (*Le marché des femmes*)," 180, 181–82
Ishii, Masami, 143
Ishikawa, Tōru, 151
Itō, Ikuko, 343. See also *Princess Tutu*
Ivy, Marilyn, 331n16
Iwaya, Sazanami, 142, 163n10, 313

Jacobs, Joseph, 175–76
Jakobson, Roman, 174
Jameson, R. D., 88, 102n9
Japanese popular culture. See also Princess Princess; romantic fairy tales; *shōjo*; *shōjo manga*
  ballet in, 342–44, 352
  consumer culture, 365–68, 372–73
  girl culture, 322–27, 330–31n14, 342–43
  princess culture, 340–42, 351–52
Japanese tales. See also *Alice's Adventures in Wonderland*, Japanese appropriation of; doll narratives; *mukashibanashi*; romantic fairy tales
  treatment of old age in, 269–70
Jenkins, Henry, 287
Jennings, Hope, 400

Jetnil-Kijiner, Kathy, 73
Johnson, David Leslie, 223
Johnson, Richard, 184–87, 188f
Jolie, Angelina, 207, 218, 220–21
Joosen, Vanessa, 286, 367
jōruri, 124
J-Pop, 376
Justice, Daniel Heath, 43

kabuki, 120–23, 124–25, 133n7
Ka'ili, Tēvita, 70, 71–72
Kakei no Arisu [*Alice in Murderland*] (Yuki), 328
Ka Kimi a Māui i ōna Mātua (*Māui Searches for His Parents*) (Wiri and Waipara), 69
Ka Makau Nui o Māui (Scorpio), 64
Kamakawiwo'ole, Israel, 47
Kamehameha Schools Hō'ike, 49–54
Kanai, Mieko, 320, 326
Kāne, Herb Kawainui, 62–63, 64
Kaneko, Kuniyoshi, 316, 319, 323
Kawabata, Yasunari, 127–29
Keetley, Dawn, 387
Keisha, Bob, 96–97, 106n32
Kelley, Theresa, 398
Kellogg, Steven, 182–84
Kim Jee-Woon, 227
Kincaid, James, 300, 304–5n2
King, Thomas, 42
Kingdom Hearts, 328
Kinoshita, Shin'ichi, 330nn5, 7
Kissing the Witch (Donoghue), 276–80
Kitchen (Yoshimoto), 372–75
Knighton, Mary, 320
Ko, Dorothy, 86
Kohn, Eduardo, 402
koi fish, 92
Komine, Shōko, 329n3
Kōnoike, Tomoko, 386
Korean film, 226–27
Korean tale, in *Youyang Zazu*, 103n10
Kotoba no kuni no Arisu [*Alice in Wordland*] (Yagawa), 319
Kubo, Kayo, 270
kugutsu, 123–24
Kusama, Yayoi, 328
Kusumoto, Kimie, 313, 314, 316
Kuwada, Bryan Kamaoli, 69

Lacan, Jacques, 174, 180
landismo genre, 235–36

Lathey, Gillian, 100, 105nn22-23
Lau, Kimberly, 27, 35n11
Lauper, Cyndi, 367-68
Law, Jane Marie, 123
Lean, David, 253
Lebeau, Vicky, 291, 302
Lee, Nick, 278, 280
Lee, Sung-Ae, 227
Legend of Briar Rose, The (Burne-Jones), 388
Lettres élementaires sur la botanique (Rousseau), 397-98
Lévi-Strauss, Claude, 173-74, 181, 189-93, 209
Lieberman, Marcia, 268
Lili'uokalani, Queen, 46-47, 48, 75n5
linguistic signs, 189
Li Shiyuan, 84-85
"Little Match Girl, The" (Andersen), 300-301, 302-3
"Little Red Riding Hood," 200, 210, 212
located wonder tales, 15, 32-33
 and home's relation to fairy tales, 22-26
 in and out of sight, 16
 and re-orientation as incitement, 26-32
 Samatar's "The Tale of Mahliya and Mauhub and the White-Footed Gazelle," 17-22
Lost Property Fairy Tales (Ogawa), 318, 322, 323-27
Louie, Ai-Ling, 103n15. See also *Yeh-Shen: A Cinderella Story from China* (Louie)
"Love Like Salt" motif, 156-57
"Loves of Lady Purple, The" (Carter), 111-12, 131-32
 Carter's relationship with Sōzō as influence on, 129-31
 comparative analysis of, 131
 "House of the Sleeping Beauties" as source for, 127-29
 and Japanese theater tradition, 120-22, 125
 prostitution in, 115-16, 118-20
 The Tale of Genji as source for, 125-27
Lure, The, 227
Lury, Karen, 297, 298

Lüthi, Max, 142, 151, 159, 160, 161
Lyons, Malcolm, 17, 18, 20, 33-34n7

Mabey, Richard, 401
Madonna, 368
magic, sympathetic, 401, 407n5
magical girl subgenre, 345-47, 350
"Magical Negro, The" (Okorafor), 35n13
magic mirror
 in *Blancanieves*, 248-49
 function of, in fairy tales, 248
 in *Tangled*, 272
 television as manifestation of, 367-68
Mah, Adeline Yen, 103n12
Mahina, 'ōkusitino, 70
Mair, Victor, 83-84, 85, 86
Maitland, Sara, 389
Mālama Honua voyage, 64
Maleficent, 207, 218, 219, 220, 222
Manaiakalani (Māui's fishhook), 63-64
Mana Moana, 72
manga, 315, 321, 325-26, 341. See also graphic novels; shōjo manga
Manga Nippon mukashibanashi, 145
Mansfield Park (Austen), 34n9
Māori culture, culturally symbolic colors in, 68-69
Marder, Michael, 389
Marie Antoinette, 340-41
marriage, Japanese heroine tales about interspecies, 146-53
Marshall, Emily Zobel, 27
Martin, Ann, 276, 277, 278, 279
Masaki, Ruriko, 159
"Material Girl" (Madonna), 368
Matrix, Sidney Eve, 208-9
Matsuoka, Kyōko, 158, 159
Māui
 call for new, 72
 Disney's portrayal of, 70-71
 function of, 71-72
 music celebrating, 47-49
 origins of, 44
 plays and hula dramas celebrating, 49-57
 visual depictions of, 57-71
 wonder tales of, 45-46

Māui: Legends of the Outcast (Slane and Sullivan), 67f, 68-69
"Māui Snaring the Sun" (Kāne), 62-63, 64f
Māuiakamalo, ka Ho'okala Kupua o ka Moku, 51-53, 54-56
Mauss, Marcel, 407n5
McKay, Hilary, 274
Méliès, George, 258
Melody of a Street Organ, 288, 301-3
memes, 16, 209-10
Meslow, Scott, 216
metamorphosis
 and divide between human and nonhuman, 385-86
 and forest in Carter's "Penetrating to the Heart of the Forest," 400
Metamorphosis (Ovid), 112, 116
middle ageism, 275
Miller, Laura, 340
mirror. See magic mirror
Mirror Mirror, 238, 271-72
Mishima, Yukio, 133n8
Miyairi, Kyohei, 365-68
Moana (Disney), 42, 70-71, 73
Moana, the Rising of the Sea (Hereniko), 73
modern literary theory
 deconstruction, 193-97
 and feminist and queer retellings of "Three Little Pigs," 182-89
 and masculinist bias of "Three Little Pigs," 178-83
 New Criticism, 170-73
 psychoanalytic theory, 173, 174-76
 structuralism, 173-74, 189-93
 "Three Little Pigs" and teaching, 169-70, 200-202
Moen, Kristian, 257
Moglen, Helene, 272, 274
Monden, Masafumi, 327
monstration, 251
mo'olelo kamaha'o
 animated videos and graphic novels depicting, 65-70
 art depicting, 57-64
 and cultural and political renaissance of 1990s, 46-47
 defined, 39
 development of, adaptations, 40-41, 44-45, 74

of Māui and Hina, 45–46
and misrepresentation
  of Indigenous people,
  42–43
and music celebrating
  Māui, 47–49
and plays and hula dramas
  celebrating Māui and
  Hina, 49–57
re-orientation of, 40,
  41–42, 44–45, 62
transmission of, 39–40
understanding political
  underpinning of, 73–74
Morita, Iori, 329n3
Morrison, Toni, 27, 28–32,
  35nn12, 15–16
movie adaptations, fairy-tale,
  207–9, 224–29
  appeal to origin and
    darkness in, 208–9, 214–
    23, 225, 226, 228
  evolution of, 211–12
  and evolution of fairy tale,
    209–10
  and genre mixing, 212–14,
    217–18, 227
  MPAA ratings of, 229n2
  redirection of, 228–29
mukashibanashi, 139–40,
  160–62
  characteristics of canonical,
    142, 144
  children's love of, 158–60
  definition and transmission
    in Japan, 140–44,
    163n11
  heroine tales, 144–46
  and significance of
    storytelling in
    contemporary society,
    158–60, 161–62
  tales about stepdaughters
    and interspecies
    marriage, 146–53
  tales about women with
    great strength, 153–58
Muñoz, Jose Esteban, 375
Murai, Mayako, 269–70,
  330n8, 353, 363, 386
Murakami, Takashi, 331n16
Muratova, Kira, 301–3
Murphy, Louise, 273
Murphy, Pat, 273
musicology, popular, 363,
  378. *See also* Princess
  Princess
Myers, Natasha, 386
myth, structural study of,
  189–90

Nagayo, Shizuo, 314
Naithani, Sadhana, 3
Nakahara, Jun'ichi, 323

Nakahara, Ryō, 316
Nakayama, Kanako, 366,
  368
Nara, Yoshitomo, 328, 331n16
Nara-ehon, 151–52
narcissistic desire, in doll
  narratives, 113–14
national stereotypes, 42–45,
  225, 235–43
necrophilia, 113–14, 115,
  119–20
Nederveen Pieterse, Jan, 357
*New Approaches to Teaching
  Folk and Fairy Tales*
  (Jones and Schwabe),
  1–2
New Criticism, 170–73
Nihon mukashibanashi
  (Iwaya), 142, 163n10
Nihon mukashibanashi taisei
  (Seki), 140
Nihon mukashibanashi tsūkan
  (Inada and Ozawa),
  140, 143
Nihon ryōiki, 155
Niiro, Moemi, 329n3
Nikolajeva, Maria, 82
Nishinomiya Shrine, 123
Nomura, Hiroshi, 162n2
Nordstrom, Georganne, 53
nostalgia, 224
November, 227
*Nursery Rhymes and Nursery
  Tales* (Halliwell), 175

Oceania. *See also mo'olelo
  kamaha'o*
  cartographic division of,
    72–73
  cultural and political
    renaissance of 1990s in,
    46–47
  and origins of Māui, 44
  settlement of, 42
Ōe no Masafusa, 123
Ogawa, Yōko, 310–16, 318,
  322–28
Ōgi, Fusami, 326, 350
Ohanashi no rōsoku [*The
  Candle of Stories*]
  (Tokyo Children's
  Library), 159
Okamura, Keiko, 336
Okorafor, Nnedi, 35n13
Okui, Kaori, 366
Okuni, 124
"Old Man Next Door, The"
  tale type, 164n13
Oliveira, Katrina-Ann, 50–51
"O Māui ti'ii o te Rā"
  (Holcomb), 76n9
"O Maui Titii o te Ra e o
  Hinahina Toto Io"
  (Holcomb), 57–62

Once Upon a Time, 211,
  230n5, 238
*Once upon a Time: A Short
  History of Fairy Tale*
  (Warner), 22–23, 25f
"Onnagata" (Mishima), 133n8
Onodera, Arisu, 329n3
Orenstein, Peggy, 351–52
Orientalism, as structuring
  fairy-tale mapping and
  journeying, 24
Orientalist stereotypes, 96–98,
  101
origin(s)
  appeal to, in fairy-tale
    movie adaptations, 208,
    216–23, 225, 228
  darkness of fairy-tale,
    214–16
Orwell, George, 202–3n2
Otésanek (Svankmajer),
  388–89
"Otohime," 155–56
"Otsuki, Ohoshi" ("Little
  Moon, Little Star"),
  147–53
Ovid, 112, 116
Oxenbury, Helen, 198–200,
  201f, 202f
Oyeyemi, Helen, 27, 35n11
Ozawa, Toshio, 140, 143, 159
Oziewicz, Marek, 32

Pacific Resources for
  Education and Learning
  (PREL), 65–66
Paglia, Camille, 405
Pang Yi tale, 103n10
Parker, Lehua, 74
passive female archetype,
  336–40
Patterson, Ray, 106n31
"Penetrating to the Heart of
  the Forest" (Carter)
  forest in, 400–405
  garden in, 397–99
  interspecies relationalities
    in, 391–93
  plantation in, 393–97
performance cartographies,
  50
Perrault, Charles, 88–89, 90,
  104n16
phallus, 180
Picture of Dorian Gray, The
  (Wilde), 271
picture scrolls, medieval
  Japanese, 150–52
pidgin, 52–54
Pinocchio (Disney), 292, 293
plantation, in Carter's
  "Penetrating to the
  Heart of the Forest,"
  393–97

plant horror, 387–89
plants
 and forest in Carter's "Penetrating to the Heart of the Forest," 400–405
 and garden in Carter's "Penetrating to the Heart of the Forest," 397–99
 and interspecies relationalities, 385, 386–89, 406n2
 and plantation in Carter's "Penetrating to the Heart of the Forest," 393–97
play, and deconstruction, 193–97
poetry, "Three Little Pigs" and teaching, 170–73
popular musicology, 363, 378. *See also* Princess Princess
post-*españolada*, 253
Pretty Woman, 212, 214
Primavesi, Anne, 403
princess culture, 343, 351–52
Princess Princess, 362–63
 "Diamonds" in reference to Tanaka's *Somewhat, Crystal*, 369–72
 "Diamonds" in reference to Yoshimoto's *Kitchen*, 372–75
 history of, 363–65
 and Japanese consumer culture, 365–68
 and re-orientation of fairy-tale studies, 377–78
 reunion of, 376–77
Princess Tutu, 336, 343–44, 356–58
 critiques of fairy-tale conventions and plots in, 353–56
 gendered reading of, 349–53, 357
 and magical girl subgenre, 346–47
 retelling of fairy tales in, 344–46
 treatment of girl characters and agency in, 347–49
"product," 336
Propp, Vladimir, 209, 254
prostitution
 and doll narratives, 116–20, 122, 131–32
 in "House of the Sleeping Beauties," 127–29
 and Japanese theater tradition, 122–25
 in *The Tale of Genji*, 127

Prout, Alan, 290
psychoanalytic theory, 173, 174–76
Pygmalion (Shaw), 114, 116–17, 133n4

queer film, *Frozen* as, 361
queer futurity, 375
queer studies, 362
queer theory, 184, 187–89

"Rabbits" (Kanai), 320, 326
racism
 and Morrison's *God Help the Child*, 28–32
 as problem in mainstream fairy-tale culture, 35n11
 as structuring fairy-tale mapping and journeying, 24
rampion, 388
"Rapunzel," 271
rapunzel (plant), 388
"Reading Snow White: The Mother's Story" (Barzilai), 267–68
red, in Māori culture, 68–69
Red Riding Hood, 217–19, 222–23, 229n3
Reed, Carrie E., 86, 102n4
Reichel-Dolmatoff, Gerardo, 401
"Remarriage with Good Fortune Evenly Divided between Man and Woman" tale type, 157–58
"Re-Orienting the Fairy Tale: Contemporary Fairy-Tale Adaptations across Cultures" conference, 4–5, 8, 10
reverse flows of culture, 357
Reynolds, Simon, 224
Ribon no kishi [*Princess Knight*] (Tezuka), 315
Riviere, Joan, 352–53
Roemer, Danielle, 392
Röhrich, Lutz, 142
romantic fairy tales, 335–36, 356–58
 and ballet in Japanese popular culture, 342–44
 critiques of fairy-tale conventions and plots in *Princess Tutu*, 353–56
 and femininity in fairy tales, 336–40
 gendered reading of *Princess Tutu*, 349–53
 and princesses in contemporary Japanese culture, 340–42

 Princess Tutu and magical girl subgenre, 346–47
 Princess Tutu's retelling of fairy tales, 344–46
 treatment of girl characters and agency in *Princess Tutu*, 347–49
Romero de Torres, Julio, 251–52, 254f
Rose, Deborah Bird, 403–4
Rousseau, Jean-Jacques, 397–98
Routledge Companion to Media and Fairy-Tale Cultures, The (Greenhill, Rudy, Hamer, and Bosc), 2, 7
Runa, 402

Sadayakko, Madame, 133n4
Sadeian Woman, The (Carter), 117–18, 122, 132–33n2, 404–5
Said, Edward, 17, 33n6, 34n9
Sakuraba, Kazuki, 321
Salamanca, Alex, 215
Samatar, Sofia, 17–22, 24, 34n8
Sandilands, Catriona, 387, 389
"Sandman, The" (Hoffmann), 113–14
Sarnet, Rainer, 227
Saura, Bruno, 60, 62, 64
Saussure, Ferdinand de, 173–74, 189, 190
Schama, Simon, 389
Scott, Carole, 82
Seaman, Amanda C., 373
"Search for the Nara Pear, The," 146
seesaw effect, 276
Seifert, Lewis, 385–86
Seiyō koji shinsen sōwa (Suga), 162n2
"sekai de ichiban," 373
Seki, Keigo, 140
sentimentalism, aesthetical, 299–303
sequels, 274–75
settler colonial storytelling, 42–43, 50, 74, 75n8
sexism, as structuring fairy-tale mapping and journeying, 24
Sexton, Anne, 273
Seyfried, Amanda, 219
Shahriari, Lisa, 116
Shaw, George Bernard, 114, 116–17, 133n4
Sheldon, Anne, 274–75
Shikibu, Murasaki, 156
Shōgakkan *Mukashibanashi* series, 144

shōjo, 313–14, 315, 319–21, 325, 327, 350, 374–75
shōjo manga, 315, 321, 325–26, 328, 341, 350, 355
Shōjo-tachi no 19seiki: Ningyohime kara Arisu made [*The Girls' Nineteenth Century: From The Little Mermaid to Alice*] (Waki), 321
Sholock, Adale, 362
Shōnagon, Sei, 156
Shrek, 212
Silva, Noenoe, 40
"single story," 93, 102n3
sister, envious, motif, 152
Slane, Chris, 67f, 68–69
Sleeper and the Spindle, The (Gaiman), 26, 34–35n10
Sleeping Beauty (Disney), 406n2
Sleeping Beauty castle at Disneyland, 27
Smoczyńska, Agnieszka, 227
"Snow Maiden, The," 145
"Snow White". See also *Blancanieves*; *Snow White and the Seven Dwarfs* (Disney)
feminist critique of, 337
as heroine tale, 145
movie adaptations of, 238
Snow White (Grimm), 254, 255, 267–68
"Snow White" (Sexton), 273
Snow White and the Huntsman, 207, 216, 219–22, 225, 238, 271–72
Snow White and the Seven Dwarfs (Disney), 211, 406n2
"Snow White turns 39" (Sheldon), 274–75
societal transformation
and building just and sustainable future, 31
as function of Māui, 71–72
Solnit, Rebecca, 398–99
Somewhat, Crystal [*Nantonaku, kurisutaru*] (Tanaka), 370–72
"Souvenir of Japan, A" (Carter), 130
Speculum of the Other Woman (Irigaray), 180
Spielberg, Steven. See *A. I. Artificial Intelligence*
Stanlaw, James, 368
Stannard, David, 43
stepdaughters, Japanese heroine tales about, 146–53
Stevens, Wallace, 130

Stone, Kay, 218
"Story of Grandmother, The," 230n5
Stowe, Harriett Beecher, 293
Strange Child, The (Hoffmann), 305n6
"Straw Millionaire, The," 146
strength, Japanese tales of women with, 153–58
structuralism, 173–74, 189–93
"Structural Study of Myth, The" (Lévi-Strauss), 189–93
"Structure, Sign, and Play" (Derrida), 195
sugar cane plantations, 395
Sugawa-Shimada, Akiko, 346, 352
Sullivan, Robert, 67f, 68–69
Sumako, 314
survivance, 74
Svankmajer, Jan, 388–89
Sydney White, 212
sympathetic magic, 401, 407n5

Takamoto, Iwao, 106n31
Takayama, Hiroshi, 310, 329n3
Takehisa, Yumeji, 323
"Tale of Alice, The" (Sumako), 314
Tale of Genji, The, 125–27
"Tale of Mahliya and Mauhub and the White-Footed Gazelle, The" (Samatar), 17–22
"Tale of Princess Kaguya, The," 144
Tale of Two Sisters, A, 227
Tales of the Marvellous and News of the Strange (Lyons), 17, 18, 20, 33–34n7
Tamadechi, Michugo, 92
"Tanabata," 152
Tanaka, Yasuo, 370–72
Tangled (Disney), 271, 272–73
tapa designs, 62
Tatar, Maria, 27, 388
Taylor, Jodie, 362
Teaching Fairy Tales (Canepa), 1–2
Teaiwa, Teresia, 57
television
and Japanese heroine tales, 145
as manifestation of magic mirror, 367–68
Yeh-Shen: A Cinderella Story from China adapted for, 83, 96–100, 101, 106nn31–36
Temple, Emily, 215

Tenniel, John, 327
Te Puia, Jason, 69–70
Teverson, Andrew, 2, 7
Tezuka, Osamu, 315
Thaman, Konai Helu, 71
Theron, Charlize, 207, 220–21
"Three Little Pigs". See also "Blowing the House In" tale type
deconstruction and, 193–97
and feared father and fearful sons paradigm, 174–76
feminist and queer retellings of, 182–89
Kellogg's adaptation of, 182–84
masculinist bias of, 178–83
structuralism and, 189–93
used in Modern Literary Theory course, 169–70, 200–202
Three Little Pigs, The (Child's Play), 184–87, 188f
Three Little Pigs, The (Galdone), 176, 177f, 178f, 179f
Three Little Pigs: An Architectural Tale, The (Guarnaccia), 190–93
"Three Little Wolves and the Big Bad Pig, The" (Trivizas), 198–200, 201f, 202f
Three Pigs, The (Wiesner), 195–97, 198f
"Tiger's Bride" (Carter), 115
Tomita, Kyoko, 373
"Tongue-Cut Sparrow, The," 146
Torremolinos 73, 235, 236
Totem and Taboo (Freud), 174–76
Trask, Haunani Kay, 43
Treat, John Whittier, 373, 374
triangulated mirroring, 16, 33n4
Trivizas, Eugene, 198–200, 201f, 202f
"True Story of Hansel and Gretel, The" (Murphy), 273
Tsing, Anna, 383, 384, 390, 394–95, 396, 406n3
Tukano Indians, 401
Turk, Mariko, 343
tutu, 342

uncanny, 288, 291, 295, 298–99, 302
Uncle Tom's Cabin (Stowe), 293
"Urashima Tarō," 151, 156

"Urikohime (Princess Melon)," 165n22

Valentine, Gil, 292
Veraci, Rocco, 69
Verdú, Maribel, 247
Vertov, Dziga, 253
Vizenor, Gerald, 74
vodevil, 254–55
Volksmärchen, versus *mukashibanashi*, 140

Waipara, Zak, 69
Wakakuwa, Midori, 337
Waki, Akiko, 321
Waley, Arthur, 84, 85–86, 88
Wang, James, 106n31
Warner, Marina
  artwork illustrating *Once upon a Time: A Short History of Fairy Tale*, 22–23, 25f
  on ballet, 342
  on boundaries and circulation of animate forces, 384
  on fairy-tale movie adaptations, 211
  on good/bad women binary, 352
  on intergenerational relationships in fairy tales, 268–69
  on magic in classic fairy-tale tradition, 401
  on nonrealist tales, 22
  on wise old woman, 279
Watanabe, Atsuko, 364
Waziyatawin, 43
wealth, symbolic pairing of fish and, 95
Weems, Carrie May, 28
Whelan, Bridget, 357
white, in Māori culture, 68–69
"whiteness, habits of," 35n13
Whitney, Henry, 75n8
Why Māui Snared the Sun (graphic novel), 65–66
Wiesner, David, 195–97, 198f
Wilde, Oscar, 271
wind-breaking tales, 145, 153–55
Winduo, Steven, 44
Wiri, Robert, 69
Wirkola, Tommy, 219, 223, 230n9. See also *Hansel and Gretel: Witch Hunters*

wise old mentor trope, 277–78, 279
Wohlmann, Anita, 271–72
Wolf (Cross), 273–74
"Wolf and the Seven Young Kids, The," 200
Wolfe, Patrick, 42
women. See also femininity; feminism
  and ageist stereotypes in fairy tales, 268–69, 271, 272–73
  as authors of *hiragana* prose literature, 151–52
  in "classic" fairy tales, 335, 336–40
  excluded from *bunraku* and *kabuki* theater, 120–21
  expectations for Japanese, 155–57
  in fairy-tale movie adaptations, 225–26
  and feminist and queer retellings of "Three Little Pigs," 182–89
  and gender ramifications of interspecies relationalities, 386
  Japanese tales of, with great strength, 153–58
  and masculinist bias of "Three Little Pigs," 178–83
  in plantation zones, 396
  plants' associations with, 385, 387–88, 406n2
  as protagonists in *mukashibanashi*, 151
Women and Madness (Chester), 180
"Women and Madness: The Critical Phallacy" (Felman), 179–81
"Women on the Market (*Le marché des femmes*)" (Irigaray), 180, 181–82
wonder curse, 19
wonder tales. See also fairy and folk tale(s); located wonder tales; *moʻolelo kamahaʻo*
  definition of Hawaiian, 75n2
  function of, 22
"Woodcutter's Hut, The" (Blackwell), 22–23, 25f
Woodward, Kathleen, 272, 279

Woźniak, Monika, 100, 105nn22–23

Yagawa, Sumiko, 318–19, 330n9, 339
Yamashita, Kōsaku, 124
Yeh-Shen: A Cinderella Story from China (Louie), 81–83, 100–101
  cross-cultural origins of, 83–87
  and cross-cultural transformation of Duan's Yexian tale, 88–96
  differences between Duan's Yexian tale and, 105–6n21
  and political and cultural conflicts pervading 1980s United States, 81, 83
  TV adaptation of, 83, 96–100, 101, 106nn31–36
  word-image interaction in, 82, 90–92, 96
"Yeh-Shen: A Cinderella Story from China" (TV adaptation), 83, 96–100, 101, 106nn31–36
yellow, 105n27
Yim, Pil-Sung, 226–27
Yoshimoto, Banana, 321, 372–75
Yoshiya, Nobuko, 314–15
Young, Ed, 81, 82, 90–96, 97, 100–101
Young, Helen, 35n13
Youyang Zazu (Duan), 83–85, 86–87, 89, 102–3nn6–8
Yuki, Kaori, 328

Zenani, Nongenile Masithathu, 24
Zipes, Jack
  on Andersen, 300
  calls for looking beyond Disney, 72
  on Disney's *Pinocchio*, 293
  on fairy-tale films, 287–88
  on fairy tales as civilizing tool, 289
  of forest in Grimms' tales, 389–90
  on Méliès's revolutionizing fairy tale, 258
  on survival of fairy tales, 209

www.ingramcontent.com/pod-product-compliance
Lightning Source LLC
Chambersburg PA
CBHW070257240426
43661CB00057B/2575